D0913407

AN WE OB JUBILEE

AN WE OB JUBILEE

THE FIRST SOUTH CAROLINA VOLUNTEERS

JOHN SAUCER

AMERICA
THROUGH TIME®
ADDING COLOR TO AMERICAN HISTORY

America Through Time is an imprint of Fonthill Media LLC
www.through-time.com
office@through-time.com

Published by Arcadia Publishing by arrangement with Fonthill Media LLC
For all general information, please contact Arcadia Publishing:
Telephone: 843-853-2070
Fax: 843-853-0044
E-mail: sales@arcadiapublishing.com
For customer service and orders:
Toll-Free 1-888-313-2665
Visit us on the internet at www.arcadiapublishing.com

First published 2019

Copyright © John Saucer 2019

Cover illustration: 1st South Carolina U.S. Volunteers 1863. *Courtesy of Historical Art*

ISBN 978-1-63499-126-1

All rights reserved. No part of this publication may be reproduced, stored in a retrieval system
or transmitted in any form or by any means, electronic, mechanical, photocopying, recording or
otherwise, without prior permission in writing from Fonthill Media LLC

Typeset in 10.5pt on 13pt Sabon
Printed and bound in England

Preface

Over the course of the American Civil War, more than 2,000 regiments of infantry, cavalry and artillery were organized on both sides to fight in the conflict. Just as in all wars prior to this one, a few would stand out, not because they fought harder than the majority of regiments, which left on the battlefield just as distinguished a record, but because of where they were at a certain moment in history. For example, there was the 20th Maine Infantry that held the extreme left flank of the Union line on a hill known as Little Round Top on the second day of Gettysburg against repeated assaults by the Confederates. If the Rebels had been able to take this critical piece of terrain, it could have threatened the rest of the Union line with disastrous consequences and possibly changed the outcome of the war.

There was also the Rebel 18th North Carolina Infantry, which just happened to be in the path of Confederate General Thomas J. "Stonewall" Jackson on an evening reconnaissance after his stunning annihilation of the Union right flank at Chancellorsville. Thinking that Jackson and his staff were Federal cavalry, the Carolinians opened fire, wounding him and ultimately causing his death. This would be a major blow to the Confederate war effort.

Another significant unit that achieved fame was the 54th Massachusetts Infantry, the first organization of black soldiers from the Northern states. It became one of the renowned by being the lead regiment in a failed attack against a Rebel redoubt named Battery Wagner near Charleston harbor. This was important because many in the military doubted the 54th would really fight. These black soldiers' bloody sacrifice proved their skeptics wrong.

Regardless of how these three regiments reached fame, there was also another one that happened to be at the right place and time in history though very little is known about it—the 1st South Carolina Volunteers, the first regiment of black soldiers recruited for the Union Army during the Civil War.

In the process of writing this book, I have traversed many a path to bring about its conclusion. However, it had not been my original intent to write about this subject. In fact, I had previously planned to write about two other regiments; but to prove that adage how one thing can lead to another, in the process of discovery I came across the 1st South Carolina Volunteers. How did this come about?

In May of 1993, while visiting a cousin with my mother in Jacksonville, Florida, Mrs. Eva Russell, she showed me a list of the campaigns of the regiment of a mutual Civil War ancestor. Having known of this soldier since childhood, I did not, however, know the details of the unit's history. When I saw that the unit had been in the major battles of Chancellorsville and Gettysburg, it clicked in my mind to write a regimental history. So, much to my mother's dismay (as a child I was an avid fan of the Civil War, which drove her nuts), I was off and running to write about the 107th Ohio Volunteer Infantry, the regiment of my maternal great-great-grandfather, Major Ferdinand C. Suhrer. In October 1994, I came across the Museum of Southern History in Jacksonville. While looking through its voluminous book collection, I saw a set of books about Georgia soldiers in the war, *Roster of the Confederate Soldiers of Georgia, 1861–1865*, by Lillian Henderson. Out of a whim I looked to see if there was anybody with my last name. Lo and behold, I came across three names, one of which turned out to be my paternal great-great-grandfather, of whom I had never heard. So, excited at this new discovery, I decided to change direction and write a regimental history about my Confederate ancestor's unit, Sergeant William Joseph Saucer's 4th Georgia Cavalry (Clinch).[1]

Over the succeeding years I tracked the 4th Georgia's movements. While researching what has become known to history as the third occupation of Jacksonville by Union forces, I came across the 1st South Carolina Volunteers for the first time. Reading *Army Life in a Black Regiment*, I saw that this unit had previously gone up the St. Mary's River, one of the areas that the 4th Georgia guarded on the Georgia coast. Since it was also my intent to find what Union units operated in this area against which the 4th responded, I read the chapter on the St. Mary's.

While still researching about the third occupation, I decided to make an article about it for submission to a scholarly publication. In the process of doing this, the idea came to me to include the St. Mary's operation of the Volunteers, since they were the primary unit in the Jacksonville expedition. It was from there that another idea came—not to just write an article about the 1st South Carolina's early experiences, but a book. So, for a second (and final) time, I changed direction.

Acknowledgements

I would like to thank the staffs, both past and present, of numerous institutions for their assistance through the years. They are the Department of Special Collections, George A. Smathers Library, University of Florida, Gainesville; Florida State Archives, Tallahassee; Special Collections Section, Thomas G. Carpenter Library, University of North Florida, Jacksonville; Jacksonville Public Library; Jacksonville Historical Society, Jacksonville University; Museum of Southern History, Jacksonville; Amelia Island Museum of History, Fernandina Beach, Florida; Georgia State Department of Archives and History, Atlanta; Bryan-Lang Historical Library, Woodbine, Georgia; Southern Historical Collection, University of North Carolina, Chapel Hill; United States Army Military History Institute, Carlisle Barracks, Pennsylvania; and the Kansas State Historical Society, Topeka. I am ever so grateful for their assistance.

I would also like to thank the staff, past and present, of the Marion County Public Library, Ocala, Florida, for putting up with my too numerous requests for interlibrary loans. This also goes to the Waynesville, North Carolina, Public Library. I would also like to show my gratitude to my maternal grandfather, Mr. Harry D. Lohman, from whom I inherited my love of history; to my mother, Mrs. Yvonne L. Saucer, who taught me to set a high standard for myself; to my father, Mr. John M. Saucer, who set the example to never be afraid to work hard to achieve a goal; and to my sister, Mrs. Katherine L. Shrum, who taught by example the virtue of patience.

Finally, I would like to thank three people from my college days who influenced me tremendously: Captain Charles Knowlton, U.S. Army R.O.T.C. instructor, University of Florida, who set high standards for and demanded them from his students; Sergeant First Class Troy Graham, Special Forces, U.S. Army R.O.T.C Advance Camp, Fort Bragg,

North Carolina, 1980, whose wise counsel guided my thoughts when I later served as an officer in the Army; and to Professor Geoffrey Giles, Department of History, University of Florida, whose demanding standards taught me to finally think like a historian.

"I look out from the broken windows of this forlorn plantation-house, through avenues of great live-oaks, with their hard, shining leaves, and their branches hung with a universal drapery of soft, long moss, like fringe-trees struck with grayness. Below, the sandy soil, scantly covered with coarse grass, bristles with sharp palmettos and aloes; all the vegetation is stiff, shining, semi-tropical, with nothing soft or delicate in its texture. Numerous plantation-buildings totter around, all slovenly and unattractive, while the interspaces are filled with all manner of wreck and refuse, pigs, fowls, dogs, and omnipresent Ethiopian infancy. All this is the universal Southern panorama; but five minutes' walk beyond the hovels and the live-oaks will bring one to something so un-Southern that the whole Southern coast at this moment trembles at the suggestion of such a thing,—the camp of a regiment of freed slaves."

Colonel Thomas Wentworth Higginson

Army Life in a Black Regiment

CONTENTS

Introduction

This is the first installment in a regimental history of the 1st South Carolina Volunteers, later the 33rd United States Colored Troop, the first black unit created during the American Civil War. It covers the days when this regiment of ex-slaves first saw combat, a critical time period in the early creation of segregated black units when there was plenty of hostility towards them. The experience the Volunteers obtained during this time frame would give them the knowledge they needed to solidify themselves as a cohesive infantry organization. Their successes there from would help in the recruitment of thousands more in the second half of the war. Nearly 200,000 would have enlisted by war's end. This would mark a significant break from the past.

In any American conflict prior to the Civil War, any use of blacks in the military was seen only as an expediency; once their services were no longer needed, the senior military leadership quickly got rid of them. The use of blacks in this war started out no differently, only as a wartime necessity. However, their usage in this one would not end the same way.

As the war progressed into its second year, thousands of casualties were inflicted upon the Union forces. Never before had the U.S. Army suffered such losses in a similar time span. To make up for them quickly, regiments from less active theaters were withdrawn to replenish the battered Federal ranks. This left these secondary Union commands on the periphery of the Confederacy (South Carolina Sea Islands, New Orleans and Kansas/ Missouri area) short. In an attempt to make up the differences, the commanders saw opportunity in the many blacks in their respective areas of control. If allowed to, they could tap into this reservoir of manpower to solve their shortages.

What began as a trickle in late 1862 and early 1863 in these secondary theaters of operation became an Army-wide flood by 1864, as it became more difficult to obtain white recruits (even with a draft). This momentum would continue unabated until the war's end.

The Civil War would be the last war in which blacks would be used only as a wartime necessity. By 1865 the political landscape in Washington and opinion of senior military officers had changed enough that permanent black army units would be created. This meant that in future conflicts, blacks would be involved right from the beginning, though still in segregated units.[1] Though this change would be a major leap forward, it would not end the overt discrimination they had to endure. It would take decades for change to occur, but it would happen.

The story of the 1st South Carolina Volunteers' early history can be divided into three parts. The first one was the unit's creation and company-level operations it conducted along the Georgia and Florida coastline[2] in August and November 1862. The second was the regiment's two trips up the St. Mary's River on the Florida–Georgia border in January 1863 and the third one up the St. John's River to Jacksonville, Florida, and its environs in March. These operations were designed to prove the fighting viability of the black soldiers by exposing them to combat in what were perceived as low-key deployments. However, the third deployment would prove to have a greater impact than originally thought.

The creation of the regiment in May 1862 was without official sanctioning, and was unfortunately disbanded three months later except for one company. That company was sent to a remote island on the Georgia coast in August to protect slaves who had previously escaped. It would remain there for several months, but would have the opportunity to fight off a Confederate raid. In October, the regiment was resuscitated under different leadership, and the one company of the previous organization was brought back to serve as the nucleus of the reconstituted Volunteers. As the unit grew, two excursions were conducted along the Florida/ Georgia coast in November. The first one used only one company, but the second excursion involved two.

The first foray up the St. Mary's in January 1863 culminated in a skirmish that became unofficially known as the battle of the Hundred Pine when a detachment of the 1st clashed with a Florida cavalry company. The Hundred Pine was the first significant "crossing of swords" between former slave and "master" in Florida. This was only a minor tactical engagement. However, it represented one of the opening salvos against Johnny Reb after the shift in the Lincoln administration's policy in the arming of blacks from one of cautious stepping, to one of open embracement.

The second excursion up the river increased the 1st South Carolina's exposure to Rebel fire when the Volunteers took on several companies of Georgia cavalry this time in addition to the same Florida unit. The trip to Jacksonville two months later was designed to find more recruits to help fill out a newly organized 2nd South Carolina regiment and possibly enough for a 3rd. However, most of their exertions were stymied by determined Confederates counter-efforts. Though not successful in their original intent, the Volunteers did receive national attention for all their work in several Northern newspapers and even got the attention of President Lincoln.

The first commanding officer of the reconstituted 1st South Carolina, Colonel Thomas Wentworth Higginson, called his experience commanding black troops, "... the beginnings of a momentous military experiment, whose ultimate results were the reorganization of the whole American army and the remolding of the relations of two races on this continent."

Writer Christopher Looby also put it quite eloquently when he said that, "The 1st South Carolina Volunteers had as one of its most important missions a symbolic or expressive one: These ex-slaves were meant to display, before the skeptical eyes of the national white public a model of perfect military valor and thus persuade the world that black men were the fighting equals of white men." Colonel Higginson would definitely see to this.

The creation of this unit, with its subsequent experiences, involved numerous people from different backgrounds, both soldier and civilian, enemy and supposed comrades-in-arms. There were glory seekers, war profiteers and individuals involved for idealistic and religious reasons. There was the professional soldier trying to do his duty and the politician riding the wave for further advancement. There was the ex-slave fighting to free his fellow bondsman. There was also the Confederate soldier fighting for what he believed to be a just cause and the Union soldier opposed to the use of blacks as soldiers. Over the course of this book the names of individuals seen in it will readily fall into one of these categories.

In the confusion of combat, its participants can interpret events differently. This is evident when the participants' experiences are later written down. Writing a narrative from conflicting accounts can make it difficult to untangle the truth, so including all the accounts may be the only way to describe what took place to give the most accurate picture possible. For example, when Colonel Higginson wrote about his first encounter with the Confederates at the Hundred Pine, he used three different venues: his official report of the St. Mary's expedition, a journal he kept of his daily experiences with black troops and an article in the magazine *Atlantic Monthly* in 1866, which was republished in his regimental history, *Army Life in a Black Regiment*, four years later. Each account has dissimilarities from the others, but at the same time they build upon each other by adding more detailed information.

In a letter by a Confederate soldier named Davis Bryant, he described what he witnessed when his company clashed with Higginson's sable soldiers at the Hundred Pine. Though his account is different (as to the details of this engagement in many ways), the exigencies of war can easily cause people to have different experiences based upon where they were during the action and how long it was. Another influential factor is when the participants wrote their experiences down. Bryant wrote this letter to his brother about two weeks after the engagement.

Is this book inclusive of all information that is available on the 1st South Carolina Volunteers' early operations? To answer this question, I had looked for primary sources in every repository that I could think of that might have applicable materials on the theme. I had also consulted the bibliography of every book that I could find on black soldiers in the Civil War and in every biography of Thomas Wentworth Higginson. If there is any other information that is still "out there," it has yet to make itself known.

I take full responsibility for the primary sources' usage and interpretation. Some of them are contradictory, but I firmly believe that I have used them correctly.

In the process of using these primary sources, I paraphrased some, which did not cause them to lose any of their meaning. However, there were others that had to be quoted because of their content. To have paraphrased them would have greatly diluted the impact of their authors' thoughts.

Also in the process of using these original documents, I sometimes had to extrapolate information not directly stated. For example, in Davis Bryant's letter, he talked about events that he experienced. In order for them to have happened, previous events not mentioned had to have taken place in order for his written experiences to have occurred—in this case, orders issued and actions taken by his commander which directly and indirectly influenced events experienced by Bryant and others in the company.

No attempt has been made to delete any racially offensive language from those being quoted. The historical record must remain true as it is found, both the good and the bad. To have deleted these words would have caused the reader to get an improper historical understanding of the individuals using them. The epithet "nigger" was commonly used during this time, not only by those who intentionally meant it as an insult, but even by those who were helping the former slaves. Though the latter's intent may have been only for descriptive purposes in their private writings, offensive is still offensive.

To understand why these terms were commonly used, one needs to understand the historical context in which they were used. During the mid-nineteenth century it was common to believe in the superiority of the white race over the black. Though certain politicians (to include Lincoln) did express the equality of man, they had to say that the white man was a little more equal than the black man if they wanted to be elected. This was the political reality of the time, and though many of their actions ran counter to their words, the politicians had to take these actions if they wanted to remain in office.

The reader will notice that certain individuals and events were not detailed. I had to omit areas considered unnecessarily distracting information not relevant to the theme of this book. If any reader would like to know more about these individuals and events, then he can read the sources about them provided by me.

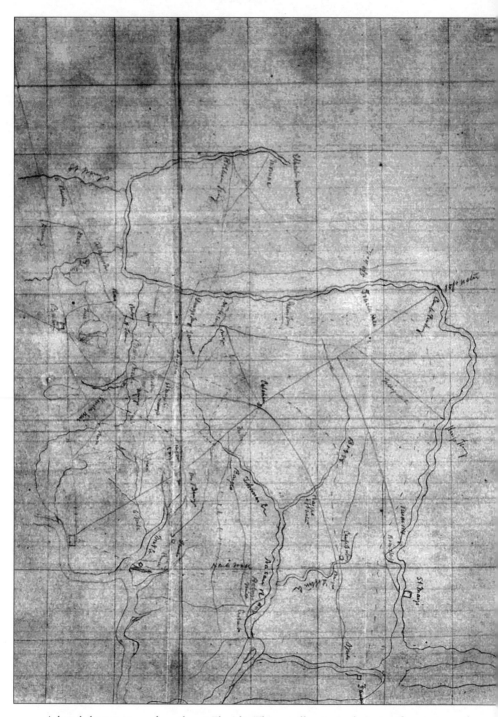

A hand-drawn map of northeast Florida. This small, seemingly insignificant piece of Confederate territory would be the initial testing ground for the 1st South Carolina as a regiment (see Chapters 9 and 10 to put the map more in context). *Courtesy State Library and Archives of Florida*

A White Man's War?

In 1866, a civil war veteran named Charles G. Halpine published under a *nom de plume* a collection of different subjects in a book which covered the various aspects of his experiences in the conflict. In the opening sentence of one chapter, he wrote in part: "Black troops are now an established success ... " Further on he added: "Looking back, however, but a few years to the organization of the first regiment of black troops in the department of the South, what a change in public opinion are we compelled to recognize! In sober verity, war is not only the sternest, but the quickest of all teachers and contrasting the Then and Now of our Negro regiments, as we propose to do in this sketch, the contrast will forcibly recall Galileo's obdurate assertion that 'the world still moves'." Just exactly what did he mean by all this?

The opening shots of the Civil War heralded in a conflict that had been simmering for decades over the subject of slavery between those who wanted to abolish the institution and those who wanted to perpetuate it. In years past, certain slave states had threatened secession from time to time to get their way, but a compromise for its continuance would be found to preclude this from happening. However, by 1860 the road to any more compromising had finally run out because of a major event that was occurring. This was a presidential election year, and the recently new Republican Party had nominated an individual who had been a vocal critic of slavery over the years. Though the candidate did say during the campaign he would respect the right of the slave states to continue the practice, his promises did not do any good because of his past statements. If he were elected, several states said they would secede from the Union. Who was the Republican candidate for president? Abraham Lincoln.

The election took place on November 6, 1860. When the votes were tabulated, Lincoln had won with a plurality of them, defeating three other candidates.[1] The first slave state to keep its word and take the plunge into the secessional abyss was South Carolina on December 20. In the succeeding weeks six more states followed suit in 1861: Mississippi, January 9; Florida, January 10; Alabama, January 11; Georgia, January 19; Louisiana, January 26; and Texas, February 1. These efforts in turn set off another series of actions that would culminate into the beginning of a major land war, the seizure of Federal property pertaining to the military in these states.

Shortly after they left the Union, state and local authorities began seizing forts, installations, naval yards and arsenals in their respective areas. By April 1861, there were few properties remaining in Federal hands, among which were Fort Pickens near Pensacola, Florida, Fort Jefferson near Key West, Florida, and Fort Sumter centrally located in the harbor of Charleston, South Carolina.[2]

Also by April, the seven seceded states had come together to form a new nation, the Confederate States of America, with its capital in Montgomery, Alabama. Assessing the situation of their new acquisitions the Confederate leaders decided that they had to have Fort Sumter too, since it resided right in the middle of the harbor of one of "their" cities. Having it occupied by a "foreign power" was not acceptable. They therefore instructed Brigadier General P. G. T. Beauregard, the commander of the recently activated Charleston defense forces, to demand that the fort be turned over to them or face the consequences of refusal. When Major Robert Anderson, commander of the garrison, did not acquiesce to Beauregard's emissaries by 3:15 a.m. on April 12, Rebel batteries surrounding the harbor opened up at 4:30. After a 34-hour bombardment Anderson was finally forced to capitulate.

The news of the attack on Fort Sumter spread quickly. On April 15, President Lincoln formerly declared that a state of insurrection existed and put out a request to the remaining states in the Union for 75,000 militia to augment the small Regular Army to help put down the rebellion. In the following weeks thousands of men would heed the call of the president. However, there would be some who quickly found out that this call to arms only meant white men.

Political Considerations amid Military Strategy

Many blacks across the remaining states in the Union volunteered to serve,[3] but they were told they were not needed. Since many people believed that this new conflict would be a short one, the general consensus of refusal was that it was to be "a white man's war." Though black men had fought in the American Revolution and the War of 1812,[4] these facts did not sway this generation of Americans. Many felt that blacks did not have the intelligence to be in the military. There was also a general belief that white soldiers would refuse to fight alongside them. Though many abolitionists, both black and white, urged that blacks be allowed to enlist, with all the logic that they could muster as to why it made sense, these requests fell on deaf ears. So, as blacks were denied enlistment at the state and local levels, a more urgent and strategic aspect of it was unfolding nationally to deny them also the ability.

A major political concern in the beginning that had to be dealt with was why this war was being fought. After the bombardment of Fort Sumter and Lincoln's call for troops, four more slave states seceded: Virginia, April 17; Arkansas, May 6; Tennessee, May 6; and North Carolina, May 20. Though this brought the total number of slave states so far to leave the Union to eleven, there were still four more that hadn't decided yet: Delaware, Maryland, Kentucky, and Missouri.[5] For Lincoln, it was most important that neither he nor his government say or do anything that would push these remaining slave states into the secessionist camp; therefore, he said his goal was to preserve the Union and that only. These were border states which separated the free states from the new Confederacy,[6] thus acting as a strategic buffer. He could not take the risk of adding them to the Rebel fold.[7] Though there were people in these states who wanted to secede also, they were at this time in the minority, but a perceived radical move on the part of Lincoln could quickly change that number, with possibly thousands of more men going into the Confederate Army.

Another vital aspect that Lincoln also had to take into consideration, with regard to the Border States, was the location of the nation's capital, which was surrounded on three sides by the slave state of Maryland and laid across the Potomac River from Virginia. If Maryland went, Washington would be isolated from the rest of the country and put the Federal government in grave peril. Therefore, Lincoln had to tread lightly on the one common denominator for these four states: slavery. Putting blacks (mainly free ones) in uniform would not have helped.

While the issue of black enlistment gained no traction in the opening months of the war, both sides continued to build up for a showdown they thought would quickly end the fighting. As the weeks passed, both the Union and the Confederacy sent many of their newly organized regiments to the Virginia/Maryland area. After the secession of Virginia, the Rebels moved their capital from Montgomery to Richmond. This then placed the two capitals just over 100 miles from each other. Each side was determined that its seat of government would not fall into its opponent's hands.

As spring turned into summer, those on the Northern side clamored for action. "On To Richmond!" became their battle cry. However, this call for action did not take into account that the assembling Federal army was nowhere near being ready for combat, but that did not sway those who were calling for it.

Though other minor engagements had already occurred around the northern periphery of the Confederacy, the expected big show had yet to take place. Finally in July, the commander of the Union force, Brigadier General Irvin McDowell, decided (most likely for political reasons) it was time to move, so he gave the order and his men started to march towards Richmond on July 16, 1861.

McDowell took his time moving, thus giving the opposing Rebel army the opportunity to be augmented by reinforcements sent from the Shenandoah Valley not far from their capital. Finally on July 21, the two sides met at a small river in northeastern Virginia called Bull Run near the small town of Manassas Junction. Fortunately for McDowell, the Confederate forces were no better trained than his own, so when they came into contact with each other, it would be an engagement later described as no more than armed mobs duking it out. Though the battle seesawed back and forth during the day, the Rebels won in the end with the beaten Yankee army retreating back to Washington. This defeat quickly proved to many on the Union side that this war was going to last much longer than they had originally anticipated. Later on, when the North had suffered thousands of casualties, it would get people to start thinking that this conflict could not just remain "a white man's war."

Since it was the policy of the Lincoln administration in the beginning of the war only to preserve the Union and not interfere with the institution of slavery, this appeared on the surface to be a very simple strategy to follow. However, events would soon outpace this position, rendering it obsolete and demonstrating that the dictates of war wait for neither man nor policy. These events would cause the abolitionists to celebrate.

In the weeks following the opening of hostilities, with regiments from the various Northern states coming to Washington, the national command authority was able to form a tight cordon around the city. Not only was the Army able to do this on the Maryland side of the Potomac River, but the Union forces established a beachhead on the Virginia side too. They also had enough men to shore up a Federal installation called Fortress Monroe at the confluence of the James River and the Chesapeake Bay. It was vulnerable to Rebel attack since it was in Virginia.

For the rest of April and into May 1861, Union commanders enforced Lincoln's order. A politician turned general named Benjamin Butler offered to help slave owners in Maryland suppress a rumored slave revolt. Another general in Missouri, William Harney, commended what Butler did and offered his services if slave owners there required it. This also happened as Union forces moved into eastern Virginia from Maryland to occupy the Federal arsenal of Harper's Ferry as Union troops under one George B. McClellan advanced. However, it would soon become clear, "that preserving the Union required an assault upon chattel bondage."

In late May, several slaves escaped to Fortress Monroe where they were taken in. General Butler, whom was in command here at the time, soon found out they had been used for the Confederate war effort. It was because of this he came up with a novel idea for their use, to solve a labor shortage problem he was having. Though Butler had supported the suppression of any slave rebellion in a loyal slave state, the fact that these bondsmen were being used by a rebellious slave state gave him the legal justification, he believed, to confiscate them just like any other property to deny their use to the Rebels.

When the Confederate owner of the escaped slaves requested their return under the Fugitive Slave Act,[8] Butler told him since his property was being used to bolster the Confederate military, he declared them contraband of war and confiscated them. He then sent this Southern gentleman packing. Butler's declaration did not free these slaves, but only denied their owner the use of their labor. Though far short of emancipation, declaring slaves as contraband would soon have a far-reaching effect as a prudent wartime necessity, therefore making it quite legal.

Butler knew that he could use any confiscated Rebel property for his own legitimate military needs, so he put these new "contrabands" to work on his own fortification requirements. Word soon got around to other slaves in the vicinity that they too could escape bondage by being declared contraband of war, so they started to arrive. By July, the number of blacks at Fortress Monroe had swelled to over 600. They were given various jobs depending upon the needs of the Army. They became teamsters, cooks, laundresses, servants and laborers.

It did not take long for Butler's contraband idea to reach the desks of Army General-In-Chief Winfield Scott and Secretary of War Simon Cameron. Justifying his position as a necessity of war, they approved Butler's action. It was also ultimately sanctioned by Lincoln, who saw that it did not interfere with his policy. Soon the contraband policy became popular in the North, as it gave commanders in the field the authority to refuse to return any runaway slaves from rebelling states whether they had been involved in the Confederate war effort or not, since it would have been next to impossible to prove that they had not. The new policy also became a hit with Congress, which decided to codify it into law as part of a general Confiscation Act in early August. It said that any property aiding the Confederates could be denied its usage by its owners. Though the new law continued to label runaways as contraband and only as a wartime necessity, it still did not deal with the institution of slavery itself. Those who were declared as contraband were still subject to be returned into slavery if there were a reconciliation of the rebelling states with the Union states, because the U.S. Constitution as then written would require it. This legislation was soon put to the test as to its intent when the planned Federal strategy to win the war was put into operation. Though the law was clear in its meaning, one general would use it far beyond its scope.

Major General John C. Fremont, the new commander of the Department of the West in the border state of Missouri and an ardent abolitionist, decided on his own that this new legislation gave him the authority to free slaves that were in the area of his command. Citing civil unrest and widespread disloyalty as a pretext, he declared martial law in the state on August 30 and said the slaves of all disloyal owners were free without any proof that they were being used in any wartime activity. As expected, this decision set off a firestorm of controversy. There were those who lauded it and those who opposed it for military and political reasons. However, there was only one opinion that Fremont had to worry about; Lincoln's. When the president requested that he modify his position to conform to the language of the Confiscation Act, because of the possible backlash from the still loyal Border States, Fremont refused. Lincoln then ordered him on September 11 to change it, and he had to comply. Though Fremont's decision was squashed by the president, the idea of a subordinate unilaterally issuing an edict of emancipation would crop up again as Union forces struck deep into Rebel territory.

Attack on Port Royal

Part of the Union strategy at the beginning of hostilities was to conduct a naval blockade of the Confederate seaports to prevent any type of supplies arriving for the Rebel war effort. Since the Southern states had very little heavy industrial capacity at the start of the conflict, as opposed to the already heavily industrialized Northern states, importing materiel of war was vital.

In spite of the Confederacy's industrial deficiency, one thing it did have was plenty of coast line, from the Chesapeake Bay to the Mexican border. This would give the Rebels an immense advantage for a while. To cover this span of territory required many armed vessels, plus all the support ships to keep them supplied. However, at the beginning of the war, the U.S. Navy had only a small fleet scattered around the world on various missions. It would take time to bring these ships home, plus much more time to build up a sizable fleet with all needed logistical support vessels.

Until this could be done, the Federal blockade would be ineffective, and Rebel steamers would be able to keep the Confederacy supplied.

For the blockading fleet to be sustainable once it became operational also required bases from which to operate, since the seaports in the Northern states were too far away to support the ships effectively. With nearly 2,000 miles of coastline in the South Atlantic and Gulf of Mexico to cover, this meant having deep-water harbors near enough the blockading stations to supply all logistical requirements. These ports also had to be easily defended from Confederate attack, so the Army would have to be involved too.

A board was established to determine which areas along the Confederate coast would meet all requirements. Made up of Army, Navy and civilian experts, it concerned itself initially with the Atlantic portion of the Confederacy. Different candidates were considered. The board thought about capturing more than one port at a time, but it decided that it was best not to split the force, but to capture one then use it as a springboard to get others later. After weighing all the options, the board decided on a location in South Carolina called Port Royal Sound, a deep-water inlet which was about halfway between Savannah, Georgia and Charleston. However, as U.S. forces began to move deep into Rebel coastal territory, they would quickly be inundated with a problem they most likely did not anticipate, even with the recent experience of Fortress Monroe.

While the board was contemplating where to attack, a naval and army task force was being organized to carry out the mission. The fleet portion, under Commodore Samuel Francis Du Pont, would be composed of regular Navy and civilian-converted vessels. The army contingent under Brigadier General Thomas W. Sherman would have about 12,000 men,[9] composed of 13 infantry militia regiments primarily from four Northeastern states, an engineer militia regiment and an artillery militia regiment. The only Regular Army unit in this otherwise state-provided contingent was an artillery battery. The infantry would be divided into three brigades. The engineers and artillery were kept separate. The expedition got under way in late October 1861 and arrived at Port Royal Sound on November 3. Though the Confederates had erected two forts at the entrance, they were only able to put up feeble opposition to the Union naval attack. The Rebel forts fell on November 7, with the Army landing shortly thereafter.

One of the reasons that Port Royal was considered along with the other possible locations was the ability to defend it against an attack. Though each candidate had strengths and weaknesses, they were all islands separated from the mainland by rivers of various widths and thick marshes. If a harbor had been taken on the mainland, it would have been vulnerable to direct attack. By having these natural waterways

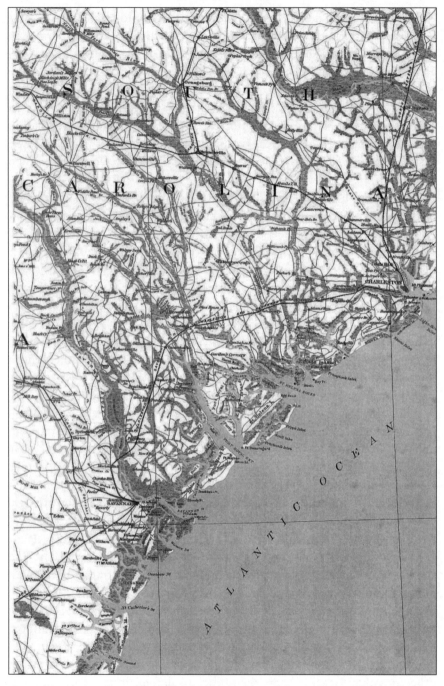

Coastal South Carolina. *The Official Miltary Atlas of the Civil War, Plate CXLIV*

as automatic barriers, plus the fact that gunboats of different sizes and draughts would be patrolling them and all points of vulnerability on the islands would be manned by guards known as pickets, made the islands easy to defend.

Port Royal Sound consisted of four large islands, plus several smaller ones. The large ones were Hilton Head, St. Helena, Ladies and Port Royal. The initial target was Hilton Head. Once the troops landed, they began to build entrenchments. After securing the initial beachhead, they occupied the other islands too. More regiments would be added to the Union force here in the following weeks as other islands deemed important were taken over, so by January 1862 the Northern force would have nearly 15,000 men. However, as the islands fell, what the Federals found was not what they had expected. The soldiers primarily saw only black faces.

One of the assignments given to General Sherman and Commodore DuPont prior to the invasion was to impress upon the residents of the Port Royal area—mainly the white plantation owners—that the occupying Union forces would not interfere with the "social and local institutions." Only if any slaves were being used in the Confederate war effort would the Confiscation Act be implemented. Though the islands would be under Union rule, life on them would go on as usual, with master and slave continuing in the same relationship. However, when the planters and other whites saw that a naval task force was preparing to attack, they decided that it was not in their best interest to stay, so they evacuated to the mainland with what they could carry with them. Some tried to take their slaves too, but many slaves resisted on the knowledge of the presence of the task force and several were shot and killed. Those the owners were able to take were primarily house servants. When Sherman's force began overrunning the islands, he quickly found there were hardly any white people to receive the message. What he did have was thousands of slaves without their masters.

The Federal armada's attack on Port Royal had brought down in one quick thrust a social institution that had been embedded since the late 17th century. What Sherman and Du Pont had thought that was going to be a continuation of the daily life on the Sea Islands turned into a chaotic upheaval. Not anticipating something of this magnitude to happen, the Union leadership entered into unchartered waters, not only militarily of having to deal with this sudden mass of people because of the invasion, which was many times greater than what Butler had to be concerned with at Fortress Monroe, but also constitutionally of how to handle the situation. Since the slaves were still legally owned property, but the property owners were not there to oversee them, Sherman and Du Pont had to adapt to this unexpected situation.

Though the legal aspect of the slaves as things stood in November 1861 was a problem that was going to have to be solved, it was something Sherman and Du Pont could not worry about at the moment. They tried to do what they had been instructed, to bring to the white planters a proclamation that the Union military would not interfere with slavery, but it was not their fault the whites had left before they could be told of the Federals' intent. Since events had now far outpaced the War and Navy Departments' policy on slavery via the Confiscation Act, Sherman and Du Pont had to gain control of the situation and act according to what they felt was best, given their particular set of circumstances, until clarified policy came from Washington.

Since the military had to worry about the possibility of a Rebel counterattack to regain the islands, this meant that the 12,000 soldiers who composed the landing force of the expedition had to concentrate on building fortifications and other defensive requirements on the islands they controlled up to this point. The Navy too was busy with blockade duty and patrolling the waterways among the islands. Though these were highly important, another important task was the required logistical support to keep the soldiers and sailors supplied with what they needed to do their jobs. This meant moving massive amounts of materiel and performing other duties requiring a lot of muscle. This need would provide the solution that Sherman and Du Pont required to bring order to the chaos because of the flight of the planters.

In short fashion the Quartermaster, Engineer and Subsistence departments of the Army put the able-bodied to good use. The Navy did too; since the wharves could not accommodate the supply ships, labor gangs were organized to move the supplies from ship to shore. Initially, the workers were only given food and clothing for their labor plus rations for their families. By December, the military started to pay them three to five dollars per month for common laborers and eight dollars for carpenters. Those who were unfit to work were also issued rations. In the upcoming months, however, others too would be availing themselves of this labor pool at Port Royal, both military and civilian, government and private individuals.

While the occupations of Fortress Monroe and Port Royal took advantage of this available manpower, the controversies of emancipation and blacks in uniform continued. In Congress, several bills were introduced in both the House and Senate during a December session floating ideas of abolition and emancipation under varying circumstances, but they got nowhere. They were yet to be deemed viable war aims by the majority of Congress. Secretary of War Simon Cameron had publicly proposed previously in November to put blacks in uniform and free slaves of rebellious masters. Not anticipating the reaction of the Border States, even with the recent experience from the Fremont episode, Lincoln forced him to resend his proposals. In the border state of Kentucky, Brigadier General William T. Sherman, following the lead of the other generals who had previously barred slaves from entering Union Army lines, had ordered on November 8 that forces under his command would return escaping slaves to their owners. Even Lincoln officially took no position on slavery and emancipation in a message to Congress in December. The little bit that had been done in 1861 in favor of the slaves, as opposed to all that had been done to advance slavery itself, was met with cries of derision by the radical abolitionists. This year may have ended with very little having been done to free blacks, let alone putting any in uniform, but 1862 would be quite different.

The Reason for
a "Colored" Regiment

Though 1861 ended with an impulse seemingly towards emancipation with the Confiscation Act, the year still had other setbacks. General Fremont had been replaced as commander in the western theater by Major General Henry W. Hallack, who had previously refused to allow escaping slaves to enter his lines. In November, General Scott, because he had been in the Army for over 50 years and was showing his age, was replaced as General-in-Chief by Major General George B. McClellan, who was an ardent foe of emancipation. However, these actions would soon be balanced by a major political decision.

By December it had become quite clear to President Lincoln and others that Secretary of War Cameron was not working out. Appointed to his position because of political considerations, he turned out to be a weak administrator and ignorant in the rough and tumble of Washington politics. The decision to replace him came shortly after his recommendation to arm blacks. Lincoln replaced Cameron with a Democrat named Edwin M. Stanton. A lawyer with proven executive and political acumen,[1] he would demonstrate to be the right man for the job during this national crisis. He came into office in January 1862 and soon made it clear to all that he was going to run the War Department quite differently than Cameron. He would also quietly demonstrate that his views on slavery were different from his generals, especially McClellan, who, as historians Benjamin B. Thomas and Harold M. Hyman put it, "consistently asserted that the war must not alter existing race relations; that the Army must remain outside the controversy. But Stanton soon saw that it could not hold aloof."

The first eight months of the war showed clearly that the decision not to interfere with "social and local institutions" in the rebelling states was not working. The continuing inundation of slaves into Federal lines fleeing bondage could not be ignored. The planned advances into the Confederacy in the upcoming months would only make things even worse and to deny slaves entry into Union-controlled territory just would not be feasible. Thousands would be acting on impulse to change their conditions, thus causing a major social upheaval, something that no Federal policy stemming from Washington could prevent, let alone ignore. The Lincoln administration would have to adapt to these changing conditions so the commanders in the field would have clear and concise guidance. Though this would be better in terms of how the commanders were to react, things would still be bumpy along the way, especially when some commanders started to put blacks in uniform on their own initiative.

Port Royal

Once Sherman's Expeditionary Corps had secured the main islands of Port Royal Sound, it started to branch out and take over other islands along the coast for tactical and strategic reasons. St. Helena Sound, just north of the Port Royal, was secured in mid-November 1861 with the occupation of Edisto Island. Tybee Island, near the entrance to the Savannah River, was seized in early December in preparation for a later assault on Fort Pulaski, which overlooked the approach to Savannah. St. Simon's Island, which guarded the entrance to Brunswick, Georgia, fell on March 9, 1862. Fernandina, Florida, the first of the additional deep-water harbors, was occupied on March 5, with St. Augustine as another one, a week later. Jacksonville fell on the 12th but would be abandoned in April. So, as Sherman's troops took over more and more Confederate coastal territory, this meant that more slaves would be making a break for freedom, and Stanton's prediction that the Union Army could not remain aloof would come true.

As other slaves joined the contrabands in the immediate islands of Port Royal or created their own colonies because of the expanding Union blockading efforts along the south-Atlantic coastline, chaotic conditions continued to be present. These people were uprooting themselves from their homes (irrespective of their bondage) and making a dash for freedom. This is very typical in war, to cause a flood of refugees who have little or no food and shelter regardless of the time of year, thus creating a very tenuous situation. Freedom for these bondsmen, however, was more important than knowing that their daily lives and security were being turned upside-down. Most of them probably considered this a one-time opportunity and therefore were willing to chance it all and endure the possible privation that could last for some time.

The initial reaction of slave owners along the southern seaboard to the fall of Port Royal differed, with the least effect of the backlash at the time coming from Florida. Many planters in South Carolina and Georgia on the islands not yet affected by the Yankee invasion began withdrawing their property onto the mainland and into the interior. Others with plantations on the mainland coast would also move their chattels further inland.[2] Once the Federals extended their line of occupation down the Georgia coast and to St. Augustine, this finally galvanized many planters in northeast Florida to move their slaves too. Though these forced migrations stifled the ability of slaves to escape, they only delayed the flight to freedom for many.

While many slaves were moved inland after the fall of Port Royal, others would still be at the places that the Federals later occupied. Many more would flee to these places in the following months and join the colonies established there. Many escapees would get to Yankee vessels plying the coastal and inland waterways when possible. This continuous influx to all points of Union occupation would also cause further problems that the Federals would have to solve. This was clearly seen by a Union officer in March. Writing to his father on the 11th, Charles Francis Adams, Jr.,[3] an officer in the 1st Massachusetts Cavalry stationed on Port Royal Island, said that "the problem is a difficult one. We have now some 7,000 masterless slaves within our lines ..." He then speculated that "in less than two months we should have nearer 70,000 and what are we to do with them?"

Though this problem vexed Adams, programs to help bring about some semblance of order to the seeming chaos at Port Royal were already in progress on the islands, which in these cases were under civilian control.

The fall of Port Royal Sound not only produced a strategic base for the Union blockading fleet, but also the islands captured in the process made available a commodity that was in short supply in the North since the war began—cotton. The crop for 1861 had already matured but fell into Yankee hands before it could be completely harvested and shipped to a cotton-hungry foreign country like England. Since it came from the Sea Islands, this made it all the more valuable, since this type of cotton was a better quality than that produced on the mainland. The cotton mills in the northeastern states would also pay handsomely for this commodity, with the bulk of the proceeds going to a cash-strapped Federal treasury to help finance the war.

Since the confiscation and selling of the cotton fell under the auspices of the Treasury Department, Secretary Chase appointed an experienced individual in the field named William Reynolds in December as the cotton collection agent. He would see to it that the commodity was harvested, baled and readied for shipment north. He would work on this for the next several months. While this was going on, Chase appointed another individual to oversee the abandoned plantations of the Port Royal islands, since this task fell under the Treasury Department's purview too. Edward L. Pierce, a friend of the secretary and a fellow abolitionist, went to Port Royal in January and did a detailed report.

In February 1862, Pierce put out a call for help with administering the islands from different freedman's aid societies that had been recently established in several Northeastern cities. Abolitionists, missionaries, teachers, theological students and others answered the call with zeal. The ones who were chosen went to the islands in March. They would supervise the work of the freedmen on the plantations, teach those who wanted to learn and see to their spiritual needs too. However, these two separate enterprises under Reynolds and Pierce soon fell into disagreement over different goals and use of available manpower. Add to this the requirements of the Army and Navy and the non-cooperation of the freedmen too, over how they felt they were being treated, and chaos was bound to happen if things did not change soon. By April, Secretary Chase saw that things were not working out though he had tried to referee the two civilian factions from Washington, so he agreed to turn over the administration of the islands to the War Department.[4] This change would add a whole new dimension to the wartime experiences of Port Royal.

The Ascension of General Hunter

After the acquisition of the final necessary ports in Florida, the War Department decided to change the name of the Army organization from Expeditionary Corps to one that denoted permanence. On March 15 it became known as the Department of The South. Consisting of all the Rebel territories the military controlled in South Carolina, Georgia, and Florida,[5] this new organization would exist until after the war.

Besides the creation of this new department, another significant event also occurred on the 15th. General Sherman was removed from command and Major General David Hunter was named as his replacement. This was done because of three connate reasons. Ever since the capture of Port Royal in November 1861, Secretary Stanton believed that Sherman was just sitting on his laurels and not trying to capture anything else of a significant nature. The fact that he had acquired Fernandina, Jacksonville, and St. Augustine in March was not enough. Though he had several regiments working since December to construct heavy artillery batteries on mud flats and islands near the Confederate bastion of Fort Pulaski to reduce it as a necessary first step to attempt the capture of a significant target—Savannah—this was too little too late. Also, to Stanton it was clear by March that Sherman was also the wrong commander to govern the islands in reference to civilians. Seen as a martinet, he could probably have remained in command if the situation had been purely military, excluding his slowness to capture another major target. Sherman had also expressed to Stanton his dislike of the many slaves making it to his lines.

Secretary Stanton's decision to appoint General Hunter as commander of the Department of the South was not his first choice. His intent was to have someone who knew how to command troops, not just appoint someone because of his administrative abilities or abolitionist views. He wanted to give command to Brigadier General James W. Shields. However, Stanton was overruled by President Lincoln, who wanted Hunter because of his long-held and well known abolitionist beliefs and felt that he was the right man for the job given the particular circumstances of the department.

The orders of March 15 assigning Hunter to Port Royal stipulated that he was to continue the mission of capturing Fort Pulaski and Savannah. They also said for him, "to attack and beat the enemy whenever and wherever an opportunity offers." Unfortunately these orders were flawed, since they did not reflect the reality of the situation of this time frame.

Major General David Hunter, whose need for soldiers in the Department of the South led to the creation of the first black regiment in the Union Army. *Massachusetts Commandery Military Order of the Loyal Legion and the U.S. Army Military History Institute*

Though the capture of Fort Pulaski was achievable since it could be isolated because of its location in the Savannah River,[6] and the fort could be attacked at the discretion of the Federals, to capture the city was a different matter. At this stage in the war, there was no way it could have been taken with the Union forces at hand (less than 20,000 men), since they were spread out protecting the Port Royal area and the occupied enclaves in Georgia and Florida. The Confederate reaction to a Federal attack on the city would have been too strong, because the Rebels had plenty of manpower in the state beside what already protected it. At the time of Hunter's appointment in March no big battles had been fought since Bull Run, therefore the Confederate High Command did not have to draw down on troop reinforcements in Georgia to replace any casualties. Though several thousand Georgians had already gone to Virginia and other active parts of the Confederacy, thousands more were still untapped (let alone the thousands also available in the neighboring states of South Carolina, Alabama, and Florida) and could easily be called upon to help defend the city.

Hunter tried several times to obtain reinforcements after learning how many men he would command, so he would have enough to increase his chances of capturing a major target. From late March to early May he communicated several times with Stanton on this issue. He also had the audacity to request 50,000 muskets and 50,000 pairs of scarlet pantaloons "with authority to arm such loyal men as I can find in the country." Though Hunter did not say so, he was implying the recruitment of the freedmen. Unfortunately for Hunter, Stanton did not approve any of these manpower or supply requests. For good reason, the secretary was not able to. In Virginia a major operation was already under way in the reorganized and newly named Union Army of the Potomac under Major General McClellan. In what would become known as the Peninsula campaign, this operation was using up just about all the available manpower, materiel, and shipping to support it.[7] Besides, a major battle had finally been fought on April 6 and 7 in western Tennessee. Called Shiloh or Pittsburg Landing, it caused thousands of Federal casualties and damaged much military equipment, thus putting a further strain on the supply line. With these realities facing him, Hunter could not get what he needed to accomplish his mission. As historian Edward Miller put it, "it was perhaps these same events that convinced Hunter that he could not depend on Washington and that he had to find his own solutions."

Hunter's Regiment

Although he understood that he was not going to obtain more reinforcements from outside the Department of the South, General Hunter knew he still had to act and take some sort of offensive action soon. He had no choice. The reality of his responsibilities as commander left him with a conundrum. He had to capture a significant target while at the same time hold on to the gains of the Union military to date. He had enough men to garrison the areas the Army controlled, but not enough to do that and take any serious action against either Charleston or Savannah. This contradiction forced Hunter to look hard at his situation to see where he could effect change, rearrange his assets where possible, and make available more men while still denying the Rebels any use of the southern seaboard.

The only place at the time Hunter saw that met his criteria was Jacksonville, Florida. Since the Union naval blockading fleet easily controlled the mouth of the St. John's River, over which the city looked, he ordered it evacuated on April 9, 1862. However, just when Hunter thought he had more men available, Fort Pulaski fell on the 11th, after a bombardment of less than 24 hours. This meant that it would have to be garrisoned for the duration of the war, thus diluting to a point the gain he had realized from the withdrawal of his forces from Jacksonville. Whether or not the fall of Pulaski was significant enough for Washington was to be seen, this victory only temporarily solved part of Hunter's dilemma. He still needed more men.

Hunter's realization that he would have to look elsewhere to help solve his manpower problem had in fact already germinated right after he took over command from General Sherman. Having been in the U.S. Army for 34 years, he understood exactly how the military system worked, especially the politics of it, and knew what he had to do. Though no evidence states it, he probably made his several requests to Stanton for reinforcements, knowing full well that he would be turned down, so he could justify raising a regiment of freedmen.[1] It is also possible that Hunter made his request for the 50,000 pairs of pantaloons and 50,000 muskets "with authority to arm such loyal men as I can find in the country" with the expressed intent to see what kind of reaction he would get from Stanton in Hunter's implication of recruiting former slaves. As Hunter expected, his requests for the weapons and uniforms were denied, but at the same time he got no further instructions as to arming "such loyal men." Since Stanton did not say one thing or the other about it, this gave Hunter the green light he believed he needed to create a regiment of black soldiers. While he was building a case to justify officially its creation, he had already begun laying the groundwork to recruit.

The first thing Hunter did after he took over command was to speak to an influential black minister he got wind of on Hilton Head named Abraham Murchison.[2] He was employed at the time as chief cook with the department's Headquarters mess. Hunter told him what he wanted to do and asked his opinion about it. The minister was immediately enthusiastic about the idea and agreed to help. Hunter wanted to know how the black males on the island would feel about military service. Murchison said he would call a meeting and inquire of the others' opinion. He did this on the evening of April 7 but given the grave sensitivity of the subject, it was done in secret. At the meeting the minister told those who attended it was their responsibility to help the government put down the rebellion. He then offered them the opportunity to enlist. No one refused. Of those who attended that evening, 105 men had their names entered on a volunteer list. Only the old men and boys were rejected. The next day 25 more names were added to the list, with 20 more by week's end for a total of 150.

Though the initial enlistment drive went well,[3] things soon stalled and very little happened for the rest of the month,[4] even though word had already spread around to the other islands at Port Royal that Hunter wanted men to enlist for a black regiment.[5] While this endeavor was going on, Hunter wrote to Secretary Stanton on the 22nd, saying his intelligence estimate of enemy strength to be at 65,000, more than three times what he had spread out from Edisto Island to the now invested Florida Panhandle (which included Key West and Pensacola). Whether these figures meant only South Carolina or that they also included Georgia and Florida, Hunter could have easily used them as another pretext to request reinforcements, knowing full well that he would be turned down again and therefore have another reason to create a regiment of contrabands. However, without waiting for any reply about his numerical inferiority from the War Department, Hunter decided to act unilaterally.

On April 25, Hunter declared martial law in his command and also invoked the instructions given by former Secretary of War Cameron to his predecessor on the use of blacks in an emergency situation, if "special circumstances seem to require it." Hunter would then be allowed to organize them into "such organization (in squads, companies, or otherwise) as you may deem most beneficial to the service, this however, not being a general arming of them for the service." The most interesting aspect of his instructions for him to successfully organize the freedmen into "squads, companies, or otherwise" was the requirements necessary for him to do so. In order for them to be effective, the men filling out these units would have to be armed, drilled and trained like any other military organization. Hunter also decided to throw in uniforms for the sake of organizational completeness. He would make sure that he would interpret his instructions to the widest possible limit as he "may deem most beneficial to the service," but his interpreting wouldn't do any good if he did not have the required number of men to fill out the "squads, companies, or otherwise."

General Hunter had to have been at a loss for words to understand why what had started out so well in early April had basically fizzled out by the first week in May. Though he had the full endorsement of a popular black minister and 150 men had volunteered within a week's time, this enthusiasm did not go beyond Hilton Head Island. Someone who would later be an important advocate for black enlistment described it this way: "Enlistments came in very slowly, and no wonder.[6] The white officers and soldiers were generally opposed to the experiment." Given how these Northern regiments felt about blacks in general, this opposition was not surprising. To have an initial meeting in secret about enlisting was one thing, but to raise a regiment in secret was impossible and it did not take long for word to spread to the white regiments as the enlistment effort got around to the other islands. To sabotage Hunter's idea these soldiers:

> filled the ears of the negroes with the same tales which had been told them by their masters,—that the Yankees really meant to sell them to Cuba, and the like.[7] The mildest threats were that they would be made to work without pay (which turned out to be the case), and that they would be put in the front rank in every battle. Nobody could assure them that they and their families would be freed by the Government, if they fought for it, since no such policy had been adopted.

A missionary who arrived in April confirmed this mistreatment. Writing in her diary on May 5, 1862 Laura M. Towne, who worked and lived on St. Helena's Island across the bay from Hilton Head said, "General

Hunter has offered to arm the Negroes and train them. But as they think it is a trap to get the able-bodied and send them to Cuba to sell, they are not anxious to be soldiers. They hate Hilton Head. So they will probably seem to be cowardly to folks at the North, and perhaps will prove so. Why shouldn't they, under their training."[8] Another missionary, Susan Walker, "tried in vain to inspire desire to fight but none wish to volunteer. This is a sad truth and full of deep meaning. All spirit has been so crushed down there is nothing left to rise up in defence of their just rights or to secure freedom." She added that they "could be forced to fight, but none will volunteer to leave their homes." Miss Walker did not know how prophetic her statement, that they might "be forced to fight," would be.

Emancipation and Impressment

During the first week in May, General Hunter was beside himself in the failure of his recruitment effort. In about a month's time, he did not even have 200 men signed up. Of course, it did not help if he was being undermined by many of his subordinates.[9] By this time he had expected to have two regiments worth of men, but they failed to materialize. Finally, in a fit of exasperation, he decided that he had to take more drastic measures in order to achieve what he wanted. A key subordinate and aide, Major Charles G. Halpine, vividly remembered the backdrop that led Hunter to this conclusion. He said:

> No reinforcements to be had from the North; vast fatigue duties in throwing up earthworks imposed on our insufficient garrisons; the enemy continually increasing both in insolence and numbers; our only success the capture of Fort Pulaski, sealing up Savannah; and this victory off-set, if not fully counterbalanced, by many gains of the enemy;—this was about the condition of affairs as seen from the headquarters fronting Port Royal bay, when General Hunter one fine morning, with twirling glasses, puckered lips, and dilated nostrils—(he had just received another 'don't-bother-us-for-reinforcements' dispatch from Washington)— announced his intention of 'forming negro regiments', and compelling 'every able-bodied black man in the department to fight for freedom which could not but be the issue of our war.'

The actions he decided to take to put this into motion would have far-reaching consequences for the course of the war and having blacks in the military.

Before General Hunter made it known that he was going to initiate a draft of all eligible black males in the Port Royal islands, he decided first to make an announcement that he hoped would ease the reaction of the contraband to his notice of induction. However, what it actually did do was to set off a bombshell that would ripple across the Union. On May 9, 1862 Hunter publically declared free all the slaves in the states in which his command encompassed. Whereas General Fremont had only declared free slaves of rebelling owners in Missouri the previous September, Hunter's declaration covered both loyal and rebellious owners. This decision was so sudden in its announcement and implementation that not even Commodore Du Pont heard about it until later. He wrote on the 11th:

> And speaking of the General brings me to a point which really startled some of us and, in reference to which, I wait with some degree of anxiety as well as curiosity. I allude to General Hunter's General Order declaring the slaves free in South Carolina, Georgia, and Florida! No one knew of it, no word whispered to me. I laughed outright when I first saw it— then I felt as if it was no laughing matter, it was calculated to make one hold his breath, rather I speculated whether a commanding general, sixty hours in time from Washington, not even operating in the field, could do such a thing, without orders.

The text of Hunter's emancipation message was clear and unambiguous:

> The three states of Georgia, Florida, and South Carolina, composing the Military Department of the South, having deliberately declared themselves no longer under the protection of the United States of America and having taken up arms against the said United States it becomes a military necessity to declare them under martial law. This was accordingly done on the 25th day of April, 1862. Slavery and martial law in a free country are altogether incompatible; the persons in these three states—Georgia, Florida, and South Carolina—heretofore held as slaves are therefore declared forever free.

It did not take long for Hunter's unilateral declaration to make it to all corners of the Northern states. Opinions in the various newspapers, both large and small, either praised or condemned his action. Though he had previously declared free on April 13 the slaves that were at Fort Pulaski when it fell on April 11, 1862, this decision was not as important as the fact that the fort had fallen. In this new action, both Lincoln and Stanton decided to wait for a while to gauge public opinion after they got wind of it. Deciding after a few days that they could proceed, Lincoln issued on May 19 a formal proclamation nullifying Hunter's declaration and at the same time for political reasons disavowing any prior knowledge of his intentions, meaning that Hunter did this without consulting either the War Department or the White House. Furthermore,[10] Lincoln made it quite clear this time that he as the president, should he elect to do so, would alone make the decision to issue a declaration of emancipation. He would do so for national security policy reasons, in some or in all of the current states in the rebellion. The president could not "feel justified in leaving to the decision of commanders in the field.[11] These are totally different questions from those police regulations in armies and camps." However, neither Lincoln nor Stanton said anything about the contraband regiment.

Though Hunter caused a firestorm of controversy, his declaration was more symbolic than substance for the vast majority of the slaves it meant to free, because the mainland portion of the states which it covered was still Rebel-controlled territory. This was, however, politically another thorn for Lincoln, as another of his generals made policy without permission. It was not also the fact that Hunter's decree in reality was limited to the areas of his command, but the larger issue that a subordinate could do such a thing independent of his superior's approval was politically unsound, even though it might have been morally correct. Policy, regardless of what time in history,[12] emits from the top down, not the reverse.

Unlike Fremont, Lincoln did not first ask Hunter to nullify his order. Also unlike Fremont, Lincoln did not relieve him. This second unlikeness was for far different political reasons. Lincoln had to act decisively in Fremont's case after he refused to recant his emancipation order, because this was still early in the war and nobody could tell then which way the Border States would go. By the time of Hunter's declaration, several things had occurred, therefore not requiring Hunter's removal. During the first several months of 1862, several federal legislative initiatives had been taking place in reference to escaping slaves and emancipation. For example, Congress passed a law in March forbidding any officer in the Army or Navy from returning escaping slaves.

Since the previous November, Lincoln had also been working on the idea of compensated emancipation. The idea was to lessen the chance of a border state wanting to join the Confederacy by providing the mechanism that if any of these states did free their slaves the federal government would pay $400.00 per slave. The first border state that this was tried in, Delaware, failed when it was rebuked by its legislature. In March, Lincoln introduced the idea to Congress as a resolution offering again to the Border States compensation if they would free their slaves. All the border legislatures refused the offer. However, Congress did pass a version of it providing for the compensated emancipation in the District of Columbia, where it had legislative jurisdiction, thus eliminating slavery in the district. Though the political mood in Congress and in Lincoln was slowly changing in regard to emancipation as the war progressed, i.e., necessity begetting opportunity, the idea about having blacks in uniform was still another issue. Neither Lincoln nor Stanton may have said anything to Hunter about this other decision of his, but it still would prove to be a highly controversial issue at that, especially back at Port Royal.

Until General Hunter's edict of manumission had been invalidated by the president, his idea to round up men of military age was going on as planned. Prior to his dual announcement on May 9, he had already begun to lay the groundwork. He appointed a nephew and aide, Captain Arthur M. Kinzie, as colonel. Though it could be viewed as nepotism, Major Halpine said that Hunter appointed Kinzie "partly to prove—so violent was then the prejudice against negro troops—that the Commanding General asked nothing of others which he was not willing that one of his own flesh and blood should be engaged in." For the freedmen who would compose the first company of his regiment, Hunter appointed three enlisted men on May 7 from the 1st New York Engineers as the company officers: Sergeant Charles T. Trowbridge as captain, with his brother John T. Trowbridge and George D. Walker as lieutenants.[13] On the 8th he wrote to one of his key subordinates, Brigadier General Isaac I. Stevens, who commanded the army units in the immediate islands of Port Royal, for recommendations of enlisted men to become officers in the other companies. "I have concluded to enlist regiments to be officered from the most intelligent and energetic of our non-commissioned officers; men who will go into it with all their hearts. If you have any such, please appoint them to officer all the companies you can furnish me except the first."

Hunter told Stevens about Trowbridge and the other two officers. He then went on to say, "Captain Trowbridge has orders to report to you, and you will very much oblige me if you furnish him with a good company as soon as possible, and then send him down to report to me. And send, also, other companies as fast as you can have them organized. The non-commissioned officers appointed as officers will not be dropped from the rolls of their respective companies till their new appointments shall have been approved by the President."[14]

Hunter had previously tried to get experienced line officers from the white units to transfer while he was trying to get the freedmen to enlist voluntarily, but this too was not popular. It was not an uncommon scene the way Major Halpine described how many junior officers felt. "On the very threshold of this novel enterprise, came the first—and it was not a trivial—difficulty. Where could experienced officers be found for such an organization? 'What! command niggers' was the reply—if possible more amazed than scornful—of nearly every competent young lieutenant or captain of volunteers to whom the suggestion of commanding this class of troops was made."

Hunter's reaction to this rebuff of his offer for advancement was quick. "The fools or bigots who refuse are enough punished by their refusal. Before two years they will be competing eagerly for the commissions they now reject."[15] However, getting officers from the next tier of possible candidates was just as daunting. Halpine said, "Non-commissioned officers and men of the right stamp, and able to pass the examination requisite were scarce articles. Few had the hardihood or moral courage to face the screaming, riotous ridicule of their associates in the white regiments."

This was proven in the experience of one Sergeant Biggs in the 48th New York Infantry. Though he had been promised a commission as a first lieutenant with a quick advancement to captain, he could not overcome the ridicule he received and turned down the commission for which he had qualified. Halpine added also this "was but one of many score of precisely similar cases."

William Todd of Company B, 79th New York Infantry said:

We heard that General Hunter was organizing such a regiment, and several of our non-commissioned officers had been offered commissions in the new organization, but the honor had been declined. Candor compels us to place on record the fact, that at this time the Highlanders, with possibly a few exceptions, were bitterly opposed to raising the Negro to the military level of the Union soldier.

The men of another unit, the 11th Maine Infantry, which would be transferred later to the Department of the South, would hold similar sentiments: "There was a reluctance among the best men in white regiments to accept commissions in which they would have rank and pay, but not a standing among officers of white regiments."

Regardless of the difficulty of finding qualified enlisted men to become officers, enough finally came forward to accept commissions, pending final approval from the War Department. Of the 25 available regiments from which to draw the candidates,[16] which included infantry, cavalry, artillery and engineers, only three provided enough volunteers to appoint as officers. These were the 100th Pennsylvania Infantry, the 48th New York Infantry and the 1st New York Engineers. The men who volunteered were as followed: from the 100th Pennsylvania, Sergeants William James, James Pomeroy, W. J. Randolph, Alexander Heasley, and Harry C. West; the 48th N.Y., Sergeants William H. Danielson and Henry A. Beach; and the 1st N.Y. Engineers, James Harrold and John Goddard,[17] besides

Captain Trowbridge and Lieutenants Trowbridge and Walker.[18] They would have their hands full.

General Hunter's initiative to augment the number of men assigned to his command, regardless of how controversial it may have been to many of his subordinates, was not without related activity going on in other areas. On April 30, Secretary of the Navy Gideon Wells had authorized his commanders to enlist blacks "To make use of able bodied fugitives in all capacities on board their warships, enjoining them to obtain the services of these persons for the country by enlisting them freely in the navy, with their consent." As opposed to the Army, the Navy had a history of recruiting blacks during wartime. This action of Wells then led radical abolitionist Senator James W. Grimes of Iowa to say on May 4, 1862 that "this must be finally followed up, by an army order, sooner or later, and then comes the end of slavery." He felt that the use of freedmen in the military "as of vastly more importance" than any legislation passed by Congress. Hunter's action would give bite to Grimes' statement.

After Hunter issued his emancipation decree on May 9 and then announced later that day his intent to draft the freedmen, he sent instructions to Brigadier General H. W. Benham, commander of the Northern District, Department of the South,[19] "that you will order the commanding officers in your district to send immediately to the headquarters [on Hilton Head Island], under a guard, all able-bodied negroes capable of bearing arms within the limits of their several commands."

On the 11th, Benham was ready to issue his own orders and sent them to Brigadier General Isaac Stevens, whose command included the islands of Port Royal, Ladies and St. Helena; and Brigadier General H. W. Wright, commander on Edisto Island. Reiterating Hunter's directive, he said that they were to:

> Immediately take the proper steps for carrying it into effect within your command and that they will report at the earliest moment to these headquarters [also on Hilton Head] the probabilities as to numbers. This order will not include the servants of officers or those now actually in the employment of the Quartermaster's Department.

Not wanting to disturb the advantage of his officers having servants and disrupt the required manpower necessary for military supply operations, Benham would simply take the men working on the plantations. Upon receiving their orders, Stevens and Wright organized their men so they could start collecting the freedmen on the 12th. This would cause an immediate reaction from the whites who were working with them.

From the time that Hunter made his decision to draft the freedmen, send out the word to the various regiments in his command that he wanted volunteers to officer his new contraband regiment, and order his subordinate commanders to start rounding them up, it is very surprising that word did not leak as it had before when Hunter first tried to get men to volunteer and many disappeared. On this occasion the superintendents of the various plantations were not informed of this draft until the last possible moment, therefore preventing anyone from giving the alarm, because it would have been obvious who did it when soldiers would arrive at a certain plantation and nobody they wanted would be there. Hunter did not even have the courtesy to inform Commodore Du Pont of this, just as with his emancipation order. Du Pont said, "The organizing and arming the contrabands here also caused some surprise."

In General Stevens' command, a circular was prepared also on May 11 at his headquarters in Beaufort to be delivered to the superintendents of the various plantations so they would know to "send to Beaufort to-morrow morning every able-bodied Negro between the ages of eighteen and forty-five, capable of bearing arms, under their charge." The overseers would also provide a descriptive list of the males on their respective plantations who met the age requirements. These instructions would be carried out and supervised by the general's Assistant Adjutant-General and son, Captain Hazard Stevens.

Captain Stevens then wrote to Edward L. Pierce, who at this time was still in charge of the plantations, that he had prepared this circular in his father's name for the superintendents in charge of the plantations within his command about General Hunter's order. Stevens required that Pierce "Have these circulars distributed among the several agents with instructions to pay the greatest attention to the enforcement of the order. Any assistance that you may require to distribute the circular, or otherwise, will be cheerfully rendered." Needless to say, Pierce complied with General Stevens' instructions by informing his supervisors of the pending roundup for transfer to Beaufort and ultimately to Hilton Head, but he would not do this without the most strongly worded protest he could write to General Hunter.

Pierce did not mince words:

General: This evening, I received from Brigadier-General Stevens, through his adjutant, while I was at my headquarters on Saint Helena Island, a circular requesting me to aid in executing an order issued by your command for the collection of all negroes on the plantations able to bear arms. I issued prompt instructions to the superintendents to aid in the execution of the order. While thus yielding ready obedience to military authority, which must of necessity, be paramount to all civil interests in your command, I must respectfully beg leave, as the representative of another Department, to express my great regret for the order and my reasons for such regret.

Pierce's protestations included the facts that as a representative of the Treasury Department, he had been placed in charge of the plantations on the Sea Islands. He had the authority of President Lincoln through Secretary Chase to be responsible for the freedmen. Pierce mentioned what he had done to date in organizing the plantations with the help of the missionaries, how much money the Treasury Department had spent for farm equipment and labor costs, the fact that the spring crops had already been planted, and that removing all these men from the fields would be devastating, leaving him only women, children, and the elderly to attend to them. If the collection of all these freedmen able to bear arms was carried out, everything that Pierce and the missionaries under the auspices of the Treasury Department had done to date would be wasted.

Though Pierce approved of a voluntary unit, he felt that forcing the freedmen to serve would be counterproductive. "I deplore the probable effects of this on their minds. They are ignorant, suspicious, and sensitive. They have not ac-quired [*sic*] such confidence in us. I fear also that an enforced enlistment will give color to their masters' assurance that we were going to take them to Cuba."

Pierce was also worried about how slavery might have had an adverse effect on the freedmen's ability to become soldiers:

They have not so far recovered the manhood which two centuries of bondage have rooted out; they do not yet so realize that they have a country to fight for, as to make this, in my judgment, a safe way of dealing with them. I have been struck, and so have others associated with me been struck, with their indisposition to become soldiers. This indisposition will pass away, but only time and growing confidence in us will remove it ... They should be instructed in due time, and as they grow to it, in every right and duty, even that to bear arms in the common defense.

While Pierce may have felt correct in his observation that the freedmen would make good soldiers in due time, future events would prove that he was completely wrong in his assessment.

So, as Edward Pierce finished his letter of protest to General Hunter on the evening of the 11th, a specifically chosen regiment of General Stevens' command was already on the march to carry out Hunter's decree, which in this case was the 79th New York Infantry, also known as the Highlanders.

Just as General Stevens had selected his son to oversee this operation since he knew he could trust him, he chose the 79th New York because he used to be the regiment's commander before he was promoted to brigadier general. He still had a special relationship with the unit.[20] His intent was to have them in place on the various plantations on the morning of May 12 so they could quickly execute General Hunter's order and prevent too many men from slipping away once they found out what was going on. As the soldiers arrived at the different places where they were supposed to collect the freedmen in the morning, several of the missionaries recorded what they witnessed and their thoughts about this operation.

Harriet Ware:

> Young Hazard Stevens came over with dispatches from General Hunter ordering all the agents to send him in the morning all the able-bodied black men between the ages of 18 and 45, capable of bearing arms, on the plantations. There was no explanation whatsoever of the reasons for the demand, no hint of what was to be done with them and nothing but our confidence in General Hunter's friendliness to the race gives us a shadow of comfort. But that would avail little to the negroes, who would lose the confidence they are beginning to feel in white men. Yet there was but one thing for us to do, and it was with heavy, aching hearts that at midnight we separated. Companies of soldiers were to be sent from Beaufort in the night and distributed to the different plantations to prevent the negroes from taking to the woods, so that we were not surprised at being roused about two hours after by thundering knocks at the front door, echoing through all these empty rooms with a ghostly sound. This proved to be Captain Stevens again, alone, who had stopped to enquire the way to some of the other plantations he had to notify, and say that the soldiers would be here in about an hour. We had scarcely got to sleep again before we all were roused by their arrival, and eight men, a Captain and Sergeant of the New York 79th Highlanders, tramped through the house. Mr. [Edward S.] Philbrick [another of the missionaries] gave them a pail of water and some hard tack, for they had had a long walk, and then they stretched themselves on the floor of one of our empty parlors as quietly as could be, considering themselves in luxury."

Laura M. Towne:

> Monday, May 12, 1862
> The Black day

> Yesterday afternoon, Captain Hazard Stevens and orderly came here with an order from General Hunter, commanding Mr. Pierce to send

every able-bodied negro down to Hilton Head to-day. Mr. Pierce was alarmed and indignant and instantly went to Beaufort to see General Stevens who told him that he knew nothing of this but the order, and that he considered it very ill-advised. Meanwhile, last night were anxious and depressed at tea-time and talked in a low tone on this extraordinary proceeding ... By the moonlight soon after when I looked out of the window, I saw a company of soldiers marching up to the house. They stood for some time about the yard and then marched off to go to the different plantations in squads ... We were astir early and up very late, for after twelve o'clock we heard a horse gallop up and a man's step on the porch. I got out of the window and peeped over. It was Stevens' orderly with his horse. I went down, let him have Mr. Hooper's bed on the parlor floor,[21] and tie his horse in the yard."

Susan Walker:

11th May Sunday

Great excitement! Capt Stevens brings order from Gen Hunter that all colored men between 18 and 45 capable of bearing arms should be taken to Hilton Head—no explanation. What can it mean? Are these men contrary to all American usages—U.S. usages rather, to be impressed against will to military service?[22] I am filled with amazement, indignation and sorrow. I am called upon, as superintendent of this plantation, to select the persons coming within Gen Hunter's requisition. How can I do it? Blinded by tears that will not be kept back, I write the names almost as signing their death warrants. The saddest duty I ever performed. If I could but speak to them before hand, I would prepare them, if possible, for any duty, but this is not permitted.

12 May Monday

Cap Stevens last night brought a company of armed soldiers and paraded before our door previous to distribution over the Islands.

All over the islands these scenes repeated themselves as the soldiers arrived at the plantations where they were supposed to be and waited for morning. When the sun rose on Monday the 12th, they began the next phase of General Hunter's order.

At "Mrs. Jenkins" plantation on St. Helena Island, the superintendent, G. M. Wells, reported that as he and the soldiers:

... left the house we saw where had been but a few moments before field hands, hard at work, but horses and plows without drivers, and idle hoes. On inquiry we found that no one could tell the whereabouts of any of the 'able-bodied men.' The fact was they had 'smelt a very large rat,' and according to the expression of an old man on the place, had found it 'very necessary to go to the woods to split rails.' The soldiers went to the cabins and to the woods some quarter of a mile distant and brought in all but two of the men ... The people were not told the object for which they were taken until they were brought to me. I tried to explain to them why they were being carried away, cheering and encouraging them by every means in my power. All seemed dishearten and sad, though none were stubborn or used harsh words. The soldiers used them very kindly and made no decided demonstration of authority ... At the Doctor Croft plantation but two men were taken, the others with the foremen escaped to the woods, having gained information in regard to the movement from a woman who had seen the soldiers at Mrs. Jenkins' plantation.

On "Doctor Pope's" plantation, also on St. Helena, L. D. Phillips gave a different scene:

Reaching the negro quarters before 6 o'clock, I find the people quietly at work, the men and boys grinding corn for the morning meal, the women cooking in their cabins ... I gather the men quietly and tell them that General Stevens has sent for them to come immediately to Beaufort and that we must all obey the general's orders. By this time the corporal comes up and bids them 'fall in.' They move reluctantly ... Hurrying back to Doctor Pope's, I took the sergeant and one soldier in our buggy over to Capt. John Tripp's. Here the people were at work in the field. The men were called from their work and their names taken ... The private was left to escort them, while the sergeant and I got in to drive to the next estate ... When we came to Thomas J. Tripp's I found the old foreman, but the men, as he hinted, had fled to the woods. I left a message ... to advise them to ... see me at Doctor Pope's, and in the afternoon, somewhat to my surprise, they appeared and took up their line of march without escort to Beaufort Ferry ... At Marion Chaplin's the same plan was pursued, the men being found in the fields, collected, impressed, and marched off.

Regardless of how the men were rounded up, every plantation had the same response from the elderly, the women, and the children. As the men from "Doctor Pope's" plantation were being led away.

... the whole village, old men, women, and boys, in tears, following at our heels. The wives and mothers of the conscripts, giving way to their feelings, break into the loudest lamentations and rush upon the men, clinging to them with the agony of seperation [sic] ... Some of them, setting up such a shrieking as only this people could, throw themselves on the ground and abandon themselves to the wildest expressions of grief.

When Phillips left John Tripp's plantation, "I whipped up to avoid witnessing another scene of violent seperation [sic], but for a long distance we could hear the prolonged crying and wailing.

Susan Walker said that the:

... men were called from the field and thus hurried off without time for coats or shoes or a good bye to their families. The women stood near by [sic], crying though half assured by my presence in their midst, that nothing wrong would be done. The school house scene was one of great excitement. Capt. Stevens drew up with his men to the negro quarters. Negroes quite unprepared, had no one to give them confidence. Women wept and children screamed as men were torn from their embrace. This is a sad day throughout the Islands.

Nucleus of a Regiment

Though General Stevens had entrusted the roundup within his command to his former regiment, it did not mean that it was going to be an easy task. Laura Towne said that Captain Stevens told her the job was "dirty work ... It appears that he had been up all night riding over the islands ..." The soldiers did not fare any better. "That night the whole island was marched over by the soldiers in squads, about six or ten going to each plantation. They were unused to the duty, had to march through deep sand, and some all night, to get to their destination, and without dinner or supper, and so they were grumbling at having to do this kind of thing at all." The men she personally witnessed go through this "were the Seventy-ninth New York (Highlanders), Company D."

This operation was an emotional drain on the soldiers too. Miss Towne said that "the soldiers have always been friendly to the negroes, have given them good advice and gentle treatment and they are honored and trusted all over the islands. So I have no doubt the duty was really repugnant to them."

Captain Stevens was not keen on doing this job either, though he was doing it for his father. He acted tough when he got the men to Susan

Walker's place, telling them to shoot anybody who disobeyed Hunter's order, but Miss Walker felt this was an act of bravado. "I do not think Capt Stevens meant to be so stern as he seemed. He is but a boy, and extremely diffident and in no sympathy with our work here for the Negroes. He said, when I besought him to be kind to the men so strangely and cruelly ordered to Hilton Head, 'Yes, poor devils—Before I do such dirty work again I will resign.'"

That Monday evening Laura Towne estimated that roughly "four hundred men, or perhaps not so many, were taken to Beaufort to-night and are to go to Hilton Head to-morrow." On Tuesday the 13th she wrote a revised number in her diary: "Five hundred men were sent from the islands to Beaufort yesterday and went to Hilton Head, to-day, I suppose."

While the impressment of the freedmen went on during Monday, Mr. Pierce took a steamer to Hilton Head to talk personally to General Hunter. He arrived there at nine a.m. after a half-hour ride. Hunter informed him that he read the letter of protest Pierce wrote to him on May 11. Pierce said, "To my question if he was aware that he was thwarting a plan of the Government which I had in charge, he said he could not help it if two plans of the Government conflicted." As to the draft itself, Pierce asked him, "If he intended to enroll these people against their will, he said he did not." Though Hunter gave him this and other assurances, he wasn't placated. When he returned to St. Helena Island later that day, Pierce composed a long letter to Treasury Secretary Chase apprising him of the events of the 11th and 12th, and also giving him the details of his meeting with Hunter. He hoped that this letter to Chase would cause him to intervene and get Secretary of War Stanton to override him. He added that the "arming of these Negroes by entirely voluntary enlistments is well, but this mode of violent seizures and transportation to Hilton Head alone, spreading dismay and fright, is repugnant." Pierce would find out soon enough what would take place.

Though Pierce did not mind the idea of freedmen volunteering in itself without coercion of any sort, he still felt the same way about their ability to automatically become soldiers because of their slave past when he wrote to Secretary Chase:

As a general rule they are extremely averse to bearing arms in this contest. They have great fear of white men, natural enough in those who have never been allowed any rights against them, and dread danger and death. They are to be brought out of this unmanliness with great caution and tact, and the proceedings of to-day, managed as they have been with a singular forgetfulness of their disposition, will only increase their aversion to military service.

Harriet Ware had a similar opinion when she wrote on the 12th that "if we can have blacks to garrison the forts and save our soldiers through the hot weather, every one [*sic*] will be thankful. But I don't believe you could make soldiers of these men at all—they are afraid, and they know it."

Unfortunately for Miss Ware, she had an unlikely ally, unbeknownst to her, in the form of General Stevens. Though he had to obey General Hunter's orders, it did not mean he could not vent his true feelings. Shortly after carrying out his instructions, he privately wrote to General Benham, his immediate superior. "There is very little material for soldiers in the able-bodied men of color in this department." He firmly believed that they were afraid of their former masters "... and of white men generally ... I conceive a great use can be made of the blacks in our military operations in developing upon them the menial duties, and as strictly subordinate to existing organizations."

Another of the missionaries also made his thoughts known when he wrote on May 27, "Negroes—plantation negroes, at least—will never make soldiers in one generation. Five white men could put a regiment to flight; but they may be very useful in preventing sickness and death among our troops by relieving them of part of their work ..." Unfortunately for Mr. William C. Gannett, his opinion, just like that of the other missionaries and General Stevens, would be proven wrong.

Whereas General Hunter did not consult his subordinates when he decided to draft the sea island freedmen, he did not bother to consult those who thought that they would not make good soldiers for whatever reason. As far as he was concerned, these men represented a means to an end, which was the creation of another infantry regiment that he could add to his command.

When the men were collected on May 12 they were funneled to Beaufort on Port Royal Island and then shipped to Hilton Head to begin military training. About a week later, Hunter kept his promise to Pierce and allowed those to leave who wanted to return home. However, Hunter was very persuasive and many remained. Laura Towne saw the evidence of this when she wrote on the 19th: "Our men have returned from Hilton Head and nearly all are eager to go there again and serve in the forts, though Marcus says he does not wish to fight, but only to learn to fight ..." For those who remained, their training continued. Major Halpine said that "... by a strange coincidence, [the regiment's] camp was pitched on the lawn and around the mansion of General Drayton, who commanded the rebel works guarding Hilton Head, Port Royal, and Beaufort, when the same was first captured by the joint naval and military operations ..."

While Hunter's new regiment started to take shape, related political matters were happening. On the same day that President Lincoln nullified Hunter's emancipation decree, May 19, 1862, the Governor of Massachusetts, John Andrew, wrote to Secretary of War Stanton about the federal government's urgent request for additional infantry regiments to be raised from the state. Using this reply as a forum to air his view on Hunter's decree and the use of blacks as soldiers, he said, "if the President will sustain General Hunter, recognize all men, even black men, as legally capable of that loyalty the blacks are waiting to manifest, and let them fight, with God and human nature on their side, the roads will swarm, if need be, with multitudes whom New England would pour out to obey your call."

On the 21st, Treasury Secretary Chase sent to Stanton all the materials he had received from Pierce on General Hunter's draft of the freedmen and the repercussions derived from them. Chase said, "All the papers are worth reading and are important to a correct view of the state of things on the islands. The report of Mr. Pierce is a brief summary of the whole, and will, I think, impress you with a high opinion of his discretion and capacity."

Unfortunately, neither Governor Andrew nor Chase had any effect on Stanton to either sanction Hunter's contraband regiment or stop his draft decree. The one person who could have had the stronger impact of the two, Chase, did not even put the full weight of his office behind it, because he did not, as historian Edward A. Miller put it, "… make a recommendation and so Stanton took no immediate action …" Here was a second and third opportunity that the secretary of war could have said or done something in regard to the contraband regiment after Lincoln had nullified Hunter's emancipation decree, to either sanction or stop it, but he continued to say or do nothing. Why? Though May would end with mixed results, the second month of Hunter's regiment would start to see momentum build.

In the memoirs that he wrote in 1872, General Hunter gave a very positive picture of the freedmen's performance in their transition from recently having been slaves to becoming soldiers. "The regiment of negroes which I enlisted in South Carolina on my own responsibility was a great success. The men acquired the drill with great rapidity; they were subordinate and attentive to all their duties, and particularly successful on picket duty." This firsthand account easily ran counter to the various predictions of those as to the freedmen's ability to become soldiers, regardless of their reasons for stating them. These ex-slaves would amply demonstrate that generations of servitude had neither damaged their intellectual ability nor adaptability.

Even with the proof that the freedmen were adapting to military life, there continued to be nay-sayers, especially if they had not seen them at drill. Edward S. Philbrick, another of the missionaries, said on June

3, 1862, "I don't regard the blacks as of any account in a military light, for they are not a military race, and have not sufficient intelligence to act in contact in any way where firmness of purpose is required." In regard to this frame of mind, the editor of the book *Letters From Port Royal*, from which this quote and others were derived, Elizabeth Ware Pearson, said that "… the opinion just expressed concerning the impossibility of making soldiers from Sea Island negroes was, very naturally, the view that prevailed at this time among the superintendents and teachers …" Then she added, "As the letters progress, the reader will see the development of a complete change of mind on this point."

As June progressed, Hunter tried several times to get his experimental unit recognized. He said, "I made repeated efforts in vain to get this regiment recognized and paid by the Government. It was a delicate subject, and I could get no reply approving or disapproving my conduct in this manner."

Major Halpine, his aide, was even more explicit in describing the government's muted intransigence. As the regiment trained:

> … meantime, the War Department gave no sign, and the oracles of the Adjutant-General's office were dumb as the statue of the Sphynx. [*sic*] Reports of the organization of the First South Carolina infantry were duly forwarded to army headquarters; but evoked no comment, either of approval or disapproval. Letters detailing what had been done, and the reason for doing it; asking instruction, and to have commissions duly issued to the officers selected; appeals that the department paymasters should be instructed to pay these negro troops like other soldiers; demands that the government should either shoulder the responsibility of sustaining the organization, or give such orders as would absolve Gen. Hunter from the responsibility of backing out from an experiment which he believed to be essential to the salvation of the country—all these appeals to Washington proved in vain; for the oracles still remained profoundly silent, probably waiting to see how public opinion and the politicians would receive this daring innovation.

In Hunter's attempts to get men, he soon realized that he would not have enough to form two regiments that he originally wanted, so he concentrated on filling out the first. Obtaining additional men from Edisto Island due to General Wright's efforts, plus those from Hilton Head and the smaller islands of the Port Royal area, which included Ladies, Paris, and Coosaw, the regiment swelled to about 800 men. A reporter for the *Boston Advertiser* said that the men wore the standard Union Army uniform, which was a dark blue coat and pants, with "a stout unbleached cotton shirt." The uniform was capped off with a cone-shaped broad-brimmed hat. He said that the general effect was "decidedly dark," but all of them were "clean and fresh in appearance" as opposed to wearing their previous slave attire.

On Monday the 23rd several of the missionaries left St. Helena's Island for Hilton Head to see how the men were doing.

When they arrived, Laura Towne said that:

> General Hunter drove us out to the camp ... which he reviewed ... The regiment is [his] great pride. They looked splendidly, and the great mass of blackness, animated with a soul and armed so keenly, was so impressive. They did credit to their commander ... The men seemed to welcome General Hunter and to be fond of him. The camp was in beautiful order.

Though the freedmen's training was going well, Hunter had to replace his nephew, Arthur M. Kinzie, as colonel, because he had come down with an illness that had impaired his health. He was replaced with another aide named Captain James D. Fessenden, son of a powerful U.S. senator, William P. Fessenden of Maine.

As it was, Hunter was getting mixed results in his endeavor to sustain his creation. On the one hand, his men were proving their critics wrong as to their adaptability to the rigor of military training. However, on the other he could not get any traction in having his unit recognized from the War Department. His numerous requests for recognition, logistical support, federal commissions for his officers and pay for the men were falling on deaf ears. He received no replies. As an officer with several decades of experience, Hunter knew quite well he could not push the issue but only make polite requests. This would seem to be the state of affairs with no seeming way out of the predicament. However, an opportunity soon arose that would allow him to break out of this communication stalemate with the War Department and bring it to the forefront of the national government. The most unlikely person who caused this to happen was a pro-slavery congressman.

On the evening of June 22, General Hunter was getting ready to take his usual ride along the picket line there on Hilton Head. A dispatch boat called the *Arago*, which had just arrived a short time prior, had some important correspondence for him. This was handed to him just as he was getting ready to mount his horse. Major Halpine relates:

> Hastily opening it, he first looked grave, than began to smile, and finally burst into peals of irrepressible laughter ... he literally was unable to

speak from constant interruptions of laughter ... At length he passed over the dispatch to his Chief of Staff who, on reading it, and rereading it, could find in its text but little apparent cause for merriment. It was a grave demand from the War Department for information in regard to our negro regiment—the demand being based on certain resolutions introduced by the Hon. Mr. Wickliffe, of Kentucky, asking for specific information on the point in a tone clearly not friendly.

How did this happen?

With the rumbling of emancipation that had been coming from the president and several members of Congress in the first half of 1862, this was starting to become a source of irritation for certain congressmen from the Border States. The fact that Congress had outlawed the practice of slavery in the District of Columbia, though the owners were compensated, did not help. Also, the extra fact that Lincoln had publicly repudiated Hunter's emancipation effort did not do much good either when he had added to his proclamation that the Border States should seriously consider compensated emancipation because the Border States "cannot, if you would, be blind to the signs of the times." However, when reports of Hunter's black regiment started to filter north through newspaper accounts, it did not take long for one border-state congressman to react.

In late May Democratic Congressman Charles A. Wickliffe of Kentucky had received word of Hunter's project. He privately wrote to Secretary Stanton to ask permission to deny these newspaper stories publically. In a reply letter the congressman was told that the secretary would get around to addressing this situation at the first available time. Incensed at this insulting rebuff, Wickliffe decided to take a public approach to this matter. Enlisting the aid of Senator Lazarus W. Powell, also of Kentucky, he introduced several resolutions in the House of Representatives on June 5 and 6 calling on the War Department to produce everything it knew of Hunter's activity. Though the resolutions did not pass, Wickliffe did not quit. On the 9th the House finally passed them and sent them to Stanton.

This congressional inquiry wanted to know if Hunter had in fact already organized or was in the process of organizing a black regiment; did Stanton permit him to do this; did Stanton provide them with uniforms; were the freedmen armed; and would the secretary provide any and all orders and correspondence the War Department had on this matter?

Stanton did not send a reply until June 14, during which time he worked in conjunction with Lincoln to disassociate the administration politically from the actions of Hunter. Stanton said in reply that neither he nor his department had any official knowledge of Hunter's black regiment; he had not permitted Hunter to do this. Uniforms had been allotted to all commanders without any instructions on how they were to be used. The War Department did not provide arms. Stanton would also not turn over any orders or correspondence by order of the president. However, that same day, he sent the dispatch that Hunter would not get until the evening of the 22nd, which contained the questions of the congressional inquiry minus the fifth part and directed Hunter to report as fast as possible.

Since the *Arago* would not be leaving before dawn with the morning high tide, General Hunter decided to do his inspection. It would also give him time to think about and discuss with his key subordinates how best to reply. Seizing upon this unanticipated opportunity from Congressman Wickliffe, he said as they rode along, "That old fool has just given me the very chance I was growing sick for! The War Department has refused to notice my black regiment; but now, in reply to this resolution, I can lay the matter before the country, and force the authorities either to adopt my negroes or to disband them." Once he got back, Hunter got busy on his reply.

The general worked with his chief of staff late into the night to have it ready for the *Arago*'s return voyage on June 23. Since Congressman Wickliffe had "introduced a denunciatory resolution in to the House of Representative," thoroughly convinced that "I had committed a heinous crime," Hunter wanted to make sure this gentleman from Kentucky got a fitting reply as soon as possible.

Stanton received Hunter's letter several days later. After sitting on it for a few more days, he finally sent it on July 2 without any endorsement to the Speaker of the House of Representatives after the chamber had returned from recess. In a dignified formality, Stanton wrote that "it will be seen that the resolution had been referred to [General Hunter], with instructions to make immediate report thereon. I have now the honor to transmit herewith the copy of a communication just received from General Hunter, furnishing information as to his action touching the various matters indicated in this resolution." The answers to Wickliffe, however, were anything but dignified; they were outright sarcastic.

When the Speaker, Mr. Galusha A. Grow, arranged to have Hunter's letter read before the entire assembly, it had its effect that the general meant for it to have. "The Clerk could scarcely read it with decorum; nor could half his words be heard amidst the universal peals of laughter in which both Democrats and Republicans appeared to vie as to which should be the more noisy." As to the first and most important question, whether General Hunter had organized a regiment of, in the words of Mr. Wickliffe, "fugitive slaves," Hunter said "that no regiment of 'fugitive slaves' has been or is being organized in this department. There is, however, a fine regiment of persons whose late masters are 'fugitive rebels'—men who everywhere fly before the appearance of the National flag ..." For the second question, whether he had any authority "for such organization," he referred to General Sherman's instructions from former Secretary of War Simon Cameron that "do distinctly authorizes one to employ all loyal persons offering their services in defense of the Union and for the suppression of this rebellion, in a manner I might see fit, or that circumstances might call for." To this Hunter added, also, "In the absence of any 'fugitive master law' the deserted slaves would be wholly without remedy, had not the crime of treason given the right to peruse, capture, and bring back those persons of whose protection they have been thus suddenly bereft."

For the third and fourth questions, whether the "fugitive slaves" had been furnished uniforms and other equipment and if they had been armed, Hunter's replies to them were the most comical. He said it was his:

> painful duty to reply that I never have received any specific authority for issues of clothing, uniforms, arms, equipment ... to the troops in question. My general instructions from Mr. Cameron to employ them in any manner I might find necessary, and the military exigencies of the department and the country being my only, but, in my judgment, sufficient, justification. Neither have I had any specific authority for supplying those persons with shovels, spades, and pickaxes, when employing them as laborers, nor with boats and oars when using them as lightermen; but these are not points included in Mr. Wickliffe's resolution. To me it seemed that liberty to employ men in a particular capacity implied with it liberty also to supply them with the necessary tools, and acting upon this faith, I have clothed, equipped, and armed the only loyal regiment yet raised in South Carolina.

Though Hunter was very serious in his closing paragraphs about the freedmen's ability and their officers testifying to this, his flippancy to Congressman Wickliffe's seriousness was too much for the other members of the House of Representatives. When Wickliffe entered the chamber after a portion of it had already been read, he "rose to his feet in a frenzy of indignation, complaining that the reply, of which he had only heard some portion, was an insult to the dignity of the House, and should be severely noticed." However, "the more he raved and gesticulated, the more irrepressible did his colleagues, on both sides of the slave question, scream and laugh." Fellow Congressman Schuyler Colfax of Indiana then suggested that the whole message be read again on Wickliffe's behalf, "which was instantaneously carried amid such an uproar of universal merriment and applauce [sic] ..." Though Hunter still did not get an answer from the War Department, as he had hoped, his comical retort would have a greater impact than he could have imagined.

Wickliffe may have suffered embarrassment from the uproarious behavior of his fellow congressmen, but this still did not stop him from challenging General Hunter. On July 5 he said in general session that the Lincoln administration had no authority to create any black units without congressional approval. Then contradicting himself he said that blacks in general were unfit for service, saying that "a negro is afraid by instinct or by nature, of a gun." Congressman Robert Mallary, also of Kentucky, added to his colleague's argument. To put them in the military would be "contrary to the rules that should govern a civilized nation in conducting war ... I shrink from arming the slave, using him to shoot down white men, knowing his depraved natures as I do. I would as soon think of enlisting the Indians ... as to arm the negro in this contest."

These statements of these congressmen would not go unchallenged. Radical Republican Thaddeus Stevens of Pennsylvania, in defending Hunter, said that armies of centuries past had liberated slaves and used them against their former masters; therefore, the federal government should do the same. "I do not view it as an abolition or as an emancipation question ... I view it as the means, and the only means, of putting down the rebellion." Though these border state congressmen continued to fight any federal attempt at emancipation or arming blacks, even they had to see that things were changing as Lincoln had said in May, that they cannot "be blind to the signs of the times." These changes would soon be embodied in two pieces of federal legislation and also a major decision by Lincoln.

As the future of slavery and blacks in uniform continued to be fought in the halls of Congress, other events continued to take place without waiting for congressional action in the Department of the South. On June 16, 1862 General Hunter had finally made an attack against Charleston. Needless to say, it did not work. After this failed attempt, he took his time pulling his men out and bringing them back to Port Royal. This slow retrograde continued into early July. One regiment, the 79th New York, arrived back in Beaufort on July 5. Since this unit and the other regiments involved had been in heavy action against determined Confederate forces on James Island south of the city in a battle known as Secessionville, they were not in the best of shape. At Beaufort, the 79th was only to be there for a short time while waiting to go to their next duty station on one of the islands. William Todd of Company B said that "while lying here at the dock, we had our first glimpse of colored troops," who happened to be there since leaving there in May for Hilton Head when they were drafted. After having been in combat, the men of the 79th were not in a good mood to see what they did. Todd said:

When we saw the negroes, uniformed and equipped like ourselves—except that their clothes and accoutrements were new and clean, while ours were almost worn out in active service—parading up and down the wharf, doing guard duty, it was more than some of our hot-headed pro-slavery comrades could witness in silence. For a while the air was filled with the vile epithets hurled at the poor darkies,[23] and overt actions against their persons were only prevented by the interference of our officers.

Though many soldiers of the 79th New York were shortsighted in their opinions of Hunter's men, not all those in the military shared this view, especially after witnessing them drill too. Commodore Du Pont wrote home on July 8 that he "witnessed the Sunday service and evening parade of Hunter's regiment of South Carolina Volunteers on Sunday last, and I could not but think there was another hand but that of men in this work. The battalions, after sixteen weeks, drill better than my men after sixteen months of drilling ..."

On July 11, General Hunter once again wrote to Stanton requesting that his black regiment be sanctioned. "I must earnestly beg that by return of mail you will give me full authority to muster into the service of the United States, as infantry, all loyal men to be found in my department, and that I be authorized to appoint all the officers. This has now become a military necessity in this department." As opposed to his previous requests for reinforcements and recognition of his new unit, this time it was a "military necessity." On July 3, Stanton ordered him to send to Virginia all the soldiers he could spare because of a major crisis there. For the past several weeks the Army of the Potomac under Major General George McClellan had been involved in a major effort to capture the Confederate capital of Richmond. When Rebel commander General Joseph E. Johnston was wounded on May 31 as the Federals were only a few miles from the city, he was replaced by General Robert E. Lee, who would turn the whole operation around. Aided by another general named Thomas J. "Stonewall" Jackson, Lee was able to push the Union forces back almost to their starting point through a series of brilliant maneuvers. This left the Yankees in a very precarious position and caused McClellan to send frantic messages to Washington for reinforcements. Shortly thereafter, Stanton sent Hunter his orders for transfer.

Hunter moved quickly to get what McClellan needed to Virginia. When he wrote his message on the 11th, he said that six infantry regiments were *en route* with General Stevens in command. The regiments sent were the 50th and 100th Pennsylvania, 28th Massachusetts, 8th Michigan and the 46th and 79th New York. This drawdown meant that he would have about 5,500 men less in his command, from nearly 19,000 to just over 13,000. This also meant he would have to contract his lines.

That same day when he wrote his message, Hunter ordered General Wright to abandon Edisto Island.

The order for the military to leave Edisto signified also that the freedmen there had to go too, abandoning a place that had been their home for generations. Laura Towne said that they "embarked in one or two vessels, sixteen hundred in all, with their house-hold effects, pigs, chickens …" With this many people uprooted, they had to be spread out over the other islands. For those who were placed on St. Helena Island, Miss Towne added that "these negroes will be rationed and cared for. They say they will get in the cotton here that had to be abandoned when the black regiment was formed." On Port Royal Island, Lt. William W. Geety of Company H, 47th Pennsylvania Infantry, wrote home on the 15th that as he was doing much picket duty, he saw that "there [was] lots of contrabands here." He also added, "Gen. Hunter has a regiment of them on duty at Hilton Head."

With the upheaval of the Edisto freedmen causing seeming disorder among the other islands, the transfer of the 5,500 soldiers to Virginia required Hunter's remaining units to be reorganized and transferred among the other points of control in the department to better facilitate command and control. By the end of July, the various subordinate commands had been organized: Beaufort and Hilton Head, South Carolina; Fort Pulaski, Georgia; Fort Clinch, Fernandina, and St. Augustine, Florida; Forts Jefferson, Old Town, and Taylor, Florida; Key West Barracks, Florida; and Pensacola Harbor, Florida. All of them reported directly to Hunter's headquarters, since the Northern, Southern and Western District structure that he had previously used had been discontinued in June.

On July 21, Stanton brought Hunter's latest request for official recognition of his black regiment to a cabinet meeting with the president. The fact that Hunter had said the withdrawal of those several thousand men to Virginia had created "a military necessity in this department" only heightened his request to a state of emergency. This was something that Stanton could no longer ignore, because this massive transfer gave credence finally to Hunter's request. Being the consummate politician that he was, the secretary of war decided to bring this issue to Lincoln's attention for direction so he could cover himself.

In a diary entry that he wrote that evening, Treasury Secretary Chase recorded what took place when Stanton brought up the issue:

> The Secretary of War presented some letters from Genl. Hunter, in which he advised the Department that the withdrawal of a large proportion of his troops to reinforce Genl. McClellan rendered it highly important that

he should be immediately authorized to enlist all loyal persons without reference to complection [*sic*]. Messrs. Stanton, Seward,[24] and myself, expressed ourselves in favor of this plan, and no one expressed himself against it. (Mr. Blair was not present.[25]) The President was not prepared to decide the question, but expressed himself as averse to arming the negroes. The whole matter was postponed until tomorrow.

The meeting the next day was not as profitable. Secretary Chase said, "The question of arming slaves was ... brought up and I advocated it warmly. The President was unwilling to adopt this measure ..." Though Lincoln still would not consent to this idea, Chase believed that he would leave it "... for some further consideration. The impression left upon my mind by the whole discussion was, that while the President thought that the organization, equipment and arming of negroes, like other soldiers, would be productive of more evil than good, he was not unwilling that Commanders should, at their discretion, arm, for purely defensive purposes, slaves coming within their lines." Even after this second meeting, Lincoln continued to be noncommittal on black enlistment, even though his cabinet was in favor of arming blacks, that the president had two significant pieces of legislation passed the previous week by Congress and that he revealed an important subject to them.

On July 17, Congress had passed a second Confiscation Act and a Militia Act, which Lincoln quickly signed. The first law allowed the military to seize all property of Rebels whether they were using it to further the Confederate war effort or not. The second authorized the president to receive blacks into the military for the first time whether they were free or slave. At the cabinet meeting on the 22nd, Lincoln revealed for the first time his plan to emancipate the slaves in all the rebelling states as a necessary war measure, citing his constitutional authority as commander in chief to do so. This announcement surprised everyone. His intention was to make it publicly known soon, but Secretary of State William H. Seward suggested that he wait for a victory on the battlefield. To do so otherwise might be interpreted as an act of desperation given the recent string of defeats suffered by the Army of the Potomac. Lincoln wisely followed this advice. However, he still would not commit himself to black enlistment. Why?

The momentum was building to eradicate slavery in the rebelling states,[26] but this still did not push the president to authorize the use of slaves as soldiers. The burden may have been taken off Stanton to let it rest with Lincoln, but he was not one to make a decision on a major political or war issue until he felt the timing was right, just as he did with emancipation. Though Lincoln now had legal authority to enlist blacks under the Militia Act, the time to do so in his view, still had not arrived. When it did, it would be clearly understood why he waited for that point in time.

The opinion of many politicians may have been changing in Washington, but this did not necessarily extend to other people, such as in the Department of the South. Charles Francis Adams, Jr., of the 1st Massachusetts Cavalry, wrote on July 28 from Hilton Head that:

> ... our ultra-friends, including General Hunter, seem to have gone crazy and they are doing the blacks all the harm they can. On this issue things are very bad. General Hunter is so carried away by his idea of negro regiments as, not only to write flippant letters about his one to Secretary Stanton, but even order their exemption from all fatigue duty; so that while our Northern soldiers work ten hours a day in loading and unloading ships, the blacks never leave their camp, but confine the attention to drill. There may be reasons for this, but it creates intense feeling here and even I cannot see the justice of it.

Adams also wrote another letter that same day to a family member but was more stinging about Hunter and his regiment:

> General Hunter is very unpopular—arbitrary and wholly taken up with his negro question. His one regiment is a failure, and becoming more so, and I have no faith in the experiment anyhow. I smiled audibly at your idea of my taking a commission in one of them; after all my assertion of principle to become a 'nigger driver' in my old age, for that is what it amounts to, seeing that they don't run away, or shirk working or fatigue duty. No! Hunter and you are all wrong, and, for once, the War Department was right. The negroes should be organized and officiered [*sic*] as soldiers; they should have arms put in their hands and be drilled simply with a view to their moral elevation and the effect on their self-respect, and for the rest they should be used as fatigue parties and on all fatigue duty. As to being made soldiers, they are more harm than good. It will be years before they can be made to stand before their old masters.... Under our system and with such white officers as we give them, we might make a soldiery equal to the native Hindoo [*sic*] regiments in about five years. It won't pay and the idea of arming the blacks as soldiers must be abandoned.

If General Hunter had become privy to Adams' vitriolic comments, he might have had him court-martialed for gross insubordination, but fortunately for Adams, his mail was not screened. Regardless of what many of Hunter's subordinates may have thought,[27] he continued to fight to keep his black regiment alive, though he received no reply to his letter of July 11 that emphasized the "military necessity in this department" when the six infantry regiments were sent to Virginia.

On July 31, Hunter again made another urgent attempt to obtain reinforcements. A seventh regiment, the 45th Pennsylvania Infantry, had also been sent to Virginia. Besides wanting to regain what territory he had to abandon, he also believed that other "strong posts should be established … I have therefore to request that reinforcements may be sent to this department as soon as possible, not only with a view to future operations, but also for the further security of our present positions and depots." However, as July ended, all Hunter could do, as with his previous requests, was once again wait and hope for a reply.

Rise of the Volunteers

Except for his decision not to have blacks in uniform, President Lincoln had made a major stride when he notified his cabinet of his intention to issue a proclamation of emancipation for all the slaves in the eleven rebelling states under his constitutional role as commander in chief of the armed forces of the United States. Add to this the congressional passage of the Second Confiscation Act and the Militia Act, and things considered impossible a year before were happening. As historian William Cochrane put it, "As the war was brought home to the people, constitutional barriers seemed less formidable. The concept that freeing the slaves would serve as a weapon of war was more readily accepted."

Now that Lincoln was ready to elevate the object of the war to a higher level, logic would seem to dictate that a natural consequence of it would be to begin to place blacks in uniform, both slave and free, to help make real that which he was poised to state. This was the opinion of his cabinet, but the president's seeming intransigence gave them the impression that he was not going to do anything about it, though he had signed the Militia Act into law without any hesitation. However, just as with the emancipation issue, it was a question of timing.

If General Hunter had known this, he probably would not have continued to make formal requests for his regiment, besides the additional manpower request with the recent loss of seven infantry regiments. On August 4, 1862 he once again wrote to Stanton to legitimize this unit, which in this case was to have the officers officially commissioned and the soldiers paid. He said also that though he had formally stopped recruiting, he continued to have other males readily available for this and other possible regiments if allowed to do so. This would go a long way to help replenish that which was lost to the Army of the Potomac in July and regain those islands Hunter had to abandon due to the drawdown:

> I make no doubt whatever that half a dozen colored regiments can be placed in the field within two months after my plan shall have received official countenance; and once the regiments are recognized and regularly paid as soldiers, it will require but a few additional posts to be established along the shore of the mainland … to bring many thousands of the loyal persons flocking around the standard of the Union.

However, by the following week, Hunter had finally decided that he had had enough with the War Department's intransigence and came to the decision he had hoped that he would not have to make. Except for Company A under Captain Charles Trowbridge, Hunter ordered the disbandment of his regiment. On the 10th, he wrote once again to Stanton to inform him of his decision. As in his previous communiqué, Hunter had even started to give the unit a formal name: "Failing to receive authority to muster the First Regiment of South Carolina Volunteers into service of the United States, I have disbanded them." Much to his chagrin, he added that he "had hoped that not only would this regiment would have been accepted, but that many similar ones would have been authorized to fill up the ranks of the army and afford the aid of which the cause seems now so much in need; but having failed to receive the authority which I expected I have deemed it best to discontinue the organization."

Hunter had waited a day or two to write to Stanton after he had made his decision, but it did not take long for word to spread once he did. This caused either tears or jubilation. Laura Towne heard the news on August 9 on St. Helena Island: "Hunter's negro regiment disbanded! Hunter almost broke his heart pleading for pay for them, and now that he sees that cannot obtain it, he disbands 'for a time,' he says and sends the men to 'gather crops.'"

On Port Royal Island, word reached there quickly too. Also on the 9th, Captain J. P. S. Gobin, commander of Company D, 47th Pennsylvania Infantry, wrote,[1] "I have heard of the disbanding of our famous nigger brigade at Hilton Head … Of their fighting qualities I have no idea, but I am satisfied there is not a single regiment in this department that would go into a fight with them or have any confidence in them."

One of the members of Captain Gobin's company, Musician Henry D. Wharton, wrote later on the 15th that he was happy:

> … that Gen. Hunter's Brigade of people of color, different in hue from Uncle Sam's legitimate soldiers, has been disbanded, and their

occupation now is that of hewing wood and carrying of carrying water ... The idea of clothing the contraband in the same style with the regular and volunteer, did not take well with the boys, they thinking it was an insult. The colored man may be good in his way, but he neither keep a hotel or fight along side [sic] of the Yankee boys for the preservation of the Union.

Placing his comments on a more ethereal level, Lt. Adams of the 1st Massachusetts Cavalry wrote home on the 10th that:

General Hunter's negro regiment was disbanded yesterday and now they have all dispatched to their old homes. Its breaking up was hailed here with great joy, for our troops have become more anti-negro than I could have imagined. But, for myself, I could not help feeling a strong regret at seeing the red-legged[2] darkies march off; for, though I have long known that the experiment was a failure, yet it was a failure of another effort at the education of these poor people ... What God made plain we have mixed up into inextricable confusion ... We have wrangled over arming the slaves before the slaves showed any disposition to use the arms, and when we have never had in our lives 5000 of them who would bear arms. Why could not fanatics be silent and let Providence work for a while. The slaves would have moved when the day came and could have been useful in a thousand ways.

Little did Gobin, Wharton and Adams know that this was just the opening act, the prelude before the storm. The political winds were slowly shifting to see the need to arm blacks, but it would still be a while before they would go in the right direction. When they finally did, these men would be aghast at what they would see.

Though General Hunter had to disband what he now called the "First Regiment of South Carolina Volunteers," it did not mean that he had lost his passion for it. When two superintendents complained to him on August 13 that "the negro regiment was quartered in their garden," he was not in a mood to listen to their complaints, especially when they complained about the unit in a besmirching manner. Since Hunter had "always suspected the superintendents of preventing enlistment and frowning upon negro soldiers, [he] became so exasperated by their complaints that he threatened to send them home in irons if they oppose the negro regiment any more [sic]."

On top of this, these two men failed to go through proper channels and went directly to Hunter. They should have gone first to the military governor who was in charge of the plantations where the two superintendents were located. Brigadier General Rufus Saxton, who had arrived back in June, was not happy when "Dr. Wakefield and Mr. Breed" went over his head. He considered it very disrespectful.

Hunter was also a forgiving individual. Though he was a career officer accustomed to regulations and discipline, he could not apply the same standards to his contraband unit. While it still existed, numerous men deserted, including one who did it several times. He did not severely punish them because of two reasons. Hunter "had promised the people pay for their services as soldiers and he could not keep his promise, and he thought the men did not yet understand the stringency of the military law and should be excused till more used to it."

Hunter's reluctance to disband his fledgling regiment, thus losing more troops on top of what he had already lost to Virginia, did not come without an epitaphic insult. Several days after his decision, he received word from the War Department to send his only cavalry regiment, the 1st Massachusetts, to Virginia. This directive came as the result of a recommendation by Brigadier General H. W. Wright to Stanton. Wright had transferred back to Washington at the end of July. Since he had been at Port Royal since its inception, Stanton wanted to know if any more units could also be withdrawn without hurting Port Royal's primary mission, to serve as a base for the naval blockade of Southern ports. Wright said that as many as four infantry regiments, the cavalry regiment, the engineer regiment, and two batteries of artillery could leave the department without jeopardizing operations. Without even consulting Hunter, even though he was the commanding officer, Stanton simply told him to transfer the 1st Massachusetts. This may have been a slight, but Hunter was fortunate that Stanton did not follow all of Wright's recommendations. About two weeks later, the secretary modified his order and allowed one squadron to remain that had not left yet, though the other two were already in Virginia.

With this seeming impasse at his inability to solve his manpower shortages, Hunter wrote to Stanton again on August 15, this time for reassignment to "give me a chance in some other direction." In a reply letter received later in the month, he was given only a 60 day leave of absence. He was to turn over command of the department to the senior brigadier general, who in this case was John M. Brannan. Though defeated in his quest to have black troops, Hunter still had one more card to play to see this brought about, and he set about using it, even before his request for transfer. This card was another brigadier general, a fellow abolitionist and the head of the plantations, Rufus Saxton.

Saxton appeared by background and temperament to be the right man to take over this difficult task.[3] A native of Massachusetts, he was raised by his abolitionist parents to believe that slavery was an evil. This anti-slavery upbringing would follow him throughout his adult life. He graduated from West Point in 1849. He served as chief quartermaster for the Expeditionary Corps with the rank of captain when it captured Port Royal. Since Saxton was the only officer to show any interest in the contrabands, this left a positive impression of him with the civilians who witnessed it, especially those with connections to Treasury Secretary Chase. He returned to Washington in March 1862 for further assignment since General Hunter brought his own chief quartermaster when he took over command. When Chase had decided previously in April that the arrangement he had at Port Royal in running the plantations and collecting cotton by distinct men, Edward L. Pierce and William H. Reynolds, was not working, he decided to turn the whole operation over to the military. On Chase's recommendation because of his previous work at Port Royal, Stanton promoted Captain Saxton to brigadier general on April 15, with orders to proceed to South Carolina.

General Saxton was prepared to begin his new assignment, but before he could travel south, an emergency arose that required his immediate attention. Confederate troops under Major General "Stonewall" Jackson

Brigadier General Rufus Saxton, whose leadership would steer the growth of a reconstituted 1st South Carolina Volunteers. *William J. Parry Collection at U.S. Army Military History Institute.*

began wreaking havoc against Union forces in the Shenandoah Valley in Virginia. Since General McClellan's amphibious assault on the coast of the state had tied down just about all available manpower and supplies on the eastern coast in this early phase of the Peninsula campaign, there were few assets available that could reinforce the Union forces in the valley. This included general officers. Jackson's intent was to stir up enough panic, which included threatening the important Federal armaments depot at Harper's Ferry on the Virginia/Maryland border and possibly Washington, so that the Federals would hopefully siphon off troops from McClellan's campaign to blunt his offensive capability as much as possible. Saxton was immediately tasked to head up defenses at Harper's Ferry.[4] This consumed his attention until June, when he was finally able to proceed to Port Royal.

Once he arrived, General Saxton set about organizing things to do his job. He was given the title of Military Governor with authority to run the plantations and look after the affairs of the freedmen.[5] No troops were placed under his command. This included Hunter's regiment, which Hunter still had under his personal control. The official transfer of operations from the Treasury Department to the War Department took place on July 1. Mr. Pierce had been offered a place on General Saxton's staff by Chase with the rank of colonel but turned it down. After helping Saxton get settled in, Pierce left Port Royal. Reynolds had already left. This arrangement was to encompass Saxton's area of endeavor until Hunter's decision to disband his Volunteers in August.

On August 9, the day before Hunter wrote to Stanton of his decision to disband, both he and General Saxton went to see Admiral Du Pont (since promoted from Commodore) on his flagship, the *Wabash*. They were joined by the Reverend Mansfield French, a representative of the freedmen's aid organization in New York City, and Robert Smalls, a recently escaped slave who had achieved national attention by commandeering his owner's harbor boat, the *Planter*, in Charleston and making it to the Union naval blockading fleet with his family.[6] Since French was going back north to raise funds for Port Royal and was also taking Smalls with him for support, Hunter, Saxton, and Du Pont decided that French and Smalls would take a letter to Stanton requesting approval to raise a black regiment. This time, however, it would be written by Saxton and crafted in a specific manner that would hopefully get the secretary's permission. French and Smalls did not leave until the 16th, ensuring that Hunter's letter of his decision to disband his unit got to Stanton first.

As opposed to Hunter, who had requested permission to raise a regiment of contraband for active military service (which meant serving along white regiments), Saxton tailored his letter to have blacks be used for local self-defense purposes only. They would be employed by the Quartermaster

Department, be designated as common laborers and mechanics, and be paid accordingly. However, they would "be uniformed, armed, and officered by men detailed from the Army." Using the abandonment of Edisto Island by the freedmen because of the withdrawal of Union forces as a pretext, Saxton said it was necessary to help guard the plantations against Rebel raiders, not only in the Port Royal area, but also in other enclaves where former slaves had been able to collect. By beefing up the security of these areas, other escaping slaves could use them as beacons to escape to, thus depriving the Rebels of their labor, especially the males, for the Confederate war effort. He added that these men could be used agriculturally as required. However, "in the event of an emergency calling for immediate aid from these men they could promply [sic] respond to the call."

Saxton's intent was to make this issue as politically palatable as possible, given its still volatile nature, though opinions were changing. He probably thought that Stanton would either approve his request or see it as a subterfuge of Hunter's scheme and deny it.

Stanton's reply was not long in coming. Getting his answer at the end of the month, Saxton received everything he had requested. He was able to enroll and organize up to 5,000 men "in any convenient organization by squads, companies, battalions, regiments, and brigades, or otherwise, colored persons of African descent." He was "also authorized to arm, uniform, equip, and receive into the service of the United States ... volunteers of African descent ... and ... detail officers to instruct them in military drill, discipline, and to command them." Saxton received authorization for one other thing that he had not requested. He would be able to deny the Rebels of their slave labor by being able to take offensive action. "You are therefore authorized by every means in your power to withdraw from the enemy their laboring force and population, and to spare no effort consistent with civilized warfare to weaken, harass, and annoy them, and to establish the authority of the Government of the United States within your department."

Secretary of War Stanton finally had the reason to act on this subject. Since he was the consummate politician, he had to wait for the right conditions so he could approve such an undertaking, stemming back of course from the cabinet meeting on July 22. In it Treasury Secretary Chase had said "The impression left upon my mind by the whole discussion was, that while the President thought that the organization, equipment and arming of negroes, like other soldiers, would be productive of more evil than good, he was not unwilling that Commanders should, at their discretion, arm for purely defensive purposes, slaves coming within their lines." In the scenario provided by Saxton, the secretary could finally act and still not violate Lincoln's policy.[7] The only thing the general wanted to do was to have the freedmen act as an unofficial security force for the other freedmen at Port Royal and at other places under Union control that slaves had escaped to. Training these men to act like soldiers was okay; in order for them to provide security effectively, they needed to react as efficiently as possible, thus the necessity. This necessary training also meant having the officers needed to lead them, plus uniforms and all required equipment, everything that this organization would need to be effective, except having official recognition. As far as any offensive action that Saxton was allowed to take, having blacks helping other blacks was also okay, since it did not involve white soldiers.

Though General Saxton's new orders did not authorize him to create new line units like the white regiments in the Department of the South, under the circumstances, especially with President Lincoln's current position on black enlistment, he could not have asked for anything better. He achieved everything that Hunter tried too, except the official designation and recognition. The 1st South Carolina Volunteers would be reborn. Company A of the old Hunter regiment continued to exist, but it would be the nucleus of a new organization that would be a far cry from its antecedent, especially in its leadership.

One other thing that was alleviated when Saxton received his orders was his worry about General Brannan when he took over from Hunter. Ever since his arrival in June at Port Royal, he and Brannan had clashed. When he received his new orders, they brought with them also a guarantee that he would have no problems with his new commander. Brannan was instructed by Major General Henry W. Hallack, who had replaced McClellan as General-in-Chief, to give "all possible assistance" to help Saxton in carrying out his new instructions. A few days later he received additional instructions. He was to "do everything in [his] power to hold the islands now occupied in South Carolina and to defend the negroes who are or may be hereafter under our protection."

Now that Saxton would not have to worry about any possible back-stabbing efforts on Brannan's part, he would be able to reconstitute the Volunteers without hindrance from above, let alone below, and could form his "squads, companies, battalions, regiments, brigades, or otherwise." Also, with a direct line to the secretary of war, he did not need to go through Brannan either in his capacity as commander of the Department of the South. However, before Saxton could begin the actual physical aspect of it, he would have to travel north for a few weeks due to ill health.[8] He left on September 7 on the steamer *McClellan* in conjunction with General Hunter, who was finally able to wrap up his affairs in the department and leave.

The Orphan Company

At the time of the dissolution of Hunter's Volunteers, both he and Saxton were formulating their new attempt to revive the regiment. They had no idea which way Stanton would react if he would react at all, given his penchant for not answering Hunter's past requests for recognition. With this in mind, why did Company A continue to exist while Saxton waited for a reply from Stanton? Why did Trowbridge, his brother John and George Walker still remain with the company, though they only officially held the ranks of enlisted men?[9] The only reason why they did, and why the men of the company had not returned to their previous endeavor, had to be attributed to Generals Hunter and Saxton. When the regiment was dissolved, they were performing a mission that was too important to stop, especially for the men, since they had not been paid at any time under Hunter's old creation. Prior to Hunter's decision to disband the Volunteers, Company A had been dispatched to St. Simon's Island, Georgia, near Brunswick, to help provide security for the contraband colony there that had been growing for some months. Though not authorized, let alone not recognized, this company finally had a real world mission to perform, and this would be the glue that would keep this unit together even after the rest of the regiment had been disbanded.

Hunter may have informed Stanton of his decision to disband his black regiment, but he did not tell him that Company A still existed. The job it would do on St. Simon's would give it some practical experience that others would be able to learn from in the months to come.

Captain Charles Trowbridge, who commaneded the one remaining company in its darkest days after the rest of the regiment had been disbanded. *Massachusetts Commandery Military Order of the Loyal Legion and the U.S. Army Military History Institute*

The contraband colony on St. Simon's Island had grown slowly but steadily. This included the slaves who had been left there after the Confederates, both military and civilian, abandoned the island to the extension of the naval blockade in early 1862. Even after the enforcement of the blockade had taken hold, the Rebels on the mainland were still strong and could easily make an occasional foray there, since there were no Union troops performing picket duty. The waterway that separated St. Simon's from the mainland was patrolled regularly, but the Georgians could still slip through in the dead of night and create whatever mischief they felt like. The colony had been given some muskets by the Navy for self-defense, but this was not enough to deter Johnny Reb. By the time Company A was sent there in August, the colony had grown to over 600, being primarily self-sufficient.

The Navy had been in charge of the island since its capture and had taken up station there to cut off Brunswick as a seaport. However, the few blockading ships available could not provide enough men to physically guard St. Simon's and still perform their primary mission, especially as the contraband colony grew. The patrolling of the waterway between the island and the mainland could only be done when the morning and evening tides allowed a ship to cross the sandbars in the sounds north and south of the island. It was only effective as long as the ship stayed there and if she was able to run into any enemy moving across the river, especially at night. The providing of the freedmen with the muskets was a seeming solution, but it still did not stop the intruders. It was therefore evident that soldiers were required, so Company A of the 1st South Carolina Volunteers (unauthorized, unrecognized, unpaid, and unappreciated by many) got the call.

When Commander J. R. Goldsborough, senior officer of the blockading station off of Brunswick, put in his request to Admiral Du Pont, this request went to General Hunter, who in turn got with General Saxton. Since he was the officer in charge of everything that had to do with the freedmen at Port Royal, having St. Simon's Island and the contraband colony there placed under his jurisdiction was a natural extension of Saxton's authority as Military Governor. Shortly thereafter, Company A received its orders and left on August 5 on a large vessel called the *Ben De Ford*, a relatively new ship that had both sail and steam capacity, with a water displacement of some 1,500 tons. General Saxton went also to formally take over control of the island from the Navy and assess the situation of his new acquisition so he could issue any specific orders to Captain Trowbridge if required.

When the *Ben De Ford* arrived at St. Simon's August 6, one could say they got there at the right time. Upon reaching Commander Goldsborough's location, General Saxton and Captain Trowbridge quickly found out from him that Rebels were once again on the island. Goldsborough then asked whether Company A could render assistance. Answered in the affirmative, the commander told Trowbridge that if "you should capture them, it will be a great thing for you." The first test of the Volunteers was about to commence.

When the Confederates landed, they knew they could not afford to be seen, given the size of the black colony and the fact that the blacks had weapons, but this still did not deter them. However, when they had been on the island for several days, they were finally spotted and therefore had to take evasive action. This Rebel force was a detachment of Company D, 3rd Georgia Cavalry Battalion, commanded by Captain William Miles Hazzard,[10] who was leading his men in this excursion. He was very familiar with the island since his family had a plantation on it and had led several raids before.

Once Company A disembarked, they began combat operations against Captain Hazzard and his men, action that they had been waiting for since General Hunter had drafted them back in May. Since these men had been drilling about the entire time they had been in uniform, they were not slow in following Captain Trowbridge's orders. However, the Volunteers soon found out that a contingent of the contrabands was already on the trail of the 3rd Georgia. After searching for a while for them, the contrabands finally came into contact with the Rebels on the day that the Volunteers arrived. Anticipating that the freedmen would be coming from a particular direction, Hazzard had his men prepare an ambush for them in a wooded area, hiding behind a log. When the blacks came within proper distance, the cavalrymen opened fire, killing two men and wounding several others. The two killed were Charles O'Neal and the group's leader, John Brown. Not accustomed to this kind of carnage, the freedmen quickly retreated. Hazzard decided not to stick around either and led his men in another direction.

For two days the Volunteers, aided by a detachment of sailors, looked for the Rebels but could not find them. At one point Trowbridge and his men came upon a scene where they found a canoe by a creek with a fire going with a pot on top melting tar, presumably to repair it. Later they found out that the troopers of the 3rd Georgia were nearby in a palmetto thicket, hiding there when they heard them approaching. The Rebels' boat, in which they had earlier come over, had been previously found. They were finally able to escape with the help of a former Hazzard plantation slave, an elderly man named Henry Capers, whom had remained loyal to Captain Hazzard.[11] Capers was able to get a boat for the Confederates so they could get back to the mainland.

A slave named Clarence Kennon who would later escape and become a sergeant in the Volunteers was present when Hazzard and his men returned and remembered the scene. He said they were "tattered and dirty from head to foot" in their efforts to escape. Months later Hazzard would write to a friend about his ordeal. Though describing it in an epithetic manner, he paid the Volunteers and the freedmen a compliment. "If you wish to know hell before your time, go to St. Simon's and be hunted ten days by niggers."

Captain Trowbridge said that not one of his men flinched. Company A "seemed to take delight in the pursuit, though the weather was very hot, and it was fearfully exhausting." Not knowing that the regiment would be disbanded shortly, he probably assumed that other companies would soon arrive to help him guard the island. So until then, he would have support from the Navy. Admiral Du Pont wrote to Commodore Goldsborough on August 7 to give "all support by your gunboats to the protection of the settlement as lies within your power and showing the same interest as heretofore in the colony, which owes its origin and existence to the Navy." Trowbridge and Company A settled in to do their job.

Recruitment on Other Fronts

As the "non-existent" Company A of the never authorized 1st South Carolina Volunteers went about helping to secure St. Simon's Island, a seemingly insignificant dot of military activity in this vast war, several hundred thousand men on opposite sides maneuvered to achieve victory in strategic Virginia, Tennessee and Mississippi. General McClellan had been ordered by General Halleck to reposition the Army of the Potomac to be nearer Washington after having been bottled up on a peninsula on the James River for several weeks by General Lee. McClellan would be in a better position to protect the capital and be near a newly constituted Union Army of Virginia under Major General John Pope so they both could hopefully combine and strike at Lee. In the west a rising star named U. S. Grant had his eye on a strategic Mississippi River fortress named Vicksburg and Confederate General Braxton Bragg wanted to recapture parts of Tennessee and possibly Kentucky lost to the Federals.

On the civilian side, President Lincoln issued an order to draft 300,000 militia after the Union Army had incurred thousands of casualties since spring. Though this draft would ultimately never be carried out, there was the fact that thousands of men were already available and just waiting for the call. Yet for political reasons that only Lincoln knew, he was not ready yet to issue the summons. The subject of emancipation was also another political football that up to this point had been tossed about in various forms on how to deal with it. From gradual emancipation to compensated emancipation to outright emancipation in itself, no plan had become definite. Reflecting on these issues of slavery, emancipation, and blacks as soldiers, Admiral Du Pont wrote from his flagship at Port Royal. "I do not mean that we are not released from all Constitutional obligations to the rebels—for I believe we are nearly released to loyal holders of the article who made no resistance, but under obligations to uphold it for ourselves and for the sake of free government; and I believe if we do this we will be rewarded by a wise system of gradual emancipation."

Du Pont also added what would take place if the United States were attacked externally: "Of course military necessity may after all overrule this—a foreign intervention would certainly free every Negro in the land tomorrow so far as a decree could do it. Arming the blacks will probably come up first."

As opposed to Du Pont's thoughts, the United States had already been attacked "externally." It was called Fort Sumter. These decrees for emancipation and putting blacks in uniform had yet to be made. They were only waiting for certain events to take place, one of which was military that would soon be, ironically, provided by General Lee and the Confederate Army of Northern Virginia.

Though Lincoln had publicly stated his position about blacks as soldiers, yet was waiting for the right time to take place to announce his true intentions, other generals on the periphery of the war were starting to get impatient with the president and began to take matters into their own hands. Brigadier General James H. Lane, in Kansas, and Brigadier General John W. Phelps, in Louisiana,[12] organized their own black regiments. Lane notified Stanton of his action, citing as his authority the Militia Act passed by Congress the previous month in July 1862. Stanton wrote back that only the president had the authority under this act to raise black regiments, but this rebuttal did not demur Lane from proceeding, though not as overtly as before. In the Union-occupied part of Louisiana, General Phelps had for some time wanted to recruit black troops, but was stopped by his superior there, Major General Benjamin Butler. In August, when Phelps tried to force his hand by raising five companies, Butler ordered him to stop. Phelps, a radical abolitionist, resigned his commission and left the army in protest.

Also during August, President Lincoln met with a delegation from Indiana to raise black troops in the North. Once again Lincoln cited his fear of losing Kentucky. The *New York Tribune* reported that it was the president's "opinion that to arm the negro would turn 50,000 bayonets from the loyal Border States against us that were for us." Lincoln was able to stave off this group but the call to have black soldiers would not diminish.

The drive to raise black regiments also did not fail to get the attention of the Confederate military. General Samuel Cooper, the adjutant of the Rebel army, decried on August 21 that Generals Hunter and Phelps would no longer be treated as "public enemies of the Confederate States, but as outlaws," since they had "organized and armed negro slaves for military service against their masters, citizens of this Confederacy." If either of these two men were captured "or any other officer employed in drilling, organizing, or instructing slaves, with a view to their armed service in this war, he shall not be regarded as a prisoner of war, but held in close confinement for execution as a felon, as such time and place as the President shall order."[13] General Lane did not have to worry about this proclamation since Kansas was U.S. territory.

While these peripheral activities were going on, another major operation in Virginia was under way. General Lee had gotten word that the repositioning of General McClellan's Army of the Potomac to be nearer Washington was to unite with General Pope's Army of Virginia and then make a combined attack against the Confederates. He moved quickly to prevent this from happening. On August 29 and 30, Lee's Army of Northern Virginia engaged Pope's forces on the old Bull Run battlefield and soundly defeated them. Once again Lincoln would have to wait for a Union victory before he could issue his preliminary Emancipation Proclamation. Regardless, however, of this additional setback, he would not have too much longer to wait.

Lead up to Emancipation

In a world far apart from the battlefields of Virginia and elsewhere, where armies clashed that involved hundreds of thousands of men and created tens of thousands of casualties, 38 soldiers of a non-recognized unit went about doing their job on St. Simon's Island, Georgia. Picket posts had been set up around the island to prevent any further Rebel excursions. To help keep in contact with the freedmen on the island, Captain Trowbridge would summon them on Saturdays to drill with his men. Roughly 150 to 200 of them would show up dressed in all manner of style: men, women and children. Though the Volunteers were glad they were performing a real mission, the work was starting to have its effect on their uniforms and shoes. No resupply was available,[1] therefore things were slowly deteriorating. Ever so often some of the men would go to the mainland on scouting expeditions to gather intelligence on Rebel movements. All of this they did on no pay and poor rations.

Regardless of these conditions, the presence of these black soldiers was having its effect on the Rebels, especially the psychological aspect of it. On September 19, the commanding officer of the 3rd Georgia Cavalry Battalion, Lieutenant Colonel Duncan L. Clinch, sent a letter of apology to Lieutenant Commander W. T. Truxtun, commander of the U.S.S. *Alabama*, stationed at St. Andrews Sound near Brunswick, when a picket station of Clinch's unit accidentally fired at the ship under a flag of truce. Though Clinch was sincere in his apology about the incident, he added he was still adamant about protecting his "country" from any seeming Yankee outrage. In chivalrous bravado, he said that he and his fellow Georgians "are in arms to defend our homes and families from destruction and outrages. Our defenseless towns have been plundered, our cemetaries [*sic*] desecrated, and the widow and orphan robbed of their all." It was however his next sentence that showed his displeasure at change happening that Clinch could not believe. "Our very slaves armed and excited against our women and children." Unfortunately for him, this was only part of the beginning, because many more slaves would become "armed and excited" as time went by.

Colonel Clinch may have been shocked about "our very slaves armed and excited," but the Volunteers would have to watch out for other attackers, and not just from the enemy. In a report to Admiral Du Pont written shortly after Company A arrived on St. Simon's Island, Captain Goldsborough made a comment that can only be interpreted as that he was not happy to have them there. "Their officers, I fear, repose very little confidence in them." However, if Captain Trowbridge, his brother Lieutenant Trowbridge and Lieutenant Walker did not have confidence in their men, they would not have stayed with the company after the regiment was disbanded. In fact, these officers were among the few white allies of the blacks in the military at this time. For example, one of the freedmen who had escaped to the island, a teenage girl named Susie Baker, had become acquainted with Captain Trowbridge. He saw that she could read and write, skills she learned while still a slave. Years later when she wrote of her experiences on the island, she said that he "found me ... teaching my little school, and was much interested in it. When I knew him better I found him to be a thorough gentleman and a staunch friend of my race."

As Company A went into its second month on St. Simon's, more attacks on the Volunteers' existence were on the way. Word had already leaked out again that a second effort to raise a regiment composed of freedmen was in the works. The *New York World*'s correspondent at Port Royal reported from the Sea Islands that "the arming of the negroes has hitherto proved not only unpopular with the people, but especially among the Volunteers. To again attempt the thing after its failure on General Hunter's hands appears to be unwise and injudicious." The *World* printed this for its September 8 issue. Another newspaper, the *National Intelligencer*, repeated this article on the 16th.

While the opinion of the *World*'s correspondent circulated among other Northern newspapers, General Hunter finally heard about the Confederacy's determination that he and General Phelps were now branded as outlaws and would be executed as such if they fell into Rebel hands, because they advocated the use of blacks as soldiers and had already armed and placed freedmen into uniform. Writing from Washington on September 20 a letter to Jefferson Davis that was never forwarded by the Federal government due to its vitriolic repartee, Hunter said in part that he would "proudly accept, if such be the chance of war, the martyrdom you mean."[2] However, if the Confederates were determined to carry out this threat, Hunter said that he would "reciprocate it by hanging every rebel officer who now is, or may hereafter be taken, prisoner by the troops of the command to which I am about returning." It was probably fortunate for Davis that he never received this letter.

In an earlier editorial of the *Savannah Republican*, the writer was especially vitriolic about General Hunter: "The cold-blooded abolition miscreant who, from his headquarters at Hilton Head, engaged in executing the bloody and savage behests of the imperial gorilla who, from his throne of human bones at Washington, rules, reigns, and riots over the destinies of the brutish and degraded North." No record shows that Hunter ever saw this article, or else he probably would have written this newspaper a proper response too.

Hunter and Phelps may have given the Confederates good reason to feel the way they did, but an announcement soon to be made by President Lincoln would blow the lid off and just consume the Rebels with rancor. After General Lee had won another victory at Second Manassas, he decided to carry the fight to the enemy and invade the North. In the process of moving his army, a copy of his movement orders was found by Union troops. The orders were soon in the hands of General McClellan, who quickly put his army on the path to intercept. On September 17, the two forces made contact at Sharpsburg, Maryland on Antietam Creek. Though outnumbered almost two to one, Lee was able to fight to a bloody draw before withdrawing back into Virginia. This may not have been the victory that Lincoln had been hoping for, but given the circumstances it was going to have to do. So five days later on the 22nd he issued for everyone to hear (to include the Rebels) his preliminary Emancipation Proclamation.

The decree was very simple. The eleven rebelling states which then constituted the Confederate States of America had exactly 100 days to cease hostilities and return to the jurisdiction of the United States. If not, then on January 1, 1863, President Lincoln would use his authority as commander in chief of the armed forces of the United States to free all the slaves in the states that were still in rebellion on this date as a prudent wartime measure, and these states would lose all federal constitutional protection that they would still enjoy up until midnight on December 31, 1862. Outside of freeing the slaves, the full thrust of this proclamation was to deny the Rebels the labor that the slaves provided to help fuel the Confederate war effort, which in this case would make the denial of that labor a legitimate military target. The congressional legislation granting this power was the Second Confiscation Act, which gave the Union forces the authority to confiscate all Rebel property whether it was being used or not to support the Rebel military.

The die was now cast. Lincoln had been warned that this announcement would cause the Republican Party to lose control of Congress in the upcoming mid-term congressional elections, but he knew he had to do it. With this proclamation, he also knew he had changed the goal of the war forever and there could be no going back. Lincoln was also under no illusion that the Rebel states would refuse his ultimatum. For good or bad, depending upon one's opinion, the goal of the war was now twofold, to restore the Union and also to destroy slavery as an institution in the eleven rebelling states as a means to help wage war. This proclamation did not touch the remaining slave states in the Union because they were still protected by the U.S. Constitution. Lincoln realized that his decision would go a long way to eradicate slavery in North America, but he still did not say anything about blacks in uniform.

As important events continued to unfold on the national scene, changes also occurred in the Department of the South. On September 3, this command was given an additional name, that of 10th Corps. It also received a new commander, Major General Ormsby M. Mitchel, who assumed command on September 17. General Brannan then resumed his previous command. After surveying his new domain, General Mitchel, on the 26th, ordered all enlisted men who had been acting as officers in Hunter's regiment to return to their own regiments. Just prior to his departure with Saxton on the 7th, Hunter had issued his last general order detailing these men to remain with Saxton so that when Saxton returned from Washington and began to reconstitute the 1st South Carolina, he would have the nucleus of an officer corps to help him.[3] Word got around of this new development. On Hilton Head, where Mitchel had his headquarters, Captain Daniel Eldredge, of the 3rd New Hampshire Infantry, observed that "times have changed. Gen. Hunter had gone north. Gen. Mitchel was now in command. On the 26th, he directed that all enlisted men who had been acting as officers in the colored regiment (First South Carolina Volunteers) to return at once to their regiments. Officers were over-staying their leaves of absence to such an extent that Gen. Mitchel made an attempt to stop it by ordering, on the 27th, a Board to 'sit' on such cases." However, four days later on October 1, Mitchel reversed himself and ordered them to "continue to perform duties to which they have been assigned under orders of Brig. Gen'l Saxton." No explanation was given.

In the political arena, Treasury Secretary Chase enacted legislation called the Direct Tax Law that had been passed by Congress in June. Its intent was to assess abandoned real property of Rebel owners in the Union-occupied areas of the Confederacy, advertise the taxes due and then sell the property of the delinquent owners at public auction if they did not pay them in the required time. In other words, it was punishment for leaving the Union. The key to the enactment of this legislation was the appointment of Direct Tax Commissioners, who would be responsible for the actual implementation of it. They would be appointed for each area of occupation. Besides the official role of the law, Chase also saw it as a possible means to help him achieve something that he coveted—the presidency. Outside of his current position, he was also an ambitious politician. He had lost to Lincoln as his party's nominee in 1860. If he appointed as tax commissioners men who were loyal to him, and by the time of the 1864 Republican convention these occupied areas had been readmitted back into the Union as loyal states, these men or others they controlled could be delegates who would be in Chase's camp. If the war continued and went bad for Lincoln, he could wind up being his replacement as the nominee.[4] The ones he appointed in September to cover the Union-controlled areas in the Department of the South were already aware of his presidential aspirations, especially those assigned to Florida, gentlemen by the names of John S. Sammis, Harrison Reed and one Lyman Stickney. Of all these commissioners, Stickney would have the greatest impact, especially as an influence in future military operations, in the department in relationship to Chase's ambitions. Some of these operations would include a revitalized 1st South Carolina Volunteers.

While the reorganization of the 1st South Carolina waited for the return of General Saxton, General Benjamin Butler over in New Orleans had a change of heart shortly after General Phelps had resigned his commission. During his time in command up to this point, he had determined that he had enough soldiers to perform occupation duty, even while Phelps wanted to raise black units. However, when some serious Confederate action in Louisiana threatened Butler's seemingly peaceful situation, he quickly decided to write to Stanton for reinforcements. When the secretary replied that none were available, Phelps' earlier denied requests all of a sudden did not seem so bad after all. Because of this emergency, Butler wrote again to Stanton that "I shall call on Africa to intervene, and I do not think I shall call in vain." However, the difference between him and Phelps was that his former subordinate wanted to use slaves. Since there was a sizable number of free blacks in this area, Butler reasoned that the usage of this category would not violate current Army policy. Therefore, he set about recruiting for his first regiment. In short order, it was filled and designated the 1st Louisiana Native Guards on September 27.

Once again Stanton had a general who took it on his own initiative to raise a black regiment. While he personally sympathized with Butler (because the general was trying to do his job with only the resources at he had at hand), the secretary still had to follow the president's policy. However, being the consummate politician that he was, his reply to Butler was just like that to Lane, that it was the administration's policy not to enlist blacks. Also just as with Hunter and Lane, he did not expressly order them to disband their units. Whereas Hunter did so because he got tired of what he perceived as Washington's intransigence on the issue, Lane and Butler did not. Stanton reminded them of Lincoln's policy, but he left it up to them to disband. This left him in the clear. He also implied to them that their respective units would not be officially recognized.

While Stanton worked to uphold Lincoln's current policy, he also had to continue to stave off the growing demands of others who saw putting blacks in uniform as a logical thing to do. At the same time, at the highest level of political theater in Washington, the president himself had to play a high-wire act. As historian Richard Carwaredine put it, "The Emancipation Proclamation was quite enough to ask conservative Unionists to digest for the moment; with elections in the offing in the fall of 1862, he would not ask them to swallow black enlistments, too."

General Saxton's Return

As the effort to raise black troops in the peripheral areas continued in its embryonic stage, the main area of the war to date, Virginia, was pretty much quiet after the brutal battle at Antietam. Both armies continued to recover from its bloody effect, replenishing their battered ranks with new men and materiel. Lee's forces were back in the state while McClellan's army straddled both the Maryland and Virginia sides of the Potomac River in the event Lee tried to make another move in this area. While this went on, several small engagements took place around the border state of Kentucky. The most significant action here was the occupation of the strategic Ohio River town of Louisville by the Union forces. In Mississippi, the Rebels lost at a battle called Iuka.

In the Department of the South and 10th Corps, another event was unfolding that would precipitate another clash of foes, the first since June when General Hunter made an attempt on Charleston. The Confederates in Florida had constructed an earthen fortress above Jacksonville on a bluff overlooking the St. John's River. The intent was to prevent any Union military activity in the eastern part of the state, i.e. not allowing the river to be used as an access to the state's interior. When the Federals discovered the fortress in September, they tried to subdue it through a naval bombardment. It did not work. General Mitchel then sent an expedition at DuPont's request. It arrived on October 1. The Rebels evacuated on the 3rd when they thought they were overwhelmingly outnumbered. The military force under General Brannan occupied Jacksonville for the second time on the 5th, than left it on the 13th when he decided that he could not accomplish any more there. In the process, he took along several white loyalists and "about 276 contrabands, including men, women, and children." Several of the men in this group would soon find themselves in uniform.

As Port Royal waited for the return of General Saxton so he could begin to reconstitute the 1st South Carolina, the people on the islands were reacting to the news of President Lincoln's preliminary emancipation decree. On October 1, Laura Town felt elated. "To-day the news came that Lincoln has declared emancipation after the 1st of January, 1863. Our first victory worth the name." Edward Philbrick reacted similarly. On the 7th he said that he "received ... a copy of President Lincoln's proclamation. I now feel more than ever the importance of our mission here, not so much for the sake of the few hundred [the freedmen] under my own eyes as for the sake of the success of the experiment we are now trying."

However, Philbrick was dumbfounded about the reaction he got from the freedmen he talked to when he told them about Lincoln's decision. Two days before he received a copy of the proclamation, he said that the news of it:

> ... does not seem to have made a great deal of stir any where [*sic*]. Here the people don't take the slightest interest in it. They have been free already for nearly a year, as they could see, and so little comprehension about the magnitude of our country and are so supremely selfish that you can't beat it into their heads that any one [*sic*] else is to be provided for beyond St. Helena Island. After telling them of the proclamation and its probable effects, they all ask if they would be given up to their masters in case South Carolina comes back into the Union. I tell them there is little chance of such a thing, but a strong probability that there will be a long, bloody war, and that they ought to prepare to do their share of the fighting.

With that concluding thought, Philbrick was not joking.

Though the number of units in the department had shrunk by eight infantry regiments and two squadrons of cavalry when they had to go to Virginia to reinforce McClellan during the summer, Hunter's evacuation of Edisto Island guaranteed enough manpower to cover the islands of Port Royal. There were still ten infantry regiments, one squadron of cavalry, and several companies of artillery and engineers. Even with this compact force of several thousand men, several of the plantation supervisors decided this was not enough. They took it on their own initiative to drill many of the freedmen as a ready reaction force in the event of enemy action. It was not surprising that these superintendents did this, as they did not trust the military because of the gross disrespectful way that many of the soldiers treated the freedmen. It would also make one want to wonder just how much effort the soldiers would put in to it to defend them against a Confederate attack.

The superintendents may have had the highest of intentions to organize and drill the men, but the freedmen had other ideas. One of supervisors on one of the Fripp plantations on St. Helena Island gave an apt description of what he experienced. On September 27, Edward Philbrick lamented that he had "tried in vein [sic] to get my young men to gether [sic] for self-defense; my twenty-five guns are lying useless ..." He also opined that:

> the people here are too timid to do any fighting unless driven to it. If General Hunter had not forced them in to his regiment last May, we might do more at drilling now. As it is, my men won't listen to me when I talk about it; they only suspect me of wanting to press them into service by stealth, and lose what little confidence they have in my sincerity.

On Sunday morning, the 5th of October, Philbrick complained again:

> I can't get one man to come up and drill yet. They say they would like to have guns to shoot with, but are afraid of being sent off into the 'big fight,' though willing to fight any one who comes onto this island to molest them. Of course their defense would amount to nothing unless they were organized and drilled.

On the 8th, Philbrick finally wrote of some success: "I succeeded day before yesterday in getting thirteen of the young men on this plantation to come up and drill. ..." However, "they did not come again yesterday. I don't believe there is sufficient zeal among them to enable them to go through the tedious routine of drill with any regularity, unless held together by some strange motive than now exists." He was not too keen on their intelligence level either, but Philbrick suspected that they were just pulling his leg. "I find them rather stupid. About half didn't know which their right foot was, and kept facing to the left when I told them to face to the right. They seemed to enjoy it, however."

Regardless of Philbrick's experiences with his charges, Laura Towne said that some freedmen who took the drilling seriously were successful when some Rebels tried to land on St. Helena. On October 24, she said that "three boats full of rebels attempted to land on these islands last night, two at the village and one at Edding's Point. The negroes with their guns were on picket; they gave the alarm, fired and drove the rebels off." This was positive proof "for those who have urged arming the negroes ...

Ellen [Murray] and I maintain that the negroes will fight; others think not. Our men keep guard to-day."

About the time that General Brannan decided to evacuate Jacksonville on October 13, General Saxton arrived back at Port Royal. Writing to Stanton from his headquarters at Beaufort that same day, he wanted to notify the secretary of his arrival "and that I have entered upon the work assigned to me in your general instructions." The first thing he did this day was to create a cadre of trainers per his orders he received from Stanton back in late August. This officer corps would instruct recruits "in military drill, discipline, and duty, and to command them." To start things off, nine of the original twelve officers from the old Hunter regiment had their commissions officially recognized.[5] From the 100th Pennsylvania Infantry: William James, Captain; W. J. Randolph, Captain; Alexander Heasley, Captain; James Pomeroy, 1st Lieutenant; and Harry West, 2nd Lieutenant. From the 48th New York Infantry: William H. Danielson, 1st Lieutenant. From the 1st New York Engineers: Charles T. Trowbridge,[6] Captain; George D. Walker, 1st Lieutenant; and John A. Trowbridge, 2nd Lieutenant.

Besides these nine of the original twelve, twelve more enlisted men were also commissioned on the 13th. From the 8th Maine Infantry: H. A. Whitney, Captain; J. H. Thibadeau, 1st Lieutenant; Charles I. Davis, 1st Lieutenant; William Stockdale, 1st Lieutenant; and W. W. Sampson, 2nd Lieutenant. From the 1st U.S. Artillery: James B. O'Neil, 2nd Lieutenant. From the 7th New Hampshire Infantry: J. M. Thompson, 2nd Lieutenant. From the 6th Connecticut Infantry: W. H. Hyde, 2nd Lieutenant. Also from the 48th New York: Jesse Fisher, 1st Lieutenant. And also from the 100th Pennsylvania: James F. Johnston, 1st Lieutenant; R. M. Gaston, 2nd Lieutenant; and James B. West, 2nd Lieutenant.

Of these 21 men who received their commissions, five became captains, eight became 1st lieutenants, and the remaining eight 2nd lieutenants. The twelve new men came from units that were scattered around the department: the 1st New York Engineers were split between Hilton Head, Port Royal, and Fort Clinch; on Port Royal were the 8th Maine, 1st U.S. Artillery, and the 6th Connecticut; the 48th New York was at Fort Pulaski. The 100th Pennsylvania was not even in the theater. It had transferred to Virginia back in July with the 5 other regiments due to the crisis there at the time that General McClellan said that the Army of the Potomac was in. The only explanation that can be given here is that one or more of the men from the 100th who had joined earlier had written to their former comrades, explained the opportunity, and the 100th's commander had allowed Johnston, Gaston, and West to transfer.

The most important aspect of the twelve new officers is that they were recruited while General Saxton was still in Washington. When he received permission in late August from Stanton to "receive into the service of the United States ... volunteers of African descent ... and ... detail officers to instruct them ... and to command them," either he or General Hunter (who was still in command at the time) put out the word that the 1st South Carolina was going to be reestablished and therefore qualified sergeants and privates could become officers. When Saxton returned, he immediately issued commissions to the nine of the original twelve and to the twelve others who had volunteered.

Even with these new commissions, more junior officers, especially captains, would still need to be recruited. This would become evident as freedmen enlisted. Right now only one company existed, and that was Company A of the old organization. It would be designated Company A of the new one, with nine more to go. Captain Trowbridge would have the distinction of being the regiment's senior captain.

On October 20, three civilians were commissioned. Dr. John Milton Hawks was given the title of Assistant Surgeon. G. W. Dewhurst became the regiment's administrative officer, or Adjutant, with the rank of 1st Lieutenant. J. M. Bingham became a 1st Lieutenant and the unit's supply officer, or Quartermaster. Dr. Hawks was already on the islands when he had volunteered his services, since he arrived in March with the first boatload of missionaries. Since no other information is available on either Dewhurst or Bingham, it can only be assumed here that they had already been on the islands for a while when they were commissioned.

John D. Strong, another civilian, became the unit's major on the 21st. Like Dewhurst and Bingham, no other information is available on him to say where he was when he heard about the need for officers or how he was able to get his rank with no prior military experience. On October 24, Reverend James H. Fowler, who had also been on the islands for some time like Dr. Hawks, became Chaplain. So as the regiment was taking shape officer-wise, it still needed to fill five more captain positions, several more lieutenant slots, plus the unit's position of lieutenant colonel. Most importantly, however, the billet for the regimental commander needed to be filled, which would require someone special. This meant not only a man who had the ability to command a regiment, but specifically one with the proper temperament to command one composed of former slaves.

As opposed to the trouble that Hunter had in getting officers for his regiment, Saxton was not having that problem. This only proved that Hunter was correct in the statement he had made back in May when he could not get commissioned officers to transfer, but was applicable to the enlisted men too who refused to be commissioned. "The fools or bigots who refuse are enough punished by their refusal. Before two years they will be competing eagerly for the commissions they now reject." So, while

Saxton was having no problems getting these positions filled, he knew that it was not going to be as easy to get the most important thing for the regiment—enough soldiers. In his letter of the 13th to Stanton, he told him of the trouble he expected to have to obtain enough recruits.

Though Saxton said that he would "proceed at once to organize all the able-bodied and intelligent blacks on these Sea Islands as rapidly as possible into companies and regiments," he added the Confederates were on to his intentions. "In anticipation of our action the rebels are moving all their slaves back from the sea-coast as fast as they can, and until we are able to maintain posts upon the mainland my operations will be limited for the most part to these islands, as it is extremely difficult for the negroes from the 'main' to reach our lines. Could we get positions on the mainland they would come in great numbers to join us." If Stanton could see to it "to send large re-inforcements to this department," then Saxton could recruit thousands more. This in turn, he added, would have the benefit of siphoning off Rebel troops from other fronts to prevent this from happening. Unfortunately, it was not to be. No additional troops would be sent by the end of the year.

Saxton's worry about trying to get enough men to fill up five regiments was one thing. He first had to see if he could recruit enough men for the first one. Hunter's attempt to raise troops would not make Saxton's efforts easy. However, he would get a short reprieve. Soon after his return to Port Royal, Captain Trowbridge came back from St. Simon's with the 38 men of Company A since the Navy had ordered the abandonment of the island. He had with him a prepared report "showing the services and claims of his men." Reporting to General Saxton, Trowbridge found out that there had been several significant changes since he had heard of the regiment's disbandment. Saxton informed him that the 1st South Carolina Volunteers were being reconstituted, that his command would be the Company A of the new organization and that he would be the regiment's senior captain. This also meant that his men would get new uniforms and equipment. In return, Trowbridge told Saxton that the contraband colony of over 600 people from St. Simon's came too, since the Navy had deemed it no longer worthy to hold. These soldiers and civilians had been transported on the *Ben De Ford*.[7] In addition, Trowbridge said there were also some new recruits from the colony for his company. However, this small addition did not include the few other hundred men also from St. Simon's, which made their arrival a very important windfall for Saxton. Since they had not been at Port Royal they had not been affected by Hunter and therefore could easily be recruited.

Just as General Hunter had kept his creation near him on Hilton Head, General Saxton would do the same thing for his edition on Port Royal Island. About four miles south of Beaufort on the Beaufort River, he decided to place the encampment. Situated on the old Smith plantation with its "stately magnolia avenue, decaying house, and tiny church amid the woods," the uniforming, arming, equipping and training would take place. Once the knowledge of this crossed the Broad River onto the mainland, it would once again spread like wildfire and become, as historian Thomas Wentworth Higginson put it, "something so un-Southern that the whole Southern coast" would tremble "at the suggestion of such a thing,—the camp of a regiment of freed slaves."

After Company A had returned to Port Royal with its new recruits, they were sent to this camp, which would be named Camp Saxton. The other commissioned officers were already there. One of the contraband who had been evacuated was Susie Baker. She said that once "we arrived in Beaufort, Captain Trowbridge and the men he had enlisted went to camp at Old Fort … I was enrolled as laundress."[8] As expected they received new uniforms, but with a twist. Instead of the complete blue uniform like the white regiments had, the men were issued red pantaloons, something that Miss Baker said the men "disliked very much, for, they said, 'The rebels see us, miles away.'" Now that the regiment was in its formalities of taking shape, with its cadre of officers working hard to try and get men to enlist, it did not take long for this activity to be noticed. A member of the 3rd Rhode Island Heavy Artillery named Frederic Denison wrote on October 18 that the unit "had already a quasi existence without sufficient forms of law for its equipment and pay,[9] having been enrolled by direction of General Hunter, following the general instructions first given to General Sherman. Now the command took full and regular form. This was an era in the war, and in the history of the ex-slaves."

The regiment might have been taking shape, but it was slow in coming, especially for October. Several of the missionaries rendered their thoughts on this subject. Charles P. Ware:[10]

Oct. 23. General Saxton returned, as you know, with full powers from the President to raise one or if possible five negro regiments. I think it will be difficult to induce the men to enlist. Their treatment in the spring and summer was such as to prejudice them against military duty under any circumstances. They were forcibly drafted, were ill-treated by at least one officer,—who is a terror to the whole black population,—have never been paid a cent, they suffered from the change of diet, and quite as much from home-sickness. I think if their treatment in the spring had been different, it would be possible to raise a regiment on these islands; as it is, I think it will be surprising if they fill a company from St. Helena.

On the 25th, Laura Towne said that:

Captain [William] James [came] to this plantation to recruit negro soldiers. I believe they are to be regularly enrolled in the army. All our men are going to volunteer, but with some this is a dismal forlornness about their consent to go. Nelly uses strong persuasions, and, with one or two lazy, bad fellows, even threats of expulsion from the place, if they will not volunteer. Many go willingly.

The next day was different.

At church to-day Captain [W. J.] Randolph and Colonel [?] Elwell were present. They came to see the colored men and recruit, or rather with an eye to recruiting. But there were no able-bodied young men to be seen. They had all taken to the woods at the sight of epaulets, guessing the errand.

On the 27th, Edward Philbrick was trying to pay the freedmen under his charge:

I sent Joe out to tell the people to come and get their money, but they didn't come with the usual promptness; bye and bye two men came to sound the way, the rest held back. I laughed at them and sent them off with the chink in their pockets, after which the rest came fast enough. They were evidently afraid of some trap to press them into United States service as General Hunter did.

He added:

General Saxton is striving earnestly to fill up his brigade with negroes, but finds it very slow work. The people are so well off on the plantations they don't see why they should go and expose themselves. Moreover, the way they were treated last summer is not very attractive to them. Many of their officers abused them, and they were very generally insulted by every white man they met. It will now require a good deal of time and very judicious, careful treatment to get rid of these impressions, particularly as some of the very officers who abused and maltreated the men are still in General Saxton's confidence and have places in his new organization.

General Saxton wrote another progress report Stanton on October 31. To no one's surprise it reflected what the above missionaries had already observed. To his chagrin, he said that though he was "organizing the First South Carolina Volunteers as rapidly as possible," the secretary would be "disappointed with regard to the number of recruits I shall be able to obtain." Besides Hunter's bungling of the first attempt, he had to deal with the fact that the Quartermaster and Engineer departments of the Army had siphoned off many men for their operations. The Navy also employed many "as sailors, servants, pilots ..." All the officers' servants were "negroes, and numbers of others drive a flourishing business as fishermen, workmen on steam-boats and for private traders ... I believe it is your intention that all these demands should be supplied before enlisting into the U.S. service."

Since Hunter was not able to get his men paid for the time they were in uniform, Saxton added:

> In the meantime their families suffered, those who did not enlist in the First Regiment were receiving wages all this time. Accustomed as these people are to having their rights disregarded, this failure to pay them for their service has weakened their confidence in our promises for the future and makes them slow to enlist. If I could be authorized to give them a small bounty as evidence they were really to be paid for their services, they would all readily enlist.

Saxton also reiterated his request for additional white regiments so he could occupy points on the mainland so as to make it easier for slaves there to get to Federal lines so more men could be recruited. Until then, "I shall hardly be able to fill more than one regiment." Adding that he had had numerous requests for officer positions, he concluded his report by notifying Stanton that General Mitchel had come down with malaria and was very ill. However, before Stanton would receive this information, Mitchel succumbed to his ailment, which for Saxton was a good thing.

Three days after General Mitchel had taken command on September 17, he decided that he did not like the dual command arrangement in the Department of the South and 10th Corps. He felt that General Saxton's separate operation of overseeing the freedmen as military governor of the islands would lead to friction between the two commands, since Saxton was directly controlled from Washington. He probably felt too that this would not be right since he was a major general and Saxton only a brigadier. Regardless of Mitchel's intentions, Saxton saw this as a threat to the independence of his mission. An example of this is in an October 14 letter by Charles P. Ware. He said that "a difficulty has already arisen between him and his old antagonist, Brannan, on a point of authority, and our General has gone to Hilton Head, probably to see Mitchel about it. This interference of the military authorities with our work and our privileges is going to make trouble." Fortunately for General Saxton this threat to his independent command ended with Mitchel's passing on October 30, but it put General Brannan, "his old antagonist," back in command of the department.

Return to Action

As October gave way to November in the Department of the South and 10th Corps, General Saxton did not have much to show for what he had anticipated when he returned from Washington. Though the availability of the men from St. Simon's Island helped, as would those who would volunteer from the other points the Union forces controlled at the time, to really jump-start the growth of the 1st South Carolina, the men of the Port Royal islands were critical. However slow it was turning out to be to reconstitute the regiment, this did not mean that the same problem was happening elsewhere.

Though Generals Lane and Butler in Kansas and Louisiana had been told by Stanton that it was against Lincoln's policy to have blacks in uniform, they were smart enough to realize the secretary did not order them to disband their units. They had to have noticed too that Lincoln was also silent on the issue. With the president's preliminary emancipation announced in September, they also probably thought that he was just biding his time until the right political moment had arrived to make a change in his policy, which would be January 1, 1863, the date in which the proclamation would come into force. This would give Lincoln the political justification, though he already had the legislative authority, to put blacks into uniform, saying that they had an obligation to help fight for their freedom.

Regardless of Stanton's admonition, Lane and Butler continued their efforts. The silence of the secretary of war and the president on the existence of black units told them all they needed to know. By this time Lane had organized several companies of the 1st Kansas Colored Infantry while Butler, whose supply of manpower in Louisiana was much more plentiful than that in Kansas, already had two regiments known as the Louisiana Native Guards with a third one in the process of being organized.

So, while the commanding generals in these other peripheral theaters were having success, though varyingly, Saxton was hoping that November would bring better results. While his emphasis was trying to get freedmen to enlist, he still needed more junior officers. Though he commissioned another enlisted man as a captain on November 1, George Dolly of the 8th Maine Infantry, this only helped a little bit. In an effort to try and solve both problems, Saxton offered captaincies to plantation superintendents if they would recruit companies. Edward Philbrick was one of them. He commented about this recruiting effort on the 2nd with mixed feelings:

> The last time I saw General Saxton he seemed to think our whole destiny depended on the success of this negro enlistment. It is certainly a very important matter, but I think as before that it is doomed to fail here at present, from the imbecile character of the people. I thought … that if I were to go as Captain I might get a company without trouble, but I failed to get a single man seriously proposing it to them. If I had been able to raise a company to follow me and the same men would not have gone without me, I think I should have accepted General Saxton's offer, but although I consider the arming of the negroes the most important question of the day, I don't feel bound to take hold unless I can give an impetus to the undertaking.

Regardless of this failed attempt, Saxton did manage to recruit and commission four more junior officers, three of them from the same regiment. Again from the 8th Maine: L. W. Metcalf, Captain, November 11; E. C. Merriam, 2nd Lieutenant, November 17; and Charles E. Parker, 2nd Lieutenant, also November 17. Again from the 1st New York Engineers also on the 17th: James H. Tonking, Captain. While these efforts were going on, Saxton had previously managed to recruit a civilian named Liberty Billings for the slot of Lieutenant Colonel.[1] He was commissioned on November 1. However, the billet of colonel was still open. An officer from the 48th New York Infantry who was actively campaigning for it, would go on two excursions this month to prove he could do the job, but General Saxton would not be satisfied. It was not the fact that he might have been competent enough, but whoever occupied this slot had to have one unique quality. As Dr. Hawks put it, "We needed a man to command the new regiment who was a friend to the Negro." The individual who would meet this special requirement was at this time over 500 miles away in Massachusetts. His knowledge of Saxton's interest in him would be forthcoming.

Much to General Saxton's chagrin, November started out no differently than October in the attempt to recruit the Port Royal freedmen. Once again plantation superintendent Edward Philbrick made several observations on this issue. He wrote also on the 2nd that:

there have been great exertions made this week past to fill the ranks of the first negro regiment. A Rev. Mr. Fowler has been appointed chaplin [*sic*] and is at work recruiting, appealing to their religious feelings. He spent two nights here and talked in the praise-house, both evenings. The women came to hear him, but the young men were shy. Not one came near him, nor would they come near me when he was present."

At one point Philbrick seemed to have luck with one man, but the heavy-handed methods of General Hunter were too recent a memory. "We succeeded in getting Randy to promise to go, and he seemed quite earnest, but when he came to start next morning he suddenly found he had a pain in his chest! his heart failed him and he backed squared out.

Even the help of a freedman who had been in the old organization did not do any good:

We ... .had an address from Prince Rivers, a black coachman from Beaufort, who has been in General Hunter's regiment all summer, and is of sufficient intelligence to take a lively interest in the cause of enlistment. He has been to Philidelphia [*sic*] lately and comes back duly impressed with the magnitude of the country and the importance of the 'negro question,' but has not sufficient eloquence to get many recruits. Of course, the young men kept away from church and will keep away, so long as the subject is discussed. They have made up their silly minds and don't want to be convinced or persuaded to any change.

Regardless of the failed attempts by Philbrick, Fowler, and Rivers, things did not stay this way for long, which was evident several days later with the creation of Company B and commanded by Captain William James, one of the original twelve officers. Reverend Fowler said that James "enlisted twice as many recruits as any other officer—a full company for himself and as many in other companies."

On November 8, Charles B. Ware said that "the only interesting event the day that I was in Beaufort I was obliged to leave without beholding, viz: the mustering in of the first full company of the new regiment, Captain James. They marched through the streets just before I came away, making a fine appearance. Many of them were in the first regiment, and the regularity and steadiness of their marching was very credible. They are a fine body of men." To make General Saxton happy, "the regiment is filling fast, its friends are much encouraged. A number of men from the regiment (now numbering about four hundred) have been allowed to return home for a few days, and I think they will carry back quite a number with them."

The day that Ware saw the swearing in of Company B was the 7th.
Dr. Hawks, still the only physician in the regiment, thought that it was
grandiose:

> This event, the first muster of freedmen into the United States Army was
> a very important epoch in the history of the United States, and occurred
> on November 7 ... at General Saxton's headquarters in Beaufort ...
> Captain James had his men drawn up in line; and as he read their names
> from the roll, each man answered 'Here.' Then, with uncovered heads
> and right hands raised, the men took the usual oath of allegiance, which
> was administered by General Saxton. This simple ceremony over, the
> newly made soldiers marched back to their camp. But the greatness of
> the occasion, considering its far-reaching consequences, can hardly be
> overestimated. Only a few months before, these men were chattels. They
> had no family names; they were listed by their owners under a single
> given name, as Tom, Dick, Harry, July, Friday, Plato, Homer, Jupiter, like
> other like-stock on the plantation. Now they took sur-names, which
> are ... written on the records of their Company ... Thus they became
> founders of family names which will be honored by their descendants
> through all future generations.

With several hundred men now in the regiment, this meant that other
companies were also organized. Susie Baker said that several of her relatives
enlisted in Company E. It was also in this unit she would meet her future
husband. Since she was acquainted with Captain Trowbridge, she wanted
him to be the company commander. "I remember when the company was
being formed, we wished [that he] was our captain, because most of the men
in Co. E were the men he brought with him from St. Simons, and they were
attached to him. He was always jolly and pleasing with all."

On November 12, General Saxton was able to write happily to Stanton
that the First Regiment of South Carolina Volunteers was finally taking
shape after several failed attempts. He said that he now had 550 men in
uniform. However, this did not mean that it was all drill. While these new
recruits were learning the fundamentals of soldiering, Saxton had earlier
decided to take offensive action along the Georgia and Florida coast.
This meant Company A, the only unit with enough experience to do so.
Therefore, he was exercising for the first time instructions he had received
from the secretary back in August: "You are therefore authorized by every
means in your power to withdraw from the enemy their laboring force
and population, and to spare no effort consistent with civilized warfare
to weaken, harass, and annoy them, and to establish the authority of the
Government of the United States within your department."

Saxton decided not to wait to have a fully functional, combat-ready regiment. To detour the opposition and criticism to the reconstitution of the Volunteers, he said he "had two objects in view in sending this expedition. The first [is] to prove the fighting qualities of the negroes (which some have doubted), and the other [is] to bring away the people from the main-land, destroy all rebel salt-work and to break up the rebel picket stations along the coast." Though Saxton did not state it, another purpose of his plan was to gather more recruits.

In the planning of this expedition, Saxton had to know that seeing ex-slaves in uniform would have a good psychological effect against the enemy, but only limited physical success. What the Yankees would destroy, the Confederates could rebuild. It would be the first time that the men of Company A would be in combat since St. Simon's Island in August, but with several months of training under their belts plus the fact there would be almost twice as many men. Saxton would also have good intelligence. In his regiment he had men who had lived along the coasts in South Carolina, Georgia and Florida, and would be able to glean from them what they knew about Confederate defenses, salt-works locations and population densities of slaves. However, before he could take care of the latter two, he had to know where the Rebels were weak defensively, since he was only sending one company. Once he got what information he could, he decided on specific points between Fernandina, Florida and Duboy Sound, Georgia. He was going to make sure his men stayed clear of the strong defensive works of Savannah.

Saxton appointed Lieutenant Colonel Oliver Beard of the 48th New York Infantry to head the expedition.[2] The regiment's chaplain, Rev. James A. Fowler, was assigned to go too. With 62 men now in Company A, a captured Confederate steamer, the *Darlington*, would transport them to the target area. They would begin operations in the vicinity of Fernandina and work their way up the coast. Assuming that the information on the Rebel defenses was correct, they would not pose much of a problem. Or would they?

Confederate Coast Defenses

In the beginning of the war, there was no planned military strategy for the Confederacy to take. It would evolve from being a state-controlled situation to a national one as the Union forces made their moves. This strategic evolution can be demonstrated in the seaboard states of South Carolina, Georgia, and Florida. At first in 1861 they had decided to defend all the inhabited points on the coast because of loud protests coming from the wealthy land-owners in these areas, which the governors had to appease. As events would later show, in order to survive, defense of the landed gentry would have to be discarded to consolidate Rebel forces so there would be adequate concentrations of manpower to respond to Union threats. There was just too much coastline and not enough trained and equipped troops, especially with the calls for soldiers to be sent to Virginia and elsewhere in 1862 as the war heated up with heavy casualties.[3]

Regiments in less active states would be sent to those areas that had heavy fighting. Florida, for example, would send eight infantry regiments, one cavalry regiment, and one battery of artillery during the year. Since the state had the smallest population in the Confederacy, it would not be able to replace these soldiers and would be left with a much diminished capacity to defend itself. These calls for troops also put additional pressures on these seaboard governors, who in turn put pressure on the local commanders, to protect the coasts. However, since the Confederate coastal forces would not have the means to launch any offensive actions because of the heavy troop withdrawals, their actions would have to be purely defensive.

After Fort Sumter, soldiers in South Carolina, Georgia and Florida were rushed from wherever possible to defend their coasts. As the units arrived, they were assigned to a particular area without regard from where they came. Many of these units were companies, and only after they had arrived were they further organized into battalions and regiments. There was naturally no preconceived plan on how many of these larger organizations would be created. The needs of the time dictated what was to happen. Not knowing what was to take place in the beginning, many were recruited only for 90 days, then disbanded with many of the men leaving to join other created units for three-year enlistments as it became clear that the war was going to last longer than had been originally anticipated. Many regiments were initially organized with 13 companies. Later, when the Confederate Army standardized the size of the regiments to 10 companies, many of the men in the displaced ones enlisted into other organizations.

Late in 1861, the Confederate government in Richmond decided it had to do a better job in organizing the coastal defenses of the south-Atlantic seacoast and get them away from state and local concerns due to political influence, but this would soon prove to be a little too late. Though the Rebel War Department had organized these three states into the Department of South Carolina, Georgia, and Florida, the bulk of the regiments that it was supposed to control still came from these states it was supposed to protect. This meant, however, that politics would still have a role to play. The first commander appointed to run this seeming quagmire of an organization was General Lee. He arrived on November 8, 1861, the day after Port Royal fell.

After a whirlwind tour of his new command following the debacle of the 7th, General Lee set about transforming it into a system of heavily-fortified strategic, strong points. Cavalry units were spread out along the coast for early warning of any Yankee movements. They were backed up by strong interior lines of infantry and artillery. A mobile defense system was also created using the railroad, which would allow reinforcements to augment local units in threatened areas. He did this because there were several realities that were beyond his control, the most important being his limited manpower and heavy artillery to guard the entire coast of his command and the superiority of Union naval gunfire in both quantity and quality. With these facts, Lee formulated a defensive policy that would enable the Confederates to take advantage of their interior line of communications (the railroads).[4] His plan would concentrate forces in threatened areas and neutralize the Union Navy's superior firepower by drawing the invading force inland and out of range of the naval guns, thus denying their use to the Federals. For political reasons so as to appease the planter interests, it would also have a secondary role, that to prevent slaves escaping via the easiest routes to the new Federal enclave at Port Royal or the Union blockading fleet. Though the department would have two other commanders by the time of the arrival of the Volunteers, in which they would have made several changes to his plans, Lee's basic ideas would remain in place. His defensive concept would continue to last for the rest of the war, being highly successful by defeating every Federal seaborne attack.

The area to which General Saxton planned to send the Volunteers was covered at this time by three units, an independent cavalry company in Florida called the Amelia Island Guerrillas,[5] the 3rd Georgia Cavalry Battalion, and the 1st Georgia Cavalry Battalion. Many of these units' members came from the areas they were controlling with very few of them having had any prior military experience. This of course would be remedied as time went by with training and exposure to combat. Since the majority of the officers and men had no prior experience, they had not been indoctrinated to a particular mode of military thought. They were not inhibited against using cavalry as the situation dictated, whereas standard military doctrine might call it unorthodox thinking. Besides being an early warning system for any Yankee excursion on the mainland, a key component of cavalry usage was its mobility, being able to move quickly to hot spots to engage the enemy and hopefully delay them until reinforcements could arrive. These cavalry outposts on the Florida and Georgia coasts would be soon put to the test.

The heavy withdrawals of regiments from Georgia during the summer and fall had created a major hole in General Lee's original plan of strong interior lines. Since Savannah was still a prime target for capture, the bulk of the available infantry and artillery for the coast had to go for the defense of the city. As far as the rest of the state's coast went, it had to play a secondary role. For command and control purposes, the state was organized as the District of Georgia, with the city as the focal point of defense. The rest of the coast was split into two sub-districts by the Altamaha River. The 1st Georgia would be responsible for the two counties (McIntosh and Liberty) north of the river and the 3rd Georgia for the two counties (Camden and Glynn) south of it to the Florida border.[6] The battalions were spread out in different camps with various names: Saville, Clinch, Dark Entry, Brookfield, Wayne, Gignilliat, Dorchester and Brailsford. As far as the district and department commanders were probably concerned, these areas north and south of the Altamaha had a very low probability of enemy activity compared to Savannah. This also meant a low probability of having to worry about sending any infantry and artillery augmentation.

In Florida, the eastern part had no strategic city like Savannah or Charleston to guard, but it did have a larger coast to protect. However, with no strategic asset to cover, the remaining infantry and artillery units after the heavy withdrawals would be readily available in the event of their need. With the Federal occupation of Fernandina and St. Augustine and the now twice abandonment of Jacksonville, the Rebels conceded the coast north of Jacksonville and the area east of the St. John's River to the enemy. They then placed camps near Fernandina and on the river's west bank.

The main camp covering this area was known as Finegan. It was situated several miles west of Jacksonville. The other ones were sub-camps of it. They were, as General Lee had planned, outposts of cavalry, watching for any sign of enemy activity. Camp Finegan had cavalry too, but its primary function was to serve as the base for the available infantry and artillery in eastern Florida. All the camps (including the ones in Georgia) were set back from the waterways they covered a certain distance to prevent any surprise attack. As an additional assurance, picket stations were established on the waterfronts to provide early warning.

The sub-camp that covered Federal activity at Fernandina was called Camp Cooper. This was where the Amelia Island Guerrillas were stationed. Besides the Union threat to its front, it also had two other avenues of danger north and south of it to watch: the St. Mary's and Nassau Rivers. Therefore, picket stations had to be placed in these areas too. Since Cooper's northern border was the St. Mary's, and the river was part of the state boundary with Georgia, this meant also that this Florida unit could coordinate with the Georgia cavalry to counter any Yankee movement. So, as the one company of the 1st South Carolina Volunteers prepared to sail on the *Darlington* in early November, these Confederate units were what they would face once the expedition got under way.

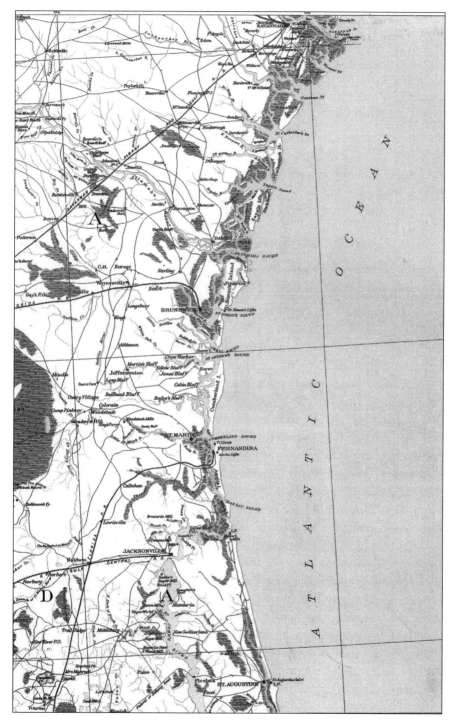

Coastal Georgia and Florida. *The Official Military Atlas of the Civil War, Plates CXLV and CXLVI*

Raid in Rebeldom

Ever since the capture of Fort Clinch and Fernandina back in March, several trips had been made by the Federals to the town of St. Mary's or farther up the St. Mary's River. This had made the Confederate forces on both sides feel a bit anticipatory that another Yankee naval excursion could happen at any time. When there had been any need for soldiers for these trips, it had always been the 9th Maine Infantry, which had been stationed on Amelia Island since the beginning. Three trips had been made to St. Mary's, one March, one in May and the other in June. However, since the last trip, the nearly five months that had elapsed had caused the Rebels to fall into a sense of lethargy. They would soon be snapped out of it.

Because this expedition to Florida and Georgia would be the first officially sanctioned one using black soldiers in the war, General Saxton knew that this would be a critical test for his men. Therefore, only the most experienced troops led by the most experienced officers of black soldiers would suffice. Of the reconstituted and reorganized 1st Regiment of South Carolina Volunteers, this naturally meant Captain Trowbridge, Lieutenants Walker and Trowbridge, and the men of Company A. Too much was riding on this to take any chance—i.e. the future use of blacks in the war—so this unit would have to be the standard-bearer.

It was fortunate for Captain Trowbridge that there was a forward combat and supply base in the area where he would be operating. Fernandina would be a safe harbor to go to if required after having been in enemy territory. Since the *Darlington* was a steamer, she could stock up on coal as needed. She could also take on fresh water or any other kind of required provisions for ships. However, because Fernandina was primarily a base of operations for the blockading fleet, the Volunteers had to make sure they brought along enough ammunition, required accouterments and other ancillary supplies necessary for the mission. Though this information on Fernandina was good to have, Lt. Colonel Beard decided to launch this operation from St. Simon's Island, which was still under the control of the blockading fleet though the island had been abandoned.

On Monday morning, November 3, the *Darlington* arrived at Amelia Island and proceeded to the Bells River,[1] one of several tidal streams bisecting the marshes between the mainland and the island. Based upon the information obtained from the freedmen who were from this area, the Volunteers would find salt-making operations along the shore.[2] Once the ship passed the marshes and arrived at the mainland, she came across the pickets of the Amelia Island Guerrillas. The Volunteers quickly fired on them and drove them back. The Rebel cavalry hardly had any time to return fire before they landed. Once the landing site was secured, the 1st S.C. proceeded to destroy and confiscate all they could before the Confederates could return in force and really give them trouble. Company A "destroyed the salt-works, and all the salt, corn, and wagons which we could not carry away, besides killing the horses." Once this was accomplished, they evacuated the shore and proceeded to the Jolly River, which connected to the Bells. There the Volunteers repeated the process, destroying "two salt-works, with a large amount of salt and corn." During this entire time, they did not see any sign of Rebel opposition.[3] Once the Jolly River salt-works were wrecked, Colonel Beard gave the order to go to St. Mary's, which was next on his list and just a few miles away. During this entire time, he had to be aware of the tide because of where the ship was. He could not afford for it to get stuck.

The first official test of the reconstituted Company A in combat conditions was an easy one, given that they did not face any more than the pickets on guard. In reality, they had no idea what they would have gone up against along the Bells and Jolly Rivers until they landed and performed their mission. Though the opposition was far lighter than what they had to deal with on St. Simon's Island back in August, they were no doubt relieved that they did not have to face any serious threat, especially the new soldiers. They might have had to engage one company initially, but the other cavalry units from Camp Finegan were only a few hours ride away, followed by horse artillery and ultimately infantry. The situation could have turned into a very nasty firefight. The freedmen did not stick around long enough to find out.

The next challenge lay not too far away as the *Darlington* made her way through the marshes to St. Mary's. Just as the Volunteers potentially had to face one company of cavalry where they were in Florida, the initial threat to them would also be the same as they made their way to Georgia. In Camden County, the unit that covered the target area was Company E of the 3rd Georgia Cavalry Battalion. The company's nickname was the Camden Mounted Rifles. Just like the Amelia Island Guerrillas, Company E had only pickets stationed in St. Mary's while the unit's main camp was several miles away at a place called Dark Entry. Also just like the Guerrillas, the Mounted Rifles could call on the other units of the 3rd Battalion to assist them if necessary. A militia cavalry company could also be mobilized if needed. Therefore, once again, time was critical.

Once the *Darlington* arrived, the pickets at St. Mary's were already alert since they were close enough to hear the sound of musket fire several hours ago. They had also sent a message to Dark Entry to warn the commander that contact with the enemy might be imminent. Though the pickets may have already been on alert, they were easily forced back by the size of Company A. The Volunteers' stay there was not long. Colonel Beard ordered them to leave after they had "brought off two families of contrabands." This raid so upset the commander of the militia cavalry company that he would later write to Georgia Governor Joseph Brown to be authorized to mobilize his unit for an extended period of time. He was mortified that "negroes were landed in St. Mary's, who ... [went about] ... insulting the few ladies remaining there and helping themselves to everything they could lay their hands on." However, once again the Volunteers withdrew before any serious enemy presence occurred. Colonel Beard decided at this point that the Volunteers had seen enough action for the day and left enemy territory.

With this level of Federal activity all of a sudden going on in the area, Rebel units all along the Georgia coast were alerted for possible enemy contact. Once the information about the Yankee activity at St. Mary had been sent up the chain of command, cavalry companies were ordered to be ready to ride if the pickets sight the enemy. Now that the Volunteers had made their intent known, they could not think that they would continue to have light resistance. This was confirmed the next day on Tuesday the 4th when the Volunteers landed at King's Bay, only a few miles north of St. Mary's. After they drove the pickets in, they marched about a mile inland and "destroyed a large salt-work on a creek ..., together with all the property on the place." In the process Company A was attacked by a force of the 3rd Georgia estimated to be about 80 soldiers.[4] Given the size of the Rebel force this time, the Volunteers were still able to keep them at bay while they finished their work and make it back to the *Darlington*. Colonel Beard believed his men killed two of the enemy. Because of the size of this engagement, he did not have his men do anything for the rest of the day and also on Wednesday.

On the 6th, the 1st S.C. had another busy day. They landed at a place called Butler Island.[5] There they "brought off 80 bushels of rice." After completing this with no Confederate troops around, the steamer proceeded on to Darien, Georgia. The Volunteers did not find anything of a military nature to destroy, but they did exchange shots with pickets of the McIntosh Cavalry, a subordinate unit of the 1st Georgia Cavalry Battalion. The company had its base at Camp Gignilliat, which was four miles above Darien. However, before the rest of the Rebel unit could react, the Volunteers left, this time with three prisoners and some arms. However, Johnny Reb, a.k.a. Johnnies, would get another crack at the Yanks the next day.

If anybody had not gotten the word yet of the 1st South Carolina's coastal activities before the 6th, after the landing at Darien, they knew it now. It had been bad enough that President Lincoln in Washington had issued a preliminary emancipation proclamation back in September, giving the Confederate States a deadline to return "to the fold" or lose their slaves, but to unleash a band of "Negro mauraders" [*sic*] on the coast was just too much. Pickets up and down the Georgia coast were on high alert and ready to ride in the event they were spotted. If they were on the 7th, the Volunteers would give Johnny Reb an added surprise—the heavy firepower of a naval gunboat.

On what would be the last day of this expedition, the target area was several miles up the Sapelo River in McIntosh County. Since Colonel Beard and Captain Trowbridge were under no illusion that the Confederates were not already on high alert up and down the coast, they anticipated that they would get heavy resistance because they would be traversing the river for several miles. This time frame would give the enemy enough of an opportunity to arrive on the scene in force to be able to engage them. Not knowing how much of an enemy force they could expect, the two officers decided that they needed additional firepower. It was time to ask the Navy for assistance. The U.S.S. *Potomska*, a civilian-converted steamer with an armament of five guns and commanded by Acting Volunteer Lieutenant William Budd, was assigned the task. It was smart for Beard to have chosen St. Simon's Island as his base,[6] because the blockading fleet was nearby, which meant he could call on assistance if required.

Of the several raids the Volunteers had conducted so far, they had come across very few slaves to carry to freedom. The few that had been liberated were placed on St. Simon's for safe-keeping while the *Darlington* would go to a new target area.[7] Not only had it been disappointing for that reason, but also for one of the main purposes why the expedition was mounted, to find more recruits among the coastal plantations. Whether the 1st S.C. would find any substantial number was once again based upon the information obtained from the freedmen from this area who had escaped to St. Simon's many months before. They would soon find out if it was still accurate when operations began on the morning of Friday, November 7.

The Sapelo River had several plantations along its banks, one of which belonged to the commander of one of the companies in the 1st Georgia Cavalry Battalion. His area of responsibility included his property. So, as the *Darlington* and the *Potomska* proceeded near mid-morning up the river, picket stations on both sides of it swung into action to warn their respective commanders. Soon, the McIntosh Cavalry under Captain Octavius C. Hopkins south of the river and the Lamar Rangers under Captain William Brailsford north of it would be on their way to prepared fighting positions.[8] As these two units of the 1st Georgia under Lieutenant Colonel Charles Spaulding would get the word to mount up and ride, information about the raiders would then be shortly sent to him at battalion headquarters. Spaulding in turn would send it to Brigadier General Hugh W. Mercer, commander of the District of Georgia in Savannah, who would pass the information to General P. G. T. Beauregard in Charleston, commanding officer of the department. Both district and department commanders would soon know whether to augment the 1st Georgia with additional cavalry, infantry and if necessary, artillery units from Savannah. If this did happen, the original defensive strategy of General Lee would fully kick in.

As the ships proceeded upriver, Captain Brailsford just happened to be inspecting one of his picket stations on the Sapelo when he noticed them. This picket station just also happened to be on his plantation. "I rode down to one of my pickets stationed at Sutherland Bluff, which is the first upon the main. Two steamboats—one a steamer, the other the old *Darlington*, I think—came up the river ... in the morning. The boats stopped about five minutes, and expected them to shell, but they did not."[9] He said also that the:

> boats went up the river to Belville (plantation), Colonel Hopkins' place, landed some men for a few minutes, then went on to Mr. King's place (Mallow plantation), stopped, landed a negro company, ... and took all of Mr. King's negroes, with a few exceptions, and would have taken the old gentleman if his daughter had not clung to him as he did. The propeller stayed there, and the old *Darlington*, with her negro company and one gun,[10] proceeded up the river to Mr. McDonald's place.

The reason why the *Potomska* did not go any further than the King plantation was that the Sapelo River was not deep enough beyond this point. Therefore it was decided that Lieutenant Budd and 10 of his men would continue on the *Darlington* while his ship would stay put. From the log of the *Potomska*: "At 10:40 anchored off King's plantation ... the captain with ten men, armed, went on board the *Darlington* and went up the river to a plantation ... " As the *Darlington* continued to the McDonald plantation, she finally came into heavy contact with the McIntosh Cavalry firing from the high ground. Captain Brailsford said that, "As they passed White Bluff, Captain Hopkins' Company fired on the boat with their small arms; when the boat could bring her gun to bear she fired four or five [times] at the bluff." Hopkins' unit had to ride seven miles from Camp Gignilliat to get to White Bluff so they could be ready to fire on the Yankees. In his report of this enemy contact, Colonel Beard said that "we were attacked by 80 or 90 of the enemy, who were well posted on a bluff behind trees. At this point the channel runs within 50 yards of the bluff. We killed 2 of the enemy and had a colored man wounded." Captain Hopkins wrote later in his unit's log: "This company engaged the Abolition forces in a gunboat at a place called White Bluff, seven miles distant from camp at 12.p.m."

Once the *Darlington* got past the gauntlet of musket fire from the McIntosh Cavalry, the Volunteers landed at a place called Fairhope. There they "destroyed the salt-works, some tan-vats, corn, and other things that might be of use to the enemy." After this Beard decided that they would not go any further upriver but return. When they came again within range of White Bluff, this time at 2 p.m., they heard once more the crack of musketry. "On return … we were again attacked by the enemy." Beard estimated this time "in greater force."[11] Hopkins said that his company began "firing upon them at a distance of from twenty to fifty yards, killing and wounding," he believed, "seven men. Having concealed ourselves behind large trees, there was no one hurt on our side."

The *Darlington* may have survived twice now the fusillade of Hopkins' boys, but it did not mean that the Volunteers and freed slaves they had below in the cargo hold were safe yet. They would have to go up against Captain Brailsford's Lamar Rangers further down river, who had had plenty of time to arrive and wait in their defensive positions. However, this time the Volunteers would have a compensating factor leading the way— the gunboat *Potomska*.

About 2:20 the *Darlington* returned to the King plantation where she met up again with her escort. The gunboat "got underway and proceeded down the river, shelling the woods as we went." At a certain point in the river the *Potomska* ran aground at 3:05 due to the low tide, thus causing both vessels to wait, but not helplessly. In order to deter any possible Rebel action, the gunboat fired various ordnance. Again from the log of the *Potomska*: "Fired 36 shells from broadside guns and 4 stands of grape; fired 27 shells from Parrott." By 4:50 the gunboat was able to move again and they continued on their way.

It hardly took 10 more minutes before the *Potomska* spotted the pickets of the Lamar Rangers. Her log: "at 5 opened fire on the enemy's pickets

...; the enemy in large numbers concealed in rifle pits." Colonel Beard said he was very grateful for her presence. "We were greatly aided here by the *Potomska*, which from a bend below shelled the woods." Under the barrage of her guns, Beard had Trowbridge land his men at Brailsford's plantation, in which they drove back the pickets and then "destroyed all the property on the place, together with the most important buildings." In his account of what took place, Captain Brailsford said "I had my men concealed about two hundred yards from the river, and took my position in the yard so as to see them when they landed. They shelled for one hour and a half, and the trees under cover of which my men were concealed, were riddled. All we did was to lay down and dodge shot and shell."[12] Once the Volunteers finished, they re-boarded the *Darlington* and left. Both ships had to make the tide while it was still high enough to allow them to get over the sand bar at the entrance of the Sapelo River and into the Atlantic.

The day's work up the Sapelo was vindication for the previous attempts to find recruits. Because of it, Beard said he was able to get a total of 94 men from the expedition. In a bit of exuberance, he said that "as soon as we took a slave from his claimant we placed a musket in his hand and he began to fight for the freedom of others."[13] As for Company A, he said they "fought with astonishing coolness and bravery. For alacrity in effecting landings, for determination, and for such bush fighting I found them all I could desire—more than I had hoped. They behaved with bravery, gloriously, and deserve all the praise."

In his report of the day's events, Lieutenant Budd corroborated Beard's appraisal, especially since he had never worked with black soldiers before:

> It gives me pleasure to testify to the admirable conduct of the negro troops ... during the day's operations. They behaved splendidly under the warm and galling fire we were exposed to in two skirmishes with the enemy [at White Bluff when Budd was on the *Darlington*]. I did not see a man flinch, contrary to my expectations. One of them particularly came under my notice, who although badly wounded in the face, continued to lead and fire in the coolest manner imaginable. Every one of them acted like veterans.

In addition to the 94 men, 62 women and children were also liberated in the expedition, the vast bulk coming from the Sapelo raid. Beard said also that his men "destroyed nine large salt-works" and an estimated "$20,000 worth of horses, salt, corn, rice ... which we could not carry away." With the expedition now over, the ships headed back to St. Simon's Island to rest, pick up the freed slaves there and then return to Port Royal.

The return of the *Darlington* to Beaufort was one of exhilaration for the men of Company A, especially the original members from the old Hunter regiment.[14] All the previous months of inactivity on St. Simon's were now behind them. The report from Lieutenant Budd of the U.S. Navy was an outside testament to their abilities and bravery under fire, not just as former slaves but as men. There was no way that any white unit with the same level of training could have done better given the same circumstances. A report that Beard wrote on November 10 was in consonance with that of the *Potomska*'s commander. In it he gave a chronology of events detailing the various landings and the results of each. According to the instructions that Beard had received from Saxton "as directed by you, I have tried a portion of the First South Carolina Volunteers" and he did not find them wanting.

Two days later on the 12th, General Saxton wrote a report to Secretary Stanton. He too lauded their achievements. "I am happy to report that in every point of view the expedition was a perfect success. Rarely in the progress of this war has so much mischief been done by so small a force in so short a space of time." As someone not directly involved in the operational part of the mission but primarily the political aspect, Saxton had to somewhat embellish the Volunteers' success to help overcome continued opposition to blacks in uniform. However, there was one part of his report that did not need any elaboration, but served as quiet testimony of her recent usage—the *Darlington*. "She returned from the expedition completely riddled with rifle bullets."

Besides his laudable comments, Saxton recommended that the Volunteers be used for a specialized mission, "one that will carry terror to the hearts of the rebels." He wanted to use them in a series of company-level operations along the coast in light-draft steamers to free slaves and obtain recruits. They would have "an abundance of spare muskets and ammunition, to put in the hands of the recruits as they come in." He added that because of their knowledge of the local areas, their usage for this type of mission would be "better than white soldiers."

Saxton also wanted to bring to Stanton's attention the logistical support problems he had if he was to succeed in any mission. Since General Brannan was back in command because of the death of General Mitchel, he had not been the most cooperative person for Saxton's charges. Because they had never gotten along, it was possible that Brannan was hiding behind the guise of officialdom just to be spiteful. "I can procure no supplies of ordnance or medical stores without an order from the commanding general, and if he thinks differently, or does not choose to give them to me, I am helpless." Though he did acknowledge the right of the commander to control his supplies and modes of transportation (the

Darlington),[15] Saxton said that unless the "military commander" gave him what he needed, he would not be able to carry out his mission.

Saxton also mentioned that more men in the Department of the South and 10th Corps were available to be recruited outside of the 550 he had enrolled to date, but they too were not under his control. "More than 1,000 able-bodied negroes are now in the employ of the Engineer and Quartermaster Departments. Were I to enlist from these I could fill up the regiment in one day; but I thus far abstained from any interference with those departments." So, with all these points brought up, Saxton sent his and Beard's reports to Washington.

The success of the 1st South Carolina's first official combat mission spread quickly in the department and the North. It even found its way into Confederate newspapers. For example, in the November 14 issue of the *Savannah Republican* a writer who called himself "Cavalry" used vitriol and lies to describe what happened:

> At the residence of Reuben King, Esq., they forced some fifty negroes to accompany them ... in spite of their piteous cries and lamentations, 'to freedom, clothe, and education' as they stated. The commander of the [steamer] ordered those shot who refused to go.... They next visited the residence of Col. McDonald ... where they succeeded in capturing Col. M., breaking up his salt-works and stealing a few things, when hearing that some cavalry was approaching, the cowardly wretches fled to their boats. These philanthropic, noble friends of the black man, at each of these places, sent armed negroes ahead to bear the brunt and receive our bullets, should any soldier be present. How Yankee! How brave!

The *Savannah Republican* was typical of a Southern response to the Volunteers, whereas Northern reaction was favorable. On November 17, *The New York Times*, in consonance with a recent action taken by the 1st Kansas Colored near Butler, Missouri, published:

> Very late advices from Kansas and Florida ... give details of engagements between the rebels and United States negro troops in which the latter behaved with distinguished coolness and brave courage, and achieved decided success.... The result of these experienced fighters is such as inspires the rebels with indescribable horror, and bids fair to work important changes in the policy of the Government toward the negroes.

The *Chicago Tribune* wrote a similar piece about the Volunteers on the 19th that:

Events of no ordinary interest have just occurred in the Department of the South. The negro troops have been tested, and to their great joy, though not contrary to their own expectations, they have triumphed, not only over enemies armed with muskets and swords, but over what the black man dreads most, sharp and cruel prejudices.

The 1st S.C.'s success also found favorable comments from some members of white regiments. A soldier in the 55th Pennsylvania Infantry said that the "colored brigade as it is called, went on an expedition to Florida, and among the captures made were three white men. On coming to Beaufort they were marched to prison by six colored guards. The humiliating part was that one of the prisoners was once the master of his captors."

Another soldier in the 47th Pennsylvania Infantry wrote that the:

negro brigade, or regiment, under the command of Gen. Saxton, have been absent on an expedition, destroying rebel salt works in Georgia and Florida and returned with a large quantity of lumber. The men of this brigade are equipped with blue dress coats and red pantaloons and are commanded by white men from the different volunteer regiments. They are encamped a few miles from here on what is known as Smith's Plantation, here they are being drilled and taught. Those who have already learned to read, show a great desire to improve and are anxious to receive reading matter.

In her diary on November 13, evangelist Laura Towne recorded that one of the freedmen made a pithy comment about the Volunteers. "Aunt Phillis is laughing and chuckling over the prowess of our soldiers. She says 'Dey fought and fought and shot down de 'Secesh,' and ne'er a white man among 'em but two captains.'"

Irrespective of the accolades that the Volunteers' commanding officers and Lieutenant Budd gave, these achievements still did not seem to impress General Brannan, especially when Saxton needed more logistical support for the new recruits brought back. On November 16, Edward Philbrick reported a conversation:

I had a talk with General Saxton. He was feeling very blue, had just been to Hilton Head to get some tents for his new recruits of which he enlisted about a hundred men on his recent trip to St. Mary's. There are some 3000 tents in warehouse there, but General Brannan refused to open it for him, alleging the advice of the Medical Department, which closed it because yellow fever had been near it. Now it is notorious that whenever one of General Brannan's men wants anything from the same warehouse, he gives a special order and it is opened for him, but not for General Saxton, the <u>Abolitionist</u>. So the new recruits have to sleep in open air these frosty nights, dampening their ardor somewhat. General Saxton agreed with me that if there is no earnestness and sincerity among other army officers than among the specimens we have had here, we should all go to the dogs. His expedition was so successful that he was in good spirits till balked by General Brannan. The best item in it was that one of the rebel prisoners taken was marched to Beaufort jail guarded by one of his former slaves! The conduct of the negro troops was very well spoken of by their officers, but is the subject of a good deal of ribaldry among the white soldiers at Beaufort, who exhibit a degree of hatred really fiendish towards the black regiment, taking their cue from their commanding officer, of course.

Regardless of Saxton's complaints about Brannan in his report to Stanton of the 12th, he did manage to get the *Darlington* for another mission. On top of it, Brannan probably wanted to make sure that Saxton knew who was boss, but did not want to push it too far because of possible repercussions from Stanton, but just enough to make sure Saxton got the message. With this mission laid on so quickly after the first one, Brannan possibly also felt he should not give Saxton any grief at this juncture but cooperate just enough to get the new one under way, which left on the 13th—but then do something again to tweak his subordinate, therefore the tent problem of the 16th.

Since this first excursion was a success with only one company, General Saxton probably wanted to continue the momentum. He authorized this next mission to have enough men by basically tripling the number of soldiers for it by using two companies.[16] With 160 men now under Colonel Beard's command, he would be hitting his target area on the Rebel coast this time with a sizable force as opposed to what the Confederates were used to. With the additional men assigned to Company A and the approximate 80 men of Company B under Captain William James, this would give Beard a mix of experience, from the combat-tested to the untried. However, once the expedition was over, he would have two companies of battle-tested soldiers.

The mission of this detachment was to procure a sizable amount of lumber they found out was at a place called Blue and Hall's Mill on the Duboy River near Darien.[17] Given the amount of lumber that they were told to expect, the large transport ship *Ben De Ford* was assigned to the mission to help bring it back. However, since she was not available at the time, she would rendezvous with the *Darlington* at Duboy Sound once she was done with her current mission. The 1st S.C. left Port Royal on November 13.

The *Darlington* did not take long to arrive at the rendezvous site. She anchored and waited for the arrival of the *Ben De Ford*. Several days went by, but the ship did not show up. Finally, Beard decided not to wait any longer. On the 18th, he commenced operations with the help of another gunboat from the blockading fleet, the steamer *Madgie*. Commanded by Acting Master F. B. Meriam, she had a serious complement of heavy ordnance: one pivotal 30-pounder Parrott, one pivotal 20-pounder Parrott, two 24-pounder S.B. howitzers and one 12-pounder S.B. howitzer.

Arriving at the target area, Beard decided to send out a reconnaissance party since the Volunteers did not run up against any initial enemy resistance.[18] Situated on an island next to the mainland, he "found it necessary to reconnoiter the land adjacent there to. To do this it was necessary to cross a narrow causeway, leading from the mill through a swamp to the main highland, a distance of about 450 yards. This highland was heavily wooded, except on the summit, which was cleaned and occupied with houses." With the *Madgie* in an over-watch position in the Duboy River, a 34-man detachment from Company B under Captain James proceeded up the causeway while the rest of the Volunteers began to organize to procure the lumber. Beard assigned them this mission to give them experience, especially if they had any contact with Rebel troops. Company A had already been under fire and it was now B's turn. It did not take long for this to occur when contact with the enemy was made.

Because the Rebels up and down the coast of Georgia had not reported any Yankee activity since the last contact that had been made on the 7th, they probably decided to cut down on their vigilance. After 10 days of inactivity when it appeared that things had gone back to normal duty, pickets spotted the *Darlington* and the *Madgie* ascending the Duboy on the 18th. The picket who rode back to camp to sound the alarm did not take long to get there, and once again the troopers of the McIntosh Cavalry, 1st Georgia Cavalry Battalion were on their way, this time under Lieutenant William Atwood. Captain Hopkins sent this small force to ascertain the situation before deciding whether it was necessary to commit the rest of his company. If the enemy decided to push inland, Hopkins would commit the rest of his unit, which was ready to ride once the order was given. Describing what they found once they got to the area, the Rebels saw that "the Abolitionists ... came up to the ridge, a village four miles distant from [Camp Gignilliat and] landed a large force of Negroes on a causeway leading from a mill to the mainland." Once the Rebs spotted them, they quickly deployed and commenced firing.

The sudden fusillade caught Company B by surprise. They did not think that they would get so quickly into firefight. They had "no sooner passed across the crossway and through the wood to the clearing beyond that they were fired on by the enemy, who were posted in the thicket in front and on both sides." Captain James said that as he took his "company some distance in land to reconnoiter and guard the landing, while on this duty, was fired on by the enemy in ambush." Though the Volunteers quickly returned fire, James said that "one of my men received a gunshot wound fracturing the bone on his left arm and was sent back" to the rear to have it attended to. Regardless of the ambush, Beard said "they speedily rallied and opened a brisk fire on the place, occupied by the concealed enemy. This fire they kept up … until ordered by me to retire to the end of the causeway."

While the firefight continued, Corporal Isaac W. Jenking, the man who had been shot, had his arm attended to by Dr. Hawks. Since the corporal had been hit "with a minnie ball," he saw the effect of it, which made "a comminuted compound fracture of the humirus [*sic*] of the left arm." At first Hawks thought he might have to amputate Jenking's arm, but James said that "our heroic and accomplished Surgeon held out that he could save both life and arm, and he succeeded and the last time I saw the soldier, his arm, though useless, was there."

When Colonel Beard finally ordered Company B to pull back, Lieutenant Atwood claimed that his men drove the enemy "back to their boats." Beard said that when he gave the order, Company B "retired … firing as they went with a slowness and deliberateness that could not have been surpassed by veteran troops." While Atwood could not determine "with what loss" the Volunteers had, Beard said that "three others were severely wounded while they were retiring. When my men reached the end of the causeway," Beard had a surprise waiting for the McIntosh Cavalry if they wanted to pursue. "I had the bow gun of the *Darlington* directed on the wood, after which the fire of the enemy ceased … "

Since the only avenue to the island was the narrow causeway, Beard had artillery fire placed on it and the mainland to prevent any Rebel encroachment while they worked day and night for the next two days to load the lumber and other useful items. From the Confederate side, Lt. Atwood said "they remained at the mill stealing lumber and shelling the village for three days and nights. Having nothing but small arms, we could not reach them. Our men in this engagement, being covered by trees, remained unhurt." From the appearance of this testimony, the higher level Rebel commands did not deem it worthy enough to send any reinforcements, especially artillery.

On the 19th, the *Ben De Ford* finally arrived. Between her and the *Darlington*, "200,000 to 300,000 feet of superior boards and planks, besides securing a number of circular and other saws, belting, corn-mills, and other property" were loaded. During this time, Dr. Hawks suffered an injury to his right ear from the constant cannonading while treating the wounded. While the "shells were being fired at intervals of a few minutes, I felt a sensation as something bursting in my right ear, and thought the typanum [*sic*] was ruptured." Once the vessels were filled, they weighed anchor and went back to Beaufort while the *Madgie* continued blockade duty.

In his report written on November 22, Colonel Beard once again praised the Volunteers. "I think you cannot fail to give them great praise for standing a galling fire from a concealed enemy so bravely and for holding the causeway referred to during the two days and nights required for loading two large steamers with valuable property in the face of the enemy. To do this, my men worked day and night without intermission." In his accolades for their performance, General Saxton said that "although scarcely one month since the organization of this regiment was commensed [*sic*], in that short period these untrained soldiers have captured from the enemy a large amount of property.... They have driven back equal numbers of rebel troops and have destroyed the salt-works along the whole line of this coast."

In some white regiments, the Volunteers found some respect after the word got around. Lt. William Geety of Company H, 47th Pennsylvania Infantry said on November 24 "the darkies fight well and whipped the Rebels again in Georgia." A soldier in the 55th Pennsylvania said they "made another expedition to [Georgia], and captured a saw mill and brought with them a large quantity of lumber, an article highly necessary in this department."

The return of the *Darlington* and the *Ben De Ford* marked the end of a second expedition of a portion of the Volunteers under Lieutenant Colonel Oliver T. Beard of the 48th New York Infantry. In both instances General Saxton gave him accolades for his performance in the general's reports to Secretary of War Stanton. On the surface this could give the appearance that Beard had earned the colonelcy of the 1st South Carolina Volunteers, but it was not to be. Once the two ships returned from the Duboy River and docked at Beaufort, Beard probably thought he had secured his promotion. However, unbeknownst to him, a captain of infantry from Massachusetts was already *en route* on a ship to Port Royal to see about that very job. His name—Thomas Wentworth Higginson.

In his quest to find the right man for the job, Saxton knew that this "first muster of freedmen into the United States Army was a very important epoch in the history of the United States." Therefore, a man of the right sort was required, "who was a friend to the Negro." The lower ranking officers might do well working with the black soldiers, but the commander had to be someone who could weather both storm and stress in the unit's inception and its forward progress. The general asked for recommendations from two men he knew he could trust, Chaplain Fowler and Dr. Hawks. One name came to mind, a radical abolitionist minister who was at this time an officer in a new infantry regiment, the 51st Massachusetts. Two days after Beard had left Port Royal on the first expedition, Saxton wrote to Captain Higginson on November 5, extending him an invitation to come to Beaufort:

My Dear Sir,—I am organizing the First Regiment of South Carolina Volunteers, with every prospect of success. Your name has been spoken of, in connection with the command of this regiment, by some friends in whose judgment I have confidence. I take great pleasure in offering you the position of Colonel in it, and hope that you may be induced to accept. I shall not fill the place until I hear from you, or sufficient time shall have passed for me to receive your reply. Should you accept, I enclose a pass for Port Royal, which I trust you will feel disposed to avail yourself at once.

I am, with sincere regard, yours truly,

R. Saxton
Brig. Gen., Mil. Gov.

The Volunteers get their Colonel

Though General Saxton's criteria for command, experience NOT being the deciding factor, was different than one might normally think, it was not uncommon during this war for men to be made colonels and generals with some or no military experience because of politics. President Lincoln, for example, played this game assiduously, handing out quotas of generals' commissions to congressmen and senators to get their support for the war. These legislators in turn would parcel these commissions out to favorites of theirs in their respective states. This practice of filling important leadership positions would have mixed results on the battlefield, with some appointees causing needless casualties because of their incompetence. On the other hand, one congressman from Illinois would make a good choice, handing out a brigadier general's star to an individual named U. S. Grant. As far as Saxton, however, was concerned, military competence in this particular unit was a secondary factor.

Outside of what Hawks and Fowler had told him, Saxton did not know much of Higginson's background. He had grown up in Massachusetts in an anti-slavery atmosphere. His college years at Harvard had been tempered by the fiery speeches of radical abolitionists William Lloyd Garrison and Wendell Phillips. He had also heard the anti-slavery sermons of theologians Theodore Parker and James Freeman Clarke. Upon graduation, Higginson taught in a boarding school and also served as a private tutor. After a while, he decided to become a minister and enrolled in divinity school. He became a preacher in a church in a small town north of Boston. These activities took up most of his time in the 1840s.

As a minister, Higginson took up what were then considered radical causes besides abolition: temperance, women's rights, public education, and labor reform. In the 1850s, he became involved in more anti-slavery activities, including some direct roles. An outspoken opponent of the Fugitive Slave Act, he took part in the planning in an abortive attempt to rescue an escaped slave from a Boston jail in 1851. He was also active in the Underground Railroad. In 1852, Higginson became minister of a nondenominational, anti-slavery church. In 1854, he and several others tried to rescue another jailed runaway slave. Though arrested for the incident, he was never tried.

In 1856 when the territory of Kansas wanted to become a state, the politicians in Washington decided to allow its citizens to decide for themselves whether it should be a slave or a free state. The end result was a bloody free-for-all, divided by pro-slavery and anti-slavery factions. Higginson took part by helping to smuggle in anti-slavery settlers through Iowa when the main river route for migration was blocked. In 1858 and 1859, he and five others plotted with the anti-slavery guerilla John Brown to foment a slave rebellion. He also raised money for him. In 1860, he planned a scheme to help break out of jail in Virginia two members of John Brown's band after their failed attempt to cause insurrection in the state, but aborted the scheme when it was found out to be impractical. The person Higginson chose to lead it was a Kansan named James Montgomery.

Colonel Thomas Wentworth Higginson. He was considered to be the right man chosen to command this regiment made up of ex-slaves. *U.S. Military History Institute*

When the Civil War broke out in 1861, Higginson did not initially enlist. In fact, for all of 1861 and well into 1862, he did not do anything because he had to continue to look after his wife, Mary, who had been an invalid since 1853 due to various ailments. However, the call to duty finally became too great. In September, he enlisted in a newly organized infantry regiment, the 51st Massachusetts, after making sure his wife was provided for.[1] Commissioned a captain, Higginson became a company commander. He continued in that capacity well into November when the letter from South Carolina arrived for him at the regiment's training camp near Boston.

At age 38, Higginson was much older than most men holding the rank of a junior officer and like the vast majority of his younger peers, he had no prior military experience. This lack of knowledge did not stop him and thousands of other men on both sides from seeking positions of leadership at the different levels when they first donned the uniform. Many would be able to adapt while others would not, but this ability would not become apparent until placed under the stress of circumstances. Higginson did have one advantage over his fellow regimental junior officers, the impression of a father figure. Given his previous civilian career as a minister, he was accustomed to dispensing advice. This trait of the cloth followed him into the Army and he used it as the situation arose.

When General Saxton's letter arrived,[2] Captain Higginson was sitting at dinner with his two subordinate officers, Lieutenants John Goodell and Luther Bigelow, with his paternal demeanor ever present. Probably thinking at first that it was just routine Army correspondence, though with a curious thought towards its Port Royal postmark, he became totally shocked when he read its contents. Higginson said, "Had an invitation reached me to take command of a regiment of Kalmuck Tartars,[3] it could hardly have been more unexpected." To be offered such a command with his background and feeling toward the liberation of slaves meant for him fulfilling "the dream of a lifetime."

However, it did not take Higginson long to realize that an active opposition still existed both in the government and in the Army. He currently had command of a company he had raised in a regiment that was near the completion of its training before heading towards an active theater. Though the offer was exciting, he needed to know if the regiment would be an active line unit and not just "a mere plantation-guard or a day-school in uniform."[4] If this latter were the case, he could still accomplish his sense of mission in his current regiment, but in order to know what to do, he would first have to travel to South Carolina.

Fortunately for Higginson, General Saxton had issued him a pass to Port Royal. Before he could use it, he first had to obtain permission to travel. Going through Massachusetts Governor John Andrew, he got approval from the War Department and left for New York on November 19 *en route* to Port Royal.[5] While he was waiting for the authorization to travel south, he wrote to his mother on the 16th to apprise her of the situation, saying that "it may change all my plans." Though the offer "is ... in itself very attractive ... I have almost decided not to sacrifice a certainty for an uncertainty, and not resign my present post till I am sure of a more important one." Before he left, his regimental commander, Colonel Augustus B. Sprague, wrote a letter to Saxton to tell him that Higginson would be an asset to his command, that though he "has never been in active service, ... he is a man of marked ability and of indomitable perseverance." After receiving this letter, Higginson then departed for the sea islands of South Carolina.

Captain Higginson arrived in New York early on the 20th and went to the Army Quartermaster in charge of transportation to arrange for passage. Since the next ship available, the *Cosmopolitan*, was already crowded, he was initially refused a place on her. However, after talking to the person in charge of the vessel, he was able to get on board, though not in the most comfortable manner. The majority of the passengers on the steamer were civilians, most of them being more missionaries. The ship departed New York on the 21st.

During the three-day voyage Higginson stayed very busy talking to various people who had already been to Port Royal and were familiar with what had been going on. He also began to keep a journal,[6] detailing his experiences and conversations. On November 22, he found out from Mrs. Elizabeth B. Hale, one of the original missionaries, some information he did not know about. Higginson found out that "Gen. Saxton sustains these missionaries and Gen Brannan ... hates them and the negroes alike. It seems that Gen Saxton has no direct control over the army here—but he and Hunter agree very well, and if Hunter returns as is expected,[7] he is over this objectionable Brannan."

Higginson was also able to get some insights about the Volunteers. "[S]o far I only hear the negro regiment well spoken of though Brannan, they say, hates even that. Recruits are constantly coming in from the main land [*sic*], and the white line officers are so far good—There has been a general belief, they all say, that the negroes will not fight—let them show that they will and the soldiers will respect them." A superintendent, Mr. H. G. Judd, "has given me much information about affairs at Beaufort. My regiment is in camp about 4 miles from Beaufort and in good condition in all respects."

After hearing this first-hand information, Higginson's doubt was starting to wane:

As I approach the mysterious land I am more and more impressed with my good fortune in having this novel and uncertain career open before me when I thought everything definitely arranged ... Every thing I hear of this opportunity the more attractive it becomes. My lot in the 51st regiment was too smooth ... Here is, on the contrary, a position of great importance; as many persons have said, the first man who organizes and commands a successful black regiment will perform the most important service in the history of the War ... it falls so remarkably into the line of all my previous preparations. To say that I would rather do it than any thing [*sic*] else in the world is to say little; it is a masterpiece of felicitous opportunity that all casualties of life or death appear trivial in connection with it.

With these thoughts he greatly anticipated what he would find once the *Cosmopolitan* arrived the next day.

"And There Is Your Future Regiment"

In the early morning hours of November 24, the *Cosmopolitan* finally arrived at her destination. The stopping of the engine aroused Captain Higginson. The ship was waiting for the high tide so she could enter the Broad River, then turn right into the Beaufort River and proceed to Beaufort to dock. By the time he came up on deck before 6, the ship had crossed the sandbar and was going upriver. He was totally amazed at what he saw and heard. "Hilton Head lay on one side, the gunboats on the other; all that was raw and bare in the low buildings of the new settlement was softened into picturesqueness by the early light. Stars were still overhead, gulls wheeled and shrieked, and the broad river rippled towards Beaufort."

By the time the *Cosmopolitan* had crossed the bar and proceeded up the Broad, other people were also up on the deck observing the same thing as Higginson. They saw the low wooded shore, and the various gunboats, schooners, and steamers, among which was the famous *Planter*. As they continued into the Beaufort, dawn occurred and soon enough daylight was present for the passengers to see their surroundings. Higginson observed, "The air was cool as at home, yet the foliage seemed green, glimpses of stiff tropical vegetation appeared along the banks, with great clumps of shrubs, whose pale seed-vessels looked like tardy blossoms." After the ship had passed a bend in the river, the object of Higginson's three-day voyage finally came into view. "Then we saw on a picturesque point an old plantation, with stately magnolia avenue, decaying house, and tiny church amid the woods ... behind it stood a neat encampment of white tents." An individual who was already familiar with the 1st South Carolina's presence and the reason for Higginson's journey, said to him as they both viewed the Volunteers' camp, "'and there,'[8] said my companion, 'is your future regiment.'"

Once he arrived, Captain Higginson immediately went to see General Saxton. To entice him to accept the colonelcy of the Volunteers once Saxton told him that that the regiment would not be just a glorified plantation guard, the general gave him *carte blanche* in running the unit; this included the selection of officers. While they were conversing, a group of soldiers arrived to be formally sworn in by Saxton. Excited that these former slaves were dressed as soldiers, something that he only could have dreamed about in his earlier abolitionist days, Higginson watched them as they took the oath. The only thing that he did not like was the red pantaloons they wore instead of the blue pants that the white regiments had. They were "the only peculiarity of their uniform as distinct from the ordinary."[9]

As the general talked to the men after the ceremony, Higginson asked one of them a question. He had been wounded in the expedition to Darien for lumber, and Higginson wanted to know if the wound he sustained had been worth it. Without any hesitation, the soldier said "'I been a-tinking, Mas'r, dat's jess what I went for.'" There was no lack of equanimity in his reply.

During the day Higginson became acquainted with the officers. He was not impressed with Lieutenant Colonel Liberty Billings and Major John Strong. "The Lieut. Col. and Major I like least as military men." He liked the captains and lieutenants, saying that they were "very ready to meet me as I wish." Later, he would recruit two men he knew back in Massachusetts to be officers, using his *carte blanche* authority. One was Dr. Seth Rogers, who practiced in Worcester, near Boston. Higginson wanted him to be regimental surgeon. Another was James Rogers, who was a relative of Dr. Rogers and currently serving in the 51st Massachusetts.

After seeing what he had this day, there was no more doubt in Higginson's mind about the 1st South Carolina's viability "and the return steamer took back a resignation of a Massachusetts commission. Thenceforth [Higginson's] lot was cast altogether with the black troops ..." He then formally accepted General Saxton's offer and became Colonel Thomas Wentworth Higginson. At 10 that evening at Camp Saxton, the headquarters of his new command. he wrote what he saw and did during the day. In the last paragraph of his journal entry, he said he found it "certainly odd to go about arming five hundred men, and not a white face—to see them go through all their cooking and talking and joking ... just as if they were white. They look so much alike at first too. I saw their 2nd dress parade, almost as good as our 2nd at Worcester and the precision of <u>time</u> which they slapped down their hands after saluting, was astonishing, so in marching." Thus ended the first day of his new experience.

Twice so far in the month of November, elements of the 1st S.C. had gone on expeditions for various reasons, but always with a common denominator, that of acquiring combat experience. Many of the officers and men probably wondered if they would continue the raids along the Rebel coast now that they had a regimental commander. It would not take long for them to get their answer. Being a quick study, Colonel Higginson realized what he had to do once he ascertained the current state of his regiment. Instead of just having the unit gain experience one company at a time, as it appeared that was going on, he decided that the Volunteers needed to train as a whole unit so it could function as a single entity when the time came. This was the only way to bring it about, since the companies were at various levels of organization and training. He said, "Of discipline there was a great need,—that is, order and regular instruction. Some of the men had already been under fire, but they were very ignorant of drill and camp duty. The officers, being appointed from … states, and … engineers—had all that diversity of methods which so confused our army in those early days. The first need, therefore, was an unbroken interval of training."

Bringing it all Together

This period of training that Higginson would set for his men would last for two months before they would once again venture into the land of Rebeldom. In his book *Army Life in a Black Regiment*, the colonel said that he "rarely left the camp, and got occasional leisure moments for a fragmentary journal, to send home, recalling the many odd or novel aspects of the new experience. Camp-life was a wonderfully strange sensation to almost all volunteer officers, and mine lay among … [the] … men suddenly transformed from slaves into soldiers …"

In a more significant description of this time frame which resonated even 46 years later,[10] Dr. Hawks said he never forgot "the impressiveness of the daily dress parade: on these occasions, when the regiment was in position, Colonel Higginson stood like a statue facing the men in line of battle, and in a loud, clear voice of command said, 'Attention, battalion, shoulder arms.'[11] … Among the other commands, that of 'Load at will, load,' when, with the regularity of a great machine, a thousand steel ramrods went ringing down into the muskets, was thrilling and assuring."

For the next several days, Colonel Higginson became acquainted with his officers and men while conducting unit drills. Being around this many blacks at one time for the first time was new for him, but with each passing day, it became less and less novel:

> Already I am growing used to the experience ... of living among five hundred men, and scarce a white face to be seen,—of seeing them go through all their daily processes, eating, frolicking, talking, just as if they were white. Each day at dress-parade I stand with the customary folding of the arms before a regimental line of countenances so black that I can hardly tell whether the men stand steadily or not; black is every hand which moves in ready cadence ...

As each day passed, Higginson also started to notice individual characteristics. "They concern me chiefly in bulk, as so many consumers of rations, wearers of uniforms, bearers of muskets. But as the machine comes into shape, I am beginning to decipher the individual parts. At first, of course, they all looked just alike; the variety comes afterwards, and they are just as distinguishable, the officers say, as so many whites."

What really got Higginson's attention was the distinction that he found among the various companies. When groups of men were recruited, they were normally placed in the same company; therefore, the regional characteristics of the men from the different states became quite apparent:

> I notice that some companies, too, look darker than others, though all are purer African than I expected. This is said to be part, a geographical difference between the South Carolina and Florida men. When the Rebels evacuated this region they probably took with them the house-servants, including most of the mixed blood, so that the residuum seems very black. But the men brought from Fernandina the other day average lighter in complexion, and look more intelligent, and they certainly take wonderfully to drill.

Yet the one thing Higginson noticed that he knew had to be there was the freedmen's adaptability to soldiering. Whether it was military deportment, musket drills, target practice, or even squad drills, the men quickly learned the required tasks. "It needs but a few days to show the absurdity of distrusting the military availability of these people. They have quite as much average comprehension as whites ..., as much courage (I doubt not), as much previous knowledge of the gun, and, above all, a readiness of ear and of imitation, which, for purpose of drill, counterbalances any defect of mental training ..."

While Colonel Higginson observed the individual and collective traits of his men, he also made observations of his officers. "The line officers (Capts and Lieuts) are without exception good, earnest, well meaning, young fellows, who understand what they have attempted and mean to do it. Half of them were in the Hunter Brigade; they are from Maine and Pa regiments chiefly and well drilled, though not up to the Sprague standard; so that the mere fact of what I have learned in a first class Masstts regiment gives me an advantage over these men; and I have been able to tighten up the reins a good deal in these few days, while forming very pleasant relations with them."[12]

Higginson found his adjutant, 1st Lieutenant George W. Dewhurst, "a very quiet pleasant fellow ..., a thorough business man and therefore perfectly reliable ..." He had also the same accolades for his quartermaster, 1st Lieutenant J. M. Bingham.

However, even after a few days' observation, Higginson still had the same opinion of his field officers, which was not good. He said that LTC Billings "is a large, soft, amiable man, with long curly black hair and blue spectacles, thoroughly well meaning, and unmilitary to the last degree." For Major Strong, Higginson said that he "has been here little, but seems still less military and less amiable. In all matters of drill and discipline they will probably be altogether useless, but they may have some usefulness among the men. But these being my only green officers I can do very well while my own life and health are secure ..."

Though he had been going hard since his arrival on November 24, Higginson was able to get a respite on the 27th, because it was Thanksgiving Day. He was finally able to write in his journal what he had experienced since the *Cosmopolitan* had docked at Beaufort. For him to be able to reflect on the proceeding three days was euphoric. He said that they "have installed me into a new mode of life so thoroughly that they seem three years. Scarcely pausing in New York or in Beaufort, there seems to have been in me but one step from the camp in Massachusetts to this, and that step over leagues of waves."

Thanksgiving was also a day of relief for the men. With games, company and regimental shooting contests, barbecues, and speeches, the day was a far cry from the training pace that the colonel had set for them. Both Higginson and General Saxton made speeches. The beef they enjoyed had been "liberated" from the Rebels. There was also a plethora of oranges, both these and the cattle courtesy of the general.

On St. Helena Island, as well as on other islands, festivities were held too. A young teacher named Charlotte Forten, a free black from Massachusetts, who only had arrived herself at Port Royal in October, attended. Having known Colonel Higginson from his abolitionist days, she was not surprised at what she heard that day when General Saxton came to make a speech:

> After an appropriate prayer and sermon by Rev. Mr. Phillips, Gen. Saxton made a short but spirited speech to the people—urging the young men to enlist in the regiment now forming under Col. T. W. Higginson. That was the first intimation I had had of Mr. H's being down here. I am greatly rejoiced thereat. He seems to me of all fighting men the one best to command a regiment of colored soldiers ... Gen. Saxton said to-day that he hoped to see him commander of an army of black men ...

Miss Forten also had a familiar impression of Port Royal's military governor:

> ... Gen. Saxton made a few more remarks. I think what he said will have much effect on the young men here. There has been a good deal of distrust about joining the regiment. The soldiers were formerly so unjustly treated by the Government. But they trust Gen. Saxton. He told them what a victory the black troops had lately won on the Georgia coast, and what a great good they had done for their race in winning; they had proved to their enemies that the black man can and will fight for his freedom.

That evening, after a full day of fun and frolicking at Camp Saxton, Colonel Higginson took a stroll about the regiment. He came upon a group of between 30 and 40 soldiers sitting around a large fire listening to an elderly gentleman named Cato recall how he was able to elude his owner once the master realized that his slave had escaped. Higginson said, "It was a narrative, dramatized to the last degree, of his adventures in escaping from his master to the Union vessels." As some of the men cooked sweet potatoes and peanuts among the ashes of the flames, they listened "with reverence to the wiles of the ancient Ulysses."[13] Higginson also gave a picturesque description of what he saw here, something that did not exist a year ago. He said here was "a bivouac of negro soldiers, with the brilliant fire lighting up their red trousers and gleaming from their shining, black faces ...," all this under "the mighty limbs of a great live-oak, with the weird moss swaying in the smoke, and the high moon gleaming faintly through."

Now that the 1st South Carolina had its colonel, it was just a matter of time to complete its recruitment of soldiers, fill its remaining officer billets, and finish its training. Then the regiment would return to combat as a complete unit under the banner of the American flag, being led by a radical abolitionist. As a member of the 3rd Rhode Island Heavy Artillery put it years after the war, "this was an era in the war, and in the history of the ex-slaves. Col. T. W. Higginson, of Massachusetts, ... became associated with this command, and gave it reputation by his talents and his sword. History is stranger than fiction. A son of Massachusetts leads a regiment of ex-slaves—volunteers from South Carolina — under the Stars and Stripes,[14] against the slaveholders' rebellion."

Another aspect of his men that Higginson learned was their willingness to work hard at night, even after a long day. On the evening of December 1, he had been alerted by an order from Beaufort that a steamboat had a cargo of lumber and would have to be unloaded. He was very surprised at the positive attitude of his men. He said, "How absurd is the impression bequeathed by Slavery in regard to the Southern blacks, that they are sluggish and inefficient in labor!" Though the job took two hours, it was one of organized manner and competition among the companies. Working by moonlight, the Volunteers unloaded the ship with a precise rhythm that the captain of the boat "declared that they unloaded the ten thousand feet of boards quicker than any white gang could have done it."[15] Later that night when Higginson was wandering about the camp, he came upon a soldier cooking an opossum. Asking him why he was not in bed after the strenuous effort put in earlier, the soldier replied with a smile: "'Da's no work at all Cunnel; dat only jess enough <u>for stretch we</u>!'" Higginson left impressed.

Now that he had been at Port Royal for just over a week, Higginson was all the more certain that he made the correct decision. With what he saw, he could not help but come to that conclusion. "I do not as yet see the slightest obstacle, in the nature of the blacks, to making them good soldiers, but rather the contrary. They take readily to drill, and do not object to discipline; they are not especially dull or inattentive; they seem fully to understand the importance of the contest, and of their share in it. They show not jealousy or suspicion towards their officers."

Though Higginson could give his men accolades over and over again, they still did not solve the problem of recruiting more men from the Port Royal Islands. Even with all the changes that had been made, the success of the Volunteers in the two excursions in November, the enlistment of men from Georgia and Florida, the work of General Saxton, and the reputation of Higginson himself, the legacy of General Hunter's high-handed draft tactics remained. He complains, "Here lies the drawback to rapid recruiting. Were this a wholly new regiment, it would have been full to overflowing, I am satisfied, ere now." Though Hunter's legacy continued, Higginson would eventually solve his manpower problems by further recruitment from outside the islands.

Men who refused to enlist also gave pause to those who were contemplating it, notwithstanding the men already in uniform. On top of this was the problem of pay that the original recruits never received. Colonel Higginson lamented, "Now, if Gen. Saxton can possibly secure the payment of the regiment, even for the month they have been in camp, all this distrust would vanish, and the recruits would at once flow in, I do no doubt. But while the plantation laborers are promptly paid and the Government laborers at Hilton Head, these soldiers are constantly twitted by their friends and families with working for nothing." He also had to combat false rumors being spread by white soldiers to "women on the plantations" that the regiment would be in the front line of any battle, just to rattle them. Though the first and third problems could be overcome, the pay part would settle recruitment. He adds, "We gain a few recruits daily, and I doubt not shall be full in time, whether the men are paid off or not, but nothing could make a difference so great." Higginson may have found these lingering problems lamentable, but a partial solution to them occurred when General Saxton returned from a trip to Fernandina on December 2. He brought back with him 76 more recruits.

When the word was spread out at Camp Saxton, the company commanders were eager to get their fair share of the new recruits. "The eagerness of the captains to secure them was a sight to see." One of the two newspapers established at Port Royal called *The New South*,[16] said that Saxton came back with the recruits on the *Ben De Ford*.[17] On top of this, the ship left Beaufort again shortly thereafter when they found out that there were more men who wanted to enlist at Georgetown, South Carolina, north of Charleston. This town had been eventually taken over also by Union forces after the fall of Port Royal.

On December 8 several men arrived from Georgetown. Colonel Higginson was not too happy with what he saw. "Such forlorn looking recruits, lame halt and blind and not clearly understanding why they were brought here or what they are expected to do. I felt like a slave driver as I partitioned them about to eager captains, each anxious to make up his number, even if the material were unattractive. So different from our fine Florida fellows."[18] He also anticipated more than he received on this day. "Next week we expect 100 more of those and then another hundred will complete the regiment to its minimum 830."

On the 10th, Higginson wrote to his mother. "My Lieut. Col. and Major are both quite efficient in recruiting, which is important. Tomorrow they go down the coast to Fernandina and St. Augustine for recruits and will probably bring back nearly enough to fill us to the minimum number 830. We are 633 today." So, judging by what he wrote, Higginson was confident that his regiment would get enough men for a full unit regardless from where they came.

After a week and a half worth of work, the effort that Billings and Strong put into their mission to Florida was paying off, especially at Fernandina. One soldier of the regiment stationed there, Daniel D. Barrows of Company E, 9th Maine Infantry, could not help but notice the exodus of the freedmen. When he wrote home on December 22, he said that "the niggers are leaving here fast to join the army at Port Royal where they have one full regiment and another is part full."[19] He also anticipated their success. "I have no doubt but they will make good soldiers."

As the training occurred through the month, Higginson made various comments. On December 3, while watching a group of men from Fernandina which became Company G, he said that they were the best company he had seen since his own in the 51st Massachusetts. "As visitors are astonished at them; yet they have only been drilled a fortnight and part only two days. The companies recruited hereabouts are far below them both in physique and intelligence." On the 16th, he said that the junior officers were very confident in them. "I have never yet heard a doubt expressed as to their superiority to white troops in aptitude to drill and discipline." One lieutenant, an Englishman named William Stockdale, trained his company on a particular drill in record time. Higginson said that he "saw them go through all the main movements in that time, which it took me a series of lessons to teach my company in the 51st ..."

After having been in South Carolina for nearly a month, Higginson also became more acquainted with men with respect to their individualities. He said on December 20 their specific characteristics were emerging "more and more, and I find first their faces, then their characters, to be as distinct as those of whites to me." He also said that "it is very interesting, the desire they show to do their duty and improve; the more they think about it, the more the importance of the things comes home to them. ... They are very ready to be attached to their officers and in some companies there is quite a beautiful relation existing between them and I think on the whole the youngest officers seem to do the best with them." Though Higginson was glad for this situation to occur, he made up his mind that evening to improve morale even more by getting rid of the red pantaloons as soon as possible, because the men do not like them. "I cannot abide these red trousers and shall get others by and by."

The areas from which the men of the 1st South Carolina had been drawn to date had been the South Carolina Sea Islands, coastal Georgia, and northeast Florida. Though the bulk of the recruits had worked in agriculture before their enlistments, numerous crafts of various skill levels were also represented. For example, in Florida there were bricklayers, blacksmiths, wheelwrights, carpenters, machinists and shoemakers. Others had worked in various forms of transportation, some as lumbermen or in mills, a few as sailors or boatmen. Quite a few worked either as cooks or waiters. Though these different occupations would be useful to the military, especially the skilled trades as the situations arose, what the Volunteers still needed were foot soldiers.

Though the Union-controlled areas of Georgia and Florida had been combed for available recruits, and could only provide men as slaves escaped to Yankee lines, the answer to finish filling the ranks quickly was still in South Carolina, with many of the available men working as civilians for the War and Navy Departments. Since General Saxton knew that General Hunter's draft attempt did not work, the only option he had, which was still the best method as far as these ex-slaves were concerned, was persuasion. Though the white officers were partly successful in overcoming Hunter's legacy and rumors spread by white soldiers, the sight of black men in the uniform of a Union soldier helped to overcome suspicion. Select Volunteers talking to possible recruits also helped. One soldier, Thomas Long, said it very plainly. "Anoder ting is, suppose you had kept your freedom without enlisting in dis army; your chillen might have grown up free and been well cultivated so as to be equal to an business, but it would have been always flung in dere faces—'Your fader never fought for he own freedom.'"[20] While these officers and enlisted men were trying to get others to enlist to help free other slaves, there would be some other men who would try to use these soldiers for their own nefarious profiteering.

In the Department of the South, the men whom Chase had appointed as commissioners as a result of the Direct Tax law, were adeptly applying their talents, particularly one member of the Florida Commission, Lyman D. Stickney. What would make him stand out among his fellow commissioners in the department would be that his thirst for gain would be greater than the others. It would not be beneath him to use the law and other people, including soldiers, to achieve his goals. His pre-war career, which was in various fields of endeavor, could easily be summed up as opportunistic. Some historians simply referred to him as a crook. When the war came, Stickney looked at it as another opportunity to exploit. Possessing a forceful personality and disarming manner, he was able to charm Secretary Chase and have himself appointed to the Florida Commission. He would soon put this public position of trust to work to satisfy his appetite for greed by committing acts of graft. To help him achieve his goals, he would not hesitate to put the lives of soldiers on the line, which would soon include men of the 1st South Carolina Volunteers. His lust for money would have a definite impact on part of their history.

As the Christmas holidays approached, the men were upbeat. They were getting attention in Northern newspapers. Chaplain Fowler "read to them some extracts from the letters in the N.Y. papers about their own expeditions." He also read to them "about the battles of the colored regiment in Kansas." Just hearing about their own exploits in print and that of another "colored" regiment made them "thoroughly stirred up." On Christmas day, Colonel Higginson read to them at the evening dress parade General Saxton's message of anticipation about President Lincoln's Emancipation Proclamation on January 1, 1863. This was well received, "for there was cheering in all the company streets after parade was dismissed."

On the 26th, Higginson received a belated Christmas present with the arrival of Dr. Seth Rogers and Captain James Rogers. He was ever glad to see them. Dr. Rogers was immediately made regimental surgeon while Captain Rogers was made commander of Company F. Because of his previous injury, Dr. Hawks was relegated to assistant surgeon. There was also good news about General Saxton. There had been information floating about that he might be removed from command. However, word was received that it was not to be. With the New Year approaching, Higginson was confident that things could only improve with the way that they were shaping up.

The Point of No Return

Ever since President Lincoln had issued his preliminary Emancipation Proclamation back in September following the battle of Antietam, he had been under severe pressure to rescind it. Though he had the concurrence of his cabinet and elsewhere, many in Congress and in the public at large were against it. He had been warned by people in his own party that the Republicans could sustain major losses in the November congressional mid-term elections. Even the cataclysmic possibility of this hanging over his head did not deter him. When the elections took place on November 7, the Republicans lost control of the Senate and had their wide majority in the House of Representatives cut to a slim one.

Even with this stinging defeat, the president did one more thing he knew he had to do. On the day after the election, he relieved General McClellan of his command of the Army of the Potomac. Lincoln did this not because McClellan did not follow up his "victory" against Lee after Antietam in September, but because of his overall procrastinating nature. Though McClellan was still popular with his soldiers and Northern opinion irrespective of his lack of battlefield success, Lincoln knew he had to go. He replaced him with Major General Ambrose E. Burnside, who failed the president too with a loss to Lee at the battle of Fredericksburg on

December 13. Regardless of these successive political and military defeats, the president knew he still had to go forward.

On the afternoon of January 1, 1863, exactly 100 days after when it was first issued, President Lincoln affixed his name to the Emancipation Proclamation, a document which forever changed the course of the war. Whereas beforehand, the object of the war was just to restore the Union, now it was this and the eradication of slavery in the eleven rebelling states as a necessary wartime measure so slaves could not be used in the Confederate war effort. Though this was the official version, the proclamation now placed the war on a moral level, that once it had been uttered, there was no going back.

However, there was one more aspect of it that was not in Lincoln's September issuance. Without mentioning race or color, the president added this: "And I further declare and make known that such persons, of suitable condition, will be received into the armed services of the United States, to garrison forts, positions, stations, and other places, and to man vessels of all sorts in said service."

So, Lincoln had finally endorsed the concept of having blacks in uniform. Just like the issuance of his proclamation, there was now no going back. The chocks were now out. Whereas previously the door stood only slightly ajar, it was now thrown wide open, and only the duration of the war would determine how many would get through it.

Though Lincoln's New Year's declaration meant that slaves could only be freed as Union armies advanced into Confederate territory, his acceptance now of blacks into the armed services did not have to wait for Yankee victories. The question as to why he waited until this day to make known his decision still remains. Just like previous political and military decisions he had to make, the president firmly believed in timing to achieve maximum effect. Now that he had formally set slaves free in the eleven rebelling states, he could imply that the new freedmen had a duty to help fight for their freedom. Nobody could argue now against having them as soldiers and sailors because of this obligation. Though the thrust of his acceptance of blacks into the military was aimed at the slaves, it meant also that free blacks could enlist.

The New Year's Day celebration at Port Royal was just as lively as the one in Washington and elsewhere around the country, perhaps even more. This was the day the thousands of ex-slaves had been waiting for, the day of jubilee that many would call it. The 100 days that the president had given the Confederacy had elapsed. Therefore, the full force of his proclamation was now in effect. They were free. The festivities took place on Port Royal Island at Camp Saxton. People from the other islands arrived there via "about ten ... steam-boats from up and down river, sent by Gen. Saxton to convoy them." After they arrived "the road was crowded with riders and walkers—chiefly black women with gay handkerchiefs on their heads and a sprinkling of men." Many of the whites were there also, but Colonel Higginson was not too impressed with some of them. He said, "Most of these superintendents do not interest me much and seem rather second rate and inefficient." Though General Saxton was there, General Brannan would be conspicuously absent the entire day.

Speeches were made, songs were sung, and President Lincoln's proclamation and General Saxton's New Year's greeting were read.[21] The band of the 8th Maine Infantry filled the atmosphere with music and the regimental colors of the 1st South Carolina Volunteers were presented to the unit. Dr. Seth Rogers, the new regimental surgeon, said that "every body [sic] was happy in the bright sunshine, and in the great hope." For the celebration's meal, the people ate ten oxen with hearty relish and drank barrels of molasses, water, vinegar and ginger to wash them down.

Different people were impressed with the sight of the Volunteers and their inclusion in the day's events. Susie Baker said "the soldiers had a good time. They sang or shouted 'Hurrah!' all through the camp, and seemed overflowing with fun and frolic until taps were sounded." *The New York Times* correspondent reported that "the most interesting part of the ceremonies was the presentation to the regiment, by Rev. Mr. French, of a set of colors ... They were received in behalf of the regiment by Col. T. W. Higginson, their commander." Harriet Ware said that the dress-parade "was excellent,—they went through the manual, including, 'load in nine times.'" Laura Towne said that as she and the other people celebrating "reached Camp Saxton ..., we arrived through the dense crowd at the foot of the platform only in time to see Colonel Higginson standing between his two color-bearers, Robert Sutton and Prince Rivers, looking small—tall and large man as he is—compared; but we missed Colonel Higginson's speech, which was stirring and eloquent." Fredrick Denison of the 3rd Rhode Island Heavy Artillery wrote that "Col. T. W. Higginson—poet, novelist, and warrior—with his historic regiment (First South Carolina Colored Troops), assisted in the New Year's Jubilation, and shared the roast-ox with intense zest."

Charlotte Forten fully captured the essence of the day's activities:

The meeting was held in a beautiful grove, a live-oak grove, adjoining the camp ... As I sat on the stand and looked around on the various groups, I thought I had never seen a sight so beautiful. There were the black soldiers, in their blue coats and scarlet pants, the officers of this and other regiments in their handsome uniforms, and crowds of lookers-on, men, women, and children, grouped in various attitudes, under the trees. The faces of all were a happy, eager, expectant look.

General Saxton spoke ... and was received with great enthusiasm. Throughout the morning, repeated cheers were given for him by the regiment and joined heartly [sic] by all the people. They know him to be one of the best and noblest men in the world ... At the close of Colonel Higginson's speech he presented the flags to the color-bearers, Sergeant Rivers and Sergeant Sutton,[22] with an earnest change, to, which they made appropriate replies. We were particularly pleased with Robert Sutton, who is a man of great natural intelligence, and whose remarks were simple, eloquent, and forcible.

The Dress Parade—the first I had ever seen—delighted me. It was a brilliant sight—the long lines of men in their brilliant uniform, with bayonets gleaming in the sunlight. The Col. looked splendid ... Dr. [Rogers] said the men went through with the drill remarkably well. It seemed to me nothing c'ld be more perfect. To me it was a great triumph—that black regiment doing itself honor in the sight of the white officers, many of whom, doubtless 'came to scoff.' It was typical of what the race, so long downtrodden and degraded will yet achieve on this continent.

Now that January 1, 1863, was over, it was time to get back to the mission at hand, to continue to prepare the men of the 1st S.C. for action against the enemy. Besides training, the one thing that would help the regiment the most was numbers. Ever since Colonel Higginson took over in late November, the number of men had been steadily climbing. On November 28, he said he had 518 in camp. On December 2 when General Saxton came back from Fernandina with 76 more men, the unit rose to 594. On the 10th when Higginson wrote to his wife, he gave a number of 633. He told her also he was sending Lt. Col. Billings and Major Strong to Florida to recruit. "Tomorrow they go down the coast to Fernandina and St. Augustine ... and will probably bring back nearly enough to fill us to the minimum number 830." When he wrote to his mother on the 26th, he said the regiment "gets on very well and numbers now 733 or properly 746." On January 2, he said "the reg't has now 750 and there are 100 waiting for us, to be sent for, at St. Augustine."

Camp life had its interesting aspects too. When people came to watch the unit train, Higginson said, "The whole demeanor of this particular regiment was watched with microscopic scrutiny by friends and foes." He "felt sometimes as if we were a plant trying to take root, but constantly pulled up to see if we were growing." He said that the camp had its own air at night "with its 250 tents glimmering in the moonlight, on the level plain which is swept smooth every day ... the dying cook fires glimmering within the picturesque palmetto enclosures." With training at a good pace, he became more confident. "I don't suppose this quiet life will last many weeks longer—we are improving fast in drill."

As the regiment was approaching the minimum number of men to complete it, there were more changes in the officer corps too. Another doctor, Thomas T. Minor, transferred from the 7th Connecticut Infantry, which was also stationed on Port Royal, on January 8. 1Lt. J. H. Thibadeau was promoted to captain, and James B. O'Neil and W. W. Sampson to first lieutenant, on the 10th. On January 12, Captain Daniel Eldredge, 3rd New Hampshire Infantry,[23] found out "there was good news for the men of volunteer regiments who had received commissions in the colored regiment … Heretofore they had been a sort of half man, half officer; but Gen. Brannan then directed (by orders from the War Department) that all such men be mustered out as enlisted men when mustered in as officers." This information he got was confirmed when it was printed in the weekly issue of one of the two newspapers at Port Royal on January 17, *The New South*.

Though the officer corps may have been nearer completion with these promotions and the transfer of Dr. Minor, it received a minor setback when Colonel Higginson requested that General Saxton rescind two commissions, one for a captain and the other for a first lieutenant. He knew the general would take away a commission just as quickly as giving one out. The captain had to leave due to ill health. However, the lieutenant had to go because Higginson had lost all "moral confidence" in him. What was even sadder was that both officers were from the same company.[24] Higginson was unsure whether he should do the same thing with regard to LTC Billings and Major Strong. He had no doubt that Saxton would remove them too "if I asked it, and if I were like him, I would do it; but now I cannot make up my mind to it; I find no fault with either of them, but that they will never be soldiers."

The transfer of Dr. Minor brought the number of physicians in the regiment to three, with Dr. Seth Rogers as regimental surgeon and both he and Dr. Hawks as assistant surgeons. Though Minor's transfer was dated January 8, he would not arrive until later in the month after he had finished up his obligation with the 7th Connecticut. Given the number of men in the unit with even more to come, it would be in better shape medically when the Volunteers went back into action. Anything less and the doctors present could easily be overwhelmed by the casualties. Besides taking care of the various ailments that the men would come down with, the doctors would conduct physicals to judge the men's fitness for military service, not only the physical aspect but also in some cases their mental fitness. Some men who had already been in uniform when Dr. Hawks arrived had to be released when he rendered his medical opinion on them as unfit to serve, though he could not render one on their enthusiasm and sincerity.

When Dr. Rogers arrived on December 26, 1862 and immediately took over as chief medical officer of the 1st S.C., he set about organizing things as he perceived needed to be done. One of the first things he did was to see about choosing an orderly to replace an elderly man named Tiff. The doctor saw that he was not physically able to do the necessary duties, "whom I should take if I had the time and strength to wait upon when he should get too tired to wait upon me. He is a dear old man who prays day and night."

Rogers was going to have one of the soldiers as an orderly, but decided upon "a shining black boy of fifteen" named Wiley Rohan, because the doctor saw that he was very intelligent.

Dr. Rogers was also well pleased that Dr. Hawks was there. Rogers said, "He is a radical anti-slavery man, somewhat older than I, and has had a large medical experience and in addition has been hospital surgeon at Beaufort during several months." Hawks had been previously examined by three doctors from New England regiments for competence and they said that he was a highly qualified physician. "I consider myself fortunate in having a man so well fitted for the place." Rogers said that he looked forward to taking Hawks with him in future operations. He was also well pleased with the hospital steward who was very experienced. However, Dr. Rogers felt his own newness in the military, hardly having been regimental surgeon for 24 hours. "All this accumulation of army experience around me makes me feel particularly green, but I guess I can work up the sticking point."

Outside of organizing his department, Rogers was kept very busy seeing to the needs of the soldiers. By the time New Year's Eve had arrived, he had been seeing 60 to 70 soldiers a day and prescribing medication as required. Besides attending to these patients, he also had hospital duties. These activities usually kept him "busy from breakfast to dinner, after that [his] assistants can 'see care' ordinarily of everybody till next morning."

The hospital they had was on the second floor of an old cotton gin building. To improve it, Rogers had the machinery removed and bed stands made, and the "beds made and filled with the dry, course [*sic*] grass that the soldiers brought on their heads from the plains." He had no pillows or sheets for his patients, but was able to improvise with the use of blankets since they were plentiful. Knapsacks also made for satisfactory pillows. The second floor had a fireplace large enough to help keep off the winter chill. At one point the hospital had a full house.

Outside of taking care of those who came down with something, Rogers' next major task was prevention, to keep to an absolute minimum those not available for duty. Having been now at Camp Saxton for about two and a half weeks, he was able to recommend certain changes, among

Dr. Seth Rogers, who provided relief and comfort to many wounded Volunteers. *Massachusetts Commandery Military Order of the Loyal Legion and the U.S. Army Military History Institute*

which were emphasis on personal hygiene and having fire pits dug in the middle of each four-man tent which was seven by eight feet so that beds of coal would keep the men warm. The tents also needed to be properly ventilated. The doctor opined, "The Colonel is not backward in favoring every hygienic measure that offers any good to the soldiers. A few days experiment with two companies will settle the question by comparison of sick lists."

Rogers also needed to obtain necessary medical instruments, medicines, and other supplies. On January 9, he went to Hilton Head "to test the honesty of a certain medical perveyor [sic], who does not incline to honor the requisitions of the surgeon of the 1st Reg. S.C. Vol's." Needless to say, this personal visit did not do any good, because the purveyor "has not yet heard of the popularity of black regiments, but Uncle Samuel will teach him that, as well as a few other things. But it will be too late for him to repeat in this world when he shall have learned the lesson." On his way back to his boat, he came across General Saxton, who had just arrived from Beaufort on his steamer, the *Flora*, and immediately informed him of "the perveyor's [sic] second refusal." It was at this point that Saxton informed Rogers of a letter he had just received from Secretary Stanton, which authorized the doctor to obtain what he needed directly from sources in New York City, thereby bypassing the medical purveyor in the Department of the South. This new authorization meant that "we shall be all right within two weeks, I hope."

Meanwhile, other changes were happening in the regiment, especially in the discipline of the Volunteers. When General Hunter had his regiment, he had repeatedly forgiven those men who had left the unit from charges of desertion because he had felt that they did not fully understand the requirements of a military organization. However, with the reorganization of the regiment under General Saxton and Colonel Higginson now in command, the men had been fully briefed about the rules of being in the military and what was expected of them. This was soon reflected in a small article in the January 17 issue of *The New South*. "Tragedy In Camp Saxton—We learn that one of the negroes belonging to the 1st South Carolina regiment, was shot while attempting to escape from the guardhouse a few days ago. He subsequently died of his wounds." Two other soldiers were involved in this attempt, though they were not mentioned.

Sergeant Prince Rivers, the unit's Provost Sergeant, was in charge of guarding these prisoners, whether they were in the guardhouse or on work detail. Like Corporal Sutton, he too had an above average I.Q. Dr. Rogers described him as "a man of remarkable executive ability." Therefore he was assigned this important task. One day he had left two guards to watch over them and some other prisoners cutting wood while he returned to camp for the evening dress parade. In his absence, these three soldiers escaped from their guards with the intent to desert. Upon learning of this, Sergeant Rivers organized a posse and went after them even though it was already sunset. He did not return until the next day about noon. The posse had one of the escapees with them in a cart because he had been shot in the abdomen when he refused to stop after he had been spotted. He died several hours later. Sergeant Rivers then went off again, this time with 28 men without rest to find the others. Seeing the requirements of discipline, Dr. Rogers said that "the feeling all through the regiment in regard to this fatal result is that the deserter received his just punishment."

As things were settling down in the 1st South Carolina, so was the situation in the Department of the South and 10th Corps. Since the massive transfer of soldiers to the Army of the Potomac during the summer, the number of men in the department continued to decrease, especially with the transfer of occupied Pensacola, FL and its units to the newly created Department of the Gulf. After September, the number of men started to climb slowly. By the end of 1862, the department had an aggregate strength of 13,337 men, with 10,875 of them present for duty. It had settled down to the islands of Port Royal; Fort Pulaski near Savannah;

Fernandina and Fort Clinch on Amelia Island, Florida; St. Augustine, Florida; and Key West, Florida. On St. Helena Island and Hilton Head under Brigadier General Alfred H. Terry were the 3rd New Hampshire, 47th New York, 76th and 97th Pennsylvania Infantry; 1st Massachusetts Cavalry, Company M; 3rd Rhode Island Heavy Artillery; 3rd U.S. Artillery, Battery E; and the 1st New York Engineers.

On Port Royal Island under the command of Brigadier General Truman Seymour were the 6th and 7th Connecticut, 8th Maine, 4th New Hampshire, 90th New York, and 55th Pennsylvania Infantry; 1st Massachusetts Cavalry; 1st Connecticut Light Battery; 1st U.S. Artillery, Batteries B, D, and M; and the 1st New York Engineers, Company H. At Fort Pulaski were the 48th New York Infantry; 3rd Rhode Island Heavy Artillery, Company G; and 1st New York Engineers, Company F. On Amelia Island were the 9th Maine Infantry; 1st New York Engineers, Company E at Old Town (just north of Fernandina); and at Fort Clinch, 1st New York Engineers, Company C. At St. Augustine was the 7th New Hampshire Infantry, and at Key West, the 47th Pennsylvania Infantry.

The reaction to President Lincoln's New Year's Day rendering of his Emancipation Proclamation had its normal complement of supporters and opponents just as his preliminary one back in September had. The Confederacy's response was nothing short of a cataleptic fit. The loyal Border States voiced their opposition though it did not include them since they were still constitutionally protected. Numerous newspapers expressed approval or disapproval. Some abolitionists still complained that the proclamation did not go far enough by excluding the Border States and certain parts of the Confederacy exempted from the proclamation. Though Lincoln did publicly state that the thrust of it was a legitimate war measure authorized by the Second Confiscation Act, he still worried about his constitutional authority to do it, even though he had been reassured by his attorney general and solicitor general that he had the power to do so as a wartime president. He felt that he might be sustained by the courts during the war, but once it was over, his action might bring on a whole host of new legal challenges. Therefore, the only sure guarantee he would later determine to prevent any of this from happening would be a constitutional amendment to prohibit slavery, not just in part but totally.

Regardless of the various reactions to Lincoln's proclamation, it was now official policy of his administration and would have behind it the full weight of his presidency. Opponents would bluster and fire broadsides of vitriol at him, but as far as the president was concerned, his announcement was a done deal. It also may not have been perfect in the eyes of many abolitionists, but they could not deny the fact that it was a major leap forward in the eradication of slavery from the North American continent.

With Union victories would come the freedom of hundreds of thousands of slaves and the building up of an abolition momentum that would be next to impossible to stop. It could only result in the deathblow to that institution not only in the eleven rebelling states, but also in the loyal Border States with the passage of a constitutional amendment. In order for any of this to happen, the Union Army needed victories, and that required men, thousands and thousands of them, from all possible sources. Thus Lincoln's January surprise comes into play.

"Men of Color, To Arms!"

When the great black orator and abolitionist, Frederick Douglass, a leviathan of thought and action, heard a rumor during the summer of 1862 that Washington had ordered General Hunter to disband his contraband regiment, he wrote a spirited piece in the July issue of his publication, *Douglass Monthly*. He said that "this terrible iron arm, more dreaded by the rebels than ten thousand men of any other color, said to be disbanded … just at the moment when the blow was most needed, and when it was about to be struck. Though thus repelled, and insulted, the Negro persists in his devotion to the Government, and will serve it with a pickaxe if he cannot with a pistol, a spade if he cannot with a sword." Lincoln's acceptance of blacks into the military put to rest any doubts Douglass had about the president now that he had made it official policy. This meant that instead of pickaxe and spade, "the Negro" would be taking on Johnny Reb with musket and bayonet.

The arrival in South Carolina, Louisiana, and Kansas of the news of Lincoln's decision meant that the regiments previously raised there would no longer be considered just as units recruited for other reasons to meet only specific situations.[25] They would now be recognized as normal military organizations existing for one purpose, to take the fight to the enemy. This formal recognition would not be long in coming, but before it did other events began to take place. On January 2, 1863 the War Department's Adjutant General's Office issued General Order No. 1, which was affixed with the president's signature. It was basically the proclamation letting the military know of his intent and for the services to be the implementers of this new policy. Most departments immediately issued their own orders once they received it, but a few would delay as long as possible.

On January 13, two significant events took place. Secretary of War Stanton authorized Brigadier General Daniel Ullmann to travel to Louisiana "to raise a brigade (of four regiments) of Louisiana volunteer infantry, to be recruited in that State, to serve for three years or during the war." Stanton also allowed an individual from Kansas named James Montgomery "to raise, subject to the approval of the general commanding the Department of the South and under his direction, a regiment of South Carolina volunteer infantry, to be recruited in that State" and serve in the military for the same amount of time as General Ulmann's recruits. Montgomery would hold the rank of colonel.[26]

Later in the month the secretary sent the Army Adjutant General Lorenzo Thomas to the Mississippi River valley to organize a recruitment drive to tap the thousands of men available in the areas under Union control at this point in the war. On January 26, the secretary authorized for the first time a regiment to be raised in a northern state. Governor John Andrew of Massachusetts was finally given the authority to do so after he had previously made repeated requests. Up to this point 53 regiments of infantry had been created, trained and sent from the state. This newly authorized black unit would get the next number available, which would give them the name of the 54th Massachusetts Infantry.

Although the timing of politics had finally allowed blacks to be formally accepted into the armed forces of the United States, it would be some time before the full weight of these tens of thousands of men in Yankee blue would begin to be felt on the battlefield. Until then, the men of the 1st Kansas Colored; the 1st, 2nd and 3rd Louisiana Native Guards; and the 1st South Carolina Volunteers would have to carry the fight to the enemy. On the island of Port Royal, S.C., the radical abolitionist colonel of that regiment of former contraband would be contemplating how to do just that, now that the organization he commanded was near the end of its training. It was just a matter of time before the men he had been with since November 24 would be trading lead once again with the Confederates. Colonel Thomas Wentworth Higginson felt that when it did happen, no matter where it wound up being, his officers and men would give a good account of themselves.

The Battle of the Hundred Pine

Plantation supervisor Edward S. Philbrick's opinion about ex-slaves in the Army had been ambivalent ever since the beginning of Hunter's regiment the previous May. He did not mind seeing them in uniform, but had feelings that it would take some time before they could be made soldiers because of what he felt that slavery had done to them mentally, and this could only take place once bondage was no longer a part of their mindset. However, his opinion of the time it would take for this to happen seems to have changed to a degree when he wrote on January 2 that he did not expect to see much:

> improvement in the conduct of the war, so long as the mass of people do not see in slavery the great cause of all the trouble. Neither do I believe that the war will terminate slavery unless the blacks will voluntarily take part in it. The 1st Regiment is in length filled here, by means of a great deal of coaxing and the abandonment of St. Simon's Island, taking all the men for recruits. They have made two raids upon the Florida [and Georgia] coast, where they met with little resistance and accomplished but little. If they can once gain [sic] a footing on the mainland and add to their numbers as they advance, they could easily carry all before them.

Unbeknownst to Philbrick, the first attempt by the regiment to add to their numbers in 1863 by invading enemy country would take place in a few weeks.

Besides training his men to be ready for combat, Colonel Higginson had been making progress in discipline. When it came to guards and their relationship to officers, he still had to worry about the old master–slave mindset. "I labor constantly to impress on them that they do not obey officers because they are white, but because they are officers." He also emphasized too "that the non commissioned officers must receive precisely as implicit obedience." Prior to his arrival, there were still desertions and absences without leave, "but this is now stopped and I am gradually getting back the older absentees. Every day they come back now, and one of the best things that has happened to us was the ... accidental shooting of ... [the] ... man who escaped from the guard house, by the men sent after him." Severe punishment was not used on the men, "accustomed as they have been to violent passion in white men; but a mild inexorableness tells on them as on children and they dread the guard house very much."

Now that Higginson was well into his second month of command, he was settling in as the commander of a regiment just he had when he had his company in the 51st Massachusetts. At this point he could not help but compare his regiment to others that he saw on Port Royal. When Higginson went to Beaufort only for the third time in the six weeks he had been on the island, he saw a review of several regiments being conducted by General Seymour, the island's commander, for General Brannan. "It is amazing how few regiments are <u>accurately</u> drilled, after the Masstts standard, that is conform strictly to the official tactics of the army regulations. The best regiments here, I find, are not as particular as I require my Captains to be ..."

Higginson also could not help but lament about the amount of paperwork required of a regimental commander. His former commander in the 51st Massachusetts told him "that for every regiment enlisted there should be another enlisted to do its <u>writings</u>. I am now thoroughly immersed in muster rolls, pay rolls, and monthly returns." Though detained much of his time with paperwork, Higginson still had time to make observations among the myriad details of his responsibilities. Religion among his men was very important, given their previous background. The more he was with them the more he respected their spiritual commitment, which contrasted sharply with the other regiments. "All the white camps seem very rough and secular ..." His observing also extended to his men's physical well-being. The winter months seemed to affect them differently than the white soldiers, "but as to general availability for military drill and duty, it is merely a question whether they are equal or superior to the whites."

Early in the morning on January 14, the 100 new men expected from St. Augustine had finally arrived under the escort of Lt. Colonel Billings. Dr. Rogers happened to be near the shore of the Beaufort River when he noticed them. "Before breakfast this morning I stood on the shore and listened to the John Brown hymn,[1] sung by a hundred of our recruits, as they came up the river on the steamer *Boston* ..." When he examined them for fitness, "We ... received into our regiment all but five, whom I rejected in consequence of old age and other disabilities." He hated to do this. "It seemed hard to reject men who came to fight for their freedom, but these poor fellows are a hindrence [*sic*] in active service ..." However much he did not want to do it, he did have some consolation when Dr. Minor finally arrived at Camp Saxton from the 7th Connecticut Infantry the next day. He was "a young man whom I was fearful we should not get."

Now that the arrival of the men from St. Augustine finally brought up the 1st South Carolina to a minimum level considered for a fully-manned regiment, Colonel Higginson decided it was time to unveil what he had been working on since his arrival on November 24. He decided to march his regiment to Beaufort and demonstrate what his men could do. What happened was impressive. "The dear 51st did not compare with them." To watch his regiment (minus the new recruits) in their blue coats and red pantaloons move in column formation with their muskets at their side and "every face steady to the front," was a sight that, had the idea of it been mentioned a year ago, could only have been laughed at. However, due to the tenacity of General Hunter and the subsequent actions by General Saxton, this day became possible.

What made this event really memorable to Higginson was the "marching through throngs of prejudiced critics, officers and privates, who had all drilled as many months as we had weeks, and who were absolutely compelled to admit how admirably the regiment appeared. Dr. Rogers and others rode about among officers who came jeering and contemptuous, and had to say at last 'they do splendidly,' one Captain in the N.H. 4th, the best drilled regiment here." Once the 1st S.C. arrived at the parade ground, it "drilled for an hour, forming squares and reducing them and doing other things which looked hard on paper and are perfectly in foot." When Higginson decided it was time to go back to Camp Saxton, the men marched back singing as they had going to Beaufort, arriving back about 5:30.

Dr. Rogers recorded a very similar account of the day's event:

This has been a triumphant day for our regiment. We have marched to Beaufort and back in such style as to turn jeers into admiration, and tonight our men are full of music and delight. The Colonel, not content with marching the whole length of the front street, actually stopped on the parade ground and drilled the regiment an hour or more and then they marched home to the music of their own voices. The different encampments at Beaufort had large delegations by the way-side, as we entered the town, and we were greeted with such language as pertains to vulgar negro haters. Our men were apparently indifferent to it and the officers could afford to wait in silence. I fell back to the rear with the major and was constantly delighted at the manly bearing of our soldiers. Not a head was turned to the right or left—not a word spoken.

This decision by Colonel Higginson to demonstrate what his regiment could do was the unit's graduation after all those weeks of training. What started out the previous May as a seemingly impulsive decision by General Hunter had culminated into the completed training of a first-class combat organization that was now ready to take on the Confederates on a grander scale than what had occurred in November. Higginson knew that the time was near when his unit would once again take part in active operations. His officers and men were ready to go on their first mission as a regiment like the other line units, but where? The answer to it would be set forth soon.

The Return of General Hunter

When General Hunter had left the Department of the South back in September, it was to be for only a 60-day leave of absence. He had originally requested a change of duty station from Stanton because of the frustration he felt when he could not alleviate his manpower shortages by either the transfer of other units to his command or the recognition of his contraband regiment. However, when he arrived in Washington, he was immediately placed on a board of inquiry convened following the battle of Antietam to look into accusations made against several senior officers in the Army of the Potomac. Once this was accomplished in November, Hunter was empaneled as a member of a general court-martial against Major General Fitz John Porter accused of disobedience by his commander, Major General John Pope, at the second battle of Bull Run.

The trial against Porter finished on January 10, but no new assignment awaited Hunter. Earlier, Lincoln had chosen him to command 9th Corps when General Burnside was elevated to command the Army of the Potomac following the firing of General McClellan, but the appointment soon fell through. His assignment status continued to be in limbo. However, since the Department of the South and 10th Corps had not had a permanent commander since the death of General Ormsby Mitchel back in October, Hunter was soon ordered back to Port Royal. He left on January 14 on the steamer *Arago*.

News of General Hunter to resume command at Hilton Head arrived before he did. Anticipating action by him against Confederate South Carolina, Dr. Rogers said on the evening of the 18th that "when General

Hunter gets here we expect to nullify the State." Shortly after Rogers had written this sentence, he got word of his arrival. "Hurrah! Hurrah!—the Quartermaster just in with dispatch from signal officer announcing arrival of the 'Arago' and a gun boat at Hilton Head and General Hunter has come."

Two days after his arrival, Hunter wrote to General Hallack, the Union Army's General-in-Chief that he had arrived safely, though he had to endure "a very boisterous and stormy voyage …" That same day he released his General Orders No. 3, detailing expectations of his subordinates. This included the penalty of death for those who would desert their units, details about who would qualify to carry wounded off the battlefield, and who was to serve on his staff. The chief benefit of his resumption of command was that now all the advocates of black enlistment did not need to worry about interference from General Brannan or any other like-minded persons. Dr. Rogers made his excitement of the general's return quite clear. "Gen. Hunter is in earnest about arming the blacks, so we may confidently expect the well-done to increase. The little opposition to our movement will fall to the ground so soon as we can prove our worthiness by marked success."

On January 21, Hunter left Hilton Head and traveled to Beaufort at General Saxton's invitation to visit the 1st South Carolina Volunteers and see how his creation had metamorphosed into a first-rate infantry organization. The regiment performed various maneuvers. When the men were done, Colonel Higginson invited Hunter to give them a speech. In an off-the-cuff manner, he expressed his hope that by spring that he would have 50,000 black troops under arms. Once he was done, Saxton added that Hunter had told him that 50,000 Springfield muskets were on their way "to this department for the black soldiers." The Volunteers cheered wildly at the news. Higginson then introduced the regiment's doctors to Hunter, who in turn gave him a tour of "our little hospital." Dr. Rogers also told him of the trouble he had in getting needed medical supplies. The commanding general than easily remedied the situation. He countersigned Rogers' next requisition, which would basically dare the department's medical purveyor to deny him what he needed. Rogers then said, "We shall see with what results."

Return to Action

The transfer of Hunter back to Hilton Head was an unexpected move for him. The War Department's most pressing need at the moment for someone holding the grade of major general was still the Department of the South.

Since Admiral Du Pont held the naval equivalent of it, that of vice admiral, the Army's presence there still required its commanding officer to hold the same pay grade. No one else appeared to be readily available among the Union Army's major generals to take over the department when General Mitchel unexpectedly died in late October 1862. Therefore this command slot remained vacant until the decision was made to send Hunter back there in January. The news of his arrival could not have arrived at a better time.

While Colonel Higginson had decided back in November not to have his men go out on any more raids until he felt he had a combat-ready organization, the unit was now rapidly approaching that point. Since General Brannan was not a proponent of the 1st S.C.'s existence, the return of the unit to active combat probably would have met some stumbling blocks which easily could have affected the Volunteers' performance in the field. General Hunter's return, however, guaranteed that this would not happen. If there ever was a time for Higginson to start planning for the first mission of his unit, it was now. In conjunction with General Saxton, he got busy.

The first thing Higginson needed to determine was what type of mission. It would not be prudent to go to places that had large concentrations of the enemy, such as the Rebel bastions of Charleston and Savannah and their surrounding areas. No, the mission needed to be somewhat low-key but at the same time should make people notice their presence and hopefully their accomplishments. Fortunately for him a situation had recently occurred that would prove to be just what he was looking for. There had been a recent attempt by a white regiment to obtain lumber in Confederate territory, but it failed. The last major success in procuring lumber was back in November when the 1st S.C. raided the coast, but the supply was now running low. To have lumber shipped in from the North was too expensive. This most recent attempt by the white troops used "four companies, with two steamers and two schooners" and "had lately returned empty-handed, after a week's foraging; and now it was our turn."

By appearance it would seem that all the places that could have provided lumber in areas that did not have huge concentrations of enemy troops had already been picked clean. Therefore, there would be no other place to go to that had lumber activities. The previous raid by the Volunteers had been successful because some of the men were from these areas and knew what they contained. For this mission, there would be an individual who knew where to look—Corporal Robert Sutton. He had been a slave on a Georgia plantation on the St. Mary's River, which serves as part of the Florida–Georgia border. He had also been a pilot on that river, so he knew it and the logging roads connecting to it quite well. Since he had been involved in the lumber business as a slave, "Sutton was prepared to offer more lumber than we had more transportation to carry." He had always urged an expedition to go after it, and now it appeared that he would get his chance. But there was a hitch; the prize was about 35 miles upriver, in which there were numerous narrow twists and turns. Add to it the potential of enemy activity and the trip would definitely be a dangerous one.

Based upon this information from Sutton, Colonel Higginson finally decided where to go for his unit's first mission. The raids in November had also been based upon the information of privates, so why not Sutton? Just like Sergeant Rivers, Corporal Sutton was a very intelligent man. Higginson realized this once introduced to him. Though smart like Rivers, Higginson said "he had a more massive brain and a far more meditative and systematic intellect." Therefore, he knew this junior non-commissioned officer would be the key to the success of this proposed operation.

Next Higginson needed to know what type of ships would be available to him. This in turn would determine how many men he could take. It was not, however, going to the area of operation that concerned him, but coming back that really determined the manpower level, because there had to be plenty of room for the lumber to be brought back. Since this mission would be an important one for the department, General Saxton was able to get for Higginson three ships which were controlled by the Army: the steamer transport *Ben De Ford*, the former Rebel ship *Planter*, and a gunboat named the *John Adams*. This last vessel, which was to play a pivotal role in the upcoming expedition, was 127 feet long, 15.5 feet wide and had a draft of 16 feet. She also had a serious complement of ordnance: a 30-pounder Parrott rifle, two VIII-inch smoothbores and four 32-pounder howitzers.[2]

To make sure that the mission had additional firepower if required, Saxton wrote to Admiral Du Pont on January 21 for it. Du Pont quickly approved the request and wrote a letter that Higginson could carry to the commanding officer of the nearest blockading station, Commander Charles Steedman, off St. Simons Island. It directed him to render "whatever assistance you can afford him through any of the smaller vessels (not inconsistent with their present duties ...)."

With the information he needed, Colonel Higginson was able to determine that he could take six companies of the ten authorized for his regiment. One each would go on the *John Adams* and *Planter* while the other four went on the *Ben De Ford*. The companies he selected were A, B, C, F, G, and H.[3] This would give him a total of "four hundred and sixty-two officers and men, and ... three invited guests." At this time Higginson also decided to order the Springfield muskets and blue pants General

Hunter had promised. "I am to send a requisition to Hilton Head for them at once." On the 22nd, Dr. Rogers took his requisition that Hunter had countersigned to Hilton Head to be filled. He was back at sunset "with my instruments and a beginning of the medicines ... [Hunter] intends to be obeyed and, I fancy, the negro hater will find it out in good season."

On the eve of the 1st South Carolina's departure, Colonel Higginson wrote in his journal of his impending mission. In it he said that in addition to acquiring lumber, he intended to recruit as well:

I am going on a trip along the shore to pick up recruits and lumber ... I am to have under my command a large steamer the Ben Deford [*sic*], and a small gunboat, to protect the former, in case we venture near any dangerous places. All this you will see in print, very likely, as it is all surmized [*sic*] in Beaufort, only they don't know where we are going, up shore or down. I have implored Gen. Saxton to be as mum as I am, and not a soul in this regiment has dared to ask me a word about it ... but if you don't hear from me for ten days you may infer that I am deep in pine lumbers, or picking up Ethiopians with their little bundles on the banks of rivers.

On January 23, the three vessels left Beaufort "at different hours, with orders to rendezvous at St. Simon's Island, on the coast of Georgia." The *Planter* and *John Adams* left at noon. Captain Trowbridge was in charge of the *Planter* while Major Strong commanded on the *John Adams*.[4] The *Ben De Ford* left at 4 p.m. with Colonel Higginson, Dr. Rogers, Dr. Minor, and the three men composing the Florida Tax Commission, who had recently arrived from Washington. They were on their way to Fernandina to "set up shop." These men were John S. Sammis, Harrison Reed, and Lyman Stickney. The *Ben De Ford* reached the open sea after dark. Dr. Rogers said that "at this moment we are outside the bar, off Hilton Head, sailing as quietly in the soft moonlight and warm atmosphere as if our intention were of the most peaceful nature."

Dr. Rogers also wrote about other things that were on his mind at this time:

The "Ben Deford" is really a magnificent steamer for transporting troops. A turn among the soldiers just now, convinced me that we can have ventilation enough to prevent illness. It is a real pleasure to go and see them so quietly wrapped in their blankets,—no quarreling, no profanity. Very much depends upon our success in this expedition, and the whole responsibility rests upon our Colonel. He has absolute authority over these three steamers. Our men were all anxious to go, and many, belonging to companies not designated for the trip, went to Col. H., and begged to go. Some have been permitted to do so. It remains to see how they will fight.

Earlier in the day Charlotte Forten had written in her diary about a note she had received from her friend she had known from Massachusetts, Dr. Rogers. "His reg[iment] goes on an expedition today. He asks me to pray for their success. And I intend I will, with my whole soul and for his safety, too—dear, kind friend that he is. I c[ou]ld have seen him again before he went. How he rejoices in Gen. Hunter's coming. And how I rejoice with him!"

The *Ben De Ford* arrived at St. Simon's Bay on the morning of the 24th at about 9 o'clock. Everybody had expected to see the *John Adams* waiting for them, but she was nowhere in sight. The *Planter* was not to arrive until much later because it was more prudent for her to stick to the inland waterways as much as possible due to engine problems. Once the *Ben De Ford* dropped anchor, Colonel Higginson and Dr. Rogers went over to the gunboat *Potomska*, still commanded by Acting Volunteer Lieutenant William Budd. He was joined by Acting Master E. Moses of the bark *Fernandina*. Since Commander Steedman was absent at the time, Lieutenant Budd was the senior officer at the scene. Higginson presented the letter from Admiral Du Pont to him. He "received polite attention from the naval officers."

As part of the conversation, Higginson found out that there was a quality of railroad iron buried on St. Simon's Island in an earthen fort built by the Confederates.[5] The iron had been used as the roofs of the ammunition bunkers and bomb-proof shelters for the men. Since it was a valuable commodity back at Port Royal, Higginson ordered that a party be organized to excavate it while they waited for the *John Adams* and *Planter*. He also found out that a trip up the St. Mary's would not be an easy one, as he had been previously advised by Corporal Sutton. He was told about the harrowing experience of the gunboat *Ottawa* ten months prior. She had to fight her "way past ... every bluff in descending" the narrow and tortuous river. No resistance would be offered going upstream, but the Rebels would be all over them "like hornets" on the way back. After the meeting, Higginson and Rogers went to St. Simon's and paid a visit to the plantation home of "a Northern renegade" named Thomas Butler King. At four that afternoon, the *John Adams* finally arrived, but still no sign of the *Planter*.

One of the naval officers who met Higginson and Rogers on the *Potomska* was the doctor assigned to the *Fernandina*, Samuel Pellman Boyer. Though he was pleasant to them at the meeting, what he later wrote in his diary was not:

All hands to quarters at 9 A.M. The suspected enemy proved to be the Army transport *Ben De Ford* with the 1st Regiment of South Carolina Volunteers on board. Col. Higginson and the surgeon paid us visit. At 4 P.M. the *John Adams* also arrived with a part of same regiment. It must be remembered that this regiment is composed of ye intelligent contrabands, the commissioned officers being the only whites. From what I have seen of the contrabands, I must confess that in my estimation they are small potatoes. Their dress is blue coat and red pantaloons. Where they are bound for I cannot tell; in fact, I don't care. I have the smallest opinion of said Gideonites.

When January 25 dawned on the waters of St. Simon's Bay, there was still no *Planter*. At the sun rose, all that the other vessels could do was continue to wait, as there was nothing to indicate her presence on the horizon. Over the course of the day, nearly 100 bars of iron were recovered and also "a quantity of five-inch plank," which was used "to barricade the very conspicuous pilot-house of the *John Adams*." It was at this point that Colonel Higginson began to worry about the *Planter*, "as the inner passage, by which alone she could arrive, was exposed at certain points to fire from Rebel batteries." Dreading a disaster to happen even before the mission to the St. Mary's River had begun, all he could do was continue to wait, even as the sun set and darkness took over.

To help his day go by on the 25th, Dr. Boyer wrote more about the men of the 1st S.C. on St. Simon's in his observation of them:

The Gideonites appear to be on a plundering expedition. They are removing everything from the Butler King place: even the window sashes and panes are taken on board their steamer.[6] When asked the question by what right they plunder, they answer, 'We take those things for the government.'— as though Uncle Sam depended upon the sale of old iron, window sashes, etc. for the purpose of carrying on the war! The black cattle were working all day, plundering ..., not having the least regard for the day. I sincerely hope that a day of retribution 'am a coming' so that the Gideonites will receive their just dues. I, for one, do not consider the officers of said regiment worthy the respect of gentlemen.

Meanwhile, back in Beaufort, General Saxton wrote to Secretary Stanton also on this day "to report that the organization of the First Regiment of South Carolina Volunteers is now completed. The regiment is light infantry, composed of ten companies of about eighty-six men each, armed with muskets, and officered by white men." He told Stanton too that not only did he send "the regiment upon an expedition to the coast of

Georgia," but that the nucleus of a second unit had begun with the arrival of Colonel James Montgomery. "I have commensed [*sic*] the organization of the Second Regiment." This would be good news to the proponents of black regiments, but it would also be useful information for future reference to an individual who was on his way to Fernandina with his fellow tax commissioners—Lyman Stickney.

Though Stickney was at this time a government employee, he would shortly open up a store there with two others not of the commission, men named Calvin Robinson and William Morrill, with Stickney serving in the capacity as a silent partner. The store would be stocked with government property and confiscated items. To demonstrate how good Stickney was at fooling people—including Treasury Secretary Chase, General Saxton, and Colonel Higginson,—Dr. Rogers wrote this about him on January 25: "Judge Stickney of Florida is with us; an able defender of the oppressed and a gentleman."

Finally on the evening of the 25th, the *Planter* arrived.[7] The next day the three ships weighed anchor for the final leg of their voyage. While the *Ben De Ford* took to the open ocean, the *John Adams* went with the *Planter* along the "inside passage." All of them were to rendezvous at Fort Clinch on the northern end of Amelia Island. This departure was good news as far as Dr. Boyer was concerned. "They left this morning ... Thank fortune they are gone." However, he did make one conciliation to one of his previous statements in taking things from the King estate: "I am told that they were ordered to do so as they have done by the government. If so, I take back, or retract, what I have written yesterday as regards them."

Post Time

After all three vessels arrived at Fort Clinch on the afternoon of the 26th, the 1st South Carolina began to organize for the mission of going up the St. Mary's River. During this time, 200 of the men of the approximate 465 that arrived were transferred to the *John Adams* from the *Ben De Ford*.[8] This included Drs. Rogers and Minor. After the transfer, the *Ben De Ford* went on to Fernandina with the Florida Tax Commission. The *Planter* was supposed to ascend the river also, but was unable to due to continuous boiler problems in her engine. She was to help transport material from upriver.

While organizing that evening, Colonel Higginson decided to alter his plans and act later that night upon some additional intelligence about Confederate troop emplacements he had received from Corporal Sutton, since he had worked extensively in the area of the river as a slave. Sutton told him about the Rebel camp known as Camp Cooper. However, what he was not able to tell Higginson was that the Amelia Island Guerrillas,[9] who had been there for some time, were now called Company K of the new 2nd Florida Cavalry Regiment. This unit had been created on December 4, 1862 as part of the state's evolving defensive strategy. The corporal also did not mention anything about the main base, Camp Finegan, which was not too far away for its infantry, cavalry, and artillery units to react if required. He probably did not know anything about it; else he would have mentioned it to Higginson as he did about Camp Cooper.

With the knowledge of the existence of this base, Higginson decided to conduct a raid on the camp to allow many of his men who had yet to see combat gain some experience, since "it seemed to me more inviting, and far more useful to the men, than any amount of mere foraging. The thing really desirable appeared to be to get them under fire as soon as possible, and teach them, by a few small successes, the application of what they had learned in camp."

Higginson also found out from Sutton that access to the Rebel encampment was by two roads, one of which was a lumber path that Sutton had helped to build. He told his commander that he could easily guide the regiment using it. To access this trail, Higginson would have to land at a small hamlet called Township Landing, some 15 miles upriver from Fort Clinch. Once they arrived the Federals would surround the house and slave quarters there to prevent an alarm from being given by the pickets, traverse the lumber path to Camp Cooper, and surprise the camp if all went according to plan. However, Higginson was also well aware of the possibility that "if they got notice of our approach, through their pickets, we should, at worst, have a fight, in which the best man must win." He and his men would soon find out that the best of plans can fall apart in actual combat, and units must adapt to the conditions at hand in order to survive, let alone win, an engagement so that "the best man must win."

Starting shortly after 10 p.m.,[10] the *John Adams* moved upriver under a full moon. In addition to the slow current, having the full illumination made the trip "easy of navigation thus far," since the water reflected the moon's brightness. As the 1st South Carolina moved upstream, Dr. Rogers recorded these observations: "We are now in the heart of secesh and before morning shall have succeeded or failed in our purpose. At this moment the men are loading their muskets with a will that means fight." He also said: "Our Colonel is cool and careful and I trust his judgment in our perilous undertaking. But if we should loose [sic] him! ... We are moving slowly and silently up the river, all lights above, extinguished, save mine and I have put my rubber blanket up for a curtain at the window."

When they neared their initial objective, Colonel Higginson had the gunboat stop just short of Township so he could dispatch a small force on shore so it could surround the houses and prevent anybody from escaping to sound the alarm. Corporal Sutton was in this advance party too. Allowing the force enough time to get there and capture the place, the *John Adams* landed shortly with the bulk of the men. As soon as Higginson stepped off the boat, Sutton was waiting on him with some updated intelligence. A slave had just returned to the landing prior to its capture from Camp Cooper so he "could give the latest information."[11] While Sutton went to get this individual, Higginson began to prepare his men for the movement on the Rebel base.

Since the operation was in the middle of winter (late January), personal ailments were prevalent, and Higginson had to separate those who were constantly coughing from catarrh from the rest, because going on a combat mission of this nature, "quiet was needed." Those who did not pass muster were sent on board, much to their dislike. He had also decided to take Dr. Minor with the detachment because Dr. Rogers "could not endure a rapid march of ten miles on foot." Rogers "reluctantly fitted our Dr. Minor with [his] orderly, pistol and sash, tourniquets, etc. ... " The expedition finally got under way after midnight. As the Volunteers moved out, Dr. Rogers said that "our men show anything but fear as [they] pass between the double line of pickets." The former slaves of the 1st South Carolina had achieved operational security and tactical surprise so far on the enemy, based upon the execution of their mission up to this point. At least that is what they thought. When Sutton met Higginson at the wharf and told him about the slave that had just returned, implying that Township Landing was secure, they (let alone anyone else) overlooked one minor detail. Where were the Rebel pickets? And in addition to this, there was also another thing that Higginson did not take into account in his planning: an early warning system which would allow the Rebels to know when an enemy boat was going upriver.

As the *John Adams* passed a certain point after it entered the St. Mary's River, some time before 11 p.m.,[12] a Confederate cavalry soldier mounted his horse to race back to Camp Cooper several miles away to warn his commanding officer that a Yankee gunboat had entered the river and was heading upstream. Captain Frank J. Clarke, commander of Company K, 2nd Florida Cavalry, had a major responsibility on his hands, given the limited assets he had to work with, and also the fact that he was not quite 21 years old yet. After the major troop withdrawals that had occurred from Florida to other theaters of operation in Virginia and Tennessee, the remaining Rebel units were stretched thin trying to cover all the places Union forces could possibly land in the state. These small Confederate detachments would only be able to offer, for the most part, token resistance until reinforcements arrived, and in some cases, only after considerable time had gone by.

Clarke's area of responsibility was fairly small, but he had the task to watch for movements at the major Union naval base at Fernandina. With roughly 70 men in his company, he had to cover at least three areas where Union forces could land on the mainland: on the St. Mary's River at Township Landing on his northern flank; at the railroad crossing of the Florida Railroad, spanning the Amelia River, tying Amelia Island with the mainland, on his eastern flank; and at a point on the Nassau River,[13] covering his southern flank.

With the two river points being potential landing areas, Captain Clarke had to keep the bulk of his men assigned to picket duty at the railroad crossing because of the Union troops on the other side. Given the fact that there was a Yankee regiment on duty on Amelia Island, his men here always had to face one of the companies on the island side of the crossing.[14] Since Camp Cooper was located on Lufkin Creek just north of the intersection of the Florida Railroad and the logging trails several miles inland, it was centrally situated to respond with reinforcements to any of these areas if required. However, his company was greatly outnumbered. At the time when the Volunteers landed at Township, he had only 29 men and two other officers besides himself available as a reaction force. Twenty five men were on picket duty, eight were on detached duty, and a few had to be left in camp to guard nine escaped slaves who had been caught a few days prior trying to make it to Fernandina.

Upon hearing the report of the picket, Captain Clarke prepared his men for action. Just how much preparation had to take place in order for his men to mount up and go, the evidence does not say. For example, were the horses already saddled and bridled, or did they have to take the time to get them ready? Besides, being as late as it was, the men must have already been in bed and had to quickly redress once they got the word from their commander. The picket stations, on the other hand, had to have at least one horse on ready alert at all times in order for the pickets to react quickly at any sign of Union activity. This unexpected presence of the enemy into what had become again a monotonous situation since the last foray in November, would also cause the tempo of the pickets' normally banal duty to increase a hundredfold, and their lethargic states of mind would snap into action at the prospect that combat might be imminent.

As his men prepared to move, Clarke had at this point two options of possible enemy intent, based upon what he was told by the reporting picket. Since his advance picket reported the boat as "passing up," she would either go further upriver for whatever reason or stop at Township Landing. If the former were the case, Clarke would take his men to Waterman's Bluff,[15] a little downriver from the landing. From prepositioned firing points on this high ground, the Confederate cavalry would be able to engage the enemy on their way back downstream. Since no artillery was stationed at Camp Cooper (what was available was stationed at Camp Finegan), the Rebels would not be able to inflict much damage on the boat, but they would make their presence known.

Clarke did not have to worry about the Confederate force on the Georgia side of the river, which was the 4th Georgia Cavalry Regiment, another new regiment which had been organized on January 23, 1863 from the old 3rd Georgia Cavalry Battalion and three independent cavalry companies, and commanded by the newly promoted Colonel Duncan L. Clinch. The 4th's Company D would monitor the enemy's movements if the boat went further upriver, and would engage them from several prepared bluffs also upriver if required. If Company K heard the sound of rifle fire in the distance, the men would know that the enemy was on the move again coming back downstream, the 4th Georgia was engaging, and to get ready to fire when the gunboat came into their sector of the river. The primary reason why the Rebel cavalry on either side of the river waited until a boat would come back before firing on her was that by the time they would have gotten to their prepositioned firing points, the boat would have already passed them.

Clarke's other option, opposing a Federal landing at Township, was tactically important to the protection of Camp Cooper, since it was most likely the target of an enemy landing there. He and his subordinates "had expected the Yanks would come that way if they came after us." He probably ruled out a simultaneous movement by Union forces on the three possible routes to Cooper from Fernandina because he had no report of enemy activity from the other picket stations at the railroad crossing and on the Nassau River (but this did not mean that other landings could not take place later). As the 32 officers and men of Company K moved out to meet the enemy, it did not take long for Captain Clarke to get the tactical information he needed in order to choose the right option.

There were three soldiers on picket duty when they heard the *John Adams* approaching Township. Not knowing the situation of the advance picket post,[16] one of them scurried back to Camp Cooper to warn the company. Captain Clarke and his contingent had gone "about one and a half mile when we met ... the picket who said the Yanks were landing just above, but the two remaining of the picket were at the gate which they must pass coming this way."[17] With this information in hand, Clarke "feeling secure carried ... on a gallop intending to dismount ... at a certain branch and there ambuscade them."

Since his unit was on horseback, Clarke took the calculated risk to forego a scouting party to ensure his men made it there first, since the intended ambush site was "about one half mile from the landing." Determining that the enemy to be infantry, he was confident that he had enough time to get to the "certain branch" first. Either this particular place was a prearranged point to fight instead of trying to oppose the enemy at the landing, or he decided to go there when he got the information that the *John Adams* had landed at Township. Either way it offered the Confederates the element of surprise in a wooded, swampy area, which would have enabled them to channel the direction of the enemy's movement. It would have also deprived the Federals of the use of the gunboat's armament, since distance and darkness would have nullified the guns' lethal advantage as opposed to the Rebels trying to defend right at the landing.[18] Even so, just as Colonel Higginson had thought the 1st South Carolina had achieved tactical surprise when it landed at Township and moved inland, Captain Clarke was to find out also that war has a way of changing the best of plans very quickly.

When Higginson's detachment left Township Landing, it had about 100 men,[19] while the rest remained behind either because of coughing or to guard the landing from surprise attack. He placed Company G in the lead, which was primarily composed of men from Florida. Being with the advance company himself, he had its commander, Captain L. W. Metcalf, and the first sergeant, Sergeant Henry McIntyre, at his side. He also had near him Corporal Sutton "with his captured negro guide, whose first fear and sullenness had yielded to the magic of the President's Proclamation, then just issued ..."[20] As the 1st South Carolina marched through the woods, the men heard nothing "but the peeping of the frogs in a neighboring marsh, and the occasional yelping of a dog, as we passed the hut of some 'cracker.'" The unit was preceded by a small advance guard, with some men on the flanks of it as the ground permitted, to prevent a surprise attack.

Moving along the logging trail in column formation, the Volunteers had to stop on occasion to tighten their line, because it had become strung out.[21] After moving inland some, Higginson decided to dispense with his guide he had obtained at the landing because he had absorbed all the information he could from the man. Thinking that things were going smoothly, he contemplated that he and his men would be able to surprise the Rebels at Camp Cooper, and with little resistance coming from the Confederates, Captain Clarke would surrender his sword to Higginson in a chivalrous manner. With this in mind, he strode on, "rapt in pleasing contemplation," but all of a sudden all hell started to break loose.

The advance guard of his detachment suddenly came to a halt. When Higginson started to find out what was going on, he said that "almost at the same instant a more ominous sound, as of galloping horses in the path before us" occurred. He was trying to make sense quickly of the unplanned action taken by his lead troops and the sound of approaching horses when it became more confusing by the sudden fire by the advance guard. Just as these events happened in quick succession, Higginson reacted fast to counter this confusion by ordering the men in his lead company to fix bayonets to their muskets and kneel on both sides of the trail under cover in expectation of what he realized was coming up the trail.

While Colonel Higginson was trying to react in a correct manner with his inexperienced soldiers in the woods at night, the Confederates were having a similar experience. As the Rebel cavalry came within shooting distance, the Volunteers opened fire. Company K was about 30 yards from where the 1st South Carolina was when the Rebels received the first mass volley of the first regiment of black soldiers in Confederate Florida. One of the individuals near the head of the column was the acting company clerk named Davis Bryant. He said "that though the moon was up that night the sky was so cloudy you could not see over 20 steps to distinguish anything, and the buggers were drawn up in front of an old fence which deceived the Captain, though he had before noticed the dark line ... imagine our surprise on being 'opened up' by a line of Yankees about 60 yards long, then whooping and yelling as soon as they fired the first volley."[22] Company K's executive officer, 1st Lieutenant John D. Jones, was the first Confederate to die from the guns of the Volunteers in their inaugural foray. Two other soldiers were wounded: one in the arm and hand, the other through the wrist. All were at or near the front of the column.

Since the presence and rifle fire of the Volunteers on the trail took the Rebels completely by surprise, Bryant said that one "can't begin to imagine a man ... under such circumstances." The surprise of sudden combat without any warning can have the most profound impact on those who were on the receiving end of a hail of bullets, since "the shock was terrible." The impact of the unplanned Union ambush had its effect on the horses too, thus seriously hampering the effectiveness of Company K as a military unit. Bryant said the action "frightened our horses so that they took us skitin' through the woods in all directions." He added, "two or three were thrown, but it is a wonder that all were not." Even for something of this nature to occur in a time frame of seconds before control is regained can cause serious repercussions and nullify a unit's ability to function at the most critical junction, when it would be most paramount to continue to be cohesive. The head of the column was almost decapitated, with 1LT Jones being killed; Captain Clarke was very fortunate he was not hit.

In the ensuing mêlée after the initial volley of musketry, Private William Parsons of Company G, standing by Colonel Higginson, was killed. With his mind occupied with the rapid chain of events occurring, Higginson "felt it no more than if a tree had fallen—I was so busy watching my own men and the enemy, and planning what to do next." Helping to maintain control of the men on the line were Company G's Captain Metcalf and Lieutenant A. W. Jackson, along with Dr. Minor. The rest of the detachment was still in column formation when the collision of the two combatants occurred, thinking the halt was just like the previous ones while marching down the trail. However, when the shooting started, the soldiers "did not know who or where their assailants might be, and the fall of the man beside me created a hasty rumor that I was killed, so that it was on the whole an alarming experience for them." According to Higginson, the enemy rode through the open pine-barren firing into the Volunteers' ranks, "but mostly over the head of the men." They returned fire rapidly, "too rapidly, being yet beginners." When Dr. Rogers heard back at the boat "volley after volley of musket off in the woods," he knew then it was time for "making final preparations for the wounded."

With each side exchanging shots, regardless of how many each side actually fired, it was over as quickly as it started. Trying to keep control of his company in the mêlée, Captain Clarke was able to effect the right command for his men as they were trying to bring their horses under control. Commanding "Right about retreat," he took his unit back about 150 yards before calling a halt. Since the unit was in column formation, the volleys of the 1st South Carolina caused minimal casualties—the death of Lieutenant Jones and the wounding of the two enlisted men. Quickly judging the situation at that point to still be untenable, he decided to put some more distance between his unit and the enemy so he could regain complete control. It would also give him enough time to evaluate what he had just run into and go over his available options.

Though they had fallen back about another 150 more yards, the Rebels were still exposed to enemy gunfire, because "the place ... [was] ... open pine woods," and "the buggers were firing all the while as fast as they could load," with "the bullets ... whizzing by and patting the back of all of us." Captain Clarke then decided to move his command a third time, since "we could not check their advance at that place." At this point the 1st South Carolina Volunteers were in a state of euphoria, because they were able to "give it back" to the Confederates. Though Company K, 2nd Florida Cavalry, did not consist of their former owners, to the Volunteers they represented the system that defended slavery, and it was against this that they were striking a blow for liberty, which gave them a good reason to fire "as fast as they could load ..."

When the Confederate company moved the second time "a little further back," the Rebels collected themselves in the road. At their first fall-back position, the Rebels were not able to ascertain the full impact of the enemy's attack. Captain Clarke was so busy with the matters of the moment, he did not realize Lieutenant Jones was not there. When they fell back to their second position on the trail, the Confederates were able to do a head count, and it was then that they found out that one man was wounded and Jones and another man were missing.

After assessing the situation, Clarke decided it was pointless to engage the enemy again, given his perception of the enemy's strength. He felt it was more prudent to fall back to a more secure position behind a swamp a mile further up the trail. The swamp on both sides would have channeled the 1st South Carolina and greatly reduced the effectiveness of its numerical superiority. He left a guard back up the road to warn the unit of the enemy's approach.

In a chance encounter with bullets flying all over the place, time can be of a secondary nature. Higginson said that he "could hardly tell whether the fight lasted then minutes or an hour," but when the enemy fire tapered off, he gave the order to cease fire, which was easier to say than do. It "was very difficult at first to make them desist: the taste of gunpowder was too intoxicating. One of them was heard to mutter, indignantly, 'Why de Cunnel order Cease firing when de Secesh blazin' away at de rate ob ten dollar a day?'"[23] Regardless of whether the soldiers wanted to continue to fire or not, they had control of the area.

Taking stock of what had just taken place as the smoke cleared away from the guns of the Volunteers, Higginson "was convinced from appearances that we had been victorious, so far, though I could not suppose that this would be the last of it." He would have loved to have continued to his original objective, as Corporal Sutton was urging him to do, but he also had to strongly consider what Saxton told him before the 1st South Carolina left for Florida—that is, not to risk too much "because of the fatal effect on public sentiment of even an honorable defeat." The use of black troops was still in its infancy. There was also much opposition in the government and military, let alone in general public opinion, as to their use, primarily because of the belief in their racial inferiority and not being intelligent enough to handle the demands of the military and combat. Any defeat would have been considered more evidence that the opponents of blacks in the military were right. With this in mind, Higginson concluded that the fight with "de hoss cavalry" was victorious enough.[24] He then decided to withdraw back to the gunboat where defensive measures would be more favorable.

Besides Saxton's cautionary advice, Higginson also had to consider the facts that he did not know the exact strength of the enemy, where the Confederates were, nor what effect if any the skirmish had on them. Besides, any attempt at surprising Camp Cooper was now long gone. He did note, however, that there were good points to this engagement, chief among them that his men gained valuable combat experience, whereas before it had been only drill and practice.[25] The junior officers in the detachment also gained first-hand experience in controlling their men. In the view of public opinion, "it was of small importance what nonsense might be talked or written about colored troops, so long as mine did not flinch, it made no difference to me." With those points in mind, Higginson started to move his command back to the river. While he did this, Dr. Rogers on the *John Adams* "appropriated the mess-room for operations and the officer's berths to receive the wounded." He said that it was "not more than one hour before we were busy dressing gunshot wounds."

Though Company K had taken up a better defensive position behind the swamp, Captain Clarke decided in the event his unit was driven back even further, he would have Camp Cooper already evacuated, having his men carry away as much as possible the most important items. He sent Davis Bryant back to evacuate the ammunition and commissary stores (food) several miles away. With the known enemy north of them, Bryant decided to go west,[26] anticipating the enemy might also come at Cooper from another direction, "which might have been done easily, as we are stationed in a narrow neck which it is impossible for us to picket."

Davis Bryant, clerk of Company K, 2nd Florida Cavalry who wrote how his unit clashed with the Volunteers at the Hundred Pine. *Courtesy of the Stephens-Bryant family of Florida*

Bryant loaded a wagon with what he could of the ammunition and commissary stores and left the camp with the few soldiers remaining and the nine runaway slaves they had caught trying to make it to Fernandina. He moved the wagon and slaves that night "8 or 10 miles" and waited until the next day when he sent one of the other soldiers back to Camp Cooper to ascertain if it was safe enough to return there.

Getting an all clear, he "returned with wagon and c[ompany]." several hours later.

The Morning After

When no more activity took place that night, Captain Clarke sent out a scouting party the next morning to probe for any Union presence. Cautiously moving up the trail, the soldiers came upon the spot where they first encountered the 1st S.C. and found the body of the missing officer, Lt. Jones. They also found the other missing man; he had been shot in the arm and had gone to a house in the confusion of the previous night's mêlée to seek help. Both the wounded man and Jones' body were evacuated. Jones was later buried in a local cemetery.

After attending to the needs of the casualties, the reconnaissance party continued up the trail looking for any signs of further enemy presence. What they saw was evidence of an enemy retrograding back to Township. They found proof of someone having been hit; also a canteen, broken ramrods, and other items that had been dropped along the trail as the Volunteers made their way back to the *John Adams*. Thinking that they had retreated, the Confederates also said that as the enemy withdrew, they fired "as they went, from the time of their first volley, as they did not advance a step over the line they first formed and the trees were cut by shot in all directions from there to the gate," anticipating that the Rebel cavalry might try to rush them as they fell back to the river.[27] Judging from the volleys they said the Yankees had fired, the recon party estimated the enemy at 250 men or more.

Retiring to Township with the casualties, Higginson anticipated that the Rebel cavalry would attack again, "for it was obvious that a mounted force would not allow a detachment of infantry to march two miles through open woods by night without renewing the fight, unless they themselves had suffered a good deal." With nothing happening by the time the 1st South Carolina got back to the boat, Higginson was all the more certain that they had won a victory in their first engagement with the enemy. He sent the majority of the men back on board to rest while he posted several men, who eagerly volunteered, as sentinels. He had decided to hold the plantation house at the river until morning. He was assisted by Lieutenants W. H. Hyde and A. W. Jackson. But much to his surprise, "we had not other enemies to encounter."

While Colonel Higginson was on shore waiting for more possible activity to occur, Drs. Rogers and Minor attended to the casualties. They worked by candlelight. Rogers said that Private Parsons was killed by a round through the heart and that seven men were wounded, one of whom he diagnosed as not likely to survive. He also described another man "with two bullets holes through the large muscles of the shoulder and neck, brought off from the scene of action, two miles distant, two muskets and not a murmur escaped his lips." Corporal Sutton had three wounds, one of which grazed his skull. Rogers said this particular wound might be fatal (which did not turn out to be the case). Regardless of his injuries, Sutton wanted to continue to do his duty. He did "not report himself till compelled to do so by his officers. While dressing his wounds he quietly talked of what they had done and what they can yet do … He is perfectly quiet and cool but takes this whole affair with the religious bravery of a man who realizes that freedom is greater than life."

Another soldier who had been wounded in the shoulders by some buckshot did not report but remained on shore as one of the volunteers for perimeter duty; he was afraid that if he told anybody, he would have been ordered to have his wounds taken care of. He later had another soldier get the shot out. As an appropriate remark for these men who wanted to remain on duty regardless of their wounds, Higginson said that any "officer may pardon some enthusiasm for such men as these." Rogers said "braver men never lived." Though there were eight Union casualties with various wounds, Rebel clerk Davis Bryant said that "three of our men fired a round each."

As morning dawned with no sign of enemy activity, Higginson and his unit had held Township Landing and its immediate surroundings for roughly eight hours. The question was what to do next. Since the Confederates were well alerted, and had probably sent someone to notify their higher headquarters, which might mean reinforcements, Higginson decided that the best course of action would be to leave and go back to Fernandina. Nothing else of military value could be achieved under these circumstances. As the unit prepared to leave, he had his men perform two more tasks.

To deny the Confederates any aid and comfort as much as possible, Colonel Higginson had his men torch the plantation house and some outbuildings there at Township, since they had been used by the pickets. Before this happened, he had them place on the boat a piano forte that was in a packing crate. Though he knew to leave private property intact, and he held his men under tight reins against "indiscriminate pilfering and wanton outrage, and to allow nothing to be taken or destroyed by proper authority," he made this one exception. He said that he only took it because it was ready to be transported, and when he got back to Fernandina, "presented it to the school for colored children."[28] After the instrument was secured, the buildings were burned. When the Rebels reoccupied Township, they found out the Yankees had "burned the dwelling of the place where they landed and took off several negroes." Dr. Rogers said there were five of them.

As the buildings burned, the *John Adams* moved back downstream to Fernandina, but before the gunboat got there, she made a stop at St. Mary's. While going upriver the night before, Higginson had noticed some lumber sitting on a wharf, since there was a full moon, and he made the decision to confiscate it on the way back after the Camp Cooper operation.

Since St. Mary's had been previously visited by Federal gunboats, Higginson had been told what to expect there if he stopped. Though the town had been deserted since Fernandina was captured the previous March, three elderly ladies still lived there. Every time the Federals landed, these women would come out to meet them, waving white handkerchiefs and professing their loyalty to the Union while carrying a portrait of George Washington. They would say there were no pickets in town, yet could not explain how fresh horse tracks just happened to be near their dwelling. Once the boat had left the dock, a hail of bullets would normally pepper her.[29] Here was an opportunity for Higginson to demonstrate to his "officers and men that, while rigid against irregular outrage, we could still be inexorable against the enemy."

As the *John Adams* moved towards St. Mary's, she fired her big guns at several bluffs to dispel any Rebel attempt to fire on her.[30] Going with the current of the river as an aid, the gunboat arrived in short time.[31] When she landed at the dock, true to what Higginson had been told, the three elderly matrons came out waving their handkerchiefs. Even with these so-called loyalists, he had his men set out as skirmishers along the principal routes into town and also placed some men in the cupola of a house so they could get a good view of the area. There were about 50 homes, two large churches, and a bank remaining, after one of the earlier trips by a Union gunboat, which had set fire to the town.

With his men in place, Higginson had the lumber loaded onto the boat. While this was going on, he had a "stately and decorous interview with the queens of society of St. Mary's." Dr. Rogers added that they:

> informed us that they were living entirely alone with their aged mother, that they were 'St. Domingo ladies,' but had not owned slaves since

England abolished slavery there. Their antecedents have been so doubtful that the Colonel thought it best to search their house very carefully in spite of their protestations and entreaties and talk of honor etc., etc. I was permitted to join him and one of the captains in the search and found it very interesting though we discovered no rebels. Of course we had a guard around the house, a guard of such color as greatly to annoy the inmates. They told me that they had not seen pickets at all and many other things which I knew to be false. But we politely left them, they avowing that they were ladies and thanking us for being gentlemen.

After the work was completed, the men withdrew to the gunboat to continue downstream. No sooner had she gotten under way than "there came, like the sudden burst of a tropical tornado, a regular little hailstorm of bullets in the open end of the boat, driving every gunner in an instant from his post, and surprising even those who were looking to be surprised."[32] Soon order was restored and the gun crews sent shells screaming into the area of the assailants,[33] which in this case were soldiers from Company D, 4th Georgia Cavalry. They had been on alert since the previous evening when their own pickets saw the *John Adams* pass the town. Since Colonel Higginson had promised his officers that if the boat were attacked as she left the dock, they would return and burn what was left of the town.

When the *John Adams* turned around and moved back to the wharf, the women came out again and did their handkerchief routine. While they did this, the small element of the 4th Georgia continued to fire at the boat.[34] Once she docked, one company disembarked and went after them, causing the soldiers of Company D to retreat. Colonel Higginson went to the women and told them he intended to burn what remained of the town. He said he "should begin burning in the house next to theirs, so that they, being women, shouldn't suffer." Though they threw accolades at him, addressing him as "Mr. Captain," he knew they were only putting on a show. Dr. Rogers wanted to take the women back to Fernandina with them, but Higginson decided it was best to leave them there, "so there will still be a screen and sympathy left there for the rebels." Once what had yet to be burned was torched, the colonel withdrew his men to the boat and continued on to Fernandina.

Raid up The St. Mary's

The 1st South Carolina arrived back in Fernandina tired but jubilant late in the morning of January 27. Though the Volunteers did not win a spectacular victory over the Florida cavalry, they did prove to themselves and others that they could successfully go toe to toe with the enemy. The Union commander of Fernandina and Amelia Island, Colonel Joseph R. Hawley,[1] and the commander of the naval gunboat *Mohawk*, Lieutenant Commander A. K. Hughes, congratulated the officers and men of the regiment.

The Volunteers may have been successful, but not all the facts of their completed mission made it to everyone. Jerome Tourtellotte,[2] commanding officer of Company K, 7th Connecticut Infantry, whose regiment had recently replaced the 9th Maine, wrote that the 1st South Carolina went up the St. Mary's in the *Planter* for lumber. He said also that the Confederates were aware in advance of their intention and were going to lie in wait to give them a lesson they would never forget.[3] "The rumor drifting back to Fernandina was to the effect that although the colored troops were defeated and lost heavily in the scrap yet they landed against heavy odds and faced the music beyond the expectation of their most ardent friends. The story floated around that some of the ex-slaves in blue uniform faced their old masters in Confederate butternut-colored uniform and in such cases the scrapping was terrific."[4] Though the Volunteers "were defeated," at least they were given credit for being able to fight, especially "against heavy odds." This was the most important aspect of the "rumor," that they were gaining credibility as soldiers even if the facts were twisted around.

Another aspect that needs to be mentioned in light of the 1st South Carolina's success, based upon the rumor of defeat before the facts were known, is that Tourtellotte said Colonel Hawley was ready to go after the Rebels. "Colonel Joe's anti-slavery sympathies were badly strained and he raved for the opportunity to turn the Seventh Connecticut loose and avenge our colored brothers." However, there were subordinate officers in his command who did not share in his opinion on black soldiers. "Lieutenant-Colonel Gardner, Captain Gray, and other officers less pronounced were McClellan democrats and laughed in their sleeves but did not hanker to take up the gauntlet on the color line."[5]

Shortly after the return of the *John Adams* and its tired passengers, more opportunities fell into their laps. Since it had been the original intent of the St. Mary's expedition to obtain lumber, the 1st S.C. would now be able to accomplish two more objectives in conjunction with its primary one. Colonel Hawley had previously received a letter from the War Department to ascertain the feasibility of obtaining bricks for Fort Clinch, based upon a request to the department by the resident engineer at the installation, Captain Alfred F. Sears. The bricks would be obtained from the place up the St. Mary's that had originally supplied the material to the U.S. Army when the fort had been under construction years earlier.[6] He showed this letter to Higginson to see if he would be interested in doing this. Since the brickyard was on the way to the place called Woodstock on the Georgia side, which Corporal Sutton had said had a large supply of lumber, Higginson agreed to do it. Commander Hughes also asked Higginson if he could find out the status of a Confederate blockade runner called the *Berosa* "said to be lying somewhere up the river," so Hughes could inform Admiral Du Pont. He agreed to do this too. With these objectives in mind, he set about getting ready for another foray up the river.

For the next two days the 1st South Carolina made preparations.[7] The wounded were offloaded the evening of their return in anticipation that Dr. Rogers would be able to get mattresses for them, but this did not happen. He was able to procure a bale of hay "so that now our men are about as comfortably placed as if they were in a hospital." Private Parsons' body had already been taken off for later interment. The men were able to catch up on their sleep. They were resupplied with ammunition, plus other accouterments that had been lost or destroyed from their first engagement, if possible. The *John Adams* took on a resupply of 20 tons of coal, courtesy of Commander Hughes. The lumber from St. Mary's was transferred to the *Ben De Ford*.[8] Sandbags obtained from Fort Clinch were added to the pilothouse to reinforce it in addition to the thick wooden planks already there. After the lumber had been transferred, 200 men were then loaded onto the *John Adams*, plus a company to work the guns on the deck; they were trained by Lieutenants William Stockdale and James B. O'Neil, "both being accomplished artillerists." With everything finally ready, "at seven o'clock in the evening of January 29th beneath a lovely moon, we steamed up the river."

Colonel Higginson had wanted to take the *Planter* too, but her engine continued to give her problems, so he decided to send her on an easier mission on the 28th, thus causing him to alter his plans. First he sent her back to St. Mary's to pick up some brick the *John Adams* did not previously get;[9] then to find an extensive salt works operation along the Crooked River in Georgia, which parallels the St. Mary's a few miles north. For the *Planter*'s mission Higginson sent Captain Trowbridge's Company A and Captain James S. Rogers' Company F. Dr. Minor was sent also along.

As the *John Adams* moved upstream, the picket station that first alerted Camp Cooper three nights prior sent a rider again to warn Captain Clarke that "the same Gunboat passed up again." After getting word that she was on the move again, he only had twenty men this time to saddle up. Though the evidence does not say it, he was probably more cautious this time moving to the river, until he got word from the picket station at Township Landing that the gunboat was "this time, however, continuing up." When he got the updated information from the second one, Clarke proceeded at a picked-up pace, passing through where Company K had first skirmished with the 1st South Carolina, and went directly to the bluff near Township to lay in wait for the boat to return down river.[10] Since Waterman's Bluff was to the right of Township, Clarke probably told the picket station to warn him if the boat landed there again at the dock, so his small contingent would not be cut off from its only escape route.

The part of the river over which the bluff looked was "about 200 yds wide, may be not even 150," which would enable the *John Adams* to stay clear as much as possible from Company K's rifle fire, as opposed to the bluffs further up on the Georgia side where the river was narrower and more crooked, thus making it harder for the gunboat to maneuver. The only thing the boat could do would be to fire her big guns in preparation as she came up to each bluff and then run the gauntlet of fire as she passed each one.

While the first picket rider was on his way to warn Captain Clarke of the *John Adams*' passing, Colonel Higginson was in heavy contemplation of venturing up the river for the first time. Though he had been told what to expect from others' experiences, doing it for the first time himself was still somewhat mysterious. As the gunboat moved up the river, he said it had a fascinating appearance. Higginson said:

> Never shall I forget the mystery and excitement of the night. I know nothing in life more fascinating, than the nocturnal ascent of an unknown river, leading far into an enemy's country, where one glides in the dim moonlight between dark hills and meadows, each turn of the channel making it seem like an island lake, and cutting you off as by a

barrier from all behind,—with no sign of human life, but an occasional picket-fire left glimmering beneath the bank, or the yelp of a dog from some low-lying plantation.

While the gunboat moved upriver, Dr. Rogers wrote that "again we are on our way into the heart of secesh. If we do not get blown to pieces before morning we shall get some distance above where any of our gunboats have been within a year."

Captain Clarke knew that the 4th Georgia Cavalry was already on alert, since its picket station at St. Mary's saw the gunboat travel upstream. The regiment would monitor its movements and take up defensive positions on the bluffs on the Georgia side of the river as required to counter the *John Adams'* return trip. With this in mind, he and his men settled down to wait for what would be a long night.

As Clarke had correctly surmised, the pickets at St. Mary's of Captain George C. Dent's Company D, 4th Georgia Cavalry,[11] saw the Yankees go upriver. One of his soldiers, William Penniman, said, "Couriers were sent for reinforcements and a couple of small brass howitzers in Waynesville, fully forty miles away." He also said the 4th's Colonel Clinch was at a place called "Brush Fort on the St. Mary's River when the news was received."

Though Colonel Higginson had a fascination with "the mystery and excitement of that night," he knew also he was going into harm's way. "I fear no attack during our ascent,—that danger ... [is] ... in our return." Before he could experience what the *Ottawa* had on her return trip the previous year, the *John Adams* had to navigate the tortuous waters of the St. Mary's River. After the 1st S.C. passed the area of its first engagement, now referred to as the battle of the Hundred Pine by Higginson's subordinate officers, the river began to take on an ominous character. The river started to curve more, the banks became steeper with protruding branches, and drift wood had to be contended with. Fortunately for Higginson, he had two advantages: one was Corporal Sutton, who as a slave had navigated the river numerous times and knew it well; the other was the *John Adams* herself. A side wheel steamer whose use before the war was as a ferryboat designed for northern waters, she could use her "powerful paddles, built to break the Northern ice, ... [to] ... crush the Southern pine as well."

Several times the boat had to navigate several sharp turns by running "the bow boldly on shore, let the stern swing around, and then reverse the motion." Eight times the gunboat became grounded in the river's upper waters, one time for forty minutes, but was always able to extricate herself. During this time, she was towing a flatboat that had been procured at St. Simon's Island prior to arriving at Fernandina. Dr. Rogers said of his experience: "This river is rebellious to the last degree. It is very crooked and sluggish and black and got us aground so many times in the long, sleepless night that rebel pickets might have picked off many of our men and officers. Again and again we had to turn points at right angles and we were never more than two rods from one or the other shore. Often the sides of our boat were swept by the boughs of the mournful looking trees."[12] Though there were "moments of tolerably concentrated anxiety," the *John Adams* finally made it to her objective about an hour before daylight,[13] having traversed about 30 miles of a tortuous river.

Arriving after the moon had set, Colonel Higginson began loading men into the flatboat. It was his intent to quietly surround Woodstock so nobody could leave once they knew the 1st South Carolina was there. He gave this assignment to Major Strong, who carried it out with Captain L. W. Metcalf's Company G and Captain William James' Company B. Strong's instructions also included to "molest no one, and to hold as temporary prisoners every [white] man whom he found." His detachment had to take turns in the flatboat to get everyone on the ground so they could surround the area. While Higginson waited for daylight before commencing the next phase of the landing, he "paced the deck for an hour in silent watchfulness, waiting for rifle-shots."

However, nothing happened in reaction to Strong's presence. When Higginson landed with the follow-on forces after sunrise, he found "a line of red legs round every house in the village" and a small group of males as prisoners, "stunted and forlorn" looking. His men were gleeful at these men's dejected look, and were all the more amused at the women's indignant reaction to their presence, one of whom was the mill owner, a Mrs. Alberti. One of the men taken prisoner was a Mr. Bessent, a former business partner of the owner's deceased husband, E. R. Alberti. Bessent "was at the house on a visit, ill with chronic bronchitis. He, being an important person, must be made prisoner, unless too feeble to be removed from the house. [Dr. Rogers] found, on examination, that he could be taken with us, without danger to himself." Bessent's daughter was there also as Rogers examined him, "too angry to sit down, standing with averted head in the background."

When he landed after Higginson, Rogers observed that:

> very few officers have voluntarily dared such a responsibility as that resting on our Colonel, but he patiently and vigilantly met all the obstacles and had his pickets and skirmishers so arranged … [they] were so placed that there was no escape for the white families at Alberti's Mills. The Col. had gone ashore and a little after sunrise sent for me to go off and take with me some copies of the President's proclamation. I found a little village, all included in the Alberti's estate and the mansion was occupied by madame Alberti and her family.

In viewing the small area with its different size buildings, Colonel Higginson was amazed at what he saw. As Corporal Sutton had promised when he first mentioned to his commander as to what he would find here, there was "lumber enough to freight half a dozen steamers." Higginson was so taken aback by what he saw that he somewhat regretted he had promised Colonel Hawley to take on a load of bricks, since his original intent had been to travel here only for lumber. Higginson said they would have to leave about fifty thousand dollars' worth of lumber, "such as cannot be bought for money now—Southern pine." He also found other things that could almost make anybody forget about the lumber.

Higginson said, "Along the river-bank I found building after building crowded with costly furniture, all neatly packed, just as it was sent up from St. Mary's when the town was evacuated." Though it was very intoxicating just to think about such easy pickings, he remained vigilant to his policy of not taking anything that was not of military value. This was hard on many of his men who had families in Fernandina or Beaufort that were destitute, but "when this abstinence was once recognized as a rule, they claimed it as an honor, in this and all succeeding expeditions."[14] The only things that were taken were beds and bedding for the hospitals as selected by Dr. Rogers, plus an old flag and an old artillery fieldpiece.

Though he felt momentarily overwhelmed by the opportunity that lay before him, Colonel Higginson realized he had a job to do, and he set about getting it done, which was lumber. Besides the amount he saw that was enough "to freight half a dozen steamers," there were also mills and lumber-wharves. Besides the buildings with the furniture, the one that stood out the most was the home of the owner, "a pretty one with picturesque out-buildings," and this is where Higginson went. Greeting him at the door was Mrs. Alberti. He said one "should have seen her come out to meet me on the step, as composedly as Goethe's Duchess met Napoleon. 'To what am I indebted for the honor of this visit, sir?'" Though she was the epitome of decorum in her initial greeting to Higginson, her demeanor quickly changed to one of repulsive indignation when she recognized the person next to him. Standing in front of her in Union Army uniform was her former slave. After Higginson introduced him as someone she should know, Mrs. Alberti "drew herself up, and dropped out the monosyllables of her answer as if they were so many drops of nitric acid. 'Ah, ... we called him Bob!'" Unfortunately for her, Mrs. Alberti's "Bob" was now Corporal Robert Sutton, 1st South Carolina Volunteers, United States Army.

Ignoring her sardonic retort, Corporal Sutton asked Higginson if he would like to see the slave jail in which rebellious slaves were kept, since Sutton had the keys to it. Higginson was glad that Mrs. Alberti's vicious remark had no effect on Sutton as he led the colonel to the building. What he saw inside shocked him: an ox-like chain for holding people down and stocks of various sizes, not only for men but women and children too. Seeing this building with its torturous means of punishment, Higginson later wrote that "I felt glad that my main interview with the lady proprietor had passed before I saw it." However, what he saw paled to what he was shown in another building near the first one. Inside was a device that neither allowed the punished to stand up or sit down, but be in a half-raised position. He said, "I remember the unutterable loathing with which I leaned against the door of that prison-house; I had thought myself seasoned to any conceivable horrors of slavery, but it seemed as if the visible presence of that den of Sin would choke me." Though the first thought by Higginson was to burn both buildings, he decided against it, since it "would have involved the sacrifice of every other building and all the piles of lumber." He took only the shackles and the keys to the jail and prepared to finish his mission at Woodstock.

The conversation between Higginson and Mrs. Alberti "rose into something more frankness when we parted—after I had just discovered the slave jail with its abominations & brought away its stocks and shackles. She & her husband ... had 'devoted themselves for years to training and elevating these poor people.'" Dr. Rogers said that:

> Madame Alberti spent much time trying to convince me that she and her husband had been wonderfully devoted to the interests of their slaves, especially to the fruitless work of trying to educate them. The truth of these assertions were disproved by certain facts,—such as a strong slave jail, containing implements of torture which we now have in our possession, (the lock I have), the fact that the slaves have "mostly gone over to the Yankees," and the yet other fact that Robert Sutton, a former slave there, said the statement was false.

Since Higginson had promised Colonel Hawley he would bring back to Fernandina as much brick as possible for Fort Clinch, he was limited in how much lumber he could load on the *John Adams*. Though space had to be reserved for the brick, he had other items loaded for military use: about 30 sheep, 40 bushels of rice, and provisions, plus tools and oars. Several slaves who were there also went on board, while an elderly couple elected to remain. The men who were rounded up in the initial landing were also placed on board, with the understanding that they would be released once the gunboat was out of danger, because none of them "were in uniform," but this did not prove that they were not soldiers.

While all of this was going on, 1st S.C. pickets reported they saw Confederate cavalrymen in the woods monitoring their activities with the expressed intent of reporting when they left so the Rebels would be ready on the bluffs. Higginson decided at this juncture against going further up the river to ascertain the status of the Confederate vessel, the *Berosa*, because of a "dangerous boom which kept back a great number of logs in a large brook that fell into the St. Mary's; the stream ran with force, and if the Rebels had wit enough to do it, they might in ten minutes so choke the river with drift-wood as infinitely to enhance our troubles."

Using discretion to avoid a possible catastrophe, Higginson moved back downstream to the place where he could obtain the required bricks. The Volunteers shortly landed at the "brickyard," finding it resplendent with the desired item. While they worked for several hours loading the *John Adams* to capacity, Higginson found out some more information on the enemy. After questioning several black and white people, he was able to ascertain the effectiveness of his unit against Company K, 2nd Florida Cavalry. He found out that a company officer, Lieutenant John D. Jones, was killed, plus "ten of their number ...,—though this I fancy to have been an exaggeration." They also told him that the Confederates admitted for the first time "a repulse at Township Landing." Dr. Rogers said that he was "told that thirteen riderless horses went back to camp after that fight in the woods the other night. That the lieutenant in command and five others were killed and many others wounded." Higginson was also told that the *Berosa* was much further upstream and not seaworthy.

Just as the 1st South Carolina had deployed its men at Woodstock, designated pickets took up positions at the brickyard once they landed to prevent any surprise attack. Sometime while the loading was going on, the pickets again reported Rebel soldiers in the woods watching them work. Also just as at Woodstock, it was the mission of the 4th Georgia scouts only to monitor the Union activity because to attack in any way would have been unwise, since they were greatly outnumbered. Once the Volunteers loaded all they could, the pickets were withdrawn to the boat and the men prepared to leave.

Since the return trip would be a gauntlet of gunfire, Higginson decided to keep only a minimum of men on deck, because he "did not propose to risk a life unnecessarily." The gun crews were readied at their stations while the Volunteers were placed in the crowded hold below. It had only a few portholes in which they could engage the enemy. This was done much to their annoyance; they wanted to take on the Rebels, but Higginson was adamant in his decision to minimize casualties. As the gunboat moved back downstream, he said that "their officers, too, were eager to see what was going on, and were almost as hard to cork down as the men." Since the *John Adams* was very crowded, there was just so much room to move around in, and Higginson had to be on the upper deck with the pilots.

Though he had control of the officers and men, he had no control of the boat's civilian commander, Captain Jack Clifton. With no sign of the enemy as the gunboat passed the first of the Georgia bluffs,[15] Clifton came out of the pilothouse "and exposed himself conspicuously on the upper deck." Higginson admitted himself that at this point everybody seemed to get into a false state of security as they passed the first one with no sign of the enemy.[16] Shortly after this Higginson decided to go lie down in a small room near the upper deck, since he had been going for almost 24 hours. However, no sooner than he had done this when the Confederates quickly made it known to the Volunteers that they were getting ready to run the gauntlet of Rebel musketry as the *John Adams* came within range at the next bluff.

Ever since the picket station of Company D, 4th Georgia Cavalry, saw the *John Adams* go up the river as she passed St. Mary's the previous night, scouts had been monitoring her activities.[17] When the Volunteers left Fernandina about 7 o'clock that evening, it was probably between 7:30 and 8 that the Georgia pickets saw the gunboat pass them. Just like the rider who reported back to Camp Cooper on the Florida side, the picket station at St. Mary's dispatched a rider back to Company D's base camp, "a place called 'Dark Entry,' five miles from the St. Mary's ..."[18] The unit's commander, Captain George W. Dent, then probably sent a small contingent to see if the boat was going to land in Florida again or somewhere on the Georgia side, which meant going further up the river, since there was not anything of significant value past Township in Florida. In anticipation of finding that the gunboat did go further up the river, Dent most likely got the rest of his men prepared to ride and take up positions on the bluffs. So until he received confirmation (which was not long in coming), he probably had his men in a ready-to-ride mode. Once Dent got the word that the *John Adams* did in fact pass Township, he ordered his men to mount up and moved out along trails that paralleled the river to take up prepared positions on the bluff where Dent decided to first engage her. Once they got there, they settled down to wait for the enemy's return.

While the rest of Company D waited, the scouts Captain Dent sent out to ascertain the intent of the Yankee gunboat were on the move to find out where the Federals intended to land and for what purpose, so they could report back to him. Though the record does not state it, the scout patrol either waited for Dent and the rest of the company to come up after reporting that the gunboat had passed Township to receive further orders to move further upriver, or they already had their instructions to continue after finding out that Township had been bypassed. Either way, the scouts moved on a parallel trail to see where the enemy was going. Based upon the evidence at hand, the only two places that the Yankees would have any interest in were the brickyard and Woodstock. Whether the scouts sent back a report that she passed the brickyard or waited until that they confirmed a landing before sending it is conjecture. One thing, however, is certain. The Volunteers beat the Rebels to Woodstock, else the people there would have been warned.

After the *John Adams* left Woodstock, the Rebels went in to find out what happened from Mrs. Alberti that they could not see from their observation point at the edge of the woods; also to learn whether anybody knew where the Yankees were going next. Once they ascertained the information they could, it was dispatched to Captain Dent. He also received word of the activity at the brickyard. When he heard that the gunboat would be arriving soon at the first bluff they were on, he got his men ready to fire on her. As the *John Adams* came within musket range, the cavalry troopers of the 4th Georgia let loose a salvo that quickly dispelled the lethargic state of mind into which the men and crew of the boat had been lulled.

The sudden deluge of fire from the bluff on the left side of the *John Adams* as she traveled downstream was devastating. There was "a mingling of shout and roar and rattle as of a tornado let loose." Being startled by this unexpected enemy contact, Colonel Higginson scrambled out of the small room he was in and back out onto the gun deck. The attack galvanized his men also. He said that "as a storm of bullets came pelting against the side of the vessel, and through a window, there went up a shrill answering shout from our own men." They surged forward out of the hold and onto the deck on both ends of the gunboat. The Volunteers fired with great rapidity, though it was hard for them to aim, given the vessel proved to be an unsteady platform to shoot from as she "glided and whirled in the … current."

In concurrence with the gun crews as they fired their heavy ordnance at the enemy on the high ground, the Volunteers continued to fire while shouting to each other, "Nebber gib it up!"

Though the men were glad to be on the gun deck firing at the Confederates irrespective of being fully exposed, Higginson was determined not to have any needless casualties. He forced them back down into the hold with the aid of his officers. The men were still able to fire from the portholes just above the waterline, though this paled in comparison with being on the deck. Fortunately for them there were no casualties while they were on top.

As Higginson worked frantically to get his men under control, Major Strong came down from the upper deck "in the midst of the mêlée" to inform him that the gunboat's civilian commander had been killed in the first volley from the Rebels. Contemplating panic if this became known among the men and passengers, Strong whispered this information of Captain Clifford's death to him "with a face of horror." As if he had been told that the boat had caught fire, "the shock would hardly have been greater." Though the sudden news caught him off guard, Higginson realized that there was a certain amount of risk and exposure to enemy fire for the captain in the piloting of his boat. He also became aware that in the midst of shock and horror of combat, one has to keep his poise and think clearly. So he told Strong to continue to be quiet about Clifford's death and then went to the upper deck himself to secure the body "from further desecration and then looked to see where we were."

The Confederate deluge from the high ground that pelted the side of the *John Adams* was the first of numerous volleys that the gunboat's crew and passengers were to experience as she traversed the river back downstream.[19] The 4th Georgia's William Penniman described what happened when the gunboat passed the Rebels' first position. He said:

> At Clark's Bluff the banks are almost perpendicular for fifty to sixty feet and the stream quite narrow.[20] The boys were in rifle pits on the bluffs and as the boat was passing they peppered the decks and pilot house... As the man in the pilot house must have been shot, at any rate the boat stuck its nose in the bank and but for the quick action of her officers would have swung across the stream and been at the mercy of the squad, but she was backed off and steerage was again gotten upon her. But, just as it was being accomplished, an officer came out on deck, exposing himself, and was immediately shot down, it was said by H.D.B.[21] Hand grenades were thrown,[22] but the elevation was such that they did not reach the boys and their guns were, of course, useless until they had sailed well down the river, when they opened fire and shelled the woods half way to St. Marys, doing no damage whatever.

After passing the first hail of Rebel gunfire almost unscathed, there was a period of quietude as the *John Adams* moved further down the river. However, this did not mean the rest of the trip was to be uneventful. During this time Higginson said that while the gunboat was "gliding past a safe reach of marsh ... our assailants were riding by cross-paths to attack us at the next bluff."[23] As she came up to the next one, her guns fired upon the high ground, but this did not stop the men of the 4th Georgia Cavalry from again raking the side of the boat. While this was going on, the Volunteers below were getting very impatient. "My men were now pretty well imprisoned in the hot and crowded hold, and actually fought each other, the officers afterwards said, for places at the open port holes, from which to aim." Though many implored their officers to land, so the Volunteers "might be 'fightin' de Secesh in de clar field,'" Higginson was

River Raid: This is a representation of elements of the 4th Georgia Cavalry engaging the *John Adams* and the Volunteers. *Courtesy of the Amelia Island Museum of History, Fernandina Beach, Florida*

adamant in not unnecessarily risking his men. "This clear field, and no small favor, was what they thenceforward sighed for. But in such difficult navigation it would have been madness to think of landing." However, contrary to this, thinking in a single act of bravery (or stupidity, depending upon how one looks at it), he said an enterprising Rebel was able to jump onto the barge the gunboat was towing,[24] only to be shot and killed by one of the unit's sergeants.

As the gunboat continued downstream, the Rebels refused to give up on her. Taking aim at her whenever possible, they were able to penetrate several times the heavy planks nailed onto the pilothouse. Nobody inside was hurt, neither Corporal Sutton, who manned the wheel, nor the first mate who took over after Captain Clifton was killed. The heavy gun crews on deck also came through unscathed.[25] They did their best to help keep the 4th Georgia off balance. Higginson said that "as we approached some wooded bluff, ... we could see galloping along the hillside what seemed a regiment of mounted riflemen, and could see our shell scatter them ere we approached." One of the gun crew commanders, Corporal Adam Allston, put it very religiously in describing later to Higginson what he experienced while this was going on: "'When I heard,' he said, 'de bombshell ascreamin' troo de woods like de Judgement Day, I said to myself, 'If my head was took off tonight, dey couldn't put my soul in de torments, percepts ... God was my enemy!' And when de rifle-bullets came whizzin' across de deck, I cried aloud, 'God help my congregation! Boys, load and fire!'" This was the pattern of action that occurred as the *John Adams* approached Waterman's Bluff, where Captain Clarke's Company K, 2nd Florida Cavalry, laid waiting.

Company K had been ready for a while for the arrival of the *John Adams*, since the men could hear the musketry of the Georgia troopers as they engaged the enemy raiders. With Waterman's Bluff sitting about 30 feet above the river, it had a good view of the area, though not as good as the 50-foot Clark's Bluff. Its main disadvantage, as opposed to the sharp and narrow turns that Clark's commanded, was that this sector of the river was "about 200 yds wide, maybe not even 150," which gave the gunboat more room to maneuver away from this bluff.

The clerk of Company K, Davis Bryant, said that the *John Adams* "came down with a rush at about dark, but the moon was full and shining brightly, shelling and graping as she came, and I can tell ... it felt kind of funny when they were passing around, for she had a long sweep at us, and directed her fire at the Bluff as soon as she came into range." However, as the gunboat got near the enemy, Higginson said that the cannonading "did not ... prevent a rather fierce fusillade from our old friends of Captain Clark's company at Waterman's Bluff."

Bryant said that "when she came within good shot the Capt. fired the signal gun at her and we all opened on her, and continued until she passed out of range when she checked down and cut away at us with a vengence [*sic*], when we 'changed base,' and waited till she was satisfied and went on down." Though Captain Clarke's twenty-man contingent gave it all they could, Higginson said that "even this did no serious damage, and this was the last." There was no more enemy action reported, even as the gunboat passed St. Mary's on her way back to Fernandina.

After Action

The raid on Woodstock had placed the Rebels in a heightened state of alert. Two trips in three days and not knowing what to expect next could only make them think that there was more to come. Anticipating further Yankee activity, other units were pulled from their assigned duties to bolster Confederate effectiveness. As far as the Rebels might have been concerned, these two excursions could have been just to test the strength of their defensive capabilities as a prelude for a larger operation in that area. However, when that did not materialize, the heightened Rebel vigilance started to wane, and soon the majority of the reinforcements left, with only a small contingent left on the Florida side.

On January 31, 1863, the day after the raid, while waiting for more Union aggression, William Penniman of Company D, 4th Georgia Cavalry, said that his unit heard about Captain Clifton's death: "The flags at Fernandina were half masted and we heard that the officer killed was a Captain, a brother of the actress 'Maggie Mitchell'!" Davis Bryant of Company K, 2nd Florida Cavalry, said that his unit got wind of Clifton's death a few days later "from some St. Augustine people who had been expelled from the place by the yanks we learn that we, at least killed a Captain of theirs, as they learn in Fernandina, gave the particulars, so I don't doubt it ..."

The Confederate reinforcements that arrived soon found out that their deployment to the river became an exercise in futility. When the elements of the 4th Georgia that were ordered to deploy anticipated contact with the enemy, they were disappointed.[1] Penniman said, "By the time they arrived the gunboat had gone ... and returned down the river." Several days later, Colonel Clinch, the 4th's commander, saw that it looked like nothing further was going to happen, so "we returned to our several camps, resuming our coast and picket duty ..." Clinch complimented the Volunteers later when he wrote that his regiment got "into a hot fight with a gunboat and some negro troops."

In Florida, reinforcements were soon on the way after Camp Finegan received word from Cooper. They were Captain Winston Stephens' Company B, 2nd Florida Cavalry; a 30-man detachment from Captain William Chambers' Company C, also 2nd Florida Cavalry; and a battery of the Milton (Florida) Light Artillery, which had two 12-pound howitzers, two 6-pound rifled pieces, and 65 men. Davis Bryant said that these extra assets came "to guard the St. Mary's river, as we had reason to believe the yankee boat intended going up (again) after a quantity of lumber and other stuff ..."

Captain Stephens said he received word on February 1 after he and his unit had been sent on another mission, when a courier arrived to say that Company B needed to return. Writing to his wife on the 2nd, he said that he was to leave shortly for Kings Ferry, another pre-war lumber point on the Florida side of the St. Mary's, which was near Woodstock. This would put the Rebels in an excellent tactical position to take on the *John Adams* again, but this time with many more rifles, four artillery pieces, and the fact that there was little or no room for the gunboat to maneuver in this part of the river. Stephens said that he "was up all night and now I am ready for a ten day trip. The telegram states that some boats had gone up the St. Mary's and that the troops in Ga. had a battery behind them & I am with my Co & a section of Dunham's battery & Capt Clark has orders to join me at this ferry. From all I can learn I will have the command on this side ..."

However, Captain Stephens returned seven days later in a less than happy mood. Writing again to his wife on February 8, he said that:

> I am again in this Camp (Finegan) after a week of hard labour, on last Sunday I started on a scout and that night I was overtaken and sent on one of much length and importance but which failed of accomplishing the object for which it was set out. It seems that a steamer went up the St. Marys [*sic*] and had on 150 negroes and some white men, they landed at Alberti's Mills near Kings Ferry and carried off some negroes, some sheep, some provisions and carried on a general thieving expedition and went out before we even got the word. It cost me a weeks hard riding when I had two large boils which made it anything but pleasant.[2]

Captain Chambers' 30-man contingent and the 65-man battery of the Milton Light Artillery remained behind, moving back to Camp Cooper with Company K until further notice to significantly bolster its reaction ability in the event of any more enemy river activity.

When Davis Bryant got back to Camp Cooper, he learned the details of the second Yankee trip up the river. On February 14, he wrote to one of his brothers who was serving in Tennessee that:

> this time they went to up Alberti's Mill took several old gentlemen prisoners who happened to be visiting there, surrounding the house at night, took off all the provisions & stock of Mrs Alberti's and every thing they could lay hands on, and what makes it most maddening is they were all nigger soldiers, officered by white men. It is said by those of the neighborhood there were at least 250 of them. It was undoubtedly the same lot that attempted to take our Camp, that I have given you an account of. What do you think of that, I guess however, it is … fortunate for us they were niggers.

In another letter to his wife later on the 24th, Stephens came to a momentous conclusion when he said that "the Federals are placing the black troops among the white ones and that is creating so much dissatisfaction that they are afraid to risk an engagement with our forces at this point." He also said that "I find on the Mississippi that they are throwing black Regiments with the whites & that the officers are resigning & the troops are so demoralized that they are afraid to risk battle, I think we are on the eve of Armastice [*sic*] & then Peace." For Davis Bryant to think that "fortunate for us they were niggers" and not white soldiers, and for Winston Stephens to conceptualize that whites would not fight with blacks—how wrong both would be in the upcoming weeks.

One thing that Colonel Higginson had meant to do while returning downriver was to put on shore somewhere the seven men he had taken prisoner at Woodstock, but he was unable to due to the constant gunfire from the Rebels, so the men had to remain on the *John Adams* while she continued on to Fernandina.[3] He did not even stop at St. Mary's, because he anticipated that the Confederates would be lying in ambush again, this time in force. He said, "I could only explain to them that they must thank our friends due to their inevitable detention."

Once the *John Adams* returned to Fernandina, Higginson wanted the post commander, Colonel Hawley, to take the prisoners off his hands, so they could be expatriated back to Confederate control. Though he thought that it would make sense just to drop them off in Fernandina, then simply allow them to cross over into Rebel-held territory, Higginson assumed incorrectly. Hawley did not want to take them over, because "he was sending no flags of truce at this time."[4] Higginson even tried to bribe him; he "offered to get his wife another piano,[5] if he would, but the 7th Ct. have their full piano rations already & the bribe was vain." Higginson offered

Hawley several of the sheep he had "liberated" at Woodstock, but "but even mutton didn't move him."[6] The appearance of the prisoners did not help either: "I felt ashamed of them, to keep them, they were such forlorn specimens ... though the men say they are a fair type of the whole." Their ragged look helping to seal their fate, Higginson had to take the prisoners back to Port Royal.[7]

After the Volunteers returned they were met by Captain Trowbridge, who had just completed his mission[8] of finding an extensive saltworks[9] operation along the Crooked River[10] in Georgia several miles north of the St. Mary's. Colonel Higginson said, "Finding that works at Kings Bay,[11] formally [sic] destroyed by this regiment, had never been rebuilt, they proceeded 5 miles up Crooked River, where salt-works were seen. Captain Trowbridge, with Captain Rogers' company (F) and 30 men, then marched 2 miles across a marsh, drawing a boat with them, then sailed up a creek and destroyed the works.[12] There were 22 large boilers, 2 storehouses, a large quantity of salt, 2 canoes, with barrels, vats, and all things appertaining."

Since the *Planter*'s engine capability was at best marginal, it required much attention just to keep it going. Higginson said her "worn-out machinery would have made her perfectly valueless but for the laborious efforts of Captain Elderidge and her engineer, Mr. Burker, aided by the unconquerable energy of Captain Trowbridge ... who had command on board. Thanks to this they were enabled ... to pay attention to the salt-works along the coast."

Just like the first time when the Volunteers returned on January 27, there was confusion again in the facts as to what happened when they returned on the 30th. Captain Tourtellotte, Company K, 7th Connecticut, said that:

this time the colored soldiers were aboard the steamer, *John Adams*, a double-ended ferry boat of large size and powerful engines. Defeat number two were scored, with the loss of the steamer's captain and eleven negro soldiers ... The Captain was well-known as an ambitious man of reckless bravery and for this reason had been chosen as a man that would not flinch with his vessel in an effort to make the expedition a success. We were within hearing of the scrimmage but not in a position to lend a helping hand owing to a lack of water transportation. How so many rumors could float without life preservers was a conundrum as we were surrounded by rivers and islands. But the air was chock full of uncomplimentary reports.

A soldier over in Company E heard both some fact and fiction. Writing a letter home on the 30th, John L. Rawley said:

the *Planter* and *John Adams* a ferry boat have been reconnoitering up the St Maries [sic] river they captured 6 guerillas a portion of the negro Brig were all the troops that were there a captain of a cavalry company was master of some of them and was immediately killed they hated to have the negroes guard them so they would not eat any thing [sic] for 36 hours when they eat a very little, one beged [sic] of them to shoot him rather than have nigers [sic] guard him.

As a result of his raid, Colonel Higginson said he was able to turn over to Captain Sears at Fort Clinch nearly 40,000 bricks.[13] He also gave to the civil provost marshal at Fernandina, Judge J. M. Latta,[14] four horses, four steers,[15] and the agricultural implements for their use. "I have also eight large sticks of valuable yellow-pine lumber, said to be worth $1700, which came from Saint Mary's, Ga. There is also a quantity of rice, resin, cordage, oars, and other small matters suitable for army purposes." On the *John Adams* were 25 of the roughly 30 sheep.[16] With "our commodities being full, coal nearly out, and time up," the 1st South Carolina left Fernandina on Sunday, February 1.

The return trip to Beaufort for the officers and men of the Volunteers was one of recuperating from an emotional drain. Though the men had been willing to stop along the river and engage the 4th Georgia Cavalry, and had previously surged up on the deck of the *John Adams* to fire back when the 4th first fired at them, knowing that they had just experienced a life-or-death situation had to have hit them after they returned to the safety of Union lines on January 30. Since they were finally able to relax from their previous exertions of vigilance, these coupled with their lack of sleep left them both physically and mentally exhausted.[17] They were so wound up after their success that it probably took them some time before they could even sleep. Fortunately for the men, Colonel Higginson allowed them 24 hours of down time before they left on the 1st. Dr. Rogers wrote the night before they left that:

while I keenly enjoy these moonlight excursions I find that like rising at three o'clock in the morning to go for pond lilies, one is satisfied with about three trips a week. You can imagime [sic] a little what an immense tax such a life makes up on the nervous system. But I find we sleep well as soon as the opportunity offers. This rough life of exposure in the open air puts an end to morbid excitability of the nerves, and one jumps at any reasonable change for a snooze.

The next day he did not have time to be tired because he had "a formidable sick list, the results of huddling so many men together in the hold of the *John Adams*, but I think nothing serious will come of it."

This exposure to combat also had to have been especially hard on the young officers, who, though having shared the same level of danger as the men, looked at fighting the Rebels from a different perspective. Both the officers and men saw the Confederates as the enemy, but to the officers they were just the enemy, whereas the men looked at them as former "masters" and had every reason to want to engage them more willingly. Though the officers did do their job, they were probably more relieved that the operation was over.

As the *Ben De Ford, John Adams*, and *Planter* moved back up the coast, they "called once more at St. Simon's Sound, bringing away the remainder of our rail road-iron, with some which the naval officers had previously disinterred."[18] The *Ben De Ford* was loaded with "250 bars of the best new railroad iron, valued at $5,000, and much needed in this department." After this was completed, the convoy continued on its way. As the ships left the sound, Dr. Boyer watched them go. Later in his diary he wrote: "Adieu, ye colored gentry of the 1st South Carolina Regiment of Volunteers. No serious objections to your remaining at Beaufort, SC."

As the ships were going back to Beaufort, several white officers and enlisted men went with them, since they had to go to Hilton Head Island. However, they were not too excited about being on the same boat with black soldiers. Dr. Rogers said "their prejudice against our soldiers is amusing. We happen to have command of this steamer and, of course, have the best places. I find white soldiers on deck rather than to go below with our men." The previous night on the 31st, a lieutenant going to Hilton Head tried to get two of the Volunteers to take his trunk to his cabin, but "he was rather informed by Lieut. West that United States soldiers were not to be called up on to do menial service."

Dr. Rogers said that another lieutenant told the commander of Company H, Captain George Dolly, a "rough and ready" individual that "'these niggers' never would fight much. Dolly, in his fearful way, said: 'You d—d fool; these soldiers have already fought more bravely than you ever will, you who have lived a couple of years on Uncle Sam without earning a cent for him.' The Lieut. did not think it safe to reply."

While the officers and men of the 1st South Carolina continued to regain a sense of normalcy, Higginson composed his report so he could turn it in to General Saxton once the convoy arrived back at home base.[19] To show his pride in what his unit accomplished, he began by saying, "I have the honor to report the safe return of the expedition under my command ..." He continued by saying that the "expedition has carried the regimental flag and the President's proclamation far into the interior of Georgia and Florida. The men have been repeatedly under fire; have had infantry, cavalry, and even artillery Arrayed against them,[20] and have in every instance come off not only with unblemished honor, but with undisputed triumph."

Higginson gave the particulars of each stage of the expedition.[21] He complimented all those who had a helping hand in the operation, plus those who either gave logistical support or advice as to what to expect. In one key reason for undertaking this operation, he was disappointed: "We found no large number of slaves anywhere ..." He credited the operation's success mostly to Corporal Sutton "of Company G, formally [*sic*] a slave upon the Saint Mary's River, a man of extraordinary qualities, who needs nothing but a knowledge of the alphabet to entitle him to the most signal promotion. In every instance when I followed his advice the predicted result followed,[22] and I never departed from it, however, without finding reason for subsequent regret."

Once Higginson had finished writing his report, he finally had time for more personal matters. At 9 p.m. that evening he composed a short letter to his mother. He gave a brief overview of his success. He also said with stark clarity that "we hv ... made one of the most daring expeditions of the war ... The men have behaved splendidly & I have enjoyed it inexpressibly. When the whole is known, it will establish past question the reputation of the regiment."

Sometime on the voyage back Dr. Rogers wrote a letter about the expedition:

> The colonel's daring bravery had deepened the love and admiration of his men and officers. I have been a constant source of annoyance to him by words of caution, but am happy to know that they were needed. The death of Capt. Clifton was a terrible confirmation of all I have said, and I doubt if the Major again puts himself unnecessarily in the way of so much danger. I could not get the ball that passed through the mess room where I was writing, but I picked one up in the prisoner's room, adjoining. Had we been the prisoners, our places would have been on the upper deck, where they begged we would not put them, and where no one dreamed of putting them. All of them, except Mr. Besent [*sic*], are now forward with the soldiers.

Dr. Rogers added also:

> Our expedition has been a capital success. We have had our soldiers three times under fire and know that they only care to face the enemy. We know also, that they can be trusted with the conquered foe. Not a single unbecoming act have I seen or heard of on part of the guards, skirmishers or pickets. It was not for want of temptation, and I am left to

wonder at their self control. The material benefit to the government, of
the expedition, is not inconsiderable.

The voyage took the rest of the night to make it back to home base. As the
sun rose on Monday the 2nd, the three ships arrived back in harbor. Once
they docked, the officers and sergeants had the men disembark and got them
ready to unload the cargo. The seven prisoners were led off for incarceration
until it was decided what to do with them. Meanwhile, Colonel Higginson
and Dr. Rogers left the *Ben De Ford* and proceeded to General Saxton's
quarters. Since he was already up, they presented to him in Higginson's one
hand the report of the expedition, and the keys and shackles of the Alberti
jail in his other. Higginson said Dr. Rogers described this scene as "a message
from heaven & one from hell ... [as Higginson] walked in to the Gen.l's bed
room & and left him reading the report."

When the 1st South Carolina returned to Camp Saxton, they were
greeted with enthusiasm. Dr. Rogers said that "the home troops were
receiving us with wild cheers of joy. All sorts of false rumors had been
reported concerning us. We had been cut up and cut down, hung and cut to
pieces and various other rebel morsels of information had been circulated
... Perhaps it is best for me to take this occasion to say that the rebel reports
are not always so reliable as their personal sympathizers could wish." Three
days later on the 5th, Lieutenant James B. O'Neil told Rogers "that during
the eight years of his military life in Texas, Utah and in the present war, he
had never been engaged in anything half so daring as our trip up the St.
Mary's River. He is one of our best officers and has seen much service."

As they settled back into camp, news of the Volunteers' success started
to filter among the islands of Port Royal. Charlotte Forten was elated when
she heard that Monday evening. Though the person who told her did not
have knowledge of the details of the expedition, Forten did find out that
they "came back with laurels and Secesh prisoners." When she found out
that Higginson and Rogers came through unscathed, she was particularly
moved. "In the joy of my heart sat down and wrote a congratulatory note,
to my dear friend, Dr. R. I knew how rejoiced he must be. Thank God that
he and the noble Col. have come back safe."

Laura Towne wrote later in her diary on Monday after getting the word
of the Volunteers' return: "The negro companies under Higginson have
fought well in Florida—four wounded. Captain Clifton killed." Though
the information was spread by many people, this also meant that the facts
could be garbled too. By the time Miss Towne received the news, she heard
also that "the soldiers—white ones—set fire to St. Mary's. Three colored
men were taken prisoners, and Higginson says if the rebels hang them he
will hang two whites for every one of them."

On the following Sunday, February 8, Harriet Ware wrote a letter that "Colonel Higginson's … expedition with the Black Regiment … was a great success." She described a former slave she knew who had deserted because of how he had been previously treated in the old Hunter Regiment and had probably felt that enlisting in the revitalized 1st South Carolina Volunteers would be the same: "January … was taken from here one night as a deserter, and who was found up his chimney, almost frightened to death at going back," since "he was so badly treated before." However, he was given a chance to redeem himself, and went on the expedition to Florida. When the regiment returned, January "came for a day or two since he got back from the expedition and told … he would not take a thousand dollars to leave now, he had such a good time."

The Northern missionaries and freedmen were very proud of the Volunteers, but none were more excited for their success than were the men of the regiment. Though they did not win any spectacular victory over the Confederates, they did sting them several times deep in their own territory and demonstrated to them that the black man as a Union soldier was going to be around, so they should expect more of the same. Colonel Higginson caught the feel of his men in their newly found pride when he wrote in his journal on February 4 after hearing his men describe the shock of the inhabitants at Woodstock that armed ex-slaves were in their midst: "I did not injure any thing [*sic*] except the feelings of the inhabitants, who did chafe at the complexion of my guards—blackguards—though the men behaved admirably—even one who threatened to throw an old termagant into the river took care to add the epithet 'Madam'—you would all laugh for 10 years if you could hear some of the descriptions the men give around the camp fires of their conversations with these women."

Esther Hill Hawks, wife of Dr. Hawks, said that Corporal Sutton was very elated in his first combat mission. And what made the experience all the more sweeter was the fact that he gave orders to his former mistress. She said, "It was a proud moment for Robert when he placed a guard of colored soldiers around the house of his former owner, 'Madam Alberti' and one of great rage to the good dame when she discovered the outrage, and heard her own nigger,[23] 'our Bob' give the order to shoot anyone who attempted to leave the house without his permission … It was great fun to hear Sutton tell the story, on his return to Camp."

On Saturday the 7th, Miss Forten wrote in her journal that another soldier told her and several others his experience of going up the St. Mary's.[24] She said no words could capture "the state of exultation and enthusiasm that he was in." To go from slave to freedman to Union soldier fighting for his and others' freedom in a matter of months was one of immense exhilaration. She asked him what would he do if his former master tried to re-enslave him. His reply reaffirmed her initial observation of him: "I'd fight um, Miss, I'd fight um till turned to dust." She also said how delighted he was as the reaction of the women at Woodstock, to see how aghast they were at the sight of the 1st South Carolina. The lady Rebels "vented their spleen by calling these men 'baboons dressed in soldiers clothes' and telling them that they ought to be at work in their master's rice swamp, and that they ought to be lashed to death. 'And what did you say to them:' I asked. 'Oh, miss, we only tell them 'Hole your tongue, and dry up.' 'You see we wasn't feared of dem, dey [cou] ldn't hurt us now. Whew! didn't we laugh ... to see dem so mad!' The spirit of resistance to the Secesh is strong in these men."

The next day on Sunday towards sunset, Dr. Rogers was visiting Miss Forten at her quarters. He brought along the notes he had made of the expedition to share with her. "Wasn't I glad to see him. He looked none the worse for his experiences." He told her they were written shortly after he had made his observations. "They are very interesting, more so to me even than Col. Higginson's excellent Report, (which the Dr. also brought) because entering into more particulars. They, and the report also, show plainly how nobly and bravely the black soldiers can fight. I am delighted. I think the contemptuous white soldiers will cease to sneer soon."

On Saturday the 21st, Miss Forten and Colonel Higginson were visiting Dr. Rogers in his tent when Corporal Sutton came in. She said it was very interesting to hear him describe the expedition's chain of events. "His manner is very simply and earnest and his words, full of eloquence and enthusiasm, flow forth with wonderful ease." She thought it was amusing to hear him say what would have happened if Higginson had listened to him. "'Now if de Cunnel had done so and so, as I told him, we c'ld a taken all dem rebels right off.'" Showing his complete respect for the corporal's knowledge and ability after his utterances, "the Col. bowed his noble head,[25] and acknowledged Robert's superior wisdom."

Listening to his men talk about the success of and their experiences in the St. Mary's operation left no doubt in Colonel Higginson's mind as to the viability of using former slaves as soldiers. He said, "Since my expedition however my hopes rest, far more exclusively than before, on the employment of negro troops." Their enthusiasm for wanting to take on the Confederates again was a direct result of their successful initial foray into combat. If there had been reservations among his subordinate officers before the expedition, these now had to have been erased. Higginson added, "No officer in this regiment now doubts that the key to the successful prosecution of this war lies in [their] unlimited employment. ..."

As for a personal note, Higginson wrote in his journal on February 15 how his first experience under fire had left a permanent imprint on him and his men:

Nothing can ever exaggerate the fascination of war; I hardly hear the crack of a gun without recalling instantly the sharp shots that spilled down from the bluffs at us, along the St. Mary's, or hear a sudden trampling of horsemen without remembering the moonlight & midnight when we were suddenly stopped by hearing it before us, at Township Landing. I never can write about those wakeful but dreamlike nights of moonlight it was all too good. My report to Ge. Saxton merely skimmed a few drops of cream & left the substance of the draught. As for the courage & all that, it is infinitely exaggerated—to stop furious runaway horses, to enter a burning house, to plunge into a boiling ocean, requires far more personal pluck than to have "dem dar bullets let loose after we" as my men describe it; the danger is so invisible, it is not nearly so hard to disregard it; I know what I say. Bomb shells are far worse, but we have only fired, not received them. Oh such superb & grotesque eloquence as I heard from some of our orators on the forward deck, as we came home after the "expeditious."

The key to the success of the expedition was the knowledge of the area by many of the men, since they knew it as slaves. A case in point was Corporal Sutton. He provided pertinent information that greatly added to the mission's overall success, especially his knowledge of the twists and turns of the St. Mary's River. Colonel Higginson wrote a fitting tribute concerning the importance of this local knowledge in his regimental history. He said, "So obvious, too, was the value, during this raid, of their local knowledge and their enthusiasm, that it was impossible not to find in its successes new suggestions for the war. Certainly I would not have consented to repeat the enterprise with the bravest white troops, leaving Corporal Sutton and his mates behind, for I should have expected failure."

To keep the momentum going, the question that had to be asked after the Volunteers returned to Beaufort was what would happen next. This had already been previously pondered by Dr. Rogers. Writing a letter the day after the regiment returned from Woodstock to Fernandina, he said that "we are more than ever satisfied that blacks must help us in this war. The next question to solve, is, how to penetrate far enough into the interior to free them. Possibly it remains for our regiment to solve this problem. Give us a gunboat and plenty of ammunition to help us into the midst of them and I think we may trust God and our determination for the result." Since one of the objectives of the St. Mary's operation failed to find any significant number of slaves, the regiment would get a chance "to solve this problem" one month later and "penetrate far into the interior."

Next Mission

On February 2, the day after the Volunteers returned, General Saxton wrote a brief letter to Secretary Stanton as an addendum to Colonel Higginson's report. His exuberance for the success of the 1st South Carolina's mission was clearly captured in his note to the secretary, specifically in his belief that it would be to the Union's advantage to tap into this vast reservoir of manpower. The success of Higginson's expedition "foreshadows clearly the very important advantage which might result to our cause by the extensive arming of the blacks." However, Saxton had to add that the availability of eligible males in the current Union-occupied sectors of the Confederacy, specifically in the Department of the South and 10th Corps, was quite limited. The bulk of the manpower reserves was still in Confederate-held territory. Though he said he was working hard to recruit more men, "the limited extent of our lines renders it impossible for them to get to me in any very great numbers."

Given this limitation of access to Union forces, Saxton implored Stanton that the next step was going to have to be extending Federal lines to the mainland. "The reestablishment of posts on the main-land would enable" more men to be recruited. He ended his letter by saying that in his opinion, "it would be no misapplication of the best energies of the Government should they now be directed toward the arming and disciplining of every one that can be brought within our lines." It was with this concluding sentence in Saxton's letter that the next major phase of the Volunteers' history began.

While General Saxton worked to find ways to increase the manpower pool by recruiting more blacks for the war effort, the schemers, the manipulators, and the war profiteers lurked in the shadows, waiting to take advantage of any military operation that could further them personally. As with his previous enterprises, Lyman Stickney continued to mix government business with opportunities to profit from them. He would not hesitate to manipulate people to achieve his goals, whether for political gain (Secretary of the Treasury Salmon P. Chase) or push for future military operations (General Saxton and Colonel Higginson).[1] He constantly looked for opportunity to apply his spurious trade. When he found out Saxton's plan to expand Union lines,[2] Stickney saw that another permanent Union base (like the South Carolina Sea Islands, Fernandina and St. Augustine) would enable him to reap the benefit that an occupation would entail. The end result that made his schemes morally bankrupt was the use of the Union soldier to help make them possible. The fact that the lives of men hung in the balance so he could profit had a repugnancy that reeked in the worse possible way. As historian David Coles aptly put it, "that whenever money could be made ..., Stickney was there to make it, and he was certainly not hesitant in using his public position to improve his personal finances." As he plotted under the official guise as head of the Florida Tax Commission, the events that led to the Volunteers' next mission unfolded.

In the days following the return of the Volunteers the routine of camp life settled in, with more drilling, picket duty, and other activities that kept the soldiers busy for the most part. There were also those who took advantage of the Northern school teachers to learn to read and write in their off-time. During this period, everybody was able to be reflective in some manner. On February 4, Colonel Higginson recorded in his journal some of his first thoughts after having commanded in combat for the first time. He said that:

> it was easy to see how little it costs to be courageous in battle. There are a thousand things that require far more daring; the reason being that the danger does not come home so vividly to the senses, in battle; there is the noise and smoke, and then besides, no matter how loud the bullets may whiz, so long as you are not hit, they don't mean you, and after they do mean you, it's too late to be frightened. To a person afraid of lightning, for instance severe storm is far more terrifying than a battle, because you sit <u>silent</u> waiting for the flash and wondering if the next will strike you— and you have not the excitement of flashing back again.

Higginson added:

> Our danger in such expeditions is not nearly so great as one would think, as we have cannon and the rebels have not, and they run from them. But, I think they would run away from our men, even without

the cannon—I should think they would—I should. They are perfectly formidable. That night in the woods they wanted to plunge off in pursuit of the enemy, which as it afterwards appeared, they might have done with safety; and coming down the river they were furious at being kept down below, "What for de Cunnel say <u>cease firing</u>, & de secesh blazing away <u>at de rate of ten dollars a day!</u>" They "supposed de Cunnel knowed best, but it was mighty mean to keep them shut in the hold, when de might be <u>shooting in de clar field</u>." They desired intensely to get on shore & fight it out.

Dr. Rogers wrote on the 5th that he:

would very much like to go up to Alberti's Mills again, with flat-boats enough to bring away lumber etc. and then set fire to what we could not take. There is not rebel force in that neighborhood to capture us. If they should block the passage by felling trees across the river, our boys would have the opportunity to do what they so much crave,—meet their old masters in "de cl'ar field." They besought me over and over, to ask "de Cunnel to let we spill out on de sho' an' meet dem fellers in the brush," There would have been bushwhacking of a startling nature and I have no doubt we could have brought off some of those cavalry horses, hitched in the rear. But the Col. is pretty economical of human life when no threat is at stake.[3]

On the afternoon of Saturday, February 7, Dr. Charles Edward Briggs and several officers of the 24th Massachusetts Infantry visited the camp to see a dress parade. He said the 1st South Carolina "numbered over 800 men and officers. They wore dark coats and red trousers. Our officers were much pleased with the drill. I was introduced to Col. T. W. Higginson. We inspected the field school-houses, thatched with palmetto leaves, where the non-commissioned officers were camped. We saw a little rust-eaten cannon, 'a nest egg for a battery,' said the colonel." Being impressed with what he saw, Dr. Briggs came to the conclusion that "this negro regiment was one of the most striking things in our country, particularly because of the courage and success of its officers."

While the routine of camp life settled in "since our own <u>expeditious</u> as the men always call it," improvements occurred for the Volunteers. By the 15th, the men had finally been able to exchange their red pantaloons for blue pants that Higginson had ordered to make them identical to the white regiments. He recorded his men's feelings of this exchange when he said that "the regiment goes on improving—now they hv. got blue pants which they like better than the odius [*sic*] red. They look very neat ..."[4]

Another officer was added to the unit on this day with the transfer of 2nd Lieutenant Niles G. Parker from the 1st Massachusetts Cavalry. Higginson said he "wanted a cavalry officer, as it may improve a great convenience; these men are such horsemen that we can extemporize a cavalry force whatever we capture the horses." On February 20, their weapons were upgraded. Though they did not get the Springfields that they had been promised, they were issued 1,000 of the Austrian Model 1854 Lorenz .54 cal. rifled muskets,[5] still giving them greater range and lethality.

The casualties from the St. Mary's operation continued to improve. Dr. Rogers said on February 5 that "Robert Sutton had quite recovered from his wounds. He told me that the flesh was healthy and I have found it so and the bone did not get involved." However, it was not the bombs and bullets which produced the most casualties; weather was the culprit.[6] He observed on the 7th that "keeping our men below so long on the *John Adams* destroyed more lives than the rifle shots would have done. It seemed a choice of evils and the least apparent was chosen. But the return of sunshine will help restore the sick." The next day he noticed that "our sick list is lessening and all will soon be as usual."

While the 1st South Carolina recovered, rearmed, and refitted from its first combat operation, the second regiment of ex-slaves began its second week of existence in the Department of the South and 10th Corps. Named the 2nd South Carolina Volunteers, the unit began when its newly authorized commander, Colonel James Montgomery,[7] arrived at Hilton Head on January 23 and received permission from General Hunter to recruit. Two days later when General Saxton wrote to Stanton that the 1st S.C. had completed its organization with about 900 officers and men, he also told him that "I have commensed [*sic*] the organization of the Second Regiment." Montgomery's orders from the War Department said that he was to get men from within South Carolina, but he quickly found out that this would not be very feasible after he arrived. Not having the advantage that Higginson had in being there first, he had to pick through what was left, minus the men who worked for the other government departments there. With the number of possible recruits scant, he had to look elsewhere.

Establishing his base camp beside that of the 1st Regiment, Montgomery obtained permission from General Hunter in early February to recruit in the one area of the Department of the South that had not been touched yet, Key West. Upon arriving there, he presented to the commanding officer, Colonel Joseph S. Morgan of the 90th New York Infantry, his authority to recruit and bring "on board the steamer 'Cosmopolitan,' every adult male negro between the ages of fifteen and fifty,[8] who is capable of bearing arms, to be found within your command." This order by Hunter was tantamount to the resumption of the draft.

Colonel James Montgomery, a follower of radical abolitionist John Brown. He would practice his own version of radical abolitionism later in the war. *Courtesy Kansas State Historical Society, Topeka*

As February progressed, no news had been received as to how Montgomery was doing in his efforts. On the 15th, while contemplating his regiment's next move, Higginson wrote that he had yet to hear anything from Key West. Eight days later on the evening of the 23rd, he finally heard the news that Montgomery had returned "with 125 men as the nucleus of the 2nd regiment."[9] With this core, Higginson said that "he will be sent with us wherever we go. Probably. His military experience will be of unspeakable value to me; how far our ideas of discipline will coincide, I don't know; it looks as if they would be less strict."

Dr. Rogers comments about Colonel Montgomery's return highlighted the importance of this second regiment, signifying that black units were destined to play an important role in the prosecution of the war: "Montgomery's arrival from Key West, with the nucleus of the Second South Carolina Volunteers is an event of importance to our life here and also to the history of the war." Arming his men with foreign smoothbore muskets,[10] he set about turning his raw recruits into a viable military organization.

Laura Towne had an interesting observation of Montgomery after she had a long conversation with him on the 25th. She had escorted a soldier named Quaker back to his regiment so he would not be charged with absence without leave,[11] since he had been gone longer than he should have. When Miss Towne and Quaker returned to camp, they found Colonel Higginson drilling his men. Montgomery was there too. In their ensuing conversation she said that he "seemed to me like a fiery westerner, full of fight and with sufficient confidence in himself. He told us about how he had been sent by General Hunter and General Saxton to recruit in Florida, and how he was ill-treated and scowled at by the officers of the steamer he was in." The colonel wanted to land at his base camp, which was set up by the 1st S.C. on the Smith plantation, "but the captain of the boat ignored his regiment and kept on up the Beaufort [River]. Meantime, General Hunter and General Saxton had both gone to Smith's to see the new men. When the steamer went past they were astonished, and General Saxton rode up to Beaufort to see why it was so. When he learned the reason, he put the steamer under Montgomery's orders, and the reluctant officers had to obey him whom they had so slighted."

While the recruitment of the black regiments had the unqualified support of General Hunter, besides that of General Saxton and Colonels Higginson and Montgomery, there were still plenty of officers in the department who harbored a deep resentment at the presence of these soldiers. Though many vented their feelings among themselves, there would be some who made their position more public. One individual, because of his rank, thought he could get away with it. When Higginson went to Hilton Head on February 16, he found out that Brigadier General Thomas G. Stevenson had been arrested by General Hunter and sent to Washington for making the statement that he would rather see the Union effort go down in defeat than see the war won with the aid of black soldiers. The responses to his open comment by the soldiers' supporters were swift and appropriate. Colonel Higginson said that General Stevenson "has begged most pathetically to be let off, they say, and perhaps will be freed from arrest. I sincerely hope not—such men need discipline." When he found out from Higginson, Dr. Rogers said that he "should like to see the gentleman this evening. Everything may go against us in the present, but these little episodes are refreshing." When Admiral Du Pont, who could go either way on black recruitment, got wind of Stevenson's declaration, he made a rather terse comment about his fellow general officer: "I heard Hunter has arrested a General Stevenson, for saying he would rather serve the rebels than in this 'nigger' department. I smiled and said if he was on that tack he had got hold of the wrong man in Hunter, who would be likely to hang him as well as arrest him."

It was, however, Harriet Ware who really brought it to ground on General Stevenson's comment when she captured the essence of the transition of thought over the use of black troops in the Department of the South and 10th Corps:

Pretty small business, anyway, though the General and most of his officers apparently are not at all waked up to the question, and oppose the idea of negro soldiers very strongly. They seem to have been living for a year with their old prejudices quietly slumbering—without coming in contact with the subject and its practical working as we have here, and so are not prepared for the change of opinion which has been silently advancing here. We did not think a year ago that these people would make good soldiers, though it might be a wise measure to organize them for garrison duty to save lives of our men in a climate they could not bear well and where no fighting would be necessary. Now it is a matter of fact, not opinion, as Colonel Higginson's report shows, that they will succeed in a certain sort of expedition when white men would fail, thus being too valuable an aid in putting down the Rebellion for us to give way to the prejudice of the mass of soldiers. But I do think it strange those prejudices exist, and they can only be removed by degrees.

However, Colonel Higginson's prediction that Stevenson "perhaps will be freed from arrest" came true and was restored to command.

In a broader observation of the subject, Higginson also could not help but see that while there was much dissension in the white regiments in the department against the use of ex-slaves as soldiers, there were also those (both officer and enlisted) who had abolitionist views in the Union Army. Though the issue of slavery fractured the unity of purpose of the Federal forces, what would be the effect if the U.S. were attacked by another country? He said, "It is slavery, not democracy, which has vitiated our army, like our politics. In every regiment here I find division among the officers about slavery. In a war against a foreign power they would be united."

As each day passed in camp, the men of the 1st South Carolina continued to get more proficient in the skills required of them to do their jobs. Experience gained from the recent combat excursion to Florida, and the passage of this knowledge to those soldiers of the regiment who had yet to see any action, especially any new recruits, gave the men a proficiency equal or better than that of the white regiments. However, there continued to be skeptics. Dr. Rogers said on February 26 that "our visitors increase and I shall not be sorry when we are beyond the reach of those who 'doubt the propriety' of arming the negroes. There is but convincing argument and I don't care how soon it comes. I am sick of talking to men whose limited capacity renders it necessary for me to explain how humanity lies somewhere deeper than the integument of the human body."

To demonstrate the seriousness of the Volunteers, Dr. Rogers said that one evening he and Captain Rogers went to see a sick soldier located in another area. When they returned later to camp, they were challenged by a guard on duty. When the guard's initial apprehension was allayed after they did not at first identify themselves to his satisfaction, but then were more specific, he allowed them to pass. This demonstrated to Dr. Rogers that the guard was deadly serious about his post. "I believe it would be fatal for any one [*sic*] to attempt to get by the guard here at night. To our soldiers, this was not play, they intend to obey orders."[12] This was amply demonstrated about three weeks later when some of the men left camp unauthorized to attend a dance. When one tried to slip back into camp, he was challenged by the guard. Dr. Rogers said the "poor fellow refused to halt, when ordered to do so ... and has lost his life for it. He was shot through the side and will die within a few days."

Besides maintaining their individual and collective skills, the men had to be healthy too. Many of them had not been previously examined by a doctor prior to enlisting. Dr. Rogers examined about 100 men on March 2 and had 30 medically discharged for various reasons. One soldier had to be released because "his mind is very torpid, though he is not idiotic. A companion of his told me that he had been overworked in the Georgia rice swamps and 'he be chilly minded, not brave and expeditious like me.'" This was hard for Dr. Rogers to do because he knew they wanted to serve. He said, "It is much easier to keep men out of a regiment than to get them out when once in."

While the officers and men of the Volunteers worked on the unit's proficiency, the next strategic use of the 1st South Carolina and its incipient sister unit was being worked out at departmental level. The impetus for this next move came to General Saxton when Colonel Higginson and his unit were in Florida. Creating new black regiments would mean going to an area on the mainland to occupy that would have sufficient quantities of slaves. The Department of the South's limitation of black males eligible for the military was not going to be solved by slaves escaping to Federal lines in the Union-controlled Sea Islands in South Carolina, Georgia and Florida. Since Confederate forces controlled the mainland adjacent to them, escape would be highly difficult and occur only spasmodically. When Saxton sent his letter of February 2 to Secretary Stanton in addition to Higginson's report, he made his thinking known to Stanton. Confident that he would see the wisdom of such a move to the mainland and approve it, Saxton now only had to answer the begging question—where?

Besides protecting deep-water harbors for the South Atlantic Blockading Fleet so it could bottle up Southern seaports, one of the primary goals of the Army-controlled Department of the South and 10th Corps was to capture the Atlantic ports of Charleston and Savannah. Though both served also as railroad hubs (and to capture one would cut in two the Confederacy's

Atlantic transportation network), the prize was still Charleston.[13] To the North the city was known as the Cradle of the Rebellion, since the war started there with the firing on Fort Sumter, and to capture it would settle a major score.

The first attack of the New Year was planned for the spring, and to accomplish this goal meant employing thousands of soldiers in the endeavor. With the assets allocated to the department at the time, General Hunter could call upon roughly 20,000 soldiers.[14] However, this would not include the fledgling corps of black soldiers. Finding out on February 4 after he got back from Florida that a major attack was in the works, Higginson was not told at the time whether it was going to be Charleston or Savannah. He felt also after being told this that the expedition he had just returned from was probably going to be the only major action the Volunteers would see for some time. "We are more likely to be left here for garrison duty. General Saxton is not anxious to make us prominent ..." Unbeknownst to him, Saxton had other plans for him,[15] though he had not shared them yet with Higginson.[16]

Since Saxton had his basic idea, he had to answer several questions that were important in the accomplishment of this proposed mission. The first one was where in the department he could take control on the mainland with his limited manpower (which in this case was just under 1000 men combining both the 1st and 2nd Regiments) that would have access to large numbers of slaves in the interior. The next one, getting into the interior with minimum effort, required the use of a river. It needed to be deep enough for miles inland for large boats that would be able to carry many slaves (both males and their families, since no way would the men leave them behind). The boats would also have to be able to move them swiftly out of the Rebel-controlled interior. Otherwise, it would be very difficult and slow to do it overland given the logistical requirements needed (especially with the young and elderly), and would also give the Confederates more time to react (cavalry units in particular). The last question that Saxton had to entertain was the number of Rebel soldiers that would be available to oppose them. He did not know the exact number of the enemy marshaled against the department, but he knew as fact that there were huge concentrations in both the Charleston and Savannah areas. Though South Carolina and Georgia had good inland waterways, the ones available were still too close to those large numbers of soldiers, and with the railroad running along the Atlantic coast, moving quantities of men and material to oppose the Volunteers would be quick. Given this information, Saxton's only other option was to look further south for an area that hopefully met his criteria. Thus his eyes turned to Florida.

Like the other two states, Florida had Confederate soldiers to resist any Union excursion, but in what number? During the previous year the major battles that had been fought in Virginia, Maryland, Kentucky, and Tennessee depleted the ranks of the Confederate armies. Outside of recruiting more men to serve in the military, the quickest way to replenish the Rebel legions was to draw units from other areas of the Confederacy that were deemed of lower priority to defend. Though South Carolina and Georgia did make some contributions, the Confederate high command continued to emphasize Charleston and Savannah as high priority in its strategic planning, thus keeping thousands of soldiers tied up. However, Florida was not considered as militarily important,[17] so it was stripped of several thousand soldiers, which left only about 1,500 men to defend the Districts of Middle and East Florida in the state.[18] With so many areas to defend on both the Atlantic and Gulf of Mexico sides, the remaining units were spread out very thin. Logically deducing that the Florida Rebels were few and far between, Saxton concluded one question answered. However, it is not known whether he thought about if Florida was tied into Georgia by rail or not to be able to receive reinforcements in a timely manner. Also not known is whether he thought how fast the scattered Florida units could be consolidated from their distant parts.

The next question to be dealt with was the ability to penetrate far into the interior with the aid of a deep river. Looking as his map, Saxton could come to only one candidate worthy of his attention—the St. John's and its several tributaries; and the base on the river from which he could let loose the Volunteers—Jacksonville.

The last and most important question of the proposed operation (did Florida have large concentrations of slaves to liberate?) was assumedly answered by the information from the Florida men in the 1st S.C. However, these men were from eastern Florida, and the knowledge they provided was unfortunately inaccurate. They could not have known that the Panhandle held the bulk of the slaves, over two-thirds of the state's pre-war population of more than 61,000. Also, it was not taken into account that during the previous year many slaves had already escaped with the Union presence on the St. John's. Many more too had been withdrawn into the interior by their owners to prevent escape. Saxton did not take as a forewarning that the very few slaves brought back from the St. Mary's operation could mean also that the St. John's area did not have the quantities desired. He therefore erroneously concluded that this vital question had been answered. When the Volunteers did arrive, they would discover that a sizable portion of the river's slave population had already been depleted.

Now that he knew where he wanted to send the Volunteers, General Saxton informed Colonel Higginson of the 1st South Carolina's next combat mission. In late February[19] he, Higginson, Lyman Stickney, and one or two others went to Hilton Head one morning to see General Hunter for approval of this proposed expedition.[20] Such was the excitement of another trip to Florida among those who would be involved that Higginson was totally elated. He said, "The St. Mary's expedition had afforded a new sensation ... the few officers of colored troops, and a larger number who wished for further experiments in the same line,[21] and the Florida tax-commissioners were urgent likewise." When Stickney was told of this new operation, he knew this was what he had been waiting for, and as head of the Florida Tax Commission, his involvement in it from the beginning was required to carry out the policies of the Treasury Department of assessing properties for delinquent taxes and auctioning them off to the highest bidders. With any Federal occupation of the new territory in Florida, this meant also that Stickney could further expand his war-profiteering sideline to enrich himself. His presence at Hilton Head was necessary in the meeting with Hunter to help ensure that the general gave his approval. So, regardless of the public or private aims of the participants of the proposed mission, they arrived at Hilton Head with the commanding officer receiving "us, that day, with his usual kindliness."[22] After a "good deal of pleasant chat ... we came to the matter at hand."

Colonel Higginson first reminded General Hunter of the first two times that Jacksonville had been occupied and abandoned: the first time in March 1862 as part of the seizure of deep-water harbors for the blockading fleet, until Hunter decided in April he felt that he needed the occupation garrison more than he needed the city; the second time in October after the capture of a new Rebel fort below the city to prevent Union river traffic, but the city was abandoned again after a short time.[23] Higginson said that since "there were fewer rebel troops in the Department than formerly, and that the St. Mary's expedition had shown the advantage possessed by colored troops, in local knowledge, and in the confidence of the loyal blacks," he proposed to take and hold the city with a brigade of less than of a thousand men, but carry arms and uniforms for twice that number, plus a month's supply of food. He said he also wanted to return his men to action and get the Florida Tax Commission onto the mainland. He ended by saying "that it was worth while [*sic*] to risk something, in the effort to hold Florida, and perhaps bring it back into the Union." Though Hunter made several reasonable objections, "before half our logical ammunition was exhausted, the desired permission was granted ..." The Volunteers were on their way again, this time the entire regiment plus the nucleus of the 2nd South Carolina.

Now that permission was granted, serious preparations for the expedition began. Three steamers were allocated for the mission: the transports *Boston*[24] and *Burnside* and once again the gunboat *John Adams*. Since the *Boston* was the largest of the three vessels, she would carry the majority of the men and materiel. Tons of equipment, ammunition, uniforms for 2,000 men (and all necessary accouterments), food for 30 days, wagons, horses, fodder to feed them, and baggage were loaded. In describing all the activity, Dr. Rogers said that "the plot thickens. Our steamers are coaling up, and the stores and ammunition are going aboard." Higginson said that since "our vast amount of surplus baggage made a heavy job in the loading, in as much as we had no wharf, ... everything had to be put on board by means of flat-boats. It was completed by twenty-four hours of steady work."

With the expedition to Florida well under way, a prime concern that had to be dealt with was operational security. A major problem to worry about in any military endeavor is that the more people that are involved, the harder it is to keep the lid on things with everything happening, especially with newspaper reporters roaming around. Higginson said, "this expedition was less within my own hands than was on the St. Mary's affair, and the great reliance for concealment was on certain counter reports, ingeniously set afloat by some of the Florida men." Since these reporters knew that something was in the works, they could not resist finding out what was going on, especially if it meant getting a major story. Being able to talk to the men, the reporters were able to obtain enough information to get a basic idea on what was happening.[25] Their stories did not, however, get back to their respective newspapers in the North until the expedition was well under way, since it would have taken a few days of travel by ship and the time required to prepare and print for the next available issue. Since it was the intent of the newspapers to sell as many copies as possible, the stories the editors received were embellished by them to the maximum possible.[26] When the reporters actually did find out the destination of the mission, their dispatches "rapidly swelled into the most enormous tales ... the expedition was 'a great volcano about bursting, whose lave [*sic*] will burn, flow, and destroy'—the sudden appearance in arms of no less than five thousand negroes,'—a liberating host,—'not the phantom, but the reality of servile insurrection.'"

However flamboyant the Northern newspapers would ultimately make this latest enterprise of black soldiers, Higginson said the operation "meant a foothold in the interior and," he believed, "an unlimited recruiting of colored troops." Though he also wanted to get the Tax Commission in the state and possibly bring Florida back into the Union, "to me personally these objects were quite secondary; what I desired was to occupy Jacksonville, then to be replaced by white troops there and go farther up the river to Magnolia, where there were large unoccupied buildings, just suited for a recruiting station ... we could recruit another regiment from the river's upper banks. For this purpose we carried arms and uniforms for twice our number and a month's rations; and it was these last facts, no doubt, which led to the newspaper tales."

In his journal that he had been sending to his family in installments, Higginson wrote on March 4: "This day the regiment begins to break camp, bound for parts unknown ..." Of course, this journal segment would not have reached home until well into the operation, but he knew he had to maintain security even in his own personal correspondence. Dr. Rogers was just a little more loose in a letter dated March 3, but his relatives would not have received it either until well into the operation. He said, "This looks southward and before this letter reaches you we shall probably be up some river, I hope not the one spoken of on the streets."

While the Volunteers of both regiments were getting ready for departure, young Charlotte Forten was hurrying home from school on the cold afternoon of March 4 when General Saxton came up beside her in his carriage. Inside with him was Mrs. Frances D. Gage, an Ohio abolitionist and lecturer. Offering Miss Forten a ride to get out of the cold, Saxton gave her some rather startling news. He said Colonel Higginson wanted her to go with his regiment to Florida in the role of teacher for his men. She said:

> the suddenness of the Gen's speech took me by surprise, and if I looked as surprised as I felt the Gen. who had of course been told that I all about it,—must have thought me a little hypocrite. I hardly knew what to say. Believe I stammered something about leaving my school. Mrs. Gage said I must get some one [*sic*] else to take it. She wants me to go to Florida ... if I go, it will be to teach the soldiers ... I shall like that.

Miss Forten said also that:

> so much depends upon these men. If I can help them in any way I shall be glad to do so. I shall be sorry to leave my dear children ... but I can really do more good by going. I am content. And then I shall have the society of my dear and noble Dr. R[ogers], and perhaps of the good and noble Col. too, and those are very, very strong individuals. The climate also is healthier, and oh how I crave good health. How can one work well without it? They think it will be safer there for me, too, but of that I do not think. I have never felt the least fear since I have been here. Though not particularly brave at home, it seems as if I cannot know fear here.

That evening Miss Forten was told by Dr. Rogers that "the Reg[iment] will leave tomorrow ... I shall not see him before he goes, perhaps never again, for it is an enterprise full of danger on which they go. Thought makes my heart ache."[27] Later that evening, however, she received a pass to go to Florida from General Saxton, which would enable her to see the doctor again. The general "highly approves my going [to Florida]. This permit, Dr. R[ogers] says, is equivalent to a Commission. So I shall go. I am determined now. Dr. R. tells me to be ready to join them at an early day."[28] The next day on the 5th, she talked over her plans with her fellow teachers. "Although they do not want me to go, they cannot help acknowledge that it would be a wider sphere of usefulness than this." Susie King, on the other hand, said that she was going to go with her husband, Sergeant King, when his unit, Company E, pulled out without having any formal approval.[29]

Harriet Ware said that one of her associates "came home at night with the news that the First South Carolina Volunteers started on an expedition to-day which Colonel Higginson considers of great importance, which will have ... [varying] ... results, from which they will probably never return."

On March 5, the brigade of Volunteers began to embark on their assigned vessels. The nucleus of Colonel James Montgomery's 2nd South Carolina[30] and Company A of the 1st South Carolina loaded onto the *Burnside*. Companies B and C embarked on the *John Adams* with LTC Billings in charge. The remaining seven companies, along with Colonel Higginson, Major Strong, Dr. Rogers, Lyman Stickney and the other two tax commissioners, the newspaper correspondents,[31] and Susie King with her husband's unit, got on board the *Boston*. Dr. Rogers placed Dr. Minor on the *John Adams*, left Dr. Hawks in charge of the hospital in Beaufort, and took with him "the hospital steward and my trusty nurse Mr. [Thomas] Spalding." Though the *Boston* was the largest of the three vessels, it too was crowded. Dr. Rogers said that there was "not much lee way on this steamer, calculated to carry less than four hundred. Besides we are blocked at every turn by camp equipage, horses, army wagons, etc." To keep the men as healthy as possible on the voyage, he said "the line officers cheerfully co-operate[d] in keeping their men where I want[ed] them."

Colonel Montgomery's fledgling 2nd South Carolina was going to an area where it would get its first taste of combat and would be doing it with a tremendous disadvantage compared to the 1st. Higginson's unit already had months of individual and unit training under its belt, plus the advantage of part of it already having been in combat against Johnny Reb. The first two organized companies of the 2nd hardly had two weeks of individual training and unit drills since the men arrived from Key West on February 23. However short their training may have been, this paled to the greater urgency of finding more men to fill up the ranks of its regiment and to be able to create more black units to help prosecute the war. The 2nd would soon have to learn under a baptism of fire.

As the Volunteers got ready to go, Colonel Higginson received his formal orders from General Saxton, whom he had asked to delay issuing for as much as possible for operational security.[32] They were as follows:

Head-quarters, Beaufort, S.C.
March 5, 1863

Colonel—You will please proceed with your command the first and second Regiments South Carolina Volunteers, which are now embarked upon the steamers John Adams, Boston, and Burnside, to Fernandina, Florida.

Relying upon your military skill and judgment, I shall give you no special directions as to your procedure after you leave Fernandina. I expect, however, that you will occupy Jacksonville, Florida, and entrench yourselves.

The main objects of your expedition are to take the proclamation of freedom to the enslaved; to call all loyal men into the service of the United States; to occupy as much of the State of Florida as possible with the forces under your command; and to neglect no means consistent with the usages of civilized warfare to weaken, harass, and annoy [those] who are in rebellion against the government of the United States.

Trusting that the blessing of our Heavenly Father will rest upon your noble enterprise,

I am yours, sincerely
R. Saxton

Brig.-Gen., Mil. Gov. Dept. of the South
Colonel Higginson, Comd, Expeditionary Corp.

Now that he had his official orders from General Saxton, Higginson only needed authorization from Admiral Du Pont that would allow him to have an armed escort up the river.

On March 6, with the men having been on board almost 24 hours, General Hunter sent his formal request to Du Pont for an armed escort to help Colonel Higginson "execute an important mission in the southernly part of this department." He asked his naval counterpart if he would "give the colonel a letter to the officers of [the] squadron on duty opposite the Florida coast to render any assistance in their power that shall not interfere with [their] other duties." Admiral Du Pont replied to the request with a short letter addressed to "the Senior Officer present at the different Blockading Stations on the Coast of Georgia and Florida." Reiterating what General Hunter said as to why he was sending Higginson, Du Pont said though he had "not been made acquainted with the objects of this mission,[33] ... any assistance that you can offer Colonel Higginson, which will not interfere with our other duties, you are authorized to give."

With the authorization for an armed escort firmly in his hands, Higginson was now ready to carry out his orders for his next combat mission. Waiting for the next high tide of the 6th, the ships were able to weigh anchor and then "we began to move down river at eight this evening." For the second time in three months, Higginson found himself "a naval as well as a military commander in a small way. There had seldom been a period in my life when I had not been master of so much as a dory or a catboat, but it was quite a step from these to the control of the two large transports Boston and ... Burnside, besides what [is] called an 'army gunboat,' this being the Boston ferry boat John Adams, heavily barricaded and armed with a few Parrott guns."

With those thoughts in mind, the convoy moved out to sea.

Combat On the St. John's

As the brigade of Volunteers steamed towards Florida, General Saxton wrote another letter to Secretary of War Stanton to apprise him this time of the mission up to this point.[1] It reflected for the most part what Higginson had already said himself, saying that there were many slaves "in that vicinity who are watching for an opportunity to join us," that the blacks in Florida "are far more intelligent than any I have yet seen," and that many of the soldiers already in the 1st Regiment came from here who "will fight with as much desperation as any people in the world."

Saxton also recapitulated the 1st Regiment's trip up the St. Mary's River, which "caused a perfect panic through out [*sic*] the State of Georgia," after it became widely known that there were armed ex-slaves on the loose. With this recent success and its geographical proximity to the Volunteers' next target, he hoped to capitalize on it so "that we shall strike a heavy blow in Florida." Also, if the "great scarcity of muskets and ammunition in this department" could be alleviated,[2] Saxton said in his opinion, "the entire State of Florida [could] be rescued from the enemy,[3] and an asylum be established for [slaves] from other states who are freed from bondage by the proclamation of freedom, from which they can never be driven." To carry out this proposed lofty goal, he would depend upon one regiment of partially combat-tested soldiers and two companies of a new one that were inexperienced in combat let alone understanding the rudiments of soldiery. This combined force numbered less than a thousand men.

While the *Boston* plowed the Atlantic along the southern seaboard, the correspondents assigned to cover the mission had scant information other than what they had been able to gather prior to embarkation. Since they knew they were going south, there were several choices among which they could guess as to where they would land: Savannah, Brunswick,

Fernandina again, Jacksonville, or St. Augustine. Maybe they could be heading for somewhere in the Gulf of Mexico. Once the destination of the convoy was finally revealed to them, this no doubt set into motion a flurry of questions that raced through their minds as to what would happen once they finally arrived. The first dispatch of *The New York Times* would say in part when it was later written: "The darkies left Port Royal on the evening of the 6th ..., the steamer *Boston* being very properly selected as the transport of the expedition."

In a follow-up report the base correspondent back in Beaufort, through whom flowed all information from the reporters in the field, said that "in a late letter, I furnished a meagre account of an expedition of colored troops in Florida. A recent arrival from the scene of operations puts me in possession of details which are interesting, and promise important results." It adds more to what the reporters already knew prior to being informed that Jacksonville was the target of the convoy. The base correspondent said, "The destination of the expedition was known to few on board, but it was generally understood that a base of operations was to be established, and measures adopted with a view of encouraging the negroes to flee their masters, and accept the protection of the United States, and this was sufficient to fill the colored soldiers with earnestness and enthusiasm."

After an uneventful trip on the evening of the 6th, the convoy arrived in Cumberland Sound early the next morning with the tide. The steamers anchored in front of Fort Clinch. Colonel Higginson,[4] in consultation with the *Boston*'s commanding officer, had previously decided to come here so they could delay "for a day, until the plans of the commanders could be properly arranged." While this was going on, the unit which was garrisoned at this time at the fort, Company K, 7th Connecticut Infantry, was able to find out that the ships had "on board a bunch of colored soldiers for an expedition up the St. John's River."[5] Though the convoy could have caught the evening high tide, the command group decided to spend the night there in Cumberland Sound under the protection of the heavy guns of the fort. The next day on March 8, Dr. Rogers recorded on the *Boston* that "at daylight this morning we left Fernandina and arrived off the bar of this river at 9:30 a.m."

The *Boston* and *Burnside* arrived at the mouth of the St. John's River within so much time of each other, but the third vessel, the *John Adams*, was nowhere in sight. All three ships were supposed to have left Cumberland Sound one at a time, but to rendezvous later at the St. John's. Having been the last ship to leave its anchorage by Fort Clinch that morning, it was naturally assumed that the *John Adams* was right behind the other two ships,[6] though they could not see her. While those on board the *Boston* and *Burnside* wondered as to what happened to her, "the gunboat 'Uncas' came off to meet us and considerably before noon we were anchored in" the mouth of the river. Once over the bar, Colonel Higginson got together with the commanding officers of the two naval gunboats at this blockading station, Commander J. M. Duncan of the *Norwich* and Lieutenant William Watson of the *Uncas*.[7] He showed them the letter from Admiral Du Pont authorizing them to give aid to the expedition as long as it did not interfere with their primary mission of blockade duty. Higginson also informed them of the missing vessel and that the expedition would have to wait on her arrival.

Both Duncan and Watson were glad to help out in this expedition. Higginson said, "Like all officers on blockade duty, they were impatient of their enforced inaction, and gladly seized the opportunity for a different service. It was some time since they had ascended as high as Jacksonville, for their orders were strict ... But they gladly agreed to escort us up the river, so soon as our own gunboat ... should arrive."

While "the sons of Mars and Neptune," i.e. the Army and Navy officers, agreed to wait until the *John Adams* arrived before proceeding to Jacksonville, "distant twenty miles up the river," this gave some of those on the *Boston* and *Burnside* an opportunity to go on shore after having been on board for about three days. Prior to this happening for some of the men of the 2nd South Carolina, Colonel Montgomery had them receive "their arms ... when they were allowed to fire a few shots to get the use of their guns."[8] *The New York Times* correspondent said that a dozen men from the 2nd later left the *Burnside* "to go ashore on a foraging excursion. They proved themselves experts in that line of business, returning in an hour with a fat beef, slung on a pole that had fallen victim to good marksmanship. This prize, with a quantity of poultry and vegetables that came with it, and a superabundance of excellent fish, which those on board the vessels took while their comrades were on shore, aided the commisary's [sic] department, and added visibly to the hilarious good humor." Dr. Rogers said he and Captain James Rogers went "ashore this afternoon and [saw] various wild flowers unfamiliar to us."

Colonel Higginson said that they "waited twenty-four hours for [the *John Adams*], at the sultry mouth of [this] glassy river, watching the great pelicans which floated lazily on its tide, or sometimes shooting one, to admire the great pouch, into which one of the soldiers could insert his foot, as into a boat ... We wandered among the bluffs, too, in the little deserted hamlet once called 'Pilot Town.'"

Though the excursion on shore was a diversion for some who were able to leave the ships, the delay of the *John Adams* caused a certain amount of consternation among those who had reason to worry. Dr. Rogers said why the ship:

has not reached here, we cannot imagine. This delay warns the rebs of our approach to Jacksonville and, if they choose to dispute our landing, I do not see why some lives may not be lost ... The Col. is deep in consultation with the gunboat captains and a steady frown indicates his impatience and perplexity about the *John Adams* ... To me the worst feature of the delay is the exposure of our men to disease. I dread confinement in close air for them much more than I do rebel bullets ... Just now I found one of our men in a collapse state which will prove fatal.

Colonel Higginson said that:

it was well to have something to relieve the anxiety naturally felt at the delay of the *John Adams*,—anxiety both for her safety and for the success of our enterprises. The Rebels had repeatedly threatened to burn the whole of Jacksonville, in case of another attack, as they had previously burned its mills and its great hotel. It seems as if the news of our arrival must surely have travelled thirty miles by this time. All day we watched every smoke that rose among the wooded hills, and consulted the compass and the map, to see if that sign announced the doom of our expected home.

As the reason why the *John Adams* was not there, only led to more speculation. Dr. Rogers said that Captain Dolly of Company H had a humorous suggestion. "His theory however about the non-arrival of the Adams is that the chaplain [James H. Fowler] had gone back [to South Carolina] for the last well to be dug. Wells are one of the chaplain's specialties and it would not be surprising if the theory proved correct."

However, when the missing vessel finally showed up at 10:00 in the morning on March 9,[9] it was a welcome relief. Higginson said that "all anxiety vanished." Dr. Rogers was most relieved from his medical point of view. He said, "The poor fellow whom I mentioned yesterday, died this morning. Were our men obliged to sleep aboard a few nights more, such deaths would be frequent. Yet I have everything done to prevent disease that, under the circumstances, can be done. Yesterday I found several ill on the *Burnside*, including Col. Montgomery and one of our best artillerists. Today all are in good condition and anticipating a fight."

The reason given to Colonel Higginson by the ship's commander and Lt. Colonel Billings why the *John Adams* was late was one that he could not approve. Dr. Rogers said that "the officers report[ed] fog so dense as to prevent running her over the bar at Fernandina."[10] Since the *Boston* and *Burnside* were able to leave without any problem, the reason for the *John Adams*' late departure was very weak. They gave no other explanation. Dr.

Rogers mirrored Higginson's dim view of the other two officers' report when he said that "if the rebels are not duller than I think them, we shall suffer for this most annoying delay. My judgment of it is more severe than I can write."

Now that the missing gunboat had arrived, the convoy could get down to the task at hand. Colonel Higginson and Commander Duncan decided later that day that they could get underway as 2 a.m. on the morning of the 10th so they would arrive about dawn. Unless the Confederates thought that something was amiss with the rifle fire that occurred while waiting on the *John Adams*, which they might have attributed to those on the blockade duty just letting off some steam, the ships would be able to catch the inhabitants of Jacksonville and its small Confederate contingent by surprise.[11] Higginson said that this particular night was chosen because "there was a moon which set early, so that we should at first have its aid and yet part with it before coming near Jacksonville." He also added, "it was necessary that the enterprise should be a surprise, as the Confederates were said to have planned to burn the town, in case of another attack."

Escorting the convoy were both the *Norwich* and the *Uncas*. The *Norwich* was the heaviest armed with four 8-inch guns, one 30-pounder Parrott, and one 11-inch rifle howitzer. The lesser armed *Uncas* had four 32-pounders and one 20-pounder Parrott. Adding the guns of the *John Adams* gave this *ad hoc* flotilla more than enough firepower to keep the Confederates at bay. By previous agreement, Higginson would land at an upper pier while Montgomery would land at a lower one, the latter behind the former, while the *Norwich* and *Uncas* would anchor in the river and provide overwatch as the other vessels would land the soldiers and supplies.

As the Union force moved upriver,[12] Higginson said that "strict quiet was enjoined on board all the vessels." He added that going up the St. John's was similar to going up the St. Mary's. He said, "Again there was the dreamy delight of ascending an unknown stream, beneath a sinking moon, into a region where peril made fascination." With the *Boston* behind one of the gunboats, he was able to see her with an early version of a night-vision device. "I looked for the first time through a powerful night-glass. It has always seemed a thing wholly inconceivable that a mere lense [*sic*] could change darkness into light; and as I turned the instrument on the preceding gunboat, and actually discerned the man at the wheel and the officers standing about him,—all relapsing into vague gloom again at the withdrawal of the glass,—it gave a feeling of childish delight. Yet it seemed only in keeping with the whole enchantment of the scene." Adding to this seeming nocturnal tranquility, Dr. Rogers said, "our fleet of five steamers moved slowly up the St. John's. Passed the yellow bluffs, the night glorious in its blue, misty moonlight, the river wide and beautiful."

However tranquil the river seemed to be in the moonlight, there were dangers that had to be avoided. Higginson said "the river was of difficult navigation; and we began to feel sometimes, beneath the keel, that ominous sliding, grating, treacherous arrest of motion which makes the heart shudder, as the vessel does." He described also, "we had heard rumors of torpedoes on the river,[13] but disregarded them with the confidence of ignorance and passed safely by spots where steamboats were later blown up and destroyed only a few months later."[14] Soon the vessels started to bottom out one at a time due to the low tide, thus causing considerable delay, but they were able to extricate themselves except for the *Norwich*, which remained stuck regardless of her efforts. This would pose a very serious problem for the convoy, because she was its main stay of firepower, and to proceed on without her would leave a serious gap in the Union force's ability to counter any concerted Rebel attack. However, no vessel continued upriver until a decision was made regarding the absence of the *Norwich*.

Commander Duncan was at first thinking that he should not have the *Uncas* go up any further, since she was a "small vessel of less than two hundred tons, and in … poor condition." With the *Boston* and *Uncas* near enough the *Norwich* for the principals to communicate with each other, Higginson and Lieutenant Watson were able to discuss Duncan's quandary with him. Though Higginson understood his dilemma, he did not want to turn around. He said, "Having got thus far, it was plainly my duty to risk the remainder with or without naval assistance; and this being so, [Commander Duncan] did not object, but allowed his dashing subordinate [Watson] to steam up with us to the city." The *Norwich* would later join them after the high tide had freed her from her stuck position.

It had been Higginson's original intent to arrive at Jacksonville at dawn, but with the problem of low tide, the flotilla would not arrive until well after sunrise. Regardless of this change in the tactical scenario, the ships continued upriver with the *Uncas* in the lead, followed by the *Boston* and *Burnside*, with the *John Adams* bringing up the rear.[15] When it became daylight, Dr. Rogers said, "we were delighted by the scenario of the shores and the cosy looking homes scattered here and there." Higginson had a similar observation of the early morning hours. He added, "We had several hours of fresh early morning sunshine, lighting up the green shores of that lovely river, wooded to the water's edge, with sometimes an emerald meadow, opening a vista to some picturesque house…. Here and there we glided by the ruins of some saw-mill burned by the Rebels … but nothing else spoke of war, except, perhaps the silence." This was the scene as the ships moved upriver. However, the silence and seeming tranquility would soon end.

As the Union convoy made progress in the early morning light, many of the Volunteers from Florida who were familiar with the river knew that they were getting closer to their objective, thus causing "our Florida men" to be "wild with delight." The correspondent of *The New York Times* took notice about the former Confederate fortification on the river. He wrote:

> A few miles from the mouth, on the left bank, is the first highland, called St. John's Bluff.[16] At this point, a former expedition was stopped last summer, by a formidable rebel battery commanding the channel. The fortification was subsequently taken by a combined naval and land force, that destroyed the works, and brought away the guns. It was reasonable to suppose that an obstacle to the passage of the fleet would be again found here, and preparations were made for a fight,[17] but no enemy appeared, and not a sign of resistence [*sic*] showed itself during the further progress of the vessels toward the town.

As each ship rounded the point below the city,[18] the soldiers and sailors were able to see Jacksonville. They saw clearly "its long streets, its brick warehouses, its white cottages, and its overshadowing trees,—all peaceful and undisturbed by flames,—it seemed, in the men's favorite phrase, 'too much good,' and all discipline were merged, for a moment, in a buzz of estacy [*sic*]." What would greet them as they got ready to dock? Higginson said, "How much warning there had been, and what resistence [*sic*] might impend, we could not guess, but there was every reason to believe that the surprise had succeeded. We drew momentarily nearer; the gunners were at their posts, the men in line."

As previously agreed upon, the *Uncas* dropped anchor in the river with its guns facing the city, and its gun crews prepared to fire a barrage of various ordnance if there was any resistance to the initial landing. With the *Uncas* in an overwatch position, the *Boston* and *Burnside* moved to dock at their respective piers,[19] with land combat operations commencing as soon as the first boatload of Volunteers disembarked. However, what the men on the ships saw was anything but a Confederate defensive battle line. They saw "children playing on the wharves; careless men, here and there, lounged down to look at us, hands in pockets; a few women came to their doors, and gazed listlessly upon us, shading their eyes with their hands." However calm this appeared, Higginson said "none knew what perils might be concealed behind those quiet buildings."[20] Not wanting to be caught in the open, even if the initial scene gave the impression that the Yankees took the remaining residents by surprise, as soon as the *Boston* docked, Colonel Higginson stepped first onto the pier. He was immediately followed by Captain Rogers' Company F and Captain Metcalf's Company G. After these two, Companies D, E, H, I, and K followed, and soon "pickets were posted in the suburbs."

While the *Boston* disgorged its human cargo, the *Burnside* docked at the lower pier and the men of Colonel Montgomery's 2nd South Carolina and Captain Trowbridge's Company A disembarked to look for evidence of any Confederate presence and "started off in the direction of the rebel camp." Once she was able to, the *John Adams* let off Companies B and C. Dr. Rogers observed that "strange as it may seem, the rebels were taken by surprise and the city was neither defended nor burned ... One man came down to the wharf and caught the line when it was thrown off." Several small boat-howitzers were taken off the ships and placed to guard several principal streets. However, when all was said and done, "not a rifle shot was heard, no bombshell rose in the air."

The New York Times correspondent had a slightly different version of the initial landing. He said Colonel Higginson landed in the *John Adams* with Captain Dolly's Company H following.[21] The rest of the description of the landing was about the same. The men scrambled:

off as best they could, neglecting, in their eagerness, to avail themselves of a gangplank. They immediately formed in marching order, and started on the double-quick for the railroad depot. The remainder of the force soon followed, and part of it advanced to the outskirts of the town, and holding the approaches. This movement was executed with such promptness, that the first knowledge of the invasion only came to the townspeople when they saw the black soldiers marching past their dwellings.

While the companies of the brigade of Volunteers moved to their assigned areas to occupy Jacksonville and set up a defensive perimeter,[22] Colonel Higginson began to take in what he saw. With a pre-war population of about 3,000 people, he estimated that there were about 500 left, primarily women, children, and the elderly, many of whom were so destitute that he would have to provide for them. A newspaper account later published in the *Philadelphia Inquirer* said, "the women and children proved to be in a wretched state of destitution, their clothes mostly in rags, and nothing to eat but a small amount of corn ecked [*sic*] out by a pretty plentiful supply of rice ... Everything else eatable had been carried off by the Rebel soldiery, or, to call them by the name which they really merit, guerrillas, whose solitary occupation in Florida seems to be stealing hogs and poultry, and carrying off every able-bodied male to swell the ranks of the army."

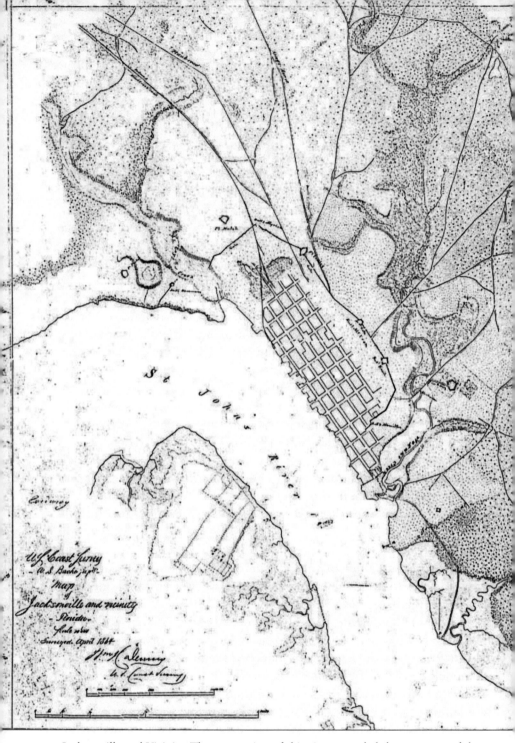

Jacksonville and Vicinity. The occupation of this city expanded the exposure of the Volunteers. The fortifications that surround the city were made later in the war.
Courtesy State Library and Archives of Florida

Besides the human element as a casualty of war, Higginson observed also the physical appearance of the city. He said before the war there had been "a rapidly growing lumber-trade, for which abundant facilities were evidently provided. The wharves were capacious, and the blocks of brick warehouses along lower street were utterly unlike anything we had yet seen in the region, as were the neatness and thrift everywhere visible. It had been built up by Northern enterprise, and much of the property was owned by loyal men. It had been a great resort for invalids, though the Rebels had burned the large hotel which once accommodated them. Mills had also been burned." He noticed also "fine rows of brick homes, all empty, along the wharf." Overall, "there was an air of substance and comfort about the town, quite alien from the picturesque decadence of Beaufort."

While Higginson knew that the empty warehouses would provide adequate quarters for his men, he elected to take over as his brigade headquarters a large brick house built by a New Yorker named Sunderland, who was the "reputed author of the [Florida] State ordinance of Secession." He said that this house, "the chief one in the town, is new and really magnificent, with beautiful gas fixtures and superb marble fireplaces."

Higginson made Captain Rogers of Company F Provost Marshal to perform military police duties. As the day proceeded the brigade continued to bolster its defenses for an expected Rebel attack, but nothing happened. When the sun set on the Volunteers for their first night in Jacksonville, this reminded him of the night spent on the St. Mary's a month and a half prior, waiting for a Confederate attack. Higginson said, "How many new night associations these forays have given me. The night at 'Township' on the St. Mary's, when I sat on the doorstep in the dying moonlight waiting for an attack till morning. Like it, but more intense, was the first night here, the most terribly anxious night I ever passed; we were all perfectly exhausted, the companies were posted in various parts of the town, all momentarily expecting attack. My temporary quarters were in the loveliest grove of trees, and as I sat and nodded on the door step, the mocking birds sang all night like nightingales, in the sweet air and among the blossoming trees." Like Township Landing on the southern bank of the St. Mary's, "day brought relief and the sense of due possession, and we could see what we had won." However, when the sun started to rise on the Volunteers' defensive perimeter on March 11, one question had to have been in Colonel Higginson's very tired mind as he sensed victory: why had not the Volunteers encountered any resistance yet from the Confederates, especially when they first landed?

Rebel Reaction

The Confederate picket that was stationed at Jacksonville on Tuesday morning of March 10 was caught unaware that a Union flotilla was coming up the river,[23] and only knew of its existence as the fleet appeared after rounding the bend and came into view just before 8:00 a.m. Since the picket was a detachment of Company B, 2nd Florida Cavalry Regiment, it would be not much of a problem getting away in a hurry from any Federal landing. On this cool March morning these Florida horse soldiers would get a chance to demonstrate just how fast they could change locations.

There had been no Yankee troops in Jacksonville since October after they had captured the Rebel fort on St. John's Bluff, a good six months earlier. Except for the occasional Federal naval foray up the river, there had not been any enemy activity to keep the pickets constantly alert. With this morning starting out like the day before, there was no reason to begin it with any change in routine. Though there were men watching the river, not everybody was needed, and the majority, like the civilians there, went about their usual morning activities.

As the troopers of Company B went about their business, they suddenly heard shouting from the pickets as "yankees and negroes in transports accompanied by three Gun boats came" into view. Seeing that this force of arms could mean only one thing— invasion—the pickets ran back to warn their detachment commander, 1st Lieutenant Henry Alexander Gray. He quickly realized that there was no time to do anything but for his men to grab their weapons and whatever else they could on a second's notice and get out of Jacksonville.[24] Lieutenant Gray moved so fast that he "lost his sword, uniform, and papers etc." and was gone with his men before they could be captured, since the Volunteers "were going in every direction trying to capture all they could." However, just as the Federals did not get any information from the elderly ladies at St. Mary's about Confederate troops being present, they would not get anything from the civilians in Jacksonville either.

Several civilians who would have left also with the retreating soldiers were captured. Among them was Jonathon Drysdale, a former army officer from St. Augustine. John G. Butler, a Duval County timber merchant before the war, barely made it. Davis Bryant, who got this information several days later at Camp Cooper, said that:

> two gunboats—I think was the number—first went very rapidly and stopped at B-and C-'s wharf before any,[25] or many, were aware of their arrival ... and immediately landed a regmt. of niggers, rushing them out to all entrances to town to "pen" all who happened to be there, and

they did catch several ... Jno. Drysdale who, has been quite sick and living there—and several less important personages, Jack Butler escaped by the skin of his teeth. As he was crossing "Brisbee's bridge" he heard the niggers "tearing" up the road behind him, whooping and yelling, to stop the outlet.

Lieutenant Gray's bedraggled command retreated to the edge of the woods where they intersected with the Lake City-bound road and railroad. He watched at a distance to see what was going to happen next. At the same time he gave his men the opportunity to get themselves together, he "sent an express out to camps" to notify his superiors of the surprise Union occupation of Jacksonville. Since Camp Finegan was only several miles away, it did not take long for the courier to arrive and inform the camp's commander, Lieutenant Colonel Abner H. McCormick, that the city had been quickly overrun. McCormick immediately ordered the remainder of Company B under Captain Winston Stephens to reinforce Gray with dispatch. He also ordered the rest of the camp to prepare to move as soon as possible. He then telegraphed Brigadier General Joseph Finegan at his Lake City headquarters to inform him of the new crisis. He also sent word to Camp Cooper for the 30-man detachment from Company C to return so Captain William Chambers would have his complete command.

When the telegraph message arrived at General Finegan's headquarters informing him of the latest invasion of Billy Yank, he set into motion of collecting his scattered command. He "immediately issued orders by telegraph and express trains for the concentration of all troops which ... could reach within the space of four or five days at the camp in the vicinity of Jacksonville." This meant that he was "compelled to leave with entirely inadequate protection many points on the coast whence negroes may escape in large numbers to the enemy and where they have easy access to the interior." While Finegan's staff moved with dispatch to implement the general's orders, Lt. Colonel McCormick was busy with his own command.

Camp Finegan had the largest concentration of Rebel combat troops in northeast Florida. Besides having five companies of the 2nd Florida Cavalry Regiment (Companies B, C, F, H, and K),[26] it had an infantry battalion, the 1st Battalion Partisan Rangers,[27] and two batteries of the Milton (Florida) Light Artillery. Though this may sound impressive, the total number of soldiers available at this time in the District of East Florida was only 803 men. These forces at Camp Finegan represented roughly two-thirds of General Finegan's available assets. To make McCormick's job more difficult, his command was not all under one roof.

Since Lt. Col. McCormick was the senior officer at the camp (he was also second-in-command of the 2nd Florida Cavalry), he was responsible

Brigadier General Joseph
Finegan, who commanded
the Confederate forces
that opposed the Union
occupation of Jacksonville.
*Courtesy State Library and
Archives of Florida*

for the entire east coast of north Florida, from the St. Mary's River to
Jacksonville and down the west side of the St. John's River as far as
Palatka.[28] He had to spread out his command to guard against any Union
encroachment and prevent escaping slaves from making it to Federal lines.
This meant the use of three cavalry companies: Company K under Captain
Clarke at Camp Cooper, Company F under Captain Samuel F. Rou in the
vicinity of Green Cove Springs, and Company H under Captain John J.
Dickison in the Palatka area. Though McCormick would have loved to
pull these units to Jacksonville in this new crisis, he still had to cover these
areas until told otherwise by General Finegan. Though the first reason
to maintain them there was now secondary to this new crisis, the second
reason to keep them where they were, to prevent slaves from escaping,
overrode it. Finegan had to play this game of politics assiduously until he
felt that the situation finally allowed him to employ them.

McCormick's only infantry unit, the 1st Battalion Partisan Rangers,
commanded by Major Theodore W. Brevard, had four companies assigned
to Camp Finegan, with a fifth one stationed in the District of Middle
Florida. The four here were Company A, Captain Asa Stewart;[29] Company
B, Captain Samuel W. Mays; Company C, Captain John Q. Stewart; and
Company D, Captain Pickins B. Bird. The Milton Light Artillery still had
one battery at Camp Cooper. So, with the remainder of Captain Chambers'

cavalry company, LTC McCormick prepared his command for movement to Jacksonville. Once there, he hoped to contain the enemy as much as possible until reinforcements could arrive from other parts of the state, let alone hopefully from out of state.

When Captain Stephens arrived with the remainder of his company at the edge of the forest where Lieutenant Gray was, he knew he was in no position to take any offensive action. All he could do at this time would be to ascertain as much information as possible about the enemy prior to Lieutenant Colonel McCormick's arrival. Gray told him that "they had thrown out their pickets about the brick church."[30] While Company B kept an eye on the Volunteers as the unit kept out of sight, McCormick soon followed up with the rest of his cavalry and artillery units from Camp Finegan, with the infantry following up as soon as possible.[31] He found out from Stephens the same information. Anticipating enemy strength to be much greater than his own, McCormick decided to wait until Finegan arrived for further instructions. So, until the general got there, he "concentrated our men on the three mile branch." The Yankees decided to oblige his decision too, because "nothing was done that day of any consequence."

Finegan left Lake City for Camp Finegan that evening after he did all he could do at his headquarters. He arrived with his staff about midnight. See that McCormick and his command had already left, he found out from the remaining personnel "that the enemy had landed from five gunboats and transport, and ... occupied the town with so much celerity and secrecy as to have surrounded it with his pickets before the people generally were aware of his presence." Finegan and his staff then proceeded to join McCormick, arriving early in the morning. After getting all the information he could as to enemy activity, he decided to wait until morning before making his next move.

The Battle is Joined

When dawn appeared on the eastern horizon, with the sun yet to start reflecting on the St. John's River, two forces opposite each other steeled themselves for what they knew the new morning would bring. The Volunteers had not had any contact with the Rebels the previous 24 hours, but this did not mean that they were not going to have any action this day. The Federals knew that Johnny Reb was lying out in the woods and were under no illusion that he was going to just let them get away with the seizure of a Southern town. The few Confederates present knew that they were going up against an unknown quantity in Billy Yank. However, each side also knew that when the sun would begin to settle, their ranks would be a little thinner.

As the soldiers of each side contemplated what was to come, they took in the frost of the early morning air as they waited for the sun to ward off the chill of the night. Since the combatants were in proximity to each other, they could not have fires when it was dark. It would have given away their positions. Only away from the "front line" a good distance could a fire be made to warm those who were lucky enough to be near them.

While the Confederate soldiers waited in those opening hours of March 11 for something to happen, General Finegan was waiting for the right moment to make that "something" occur. He had earlier decided to make a reconnaissance of the Union lines with his whole force to test enemy reaction. He told Major Brevard to place his Partisan Rangers on the western side of the Yankee defenses while he had Lt. Colonel McCormick position his two cavalry companies on the northern approach. At a designated time both sides would advance until resistance would be determined to be too great and then withdraw.[32] Finegan decided to place himself with the 2nd Florida Cavalry.

With both Brevard and McCormick having received their orders, they then had to get their respective unit commanders briefed and units into position so they would be ready to move at the designated time.[33] The men who were able to get some sleep were awakened, rolled up their blankets, and either got in line to march in infantry formation or mount horses. Finegan decided not to use any artillery for this attack; he only had one battery of the Milton Light Artillery while the other one was still at Camp Cooper. Using the best means available, the units moved until they arrived into position. Once there they waited.

By mid-morning, with the sun well above the horizon, the designated start-time arrived and the small force of Brigadier General Finegan began to advance. Riding with McCormick's cavalry detachment, Finegan watched as Captain Stephens' Company B and Captain Chambers' Company C moved slowly south in line formation towards the enemy,[34] while Major Brevard's battalion marched east. In the infantry line of battle here were Captain Asa Stewart's Company A, Captain May's Company B, Captain John Q. Stewart's Company C and Captain Bird's Company D. Whether they had seen action before or were going into combat for the first time, both wings of the Confederate advance steeled themselves for what was to come.

While the Rebels moved to get into position, the pickets of the Volunteers were able to hear them and reported accordingly. As the battle lines of Johnny Reb closed the distance to their objectives, the pickets quickly reported this too. Facing Brevard's men were the 1st South Carolina while

McCormick's horse soldiers viewed the 2nd. Unbeknownst to Finegan, his cavalry would soon come into contact with the weak link of the Federal line and thus get an incorrect impression of his opponents, which would ultimately be to his disadvantage. Very soon first contact was made.

Seeing that the advance pickets on the north side were anchored around some outlying buildings, Finegan said:

> the cavalry detachment ... advanced into the suburbs of the town, where we found the enemy in strong picket force. We were fired upon by their first pickets without effect, except the disabling of 1 or 2 horses, and drove them into the town. Proceeding farther, we encountered stronger force, which I estimated to be about two companies of infantry, drawn up in line of battle and advantageously posted. These opened on us unexpectedly, firing alternately by platoons and by file, with some degree of regularity. Our men, at great disadvantage of position, returned their fire with effect and drove them in haste and confusion from their position, killing 2 of whom we are certainly advised and wounded 4 or 5, and we have some reason to believe inflicting on them a severe loss.

Captain Stephens said on "Wednesday morning we were thrown in line of battle and the Cavalry went on the north side and the Infantry on the three mile branch and so as to cut off the retreat of the enemy and we were to charge them." Soon the advancing cavalrymen "came in where the Yankees made some sand batteries." At this point he said that "every thing [*sic*] went on quietly until we got to ... the plank road." With Lieutenant Gray and eight men acting as skirmishers, "as we entered the opening ... the [pickets] on the plank road & the sand batteries commensed [*sic*] heavy fire." Colonel McCormick then ordered Stephens to form his company "under the hail of bullets and ... moved up the road pouring a fire into their lines ..." His "men behaved very firmly but rather anxious to shoot." Company B "then advanced until near the plank road exchanging shots & then my company was halted & fired into two companies of negroes drawn up in front of me about 300 yards." As the Confederates "moved up the road pouring a fire into their lines ...," the 2nd South Carolina "began soon to give way." When "[we] commensed [*sic*] firing they began to brake [*sic*] & they ran like wild animals."

About the same time the 2nd South Carolina was being pushed back, "Capt. Chambers ... formed his Company on [Stephens'] right and across the road." When Company C started to fire, "the enemy had got in great confusion & he did not have any one to shoot at long." When Stephens started to move in Chambers' direction, "the Genl ordered the firing to cease ... then we were ordered out as was expected the Gun Boats would open on us."

When the 2nd Florida Cavalry started to engage the 2nd S.C.'s pickets, Colonel Montgomery said that as he "was engaged in consultation with Col. Higginson, in town, my men were attacked, in front, by a squadron of Mounted Carbines ... After a sharp conflict, the officers ... ordered a retreat."

Montgomery said he then "met the men just as the retreat was beginning to degenerate into a rout. They rallied, promptly, at the order, and I led them back into the fight; when, the enemy, in turn, retreated; and we reoccupied the ground from which we had been driven." As Finegan had said that his men were "under the range of the enemy's five gunboats," Montgomery said that "at this stage of the fight, the Gun Boats opened, in splendid [sic] style, throwing up the shells over our heads, and hurrying up the retreat of the enemy, most beautifully."

Since it had been General Finegan's intent to have both his units hit the Union lines simultaneously, they could only do so by moving independently of each other. However, his plans did not work out as he had anticipated. When the cavalry got to what was to be its furthest point of advance, Finegan said "at this point I had expected to meet the infantry detachment under Major Brevard, and with them to have retired from the town, capturing such pickets as were posted still farther out. The road taken was shorter than anticipated, and the two skirmishes with the enemy had accelerated our progress, so that we arrived at the place in advance of the infantry." Captain Stephens confirmed this: "The infantry had not moved up fast enough and consequently all of them got away except those that were killed."[35] What exactly did happen to the assaulting infantry formation?

Major Brevard's 1st Battalion Partisan Rangers, unknown to the cavalry, had a tougher nut to crack. When General Finegan made his plan to attack, he had no idea that his assault columns would come up against two distinct units, one experienced and the other one very green. It would be unfortunate for Finegan that he had placed his cavalry where he did and had a fairly easy time in driving them back, thus getting the wrong impression of the Volunteers' total capacity. As the infantry advanced, they were naturally able to push back the pickets of the 1st S.C. into their own defenses. However, when the Rebel battle line of 200 men came up against an experienced force of over 800, it was not hard to see why Brevard was not able to link up with McCormick, given that the Rangers were outnumbered and out-gunned four to one. Once Brevard realized that his small contingent was going up against a force too strong,[36] especially with the volleys of musketry it could put out, he moved his command back to the woods.

Casualties on both sides were relatively light, but the information available did not give a complete picture. Colonel Montgomery said that in his unit's first engagement, the 2nd S.C. lost "one man killed, and two wounded, one seriously." He also said that "the enemy confesses to a loss of one man: (Dr. Meredith) and three horses killed." One newspaper reporter said that "the casualties on our side were trifling, and doubtless not very great on that of the Rebels, for the engagement did not last over half an hour. So far as I have been able to learn, one negro only was killed, although many were wounded, and it would be difficult to estimate the enemy's loss, as he left no dead on the field and carried off most of his wounded."

General Finegan said that his cavalry killed "2 of whom we are certainly advised and wounding 4 or 5, and we have some reason to believe inflicting on them a severe loss. In this skirmish we lost a valuable life in Acting Surgeon Meredith, who accompanied the expedition ..."

When Captain Stephens had moved over in the direction of Captain Chambers at the time that General Finegan had ordered a cease fire, he said he had come across one of his men who he thought needed help. On Stephens' way over, he:

found Jessup down and thinking him wounded I rode back to him and found he could not shoot off of his horse and had dismounted. I ordered him to mount and soon saw Dr. [James] Meredith on his face apparently dead, I got down and turned him over and saw he was living, but saw he had no chance as his brains were shot out, I ordered him taken up and then we are ordered out as we expected the Gun Boats would open up on us.

Stephens said that the doctor "didn't know what hit him, he lived about five hours after he was shot but was not sensible nor apparently in pain. We have lost a good friend and a valuable Physician."

Stephens also said that one of his men "had a horse shot down under him and two others slightly wounded." Private D. C. McLeod, "a brother of Lt. McLeod was struck with a spent ball on the thigh, but was not hurt. Jessup had the strip of his pants on the thigh cut out by a ball." Stephens noted too that "Capt. Chambers lost one horse and no one hit" and later learned that the enemy lost "one officer and 15 negroes we killed." No casualties were reported from Major Brevard's command.

In the afternoon,[37] Brevard's Rangers made another foray against the Union defenses.[38] This time they made their "way into the suburbs of the town" where they "encountered in the vicinity of the same one or two companies of the enemy drawn up in line under cover of the trees and a house." General Finegan said in his official report that as Brevard advanced with a "party of skirmishers, he then opened on them with his entire command, when they broke and fled in confusion, having first, however, returned the fire." Finegan also said that as he "withdrew his command, ... the enemy opened with shell from their gunboats, escaped, without loss, having inflicted, as we believe, some loss on the enemy."

Later, Colonel Higginson sent Major Strong out with 12 men on a reconnaissance mission to ascertain the disposition of the Rebels. Strong went out "about two miles from the town, on the line of the railroad. He could see a large force of the Rebels, but they kept a respectful distance and could not be induced to leave the shelter of the woods." Besides knowing where the Rebels were, the squad "brought back one prisoner, a Rebel flag, four horses, and a fine beef."

On the Union side, there was a different interpretation of events about the second encounter. As Montgomery had said about the first firefight, the Federals considered this attack another Confederate defeat. Dr. Rogers said "at every fight our boys have put the rebels to flight." Regardless of each side's view, the first day ended with neither gaining an advantage. The Rebels were able to test the Volunteers' defenses, while the Union forces got a good idea of what they had initially to go up against.[39] However, though the Federals got a feeling for the enemy on this first day of battle, they knew that more Johnnies would be on the way.

The first day of action produced no decisive victory for each side, but it did give the impression to both combatants that they were outnumbered and would need reinforcements if any tangible results were to take place. In this respect, the Confederates did have one advantage. Whereas they could draw from other units in Florida and nearby states fairly quickly (since for the most part they were connected by rail), the Federals were limited by the amount of ships assigned to support the mission. To bring in a sizable number of troops would take longer.

When it became clear to Colonel Higginson that he was going to require more soldiers than he had originally anticipated, he made this known to the other principals of the expedition, three of whom were the members of the Florida Tax Commission. This caused Lyman Stickney great concern, since this revelation threatened to ruin his plans to further enrich himself. He realized that going back to Beaufort for more soldiers would require an extended turnaround time. Stickney said he recalled a conversation he had previously with Colonel Joseph Hawley, commander of the 7th Connecticut Infantry at Fernandina, stating that Hawley could send troops to help Higginson if needed. Since Higginson came to Jacksonville to recruit more blacks, it was his original intent not to use any white units in this operation (except later to garrison Jacksonville while the Volunteers would go out for more recruits). However, when the Volunteers arrived on the 10th, there were hardly any able-bodied blacks around (just like at

Woodstock, Georgia). Realizing now that he did not have enough men to both hold the city and go recruit upriver, Higginson needed to reconsider his original plan of not using white troops until later. Since Hawley "had offered to send four white companies and a light battery to swell our force,—in view of the aid given to his position by this more advanced post, I decided to authorize the energetic Judge [Stickney] to go back to Fernandina and renew the negotiation ..."

With Higginson's permission, Stickney left at the next available high tide to bring back reinforcements to bolster the Volunteers and, hopefully, also save his sideline enrichment schemes. While this went on, Dr. Rogers contemplated the need to keep Jacksonville. "It is the most important position in Florida for us to hold." However, this thought was tempered by the results of the two previous occupations. The city "has already been twice abandoned by our troops and it remains to be proved whether it must be abandoned a third time."

Stalemate and Reinforcement

As Lyman Stickney sailed back to Fernandina for reinforcements, defense became the watchword of the day, especially on the Union side, since Colonel Higginson knew it could be as much as two days before any of the 7th Connecticut Infantry would arrive. If Hawley was not able to oblige Stickney, it would mean having to go all the way back to Beaufort, and even then several more days would have to pass before any units could get there. So until then, Higginson had to improve his physical defenses. He had to give the impression that his force was much bigger than it actually was, which also meant he had to stay put where he was and forego any trip upriver to find any new recruits.

While Higginson waited in anticipation for the "four white companies & a battery in addition, which Col. Hawley has promised ...," he improved his defensive posture as much as possible. Numerous outlying buildings were burned down so the Volunteers could see better any advancing Rebels. The routes into town were barricaded by "constructing barriers or felling trees." He also established a "look-out in a church steeple which over-looked the line of roadrail."

Though Higginson made physical preparations, he realized that this alone was not going to be enough. In order to overcome his numerical deficiency, he developed a defensive strategy based on guile. "On our side we magnified ourselves, omitted all regular dress parades, as showing our small numbers, but sometimes marched and countermarched a few companies in stage fashion, at some conspicuous point, until they looked like a large brigade; and at night garrisoned some exposed point, with a tent and a smouldering [sic] camp-fire, in default of actual troops." He had the "gunboats and transports moved impressively up and down the river, from time to time" to make the Confederates think of a slow but continuous buildup of troops. Higginson also had the "disposition of pickets ... varied each night to perplex the enemy, and some advantage take of his distrust, which might be assumed as equally as our own. The citizens were duly impressed by our supply of ammunition, which was really enormous."

While the Volunteers worked on their defensive measures, both real and imaginary, the Rebels continued to probe their lines, looking for weaknesses and gathering intelligence. The 12th and 13th of March 1863 saw quite a bit of this, with the Volunteers always responding to the Confederate jabs.

Higginson said that "companies go out on the dangerous direction & and after a while the rebel cavalry perhaps appear & and fighting begins— or firing, at least. Messages gallop down & tell me & I mount my horse & ride to the scene of action, & usually the rebels have all disappeared; so that I have not yet seen one of them; they do not seem daring & my men are very willing to advance." Also:

> the gunboats would continue their louder share, their aim being rather embarrassed by the woods and hills. We made reconnaissances, too, to learn the country in different directions, and were apt to be fired upon during these. Along the farther side of what we called the "Debatable Land" there was a line of cottages, hardly superior to negro huts, and almost empty, where the Rebel pickets resorted, and from whose windows they fired. By degrees all these nests were broken up and destroyed, though it cost some trouble to do it, and the hottest skirmishing usually took place around them.

As these things happened, Dr. Rogers said on the 12th that "yesterday they brought in a saddle and some instruments that belonged to a surgeon of the cavalry who was shot through the head. At every fight our boys have put the rebels to flight, though they have twice made the attack with force superior to our own."

With all their efforts to give the Rebels a false estimate of their actual numbers, Higginson was able to say that "all these soon took hold." Many years later he ascertained that General Finegan firmly believed that his command was vastly outnumbered. Higginson said that his tactics were successful. He said that General Finegan wrote on March 14 that "'from the best information we can gather there may be four thousand negroes now in the place with perhaps one company of white troops.'" Gleaning this estimate from the 11th to the 13th from "reconnaissances and other sources of information that the enemy are certainly in large force in Jacksonville," the Confederate commander realized he was going to need some serious reinforcements, more than he had originally estimated from the two skirmishes on the 11th. He set out to make this quite clear to his superiors. Higginson's campaign of deception was working.

Higginson's ruse was having the desired effect of buying him some time, but he knew that bluffing would go just so far. Reflecting on his predicament later, he realized that the original plan of getting the Volunteers into Florida with the numbers at hand had been a mistake. He realized:

> This deficiency in numbers at once became a source of serious anxiety. While planning the expedition, it had seemed so important to get the men a foothold in Florida that I was willing to risk everything for it ... To hold it permanently with nine hundred men was not, perhaps, impossible, with the aid of a gunboat ...; but to hold it, and also to make forays up the river, certainly required a larger number. We came in part to recruit, but had found scarcely an able-bodied negro in the city; all had been removed farther up, and we must certainly contrive to follow them.

So, while Higginson continued his guileful tactics until Stickney returned, Finegan pushed hard to get more men to counter the perceived vast Yankee superiority.

The Confederate commander's predicament of having too few troops, with many of them scattered over a wide area, was not one of his design. He had to make do with considerably less to carry out his military assignment of countering any Union movement in the District of East Florida, which only made his other required duty all the more difficult, that of preventing slaves from escaping. The slave owners, primarily the large ones, were the main power brokers in the state. Since the politicians (many of whom also owned slaves, which included the governor) derived their power from this landed gentry, they had to pay homage to them. This meant making sure that the military in the state (or what was left by March 1863) helped to prevent their property from escaping. If any commander was not enthusiastic enough (in their view) in this task, these planters could pressure the politicians for his removal. Since Finegan could lose his job because of politics, the thought of slaves escaping to this latest Northern invasion (and given the fact that this time the soldiers were black) caused him to use this as one of the reasons to plead for reinforcements.

After three days of skirmishing with the "Abolition troops," Finegan felt he had obtained enough information on the enemy to give his boss, General P. G. T. Beauregard, a clear picture of Union strength and intent. Writing on March 14 his initial assessment, besides falling for Higginson's numerical deception tactics, he emphasized that consolidating his scattered command would "leave with entirely inadequate protection many important points on the coast whence negroes may escape in large numbers to the enemy and where they have easy access to the interior." He said that the object of fortifying Jacksonville "as we gather from our people who have been allowed to come out and indicated by the probabilities of the case, is to hold the town ... and then to advance up the St. John's in their gunboats and establish another secure position higher up the river, whence they may entice the slaves. That the entire negro population of East Florida will be lost and the country ruined there cannot be a doubt, unless the means of holding the Saint John's River are immediately supplied."

Though Finegan emphasized the economic impact of slaves escaping *en masse*, he worded very strongly the political fallout if it occurred. "To appreciate the danger of the permanent establishment of the posts of negro troops on the Saint John's River, I respectfully submit to the commanding general that a consideration of the topography of the country will exhibit the fact that the entire planting interest of East Florida lies within easy communications of the river."[1] Then again Finegan repeated that "a few weeks will suffice to corrupt the entire slave population of East Florida." He was determined to play the political angle to the hilt.

Finegan also asked for four siege guns to counter the gunboats and between 300 and 400 Enfield rifles and enough ammunition for civilian volunteers that he had put a call for the previous day to counter "our unscrupulous enemy" that had "landed a large force of negroes." He said that he hoped "the commanding general will be able to supply me with the means absolutely necessary for the preservation of the people of this district."

As General Finegan stated the grave economic and political risks of not getting reinforcements, Florida's two senators to Richmond had already beaten him to the punch. Augustus E. Maxwell and James M. Baker had previously dispatched a message to Beauregard asking that more troops and heavy guns be sent to Florida.[2] However, Beauregard had a greater problem to worry about than possibly alienating a bunch of wealthy farmers. There had been signs for some time now indicating a possible Union move against either Charleston or Savannah. There was no way that he could afford to lose the infantry and artillery he had concentrated around these cities. He replied to Maxwell and Baker on the 14th that he could "spare no troops or guns for Florida so long as enemy threatens in such overwhelming numbers this place [Charleston] and Savannah." He did however promise to do all he could to assist the state.

While General Finegan waited for his reply from Beauregard, he continued to pull other units of his command from their current assignments that he did not have when he first skirmished with the enemy on the 11th. On March 14 the battery of the Milton Light Artillery on the St. Mary's River was recalled from where it had been since early February with Company K, 2nd Florida Cavalry.[3] This would add 65 more men with their two 12-pound howitzers and two 6-pound rifled pieces to Finegan's growing arsenal. He would now have two batteries of artillery, one under Captain Joseph Dunham and the other under Captain Henry F. Abell. He had waited until the 14th to see if there was going to be any more Federal activity on the St. Mary's before recalling that battery. After waiting for four days after the initial Union landing on March 10, he decided that nothing more was going to happen, so he felt free to do so.[4]

Finegan had also recalled the two other 2nd Florida Cavalry units which had been guarding areas upriver on the west bank of the St. Johns, Company F under Captain Samuel F. Rou from the area of Green Cove Springs and Company H,[5] commanded by Captain John J. Dickison, from the Palatka area. Since no Federal activity was reported going on upriver at the time, he decided his right flank was secure. This was also the tactical information that he had been waiting for so as to protect his political flank. Though Finegan felt that the escaping slave issue was safe for the moment, this too could change at any time and he would have to give up one or both units he had just summoned. He did not recall Company K from Camp Cooper because he decided he still needed to cover that area. He could have used it, because during February Company K had 26 men enlist as a result of the 1st South Carolina's venture up the St. Mary's River.

Finegan's request for help from General Beauregard was not long in coming. Though he could not spare the forces he had marshaled around Charleston and Savannah, Beauregard was true to his word that he would "do all [he] can do as soon as practicable to assist" his Florida subordinate. Since there were other units in his command that were not assigned to the defense of these two cities, he would utilize them. In the District of Georgia he had available four cavalry units guarding the coast. The ones at this time were the recently created 5th Georgia Cavalry Regiment, the 24th Georgia Cavalry Battalion, the 20th Georgia Cavalry Battalion, and the 4th Georgia Cavalry Regiment (Clinch). Since the 4th Georgia was the closest unit, it was used. Colonel Duncan Clinch soon left with five companies and an artillery battery consisting of three small pieces, totaling 227 men. Once he arrived, Clinch would command the combined cavalry, since he outranked Lt. Colonel McCormick.

Beauregard also ordered the District of Middle Florida to help. The commanding officer there, Brigadier General Howell Cobb,[6] initially sent Finegan one artillery battery, the Leon (Florida) Light Artillery, commanded by Captain R. H. Gamble; two new infantry companies, both about 40 men each; and a 32-pound rifled gun mounted on a railroad flatcar. This heavy, mobile artillery piece would give Finegan the ability to counter in part the gunboats, since Beauregard was not able to send him any heavy siege guns. Seeing these units arrive from other districts, plus four more independent infantry companies of Finegan's command, gave Winston Stevens the feeling that "we are getting strong." He wrote to his brother-in-law, Davis Bryant, on March 16 that "we have now ten Infantry 4 Cavalry & Three artillery Companies & we are looking for more to day [*sic*]." In a letter to his wife he also wrote on the 16th, he said that "we have some 16 Companies & some Cavalry is now arriving from Ga." Believing that the Confederate cause a righteous one, Stephens added that "I think God being our helper that the Yanks & negroes will be cleared out of Jacksonville in a few days. We look to God & trust in him to sustain us in this our just cause ... Col Clinch from Ga is here with his Cavalry."

As the word spread of the latest excursion of the "Abolitionist invader" into Florida, outrage was particularly expressed when people found out it was "two negro Regiments commanded by white officers." Davis Bryant was incensed when he found out that Jacksonville was "again taken possession of and occupied by yankees," but this time "garrisoned with nigger troops." Writing on the 15th to his brother, Willie Bryant, who at this time was serving in Tennessee, Davis said that "the last account was that two regiments of the devils had been placed there and were engaged in fortifying the place ..." Though nothing was going on at this time on the St. Mary's, he said "there in no knowing how long it will remain so." However, if the current stalemate in Jacksonville were to change, with the Volunteers being able to achieve a major breakout , he promised swift retribution: "... if those niggers are brought out into the State as they intend, you'll hear of some of the 'damest fights' you ever heard of, as every man of us is determined & do his best towards wiping them out completely."

The civilian population too was aghast at the thought of armed ex-slaves on the loose. As people in other states heard of the invasion of the Volunteers, this had to have the effect of bringing to the forefront for many slave owners the one thing they feared the most—servile insurrection.[7] For many others, the thought of the North putting blacks in uniform was abhorrent enough, let alone them having the ability to be part of active military operations. The editors of the *Augusta Daily Chronicle and Sentinel* caught this sentiment in their preface to an article about Jacksonville that had been previously published in the *Savannah Republican*: "We publish below, from ... a reliable eyewitness, a full account of the recent skirmish near Jacksonville ... about which so many reports have found their way to the public, some of those to the disparagement of our brave troops in the quarter. The idea of even a handful of our men being backed down by a negro regiment, is a slander on freemen." The editors even suggested what to do with the Volunteers. "It is hoped that Gen. Finnegan will adopt a rigorous policy towards these black scoundrels, and either capture or drive them from the State." The officers of the Volunteers would not have fared better when the editors added, "Their white leaders should be forthwhile hung whenever they may fall into our hands."

Though the military occupation of Jacksonville had been a stalemate for almost a week since it began on March 10, a certain level of civilian activity also took place during this time. On the first day of occupation, Susie King said that she and a friend, one Lizzie Lancaster:

> stopped at several of the rebel homes, and after talking with some of the women and children we asked them if they had any food. They claimed to have only some hardtack, and evidently did not care to give us anything to eat, but this was not surprising. They were bitterly against our people and had no mercy or sympathy for us.

Prior to his departure to Fernandina, Lyman Stickney and the other two members of the Florida Tax Commission, John S. Sammis and Harrison Reed, set about doing their job.[8] They "secured a large number of valuable documents, which will greatly expedite the operations of the Commission." As far they knew, the commission would continue to work in Jacksonville for the foreseeable future.

Another civilian who did not arrive until a few days later was Calvin L. Robinson. Originally an assistant assessor to the Florida Tax Commission, he became later a deputy to Colonel J. M. Latta, who had been "appointed provost marshal of the State of Florida by General Saxton." This civilian position was designed to relieve the military "of the care of the refugees and noncombatants, white or black, to provide for their employment, superintendence and education, and to take charge of all abandoned or captured property."

Assigned to his position as deputy when Higginson's expedition sailed for Florida, Robinson was directed on March 13 to "take possession of abandoned property found by U.S. forces in Jacksonville." He then proceeded south on the 14th. Since Captain Rogers of Company E had originally been placed in charge of collecting all abandoned property, Robinson took over this duty when he arrived. Seeing that there was much to do in the discharge of his duty, he "took an inventory of all these articles and kept a full account of them in a book prepared for that purpose. Some of the articles of furniture were requested by the officers to furnish their quarters ... Not only household goods, but all articles of merchandise and produce found or captured were turned over to me and taken charge of by soldiers detailed for my service."

While civilian activity would slowly increase with each day of occupation, military operations continued unabated. One aspect of the occupation that would have seriously hampered the operational part would be poor conduct on the part of the soldiers, thus causing disciplinary problems. However, Colonel Higginson was able to say after the fourth day that his "men have behaved perfectly well, though many were owned here & do not love the people ... There has been no wonton [*sic*] outrages." He said on March 16 that while there "were complaints made against them, they primarily came from the white women," since the women had "insulted them most grossly, swearing at them," and so forth. For these Rebel ladies to act this way was easy to understand. "Here were five hundred citizens, nearly all white, at the mercy of their former slaves.[9] To some of these whites it was the last crowning humiliation, and they were, or professed to be, in perpetual fear."

Dr. Rogers observed similar situations. On the 14th he said that they found:

the rebel women here exceeding desirous to prove that our soldiers are guilty of all the outrages they might expect from a long-injured people now in power. Many of our soldiers are natives of this place and meet their old mistresses here. On the day of our landing, I was over and over implored by those who knew their deserts, to protect them from the "niggers." It was an awful turning of the tables. I quite enjoyed saying "These are United States troops and they will not dishonor the flag."

He added also:

Several charges have been preferred against the soldiers, but thus far, when sifted down, have proved quite as much against those who complained as against our men. The Adjutant told me of a lady of easy manner, who had been very much insulted by a soldier. Close investigation proved he actually sat on her front door-step.

That our soldiers do some outrageous things, I have little doubt. When women taunt them with language most unbecoming, as they sometimes do, I should be very sorry if they did not return a silencer. Thus far they have behaved better than any white regiment has done under such circumstances.

However, there were a few whites who did not act the way of the majority. Higginson said that there was one woman, "the wife of a Rebel captain," who had said that if Jacksonville were to be occupied by enemy troops, it would be best if she had "known them all their lives, and who had generally borne a good character, than to be in the power of entire strangers." In another example, Higginson said that one of his men had brought to his attention a German immigrant who was a small grocer. He had a bad reputation with the whites, because he had dared "lend money to the negroes, or sell to them on credit." The soldier gave the German "the highest compliment in his power," when he said "'He hab true colored-man heart,'" Though the civilians would continue to utter vitriol at the soldiers during their stay in Jacksonville, it did not stop the men from doing their duty.

By the evening of the 13th, Colonel Higginson was convinced that nothing was going to significantly change, that everything had settled into a routine. He said that "we do not go outside at night, but by day the rebel cavalry shew [*sic*] themselves beyond the hill & we go out to meet them, but then retire again." He then thought that it was safe enough of a risk to send part of his force upriver to conduct a limited raid. Since Higginson was the commanding officer of the expedition, he was not able to go, so he sent Colonel Montgomery and his 2nd South Carolina. This was the best thing to do, since it meant keeping both regiments intact. Higginson could better react to enemy action by having his own unit intact instead of having detachments from both the 1st and 2nd S.C. go upriver.

The next day, on the 14th, the 2nd Regiment traveled several miles up the St. John's to a place called Doctor's Lake in the *John Adams* and the *Burnside*. As Montgomery led his men on this raid, the men said that "he is a 'perfect devil to fight, he don't care nuttin 'bout de revels.'" Dr. Rogers added to this: "His bravery is apparently rashness but in reality, far from it. He evidently thinks the true mode of self-defense is to attack the enemy on his own ground."

About 6 p.m. the *Burnside* returned. Montgomery's men had raided a plantation and captured its owner, one Col. Bryant. The Volunteers had caught him "just as he returned to his plantation after running his negroes into the back country." They also reported "great quantities of cotton and cattle up the river." The gunboat however did not come back empty. She was replete "with horses, hogs, chickens, and prisoners."

When Colonel Higginson saw the *Burnside* return, he was very impressed with the 2nd South Carolina's results. He was on one of the wharves with several naval officers when Colonel Montgomery[10] "came down from his first trip. The steamer seemed an animated hen-coop. Live poultry hung from the foremast shrouds, dead ones from the mainmast, geese hissed from the binnacle, a pig paced on the quarter-deck, and a duck's wings were seen fluttering ..."

This raid did not set well with the Confederates. General Finegan decided to send Captain Dickison, Company H, 2nd Florida Cavalry, back to the Palatka area to try and prevent further Yankee excursions up the St. John's and cover in part this exposed Rebel right flank (and his political one). This was what Finegan had feared, that enough river raids would suffice in a few weeks "to corrupt the entire slave population of East Florida." While this first raid by Montgomery was seen as a political threat to Finegan from the point of view as the commander of the District of East Florida, it came too close to home for one of his subordinates.

Captain Winston Stephens, Company B, 2nd Florida Cavalry, had a small plantation near the village of Welaka, several miles upriver from Palatka. In a letter written on March 16 to his young wife, Octavia, he gave detailed instructions to her on what to do if the Volunteers were to go that far up the St. John's. He said:

> I want you to arrange so that the negroes can go at once into the woods if they come up as high as you are & get Clark if the Yankees stay up there to try & get the negroes across the river & send them up on the road to me, but I hope it will not be necessary to break up, tell Burrel [a slave] all about it & tell him I shall depend upon him to care of the rest of the negroes. The negroes in arms will promise him fair prospects, but they will require him to take up arms against us & he will suffer the same fate those did in Town that we killed, & the Yankees say they will hang them if they don't fight.

Stephens also wanted his wife:

> to take care that none of ... the mules fall into their hands. I hope Capt. Dickison will able to keep them from going up above Palatka as his Company will return to that point. The Yankees or negroes went up to Doctor's Lake and captured Col Bryant & three of his negroes and three horses & killed some of his stock. They threatened to do big things but they will not fight and if they come up a few resolute men can drive them back, they will steal every thing they put their hands on so you had better get Henry [another slave] to bury every thing some place & what money you keep put it around your body. I would not wear any jewelry or show any thing that will tempt the men ... The famous Kansas Montgomery is in Command of one of the negro regiments & your Mother knows his character.

Contact between Johnny Reb and Billy Yank continued as civilian activity and Montgomery's first raid took place. The Confederates would appear in small, mounted formations, go up just so far and engage the pickets, after which the gunboats would open up. However, the naval batteries' accuracy would not be too good, since "their aim being rather embarrassed by the woods and hills."

In one of the Union forays into "no man's land" on March 16, Captain Stephens was several miles behind the lines with his command on the property of a small slave holder named George Mooney. He was in the process of writing another letter to his wife when he received word that once again "the Yankees were advancing." He immediately got his unit ready to go. However, "after getting ready and going down we learned that after exchanging a few shots they returned to Town." Stephens' Company B returned by mid-afternoon and he continued with his letter. Since his ride that day did not accomplish anything, he said he would "go down this evening to ambush them and ... hope to get some of the scamps."

In another instance on the 16th in which the Rebels shot at the pickets, one of them was hit in his foot by a conical bullet. He was carried back to be treated by Dr. Rogers. While the doctor took care of him, he complained that he was not allowed to shoot because "'de cunnel stood out for ward ob we lookin at de revels wid de glass an wouldn't let we fire.'" Inquiring later about this, Higginson explained to Rogers "that the range was so long that it would have been a waste of ammunition."

Though there had been plenty of skirmishing between the Confederates and the Volunteers from the 12th to the 16th, there had also been plenty of downtime, since not everyone was needed every time shots were exchanged. One way soldiers passed the time was to write letters. Confederate Captain Stephens wrote to his brother-in-law, Davis Bryant, on the 16th, giving him up-to-date details and expressing his fears:

Five boats are in the river opposite Town, one went up the river yesterday & returned last night with a few horses ... My opinion is they intend to overrun the country with negroes & I am very anxious about my family & have tried to send a man up to notify them but could not. I dont know what will be best to do. Genl Finegan is concentrating a large force with the intention of storming the place. We can drive them out but the difficulty is the Gun boats, they can prevent us from holding this place ... I think from all I can learn that in two or three days the fight will come off. If I should be among the dead take care of my Dear family the best you can & take charge of her [Octavia's] business matters.[11] I hope no such luck to be my share but in these times we can t tell what to look for ... I forgot to tell you they have burnt up all the buildings from Bisbee to the clearing this side of Town & they continue to burn & no telling when the thing is to stop. Ours is a terrible fix as the negroes are so very insulting and cruel. They stick fire in some of the houses & the families in them & they have to get out the best they can.

All the participants in this latest invasion of Florida would express their thoughts, fears, hopes, and anticipations of what might happen next. Though some things would be similar, others would be quite different. Since Colonel Higginson was the commander of this expedition, he saw things differently than Captain Stephens. He opined:

> In respect to personal courage I have learnt nothing new, & adhere to the belief that war has not so much harder tests than peace. But the anxiety of a commander is something for which peace affords no parallel ... This of itself would be enough to keep me from any desire for high military responsibility, & if it is so with one of my easy temperament, what must it be to those as conscientious & more excitable? ... So for as love of adventure goes, it must yield less & less enjoyment as one goes up—were I a private I could do many things & run many risks which I ought not now to incur ... I have power, responsibility, rule a city absolutely, adjudicate arrests of prisoners & restitutions of old women's cows—plan defences [*sic*], go on well-escorted reconnaissances, but the propensity for personal scraps is partially corked up.

As Higginson wrote these personal thoughts on the pros and cons of command responsibility, there could also be no doubt that there was one vexing question on his mind: where were Stickney and the reinforcements? As he worried about this with each passing day, Rebel strength continued to grow.

Beaufort, South Carolina

Lyman Stickney's voyage back to Fernandina on the 12th on the *Boston* was not what he had expected. He had anticipated that he would have been able to obtain the promised reinforcements from Colonel Hawley, commander of the 7th Connecticut Infantry, and then easily return to Jacksonville. However, this seemingly simple transfer of four infantry companies and a light artillery battery did not materialize. Hawley reneged on his promise.[12] This left Stickney in an awkward position. He probably thought of going to St. Augustine where the 7th New Hampshire was stationed, but probably would get turned down there too. He could still try since time was of the essence, but if refused, more time would have been wasted. Therefore, he only really had one alternative left, which was to return to Beaufort and go see General Saxton.[13] This would take much more time, but to return to Jacksonville empty-handed would be far worse, which in this case was not an option.

When Stickney arrived back in Beaufort on March 13, he immediately went to General Saxton to explain his plight. Fortunately for him, Saxton would be able to help. When Saxton first arrived, he only had the title of Military Governor in the Department of the South after the War Department took over from the Treasury Department in the management of the plantations, the freedmen, and the collection of cotton. He also did not have any white regiments placed under his command. However, when General Hunter returned near the end of January 1863 to resume command, he made a few changes in the makeup of his staff, the most important being the appointment of Brigadier General Truman Seymour as his chief-of-staff and chief of artillery. This meant that Seymour's previous position as commander of Port Royal Island needed to be filled. Hunter gave the job to Saxton. He now had white regiments to command. When Stickney came to see him, Saxton was in a position to help.

Since the movement of troops from Beaufort to Jacksonville meant transferring soldiers from one part of the department to another, Saxton would have to go to Hilton Head to obtain permission from Hunter.[14] Stickney and Saxton went to visit him as soon as possible. Since he had a vested financial interest in the success of this Florida mission, Stickney knew he had to be prepared to make the case. With Saxton in his corner, he was ready to do so, especially in his role as the head of the Florida Tax Commission. Since Hunter was known as an impulsive individual,[15] he could quickly pull the operation out of Jacksonville just as quickly as he had originally approved it. However, once Hunter heard Stickney and Saxton, he acquiesced to their requests. This now set the wheels into motion to coordinate all activity required to send reinforcements to Florida.

On Port Royal Island, General Saxton had six infantry regiments, three artillery batteries and a battalion of cavalry, besides the 1st and 2nd S.C. Volunteers.[16]

Since he had the responsibility of protecting the island against any Rebel attack, plus the fact that there was an attack being planned against Charleston, he could only send so many troops. Of his six infantry regiments, Saxton decided he could spare two, so he choose the 6th Connecticut and the 8th Maine.[17] Giving them their deployment orders to get ready, he then coordinated with the Navy to get transportation. The *Boston* plus two other ships were used. They were the *General Meigs* and the *Delaware*. The 6th Connecticut was assigned to the *Boston*, while the

8th Maine would be transported on the other two vessels. When they were ready to go, the 6th left on the evening of March 18 while the 8th[18] would start out at noon the next day.[18]

By the time the 8th Maine began to leave on the 19th, word had already reached Washington, D.C. that the operation was not going as planned. One of President Lincoln's aides, John Hay, heard "rumors here of disaster to the colored troops. I am in hopes they may turn out to be untrue." He would eventually find out that the rumors were indeed false.

Since the 6th Connecticut left Beaufort on the evening of the 18th, it arrived the next morning at Fort Clinch. While there, Jerome Tourtellotte of the 7th Connecticut stationed there noted in his diary "Steamer Boston passed the fort from Hilton Head having the Sixth Connecticut on board on the way to Jacksonville, making a friendly call only." Later that day the *Boston* arrived at the mouth of the St. John's River. However, when the steamer tried "to cross the bar and enter [the river]," Charles Cadwell of the 6th said that they "got aground, and after several ineffectual attempts, we finally succeeded by the aid of a tug-boat, and our destination, Jacksonville, was reached on the morning of the 20th of March."[19]

When the 8th Maine boarded its transport, three companies were placed on the *General Meigs* while the other seven were put on the *Delaware*. When the *General Meigs* left Beaufort at noon on the 19th, the *Delaware* was still being prepared. The *General Meigs* went as far as Hilton Head where she anchored until the 20th with the intent of waiting for the *Delaware* so they could convoy down together. However, the sea would cause a few problems that did not allow this to happen. Charles Lord on the *General Meigs* said that "when the Deleware [*sic*] started for this place as it was rather rough weather our captain did not start from Hilton head until some six hours after the Deleware [*sic*] had started. We had a rough time of it through the night … most of the men were [seasick] … I was fortunate enough however to keep off from the sick list. Capt Roberts & Lieut Willis were completely used up with sea sickness. In fact the waves pitched us about in fine style."

When the *General Meigs* arrived at the St. John's at 8 a.m. the next morning, everybody thought their ordeal was just about over, "but it was so rough that we could not get in over the bar. The Captain ran up the signal for a pilot to come out and help in, but it was so rough that the pilot would not venture out so after cruising around a couple of hours or such another, we put back about 25 miles to Fernandina where we put in and remained until 6 oclock this morning, when we made another start for … [Jacksonville}, when we arrived …" After navigating up the river, the *General Meigs* finally arrived at the dock about 2:30 p.m. on March 22, but there was no sign of the *Delaware*.

A Brigade of Black and White

When Stickney left on March 12 on the *Boston* to procure more soldiers, he came across the gunboat *Paul Jones*, which was on her way to conduct a reconnaissance up the St. John's River. Her commanding officer, Captain Charles Steedman, said that he had been "informed by Judge Stickney ... that it was his intention to obtain a large reinforcement of troops for the purpose of holding this place permantly [*sic*]." Given the precariousness of the Union land forces, Steedman felt "obliged to remain here to give protection to the force now in possession of the town, as I did not think it adequate ... [to] ... hold it without assistance." This additional naval firepower would be a welcome relief to Higginson as he continued to build up his defensive capability while waiting for Stickney to return.

In addition to barricaded streets, burned buildings to increase fields of fire, and an ever present picket line, Colonel Higginson had two earthen works built on both sides of the railroad leading westward. The correspondent of *The New York Times* said in a dispatch that this area was "the only weak link ... on the southwest ... portion of the city ..." The work on the northern side of the railroad was named Fort Montgomery and the one on the southern side Fort Higginson. The correspondent said also that "to give range to the guns from these forts, a large forest of pine and oak trees had to be cut down, and about fifty dwellings ... destroyed ... Fort Higginson not only commands the left of the railroad, but the approach on the south to Jacksonville, by the St. John's River." By the time the 6th Connecticut arrived on the 20th, Dr. Rogers wrote that "our earthworks are so nearly completed that guns are mounted and a large force could be easily repulsed."

While these fortifications were being built, Higginson received a message under a flag of truce from Lieutenant Colonel McCormick on the morning of March 18 telling him to evacuate all women and children that were still in Union lines within 24 hours or face the consequences of being held responsible for any civilian casualties in the event of a Confederate attack. McCormick added that "if the safe return of teams is guaranteed I will to-day send to the brick-yard church or to the town for all women and children who may wish to come within our lines." Higginson did not initially respond to this. In the afternoon he got another message repeating the same thing, this time from Colonel Duncan Clinch, commander of the 4th Georgia Cavalry and the combined cavalry units. After this second transmission, Higginson sent his reply stating that "there has been no restriction upon the passage of women and children across lines nor will there be." He agreed to McCormick's demand that if any civilians wanted to go, they would be ready to leave within 24 hours and "any teams coming under a flag of truce as far as the brick church will of course be rigidly respected."

Dr. Rogers added his thoughts to this:

This looks as if they intend to approach the town with artillery and set it on fire with shells. This is feasible in spite of our gunboats. If there is any pluck in them the attempt will be made. Many of our officers think the message a mere flourish for intimidation, but I do not and shall hold myself in readiness to send my sick and wounded to the steamers at short notice.

Regardless of this, he continued to look down the river. Rogers said, "Meanwhile we look for reinforcements by the *Boston*. Her delay is unaccountable."

The next day, the 19th, the Provost Marshal [Captain Rogers] and Major Strong were kept very busy escorting those who wanted to leave. About 150 women and children left. There were about 200 more who did not leave, since Higginson had said that he would not force anyone to go. While the transfer of the noncombatants went on, Major Strong said Captain Rogers sat on his horse and whistled the John Brown hymn, a variation of the "Battle Hymn of The Republic," only to annoy the Rebels. Dr. Rogers wanted to go also to the transfer point, but was denied permission. As far as the others who did not leave, he said "the Col is under no obligation to force civilians out of town without positive notification from the enemy that he intends to attack."

To continue to keep the Rebels off balance, Colonel Higginson sent more raiding parties upriver. The *John Adams* went up on the 16th and brought back that evening "thirty contrabands, ten horses, and quantities of corn, hogs, cotton, etc." On the 17th the *Burnside* went "on a [*sic*] errand." Higginson said that "these little trips were called 'rests;' there was no other rest" while waiting for the *Boston* to return, because "an immense amount of picket and fatigue duty had to be done." None of this activity, however, was lost on General Finegan. Besides the presence of the gunboats, he said in another report to General Beauregard on March 20 that "the town is now strongly fortified ..." The Volunteers "are robbing and plundering everything on the east bank of the Saint John's River." Since "the enemy have been expecting re-inforcements of white troops," he said "their own statements and circumstances indicate that their probable policy is to occupy Jacksonville with white troops and send the negroes, with largely increased numbers, to Palatka, and then attempt to move amongst the Plantations." Though he had been clamoring for more troops, more were already arriving. On the 18th, one company of the 1st Florida

Special Battalion, commanded by Captain Edwin West, had arrived from the District of Middle Florida. On the 20th, another Georgia regiment, the 1st Georgia Regulars, received its orders to go to Florida. Though these additions would be a relief, Finegan's latest request for more soldiers would take on a new emergency when he found out also on the 20th that the Volunteers had been "largely re-inforced [sic], as we are advised by our pickets to-day, by troops supposed to be white."

The arrival of the *Boston* on the morning of the 20th with the 6th Connecticut Infantry and Stickney was a welcome relief to Higginson. As he later remembered about the first 10 days in Jacksonville, writing in his regimental history, he said "How like a dream seems now that period of daily skirmishes and nightly watchfulness. The fatigue was so constant that the days hurried by." Though he was grateful that the white soldiers were here, "I only wish they were black." However, he had now a new task to perform that had never been done before. "I had to show not only that blacks can fight, but that they & white soldiers can work in harmony together." He never mentioned anything about the 7th Connecticut Infantry, but most likely Stickney told him what took place.

As the commander of the Florida operation, Higginson had the responsibility of carrying out his mission with the means provided to him, even if there was a polarizing issue—race. Though the arrival of the 6th Connecticut gave him the badly needed manpower required, the mindset that many of the white soldiers brought with them would be a two-edged sword.[20] On the one hand he had to deal with an external enemy, the Confederates, while on the other he had to combat an internal one, racial prejudice. If not dealt with in the right manner, the latter would defeat his mission quicker than a Rebel victory on the battlefield. However, he did have one ace up his sleeve. Higginson said, "Fortunately for our own serenity, I had great faith in the intrinsic power of military discipline, and also knew that a common service would soon produce mutual respect among good soldiers." However, "the first twelve hours of this mixed command were to me a more anxious period than any outward alarms had created."

Though discipline would be the key that would enable Higginson to handle this internal problem, it did not stop those against blacks from venting among themselves, officer or enlisted man. Charles Steedman, commander of the gunboat *Paul Jones*, had said previously in an official communiqué on the 12th that he felt "obliged to remain to give protection to the force now in possession of the town." In a letter to his wife on the 20th he wrote his true feelings. He said:

> I arrived here just one week ago & found this town in the quiet possession
> of the army as the force was inadequate to hold the town without the

protection of the Gun Boats. I have been obliged to remain here this long to take care of them. The day has been by no means to my taste as the army force was composed entirely of Niggers ... you can have no idea how annoying it has been to me in being obliged to act with these people but as the old adage has it "duty before pleasure."

Two days after the 6th Connecticut arrived, "white and black soldiers, navy and army officers and civilians" attended church on Sunday the 22nd. However reverend the occasion was, Dr. Rogers could not help but make the observation that the "prejudice of the white soldiers is very strong, yet I trust there will be no serious collision. Our boys have seen hardships enough to unfit them for receiving taunts very graciously."

Once the soldiers of the 6th Connecticut had disembarked off the *Boston* on the 20th, Higginson did not waste any time in putting them to use on the ramparts of the Union forces' defensive perimeter. They did not have to pitch any tents, "but occupied the houses which had but recently been vacated." The early evening hours passed away quietly though there was rain and wind "enough to make sounds everywhere." However, General Finegan decided he would test the new arrivals with a late-night skirmish. About midnight, the Rebel reconnaissance opened up on the enemy picket line, which gave the Federals "a general impression outside that all secesh was down upon us," but the Union response was quick and decisive. "[C]annonading began at one of the forts and then followed shells from the gunboats." Higginson estimated that the Confederate attack was done by "perhaps fifty men," but it had an effect that "kept us stirred up all night. It was intensely dark, which increased the perplexity." There were no more attacks after this one that night.

The next day, March 21, Colonel Higginson sent Major Strong and a detachment of the 1st S.C. to see if the Rebels from the previous night's attack were still around. After going "far beyond the accustomed line, without opposition," the Volunteers returned. Meanwhile, back at the hospital, Dr. Rogers noticed that day the effects that the Federal return artillery fire had on his patients. "Cannonading in the night is hard for weak nerves and I dreaded the effect upon my sick. One of the convalescents was suddenly attacked with pleurisy in the night, and when I asked him about the time when the pain began, he replied, 'Just after de gun done gone shoot.' Another, who had a bullet through his leg, said he had 'enjoyed a mighty night bad rest.'" Fortunately for the wounded (and the rest of the Union force), there would be no more Rebel attacks that day or evening, since "[it] was one of unbroken quiet."

When Sunday the 22nd dawned on the Volunteers, now augmented for two days by the presence of the 6th Connecticut, quiet was still present along the defenses. As the sun rose over the horizon facing west, the pickets could see that the Johnnies were not around. As if by divine intervention on this Sabbath day, the guns of the Yankees remained silent. Commenting on the tranquil setting of this morning, especially in the knowledge that more reinforcements were on the way, Colonel Higginson said that "every day makes us more impregnable & now the enemy has drawn back & there is no more skirmishing & I think we shall be let alone unless we march out to meet him. This is Sunday; the bell is ringing for church & Rev. Mr. French ... is to preach." When the church service began, it was "densly [sic] crowded with white and black soldiers, navy and army officers and civilians." The chaplain of the 1st South Carolina had as his subject "the sword of the Lord and of Gideon." While this service was going on, the *General Meigs* containing three companies of the 8th Maine Infantry had finally cleared the bar at the entrance of the St. John's and was proceeding upriver.

When the *General Meigs* finally arrived at Jacksonville, it was about 2:30 in the afternoon. These soldiers of the 8th Maine, which were Companies E, F, and I, were glad to finally be on solid ground after several days on the ship, especially after their ordeal in the rough weather, which left many a stomach very nauseous. They were definitely not in the mood to fight the Rebels. Once disembarked, Colonel Higginson instructed the 8th's officer-in-charge, Major John Hemmingway, where to go and what to do. He also inquired about the status of the rest of the regiment, in which Hemmingway replied he did not know of the *Delaware*'s whereabouts.

When Higginson found out that the 8th Maine's commander, Colonel John D. Rust, was also on the *Delaware*, he realized that he would soon no longer be the senior officer. Though he had the same rank, Rust was senior because he had been promoted to colonel earlier than Higginson. The date of rank always settled who was in charge when officers of equal rank were present. Higginson's main worry now was that Rust would change his reason why he came to Florida in the first place.[21] He said, "Now my hope is that we may be allowed to go to some point higher up the river, which we can hold for ourselves. There are two other points which in themselves are as favorable as this, & for getting recruits, better. So I shall hope to be allowed to go. To take posts & then let white troops garrison them—that is my programme."

Though the 22nd was turning out to be another quiet day, General Finegan was already making plans to have Monday be very different. Even if Higginson knew of these plans, it would be doubtful if he would have worried about them now that more reinforcements were arriving. He also felt more confident that he would finally be able to carry out his mission. However, an equally determined enemy would also try to see to it that he would not succeed.

Retrograde or Retreat?

Ever since March 10, 1863 when the Volunteers landed in the morning and drove out the Confederate cavalry detachment, Rebal pickets had been placed around Jacksonville to watch out for and report any Federal movements so General Finegan would be able to counter them. Also, with the increase in the size of his forces as time went by, he was able to form a tight cordon around the Yankee invaders. However, except for the two engagements fought on the 11th, Finegan had not yet fully employed all the reinforcements he had acquired up to the 22nd, save using the infantry and cavalry for picketing and the occasional skirmish. He had not even used any of his artillery yet. Nevertheless, he finally made the decision on this Sunday to use his enlarged command to demonstrate in force against the Federals the next day.

Finegan ordered Colonel Clinch, who was now the commanding officer at Camp Finegan, to be ready to move at 7 a.m. the next morning on the 23rd. His force would include all the infantry and dismounted cavalry being used as infantry, any of the remaining cavalry on picket duty that could be spared, and two of the artillery batteries. He would also have the railroad gun. The Confederate attack force was to have two days' cooked rations, enough ammunition for all arms for a protracted engagement, and all necessary medical support. Finegan said that the "lines of battle will be formed on the hill on this side of the Three Mile Branch." He also instructed Clinch that "every effort will be made by our skirmishers to advance to the ground selected, and, failing in this, we will open on them with the 32-pounder rifle gun."

As Colonel Clinch set about preparing for his mission the next day, the quietness of March 22 continued into the evening. Those not on the Union defensive perimeter were either asleep, talking around fires, playing cards, or writing letters. Charles Lord of the 8th Maine wrote to his sister since he had "a spare moment to write … a few lines which I will forward by the mail which it is to leave here for Hilton Head in a few minutes. It is now about 8 oclock in the evening and we that is Companies F. E. & I. of the 8th Maine Regt. arrived here on the Genl Meigs at about half past two o clock this P.M." Describing the 8th's ordeal on their ship, he said also that Jacksonville was a "quite a pretty village—, on the St. Johns river some 25 miles from the mouth of the river." Still recuperating from his voyage, he added he did not have "the time to particularize of the present time, neither am I in a fit condition to write. I have not just got over the rolling of the ship. It seems just as if the room was rolling and front it seems as if every-thing was on the move." Lord added that the "Deleware [*sic*] with the Col. Lieut. Col. and the other seven companies of the regiment has not yet arrived here and we have not heard a word from her." He anticipated that "we shall soon have some music with the rebs as their pickets are very near to ours and there is skirmishing with the enemy every day." His expectation of soon having "some music with the rebs" would prove to be in consonance with General Finegan's plan to attack on Monday.

Now that he had the reinforcements he needed, though the seven remaining companies of the 8th Maine were still *en route*, Higginson was hopeful that Colonel Rust would allow him to continue with his original plans once he arrived. However, he still worried about having an integrated brigade. In a rather comical way gauging future successes with its current makeup, he wrote in his journal that "we can sleep sound o'nights & if the black and white babies do not quarrel & pull hair, can do very well." In a letter to his mother, he wrote seriously that the "colors are better apart, for the military service—let us take posts & the white troops garrison them."

The Rebel tune that Charles Lord anticipated commenced the next morning, March 23, after the sun was up,[1] when the Confederates had advanced sufficiently close enough for the railroad gun to be within range to hit Jacksonville's defenses. This was the first time in any armed conflict that a heavy artillery piece had been placed on a railroad flatcar to give it mobility instead of just being in a static position. Though it had the advantage of speed and could easily outdistance any advancing Federals if they attacked, Finegan wanted to defeat them on the field of battle. However, the Yankees did not react to the Rebel provocation.

When the artillery attack began, Higginson prepared his men for an expected ground assault. He moved them to the front to direct his subordinates as the situation dictated. He was certain, though still worried, that his integrated brigade, a first in the American Civil War, would hold together as they got ready to fight side by side an expected enemy attack. While the Confederate barrage continued, the *Delaware* with Colonel Rust and the remaining seven companies of the 8th Maine finally arrived.[2] When Higginson was made aware of this, he quickly sent a message to Rust telling him that he "was very sorry I could not receive him handsomely," but he was "in the middle of a fight." When the gunboats added their weight to the Federal counter battery effort, the Rebel artillery attack "didn't last long."

Now that Colonel Rust was here, Higginson had to relinquish command that he had had since the expedition's inception. He would now revert to commanding the 1st South Carolina again. All he had to do now was "merely ... fight & obey orders—not command." This change of command also meant that Captain Rogers would no longer be provost marshal. He and his company would be replaced by a company from the 8th Maine. The 8th's surgeon would also replace Dr. Rogers as post surgeon. These changes were made in this expedition because the responsibilities of rear area operations were normally given to individuals from the regiment of the ranking officer.

Once Higginson was able to, he apprised Rust of the situation and what he wanted to accomplish by going upriver. Rust acquiesced to his original plans. Higginson said that his new superior officer "felt bound to give the chief opportunities of action to the colored troops," though there were those in the 8th Maine (and the 6th Connecticut) who wanted to take part in the river operations also. They had been doing primarily picket duty on Port Royal Island for the longest time and wanted to see action. He added, "Oh how the Conn. & Me boys long for active service, from which they have always been kept back."

Though the arrival of the remainder of the 8th gave the added weight needed to repel any Rebel attack, the fact that its commanding officer was senior of all the colonels present was not too well·received. Dr. Rogers said that he was sorry "that Col. Rust ranks our Col." Higginson wrote in his journal that "the Senior officer has to take command & that there was no way of sending me reinforcements without a senior officer I being junior to all the Colonels.[3] Only the 6th Ct. has an absent Colonel, & if he returns soon, as is expected, he will supersede both Rust and me." The ranking officer that had arrived with the 6th Connecticut was Major Lorenzo Meeker. The 6th's commander was Colonel John L. Chatfield, who Higginson heard was "a fine officer which Rust is not."

There was a friendly dispute that evening between Higginson and Montgomery, about whether the Confederates would attack again with their railroad gun. Montgomery exclaimed, "Tonight the town will be shelled." Higginson replied, "They w'ont dare." However, as Higginson later observed, Montgomery's exhortation was not a rash utterance. Higginson attested, "He is commonly so little apprehensive that it meant more from him than it would from most men: it was based on their known wish to destroy the town, & their having shelled us during the day." He may have disagreed with Montgomery's prediction, but Higginson decided anyway to play it safe. He "went to bed with [his] clothes on." He would, however, prove to be correct, because the Rebels did withdraw before dark (without the Federals knowledge) and Higginson "never waked from half past nine to six."

Though the night attack predicted by Montgomery failed to materialize, this did not mean that the Johnnies would not renew their shelling of Jacksonville sometime during the day of the 24th. Anticipating this renewed bombardment also did not mean that there was going to be a cessation of upriver activity. The gunboat *Paul Jones* went to Palatka that day to continue the mission of looking for recruits. After a lengthy search, the Volunteers detached for this detail came up almost empty-handed. They only found "a single contraband." This was due to the fact, much to their dismay, that "all the slaves [had] been run back into the interior." Whether this trip was ultimately seen as a correlation to the experience of hardly finding anyone on the St. Mary's River is a good question; only having "a single contraband" after all their efforts caused the commander of this trip to return to Jacksonville that evening.

The lack of progress in finding recruits to fill out the 2nd South Carolina (let alone enough for a possible third regiment), plus the continuous efforts by the Confederates to drive the Federals out of the city, had to be causing consternation among the principals of the Volunteers. Dr. Rogers expressed his worries when he wrote on the evening of the 24th that:

> The fact is if we are ever to get black soldiers, we must make a big hole through the rebel lines so that the blacks can run back to us. Every day of waiting here is a day of strength to our fortifications, but a day of weakness for our purpose. We need nothing so much as black recruits and it seems to me that if the proclamation of emancipation is ever to be anything more than a dead letter, it must be made so before many weeks. Were the North an anti-slavery unit I should not feel at all impatient, but I believe we have more to dread from traitors at home than from their friends who fight against us here. Possibly public opinion may not continue on its anti-slavery decline at home, but if today we had fifty thousand black troops, I should feel more certain of its returning to health.

However, on an upbeat, Rogers said that he was "perfectly satisfied that there is nothing in this world so dreadful to the rebels as the enlistment of their slaves in the federal service. They will resort to every possible means to prevent our getting recruits." One "means" the Rebels did have to prevent further recruiting was in the form of a certain captain of cavalry named J. J. Dickison, who would prove very shortly to the Yankees that he was a very deadly opponent.

The Volunteers may not have been successful on this trip, but it did not mean that there would not be any more river forays. In fact, Colonel Montgomery was going to make another trip the next day, the 25th. Higginson lauded this idea, but said that Montgomery did not exactly plan it out properly. Since he was no longer the expeditionary commander, there was not anything Higginson could do except recommend against it. If he had, it did not work. Higginson called him:

> splendid, but impulsive & changable [*sic*] never plans far ahead, & goes off on a tangent. The last tangent is to leave us tomorrow—go up the river 30 miles on steamer & strike directly for the interior, where the slaves are leaving the rebels to watch us here. What makes the project odder is that in forty eight hours or so we i.e. the S.C.V. hope to be under weigh to take & occupy some upper point, so that by waiting he could strike off from us. But off he goes tomorrow unless he changes his mind.

Montgomery actually did not leave the next day but 24 hours after that, on the 26th, not because of his impulsive behavior but because Johnny Reb decided to give Jacksonville and its uninvited inhabitants an early morning wake-up call in the form of an artillery barrage with the 32-pound railroad gun.

The Bombardment of Jacksonville

To Brigadier General Joseph Finegan, it seemed that the only way he could defeat the Federals would be to draw them out of their strong defensive position, out of range of the gunboats' and forts' ability to return overwhelming fire, and engage them in open battle—i.e., General Lee's basic plan. A frontal assault was out of the question because it would be too costly to the Rebels. Since the first artillery attack on the defenses did not cause them to react, maybe lobbing several rounds into Jacksonville itself just might do the trick. Using the railroad gun as bait, he would force the Yankees to attack his position. This would be the only way, Finegan reasoned, for them to stop the Confederates from shelling the city, especially with its remaining civilian population.

On Tuesday the 24th of March, Finegan ordered his chief of ordnance, Lieutenant T. E. Buckman, to take the railroad gun to within a short distance of the city early the next morning, lob several shells, and then retire before the superior firepower of the Yankees would be able to mount an effective reply, especially if a lucky round hit something vital, like the engine or the gun itself. Buckman would have the assistance of Private Francis Soule, detached from Captain Edwin West's company of the 1st Florida Special Battalion, who would command the gun detachment. Buckman would also have a detachment of infantry for local support. "In obedience to [his orders, the lieutenant] proceeded to within 1½ miles of the town and opened on it with effect, throwing shell with great accuracy into those parts of the town where the enemy was located." As Finegan had predicted, the "firing of the enemy from a large number of heavy guns on their gunboats and some in battery, soon became concentrated and accurate, and the gun, in pursuance of orders, was withdrawn after inflicting some damage on the enemy and without loss on our side."

Since the railroad gun had been first introduced to the Union forces on Monday the 23rd, there was no doubt in the minds of the Federals and civilians what to expect in the succeeding days as long as they remained in occupation of the city. Their expectation became reality early Wednesday, with the Rebel fire being surprisingly accurate. Dr. Alfred Walton of the 8th Maine said that:

> ... at 3:30 this morning the rebels came down on the railroad and opened on the town ... The first shot went through an unoccupied house next to our medical headquarters and exploded, turning us all out in a hurry. Just as I went out of doors the second one broke over our heads. The third one struck the roof of a house where a Union man and his wife were sleeping; the shell passed through the side of the house and imbedded itself eight feet in the ground without exploding ... They got seven of these shells into town before our gunboats got a range on them, when they beat a retreat.

Sergeant Charles Cadwell of the 6th Connecticut said that:

> a shell entered a house ..., passing through the bed-room in which a man and wife were sleeping, and in its course it passed a stuffed-seat rocking chair on which lay the man's coat, cutting off the skirts and forcing them through the back of the chair. The window glass was shattered and two looking glasses hanging in the room were broken, while the occupants of the bed were litterally [*sic*] covered with plaster and splinters.

Dr. Rogers said that he had been:

... dreaming pleasantly ... when a rebel bomb-shell burst somewhere in the immediate vicinity of the town. Presently another and another, then the reply of our guns and then the 'long roll.' It seemed as if we were at last, fairly in for it. Dr. Minor came up to ask if we were to trust Providence to care for our hospital. I advised him to go back and assure them all that the Lord was on the side of our big guns. Meanwhile I crawled on the top of our observatory and watched the firing until the secesh sent a shell which burst above my head with a note so shrill that I began to think of Gabriel's trumpet and crawled down again ... I do not think it was chivalric for the rebels to wake us so early ...

Rogers added:

Several shells came into town before our guns gave the quietus. A section of one struck within a few feet of the Col. and Major, in front of Headquarters. The hospital of the 8th Maine was porforated [*sic*] by a piece of one, and two dwelling houses were terribly bored. One went through two occupied chambers ... Shells make very ugly looking holes through houses.

Susie King, being a civilian, greatly concerned Colonel Higginson when, as she wrote:

that night the rebels shelled directly toward ... [his] ... headquarters. The shelling was so heavy, that the colonel told my captain to have me taken into the town to a hotel, which was used as a hospital. As my quarters were just in the rear of the colonel's, he was compelled to leave his before the night was over. I expected every moment to be killed by a shell, but on arriving at the hospital I knew I was safe, for the shells could not reach us there.

Calvin Robinson had a near miss when an "unexploded shell passed over the roof of my house and through a little bakery building." Fortunately nobody was hurt during the Rebel attack.

Finegan's plan to draw the Federals out of their defensive works and into the open also worked. Colonel Rust and his subordinate commanders decided that something had to be done, given all the near misses of the Confederate barrage. Though nobody was killed or wounded, it did not mean they would be so lucky again. Rust ordered Colonel Higginson to form a composite force made up of several companies from the 8th Maine, 6th Connecticut, and the 1st South Carolina.[4] He did not include the 2nd S.C. because it still had only two companies. Higginson's force would be out of range of the protective umbrella of the Federals' heavy guns (and with no means to quickly communicate with them even if they were not). He decided to borrow from the Rebel playbook and have a 10-pound Parrott gun mounted on a railroad flatcar. The Federals did not have an engine, so one of the 1st S.C.'s companies provided the motive power to pull it along the rail. Rust also ordered Higginson not to go too far into the interior. His force "comprised half our garrison, and should the town meanwhile be attacked from some other direction, it would be in great danger."

When the Federals moved out and marched west into the interior, the 6th Connecticut under Major Meeker was on the left side of the railroad, the 8th Maine under Lieutenant Colonel Twitchell on the right, and the 1st S.C. "under Major Strong, in the centre, having in charge the cannon, to which they have been trained." This movement was the first offensive action taken during this occupation. As they moved along the rail, Higginson placed skirmishers out in front of the columns and on the flanks to provide early warning of any enemy presence. It was not too long before the advancing skirmishers made contact with mounted Rebel pickets. The Confederate cavalry "retired before us through the woods, keeping beyond the range of the skirmishers." Higginson knew it would not be much more time before contact with the main enemy body would be made.

As the Union columns continued their advance, they moved "through the open pine barrens and occasional thick woods." When Higginson reached what he believed to be the limit of his advance per his order from Rust, he started to have his men fall back, tearing up the tracks as they went to prevent the Confederates from being able to be in artillery range of Jacksonville again. However, as they worked, about four miles from town, "the smoke of a rebel engine was seen in the distance."

When the mounted Confederate pickets first saw the advancing Yankee force, word was sent to General Finegan who quickly put his plan into motion. "My entire force was immediately ordered with all possible expedition to proceed to the ground where they were drawn up and engage them. The rifled 32-pounder, under the command of Lieutenant Buckman, with a strong support of infantry and cavalry on left flank, protected on the right by the main body of our troops, was sent down on the railroad." Fortunately for Finegan, he also had at his disposal another infantry regiment that had finally arrived the day before, after five days of being en route,[5] the 1st Georgia Regulars. As soon as the Confederate railroad gun came within distance, Lieutenant Buckman fired.

While Finegan hoped that this action of his would finally force the Yankees out of Jacksonville, the Confederate approach became very clear to them, especially to Colonel Higginson. He said:

Straining our eyes to look along the reach of level railway which stretched away through the pine barren, we began to see certain ominous puffs of smoke … Gradually the smoke grew denser, and appeared to be moving up along the track, keeping pace with our motion, and about two miles distant. I watched it steadily through a field-glass from our own slowly moving battery … Sometime in the dim smoke I caught a glimpse of something blacker, raised high in the air like the threatening head of some giant gliding serpeant [*sic*]. Suddenly there came a sharp puff of lighter smoke that seemed like a forked tongue, and then a hollow report, and we could see a great black projectile hurled into the air.

Right after this ominous looking object came the accompanying sound of cannon fire echoing right behind it.

When the shell landed, it "fell into the ranks of Company I, Eighth Maine who were marching in four ranks … It struck the musket barrel of Thomas Hoole …, taking off his head. Passing to the next rank it took off the shoulder of Joseph Goodwin … he lived two hours. Passing to the next rank it took off the leg below the knee of another man."

The first shot of the Rebel battery caused the 10-pound Parrott gun to send a quick reply. While this initial exchange occurred, Finegan ordered "a secton [*sic*] of Captain … Gamble's battery … some distance in advance of our main body … [to open up] … on the enemy." While this happened, Lt. Buckman continued to send shells into the retiring Union columns with their Parrott providing quick counter battery fire as they withdrew. Dr. Rogers said that the Confederates:

firing was very accurate, first on the one side of the road, then on the other side a shell would come singing over and many of them exploded over our heads. Gen. Saxton believes a special Providence watches over our regiment and that not a man was seriously injured today would seem to justify his belief. I saw a whole shell that did not explode, plough into the sand under the foot of a soldier not six rods from me, knock his gun out of his hands and his cap off his head, but before I could get to him he had gathered himself up and was off uninjured.

As the Federals continued to fall back to Jacksonville, Finegan thought his actions were causing them to retreat. Higginson was puzzled by the Confederates' lack of aggression:

For some reason they showed no disposition to overtake us, in which attempt their locomotive would have given them an immense advantage over our heavy hand-car, and their cavalry force over our infantry … As it was ... they moved slowly, as we moved, keeping always about two miles away. When they finally ceased firing we took up the rails beyond us before withdrawing, and this kept the enemy from approaching so near the city again.

Once the Union forces were out of range, Finegan decided to send a reconnaissance-in-force with the intent to ascertain the Yankee disposition. Using the 1st Partisan Rangers commanded by Major Brevard, Finegan instructed him to use skirmishers to approach the enemy position cautiously while holding his main body of troops out of sight, especially from the fire of their big guns. Finegan watched to see if he could again "draw them out in force." Finding out that they had moved back into their strongly fortified position, "and having no further object to gain, I ordered Major Brevard's command to retire, and replacing and strengthing [*sic*] my pickets, returned with the main body of my force to camp, having inflicted on the enemy, as I have reason to believe, a probable loss of 10 or 15 men, without any casualties to my own troops."

Early on in the third occupation of Jacksonville, General Finegan decided that he wanted his troops close to the city so he could react quickly with them to any enemy movement. This meant establishing camps with tents, as opposed to the permanent base at Camp Finegan. He had them placed around the city to accommodate the units assigned to cover designated sectors. While pickets would watch for any enemy action, the bulk of the unit covering a particular area would remain in camp until needed. However, when Finegan later became convinced he was outnumbered, he made the decision to consolidate his forces instead of having them spread out so they would not be possibly chopped up individually. He made his decision about the 20th and had them moved back to Camp Finegan. Though this was farther in the interior, the additional space would allow him the extra time to organize his units to counter any Federal movement. He still kept pickets around the city for early warning.

One of the reasons why Colonel Rust had Higginson do a reconnaissance-in-force on the 25th was to see if what Higginson had previously heard was true, that the Confederates had pulled back from their advance camps. He said, "For several days before the arrival of Colonel Rust (on the 23rd) a reconnaissance had been planned in the direction of the enemy camp, and he finally consented to it being carried out." Rust gave him his "instructions to march as far as the four-mile on the railway, if possible, examine the country, and find out if the Rebel camp had been removed, as was reported, beyond that distance."

Higginson found this information to be true. "We passed through a former camp of the Rebels, from which everything had been lately removed; but when the utmost permitted limits of our reconnaissance were reached, there were still no signs of any other camp, and the Rebel cavalry still kept provokingly before us. Their evident object was to lure us on to their own stronghold ... With a good deal of reluctance, however, I caused the recall to be sounded, and after a slight halt, we began to retrace our steps." It was at this point that the smoke of the locomotive pushing the railroad gun was first noticed.

Finegan's attempt to lure the Federals into a decisive battle failed once again, even though his cavalry tried to egg them on besides having the railroad gun being within striking distance of the Union force. They may not have bitten a second time, but this did not mean Finegan was through trying to defeat them in a decisive engagement. He decided to try another tactic. Since the Yankees had come out of their western defenses and marched along the railroad, Finegan reasoned they would use this same direction again and, therefore, ambush them in force. He planned to do this on the Thursday the 26th. "I planned early in the morning a strong force of infantry, with a battery of artillery, under Major Brevard, First Battalion Partisan Rangers, under cover of some woods to the right of where the enemy were posted on the 25th ..., with the design of getting in their rear should they again venture out." Once again the Federals did not cooperate with Finegan's plan. Though they did venture out on the 26th, it was not on the western approach as he had anticipated, but on the northern.

On Thursday morning a company from the 8th Maine was sent out on a scouting party to ascertain if there was any more Rebel activity on the northeastern approach to the city.[6] Prior to leaving, the 8th had coordinated with Colonel Higginson for a guide who knew the area. The 8th's company had not been gone too long when "the captain sent back a message that he had discovered a Rebel camp with twenty-two tents, beyond a creek, about four miles away, the officers and men had been distinctly seen, and it would be quite possible to capture it."

Dr. Rogers said that about noon the "messenger came in for reinforcements." The messenger had been instructed to say that the camp contained "a hundred cavalry pickets." Colonel Rust decided that the 1st South Carolina would have the honors of providing reinforcements. "Col. H. and Major Strong with four of our companies should undertake the job, much to the disappointment of Lieut Col. Twitchell of the 8th Maine, who told me how certain he was of making a fine dash of it if allowed to go. But we held this town against odds greater before they came to our relief, and it was our right to go."

The relief column went several miles through open pine barren until it made contact with the 8th's company, which was in a defensive position until help arrived. After sending out a scout, Colonel Higginson decided to split his force into two detachments, one to attack the camp frontally and the other to flank the Rebels and cut off their ability to retreat. Dr. Rogers continues: "Finally the trap was handsomely and strategically set, the Major was on the left spring and the Col. on the right, and when the two jaws snapped together they found between their teeth quite a lot of drying sheets and shirts and other articles." The Rebel presence that had been reported that was supposed to be an "unsuspecting enemy" upon whom the 1st S.C. was going to swoop "down at last in triumph upon" turned out to be "a solitary farm-house,—where the family-washing had been hung to dry. This was the 'Rebel camp.'!"

Needless to say, the revelation that "the 8th Maine captain ... made [a] blunder" caused a great deal of amusement among the soldiers. Though there had been evidence of Rebel presence, this did nothing to abate the chagrin "the author of the alarm" had to endure. Colonel Higginson said the Volunteers marched "triumphantly back through the lovely woods joking at the scare for which we were glad not to be responsible."[7] This exercise in futility "was baptised [sic] the Battle of the Clothes-Line." Fortunately for them, this rare moment of comedy in the field was not interrupted by Confederate fire. So, as the 1st South Carolina marched back gleefully to the protection of their defensive line, the 2nd South Carolina, which had gone on another expedition up the river earlier in the day, would suffer a very bloody defeat in less than 24 hours at the hands of a very deadly opponent.

When General Finegan received word that a sizable Yankee force on the other side of the Jacksonville defenses had been spotted, he moved his men with all dispatch to intercept them "with the intention of cutting them off, but they retired before we got near them." There would be no more fighting between the adversaries in Jacksonville. Though he could not know this, Finegan "posted a large body of infantry under cover for the purpose of cutting off any force that might come out."

Still, "the enemy kept closely within their lines ... "

Firefight at Palatka

Colonels Rust, Higginson and Montgomery, let alone the rest of the Union contingent, anticipated that the Confederates would continue their artillery barrage on the 26th if they were able to get the track repaired in time. As Thursday dawned, it appeared that the Union efforts of the previous day were still holding. Since the Rebels would probably not attack in force without their railroad gun, the commanders assumed it would be safe enough to allow Montgomery to go upriver that he had planned for the 25th. While he prepared his two-company unit, the *General Meigs* was assigned to transport the 2nd S.C. Rust and Higginson also decided that Lieutenant Colonel Liberty Billings,[8] second-in-command of the 1st S.C., would go.

The intent of this trip, like the previous ones, was to forage and try once again to find recruits. The area in which Montgomery planned to operate again was Palatka. Though his previous trip here was not successful, it did not mean he was done with it. Once he had secured the town, Higginson would follow up with the 1st South Carolina and then the 2nd would strike out into the interior. The addition of the 1st had two advantages: Higginson's regiment would continue to secure the town strongly as a base of operations, since his entire unit would be there; in the event that Montgomery needed help, Higginson could quickly respond. There would also be naval support if needed.

Once the *General Meigs* arrived at the intended area of operations, Montgomery decided to start on the east side of the river. He "landed with seventy-five men at Orange Mills, and scouted the country ... up to a point nearly opposite Pilatka [*sic*], where we camped for the night." Though Montgomery's actions on the east side almost guaranteed him there would be little or no enemy troops to worry about,[9] this did not mean his activities would go unnoticed.

Ever since their return to Palatka about a week and a half ago, the men of Captain John J. Dickison's Company H, 2nd Florida Cavalry had been trying to counter what they saw as Yankee raiding and pillaging of plantations of their food, slaves, and anything else that the Federals wanted, but the troopers of Company H were not able to stop them. The Volunteers always left before the Confederates were able to get to them. This did not mean that this was the way it was always going to be. It was just a matter of time, these cavalrymen knew, before they would catch the Federals. When Captain Dickison's pickets saw the *General Meigs* coming up the river on March 26, it appeared this time that they might be able to surprise the Yankees when they least suspected it.

When Captain Dickison learned of the *General Meigs*, he anticipated that she would land at Palatka and therefore he would be waiting for her. Leaving his horses behind so they would not make any noise to give away the Rebels' presence, Dickison marched his men as infantry (not far from his camp) and placed one detachment "within 50 yards of the river to cover one of the positions ... [where] ... the enemy might make an effort to land." He had another detachment "cover one of the main streets in town." When he saw the Yankee vessel stop across from Palatka, Dickison decided that the Federals were going to put in there for the night, so he placed pickets above and below the town "with instructions that they would report to me at day break without fail, as I was under the impression that the enemy would make an effort to land early in the morning." This vigilance would soon pay off.

The next morning, Friday the 27th of March, Colonel Montgomery decided to cross the river to Palatka on the west bank "to bring off a colored family ... said to be there." So, "while the men were preparing their breakfast, I ran over ... in the transport (Genl Meigs) with fifteen men." Lt. Col. Billings went with them. While the 2nd S.C. detachment prepared to go, Captain Dickison's men noticed the activity, notified their commander, and got ready for possible action. Dickison said, "Having nothing to cover my men from their view but a plank fence and an entrenchment thrown up during the night, I ordered all to lie close and keep concealed, at the same time occupying a position myself as to watch every movement of the enemy."

It took but a few minutes for the *General Meigs* to cross the river and land at the main wharf. Since there were less than twenty men on the vessel, they were ready to disembark when she came up to dock. Montgomery

Captain John J. Dickison, a brilliant tactician, he commanded Company H, 2nd Florida Cavalry that inflicted on the Volunteers their first defeat. *Courtesy State Library and Archives of Florida*

said, "Just as we were landing, and when about half our men were on the dock, we were fired on by two companies of guerillas concealed in the houses, which appeared to be deserted." Because the 2nd S.C.'s men were in the open, they took heavy casualties. Those who were not hit quickly scrambled back on board to seek cover, "dragging their dead and wounded after them." This took place while the Confederates had to reload their single-shot weapons.

The men who were not wounded after the first Rebel volley then opened up on them, using the *General Meigs* as a protective barrier. They returned fire as quickly as possible in the directions from which the two detachments of Company H fired. Montgomery ordered the gunboat back across the river once everybody was on board. As he moved fast to get things under control, the men of the 2nd and those manning the vessel's guns "returned ... fire both by small-arms as well as heavy and light artillery, throwing shell, grape, and canister-shot, moving as rapidly as their steam could carry them under cover of their heavy fire." While all this conflagration was going on, the rest of the 2nd S.C. on the other side of the river could only watch helplessly, since they were too far away for their muskets to be of any use.

As soon as the *General Meigs* got to the other side of the river, the wounded were attended to. One of them was Billings. "Lt. Col. Billings of the 1st Regt. and his servent [*sic*] ... were wounded, the servant mortally."[10] Dr. Rogers would later see after the gunboat had returned that "Billings received a ball through the fleshly margin of each hand while attempting to get off the steamer." Montgomery decided soon thereafter that there was not any more he could do here to secure Palatka as a base, since he did not have enough men to overcome Confederate resistance, which he perceived as being two companies. He ordered the ship back to Jacksonville.

The Confederates were jubilant that they had severely stung the enemy. It was Montgomery's misfortune here that he went up against J. J. Dickison, because Dickison was destined to become the most talented Confederate officer in Florida during the Civil War. The ambush he organized was an early example of what he would later do in the war.

The Rebel ambush may have made short work of Montgomery's plan, but it did not stop him from going through with an idea he had thought of on the trip back. He decided to stop back at a place he had previously visited that had produced good results. He did this to try and salvage a trip that had turned out to be a disaster. However, he could rest on one note. Had he taken more men across the river, the ambush would have produced many more casualties than those actually inflicted. With the number of men Montgomery did have in his regiment at this time, having more casualties would not have been a good thing, since there were no ready replacements.

Montgomery had the *General Meigs* stop again at Doctor's Lake. Though the ship did not arrive until after dark, this did not deter him from carrying out his plan. He "made an expedition inland, with twenty five men on a night's drive" to catch off guard whoever might cross his path. Moving several miles, they came across a campfire. Upon closer inspection, Montgomery found out it was a Confederate camp and, to his delight, everybody was asleep. In a very short time the 2nd S.C. had them surrounded and in their custody; the prisoners were a lieutenant and 16 privates. Montgomery said, "The moment the Lieutenant discovered that his entire party had been captured by a company of negroes, his mortification was extreme."

The Volunteers also captured "two good army wagons, heavily laden with valuable stores, and eight mules," besides 15 new Enfield rifles from the Rebels. With these items and prisoners under his control, Montgomery had the mules hitched to the wagons and moved back to the *General Meigs*, making it just before dawn on the 28th. His expedition also netted "4000 lbs. of cotton besides a large lot of negroes." When the Volunteers got back to their vessel with the results of their nocturnal effort, they were surprised to see the *John Adams* there too. She had orders for the 2nd S.C. to return to Jacksonville at once, because General Hunter had ordered the city to be evacuated.

Since Colonel Higginson did not know that Montgomery had been defeated at Palatka on the 27th, he was naturally under the impression that he and his regiment would still be going upriver, thus leaving the 6th Connecticut and 8th Maine in charge of Jacksonville. That day he wrote a quick letter to his mother. "Probably my reg't will go farther up the river, which we shall like. The river is broad & safe, no high banks for which to fear attack, & there are two points on the right bank Palatka (75 miles) & Magnolia (35) either of which would be a good point for us. Both are health resorts in winter & have large buildings & wharves. Both give more access to the slave population than this & are farther fr. troops & railroads. There we shall be by ourselves."

Higginson also had believed that General Hunter was going to visit Jacksonville ever since Colonel Rust arrived on the 23rd. "General Hunter is expected every day, and it is strange he has not come." However, an event happened later that day that initially gave him impression that he might have finally arrived, especially with more reinforcements. "This afternoon our eyes were gladdened by the sight of the Boston and Convoy steaming up the river, but when, instead of a cavalry force and light artillery to weigh them down, we perceived they came empty, we were filled with forebodings, till our hearts actually sank within us at the intelligence that an order from Gen. Hunter had come for our forces to evacuate the town to help those further north."

Needless to say, this sudden change in mission did not go well with those glad to be here rather than in Beaufort. Higginson said, "Just as our defenses are complete & all in order for the transfer of part of our forces up river, to other points, we are ordered away. Every military and naval officer here takes the same view of the order—but it is useless to criticize; there is nothing to do but to go."

Expressing similar thoughts, Dr. Rogers said, "This may be wisdom, but I fail to see anything but that fatal vacillation which has thus far cursed us in this war. We have planted ourselves here for the definite purpose of making this state free, and have already so fortified the city that a small force can hold it while the boats are making such raids up the river as may seem best."

However, the one person who was definitely put out the most, at least from an economic point of view, was Lyman Stickney. Higginson saw that "Judge Stickney [was] exceedingly anxious to take the Convoy and go back to Hilton Head to ask for a reconsideration of the order." He was not allowed to do so. All the work that he had done for the past three weeks to get his money-making side business going, including his labor to bring reinforcements to Jacksonville, was going up in smoke because of the "impulsive nature of Major-General Hunter."

The *John Adams* was dispatched as soon as she was ready, to find Colonel Montgomery and bring him back. She left that Friday evening. Dr. Rogers did not mind if the search took some time. "I hope it will take the John Adams a week to find the Gen Meigs, for we cannot think of leaving her back, though it would not surprise me if Col Montgomery had marched his men twenty miles inland and confiscated all sorts of contrabands." Rogers would soon see just how close he was to predicting Montgomery's movement later that evening when he saw the results the next day of Montgomery's Doctor Lake expedition.

Now that he believed he had avenged the embarrassment of his defeat 24 hours prior, Colonel Montgomery got his men, the prisoners, the slave refugees, and all captured goods ready to transport back to Jacksonville. Before the arrival of the *John Adams*, he was still under the impression that Higginson's future intentions were to occupy Palatka. "I [expect] Col. Higginson up, next day, with his Regt to occupy the place ...," but the news from the *John Adams* quickly changed that idea. Even with this new information, he continued with his current mission. Montgomery had earlier found out that the captured Rebels were in Captain John Westcott's company of the 1st Special Infantry Battalion. They had been detailed to act "as an escort to the inhabitants who desired to seek safety from the Northern invaders beyond the lines of the Rebel army."[11] Thinking that being several miles inland would secure them proved their undoing. They were still incensed that they had been surrounded and forced to surrender to black soldiers, especially the Rebels' officer-in-charge, Lieutenant O. F. Braddock.

Before the prisoners were placed on board the vessel, Braddock asked if he could say goodbye to his wife who happened to be there at Doctor's Lake. Since he was going to be a prisoner for the rest of the war, Montgomery acquiesced to this request. However, as he was going through the motion of saying goodbye to her and several of her friends, he escaped.[12] Later, when the colonel related the incident to Dr. Rogers, he said that he had "a weak spot in his military nature. He could have shot the Lieut. while escaping, but would not do so in the presence of his wife." After this minor episode, Montgomery finished loading the vessels and moved out for Jacksonville. They arrived back at noon.

The suddenness of General Hunter's order caught everyone by surprise. For an operation that had been ensconced for nearly three weeks to be abruptly uprooted would not be an easy task. There were a myriad of details that had to be taken into account. Colonel Rust convened "[a] council of military and naval officers ... at once" to organize for a departure as soon as possible. The first thing, of course, that had to be done was to recall Colonel Montgomery from his operation. There were both military and civilian aspects to take into consideration. The civilians had to be notified of General Hunter's orders and organized at the appropriate in a manner with their belongings that would not induce panic. Since there were both slave refugees and white Unionists, the civilians did not want to be caught by the Confederates with the anticipated reprisals.

Another major effort that had to be undertaken was the removal of the artillery pieces on the railroad flatcar and the forts beside the track. They had to be disassembled and placed on the ships from which they came as quickly as possible, as opposed to when they were first set up with no specific time frame for being put in place. The wounded required extra space to accommodate them plus the needed medical supplies for the voyage back to South Carolina. All ammunition, food, and other necessary supplies required of four regiments and all civilians for an extended stay would need to be reloaded. Fresh water for both humans and animals would be at a premium, plus enough food for the latter. Space would have to be made for the prisoners with their guards and all horses and mules. The dead would have to be left behind. All this had to be done while still providing security from any renewed Rebel attack.

Loading on the ships began as soon as priorities were set, details assigned, and what vessels would be loaded in order. When the *General*

Meigs and the *John Adams* returned at noon on the 28th, they were organized also for departure. The Adams was designated to carry the wounded. Dr. Rogers wrote that evening: "Have worked enough for one day in getting our sick and wounded on the *John Adams*."

March 29 was just as intense, if not more so, since Colonel Rust was going to have the expedition depart on this day. Dr. Rogers relates:

> Early this morning all was hurry and excitement. Insufficient means of transportation caused a good deal of grief among families obliged to leave behind their furniture, and caused good deal of profanity among officers and soldiers obliged to be packed as you would pack pork. This little Convoy, of 410 tons has six companies of soldiers, with all their equipments, forty or fifty citizens with all the trunk we did not throw back upon the wharf; fifty horses; all the Commissary stores and all my hospital stores save those needed on the *John Adams* ... we have also all our camp tents on board.

The correspondent of the *New York Tribune* described a very succinct picture of the ravages of war as he watched the evacuation in progress on the morning of the 29th:

> I am now writing on the deck of the fine transport ship, the *Boston*. Three gun-boats, the *Paul Jones*, the *Norwich*, and the *John Adams*, are lying out in the river, with guns shotted, ready to fire the moment a Rebel appears in sight. The transport vessels, the *Boston*, the *Deleware* [*sic*], the *General Meigs*, the *Tillie*, and the *Cossack*, are at the wharves, filled with troops. All are on board, except about two hundred of the Sixth Connecticut, who are on picket duty. Three blank shots from the *Paul Jones* have just been fired, as a signal for them to come in.

The correspondent continues:

> One solitary woman, a horse tied to a fence between two fires, and a lean half-starved dog, are the only living inhabitants to be seen on the streets. Fifty families, most of them professing Union sentiments, have been taken on board of the transports and provided with such accommodations as the tubs will afford. Some of them have been able to save a bed and a few chairs, but most of them have nothing in the world but the clothes upon their backs.

Though the evacuation was the result of an official order by General Hunter, it did not mean that there were not personal views on this matter.

Colonel Higginson said that for him this precipitate action by Hunter was "the first time I have been thoroughly subjected to that uncertainty of counsel which has been the bane of the war; it defeated us in this case, just in the hour of success—but thanks to my natural bouyancy [*sic*], I can stand it. What is to be done with us I have no intimation." He added that it was also his "first experience of the chagrin which officers feel from divided or uncertain counsel in higher places ... As for the men their bouyant [*sic*] spirits are proof against everything."

Dr. Rogers was tremendously grieved that they had to evacuate, since they could not complete their mission:

> This is one of the sad days of my life. The evacuation of Jacksonville is the burial of so many hopes I had cherished for the oppressed, that I feel like one in attendance at the funeral of a host of his friends. I greatly fear we are to be put back out of active service at a moment when there is most need for us to work. I believe our retrograde movement today is an error more serious and damaging to the interests of the enslaved than appears on the surface ...

For the varied interests that composed this expedition, they were saddened for different reasons. What Susie King felt was quite unlike that of Lyman Stickney, whose only thought was that of how much money he would be losing. Then there was Captain Charles Steedman, commander of the gunboat *Paul Jones*, who was happy that he could finally leave and no longer pretend he liked what he was doing. However these people felt at the suddenness of their departure, there would be one more event that would be a calamitous epitaph to a mission that began only three weeks ago with bright prospects for the future.

As final preparations were made for departure on this Sunday morning, smoke could be seen coming from different buildings around town. The *New York Tribune* reporter witnessed the burning of Jacksonville, which had not been authorized. "At 8 o'clock the flames burst from several buildings in different parts of the city, and at a later hour still more were fired. The wind then rose to a stiff gate, and the torch of the incendiary became unnecessary to increase the fire."

However wrong this was, he could say that the black soldiers did not start the fires:

> It gives me pleasure to report that the negro troops took no part whatsoever in the perpetration of this vandalism. They had nothing whatever to do with it, and were simply silent spectators of the splendid but sad spectacle. The Sixth Connecticut charge it upon the Eighth

Maine, and the Eighth Maine hurl it back at the Sixth Connecticut. After the fires in different parts of the city had broken out, Colonel Rust ordered every man to be shot who should be found applying the torch. But the order came too late. The Provost Marshal and his guard could not shoot or arrest the wind. No human power could stay its ravages.

The correspondent of the *Boston Journal* confirmed the *Tribune* reporter's account that the Volunteers were innocent. "The colored regiments had nothing at all to do with it; they behaved with propriety throughout." Dr. Rogers was also a witness. "Quite early this morning the 8th Maine boys began setting fire to the city—a most shameful proceeding. I came near losing my hospital stores before I could find conveyance for them to the steamer."

Colonel Higginson added his own lament to Rogers' thoughts:

The only time since I entered the service when I have felt within the reach of tears was when ... the men were all on board ..., I walked back among the burning buildings (set on fire by the white soldiers, not by mine) & picked a tea rose bud from the garden of my Headquarters. To think that this was the end of our brilliant enterprise & the destruction of my beautiful city was a sadder thing than wounds or death,—as for defeat I have not yet known it—and knowing the triumphant hopes felt by all loyal Floridians & the corresponding depth of their disappointment— and the apparent aimlessness of the evacuation, it was doubly hard.

As the gunboats and troop transports picked up steam and left Jacksonville, the conflagration of the city left a most lasting imprint on those who witnessed it as they moved away and around the bend of the river. Higginson said, "The sight and roar of the flames, and the rolling clouds of smoke, brought home to the impressible minds of the black soldiers all their favorite imagery of the Judgment Day; and those who were not too much depressed by disappointment were excited by the spectacle, and sang and exhorted without ceasing."

The departing soldiers, sailors, and civilians were not the only ones to see black smoke billowing high in the air. The Confederates were already investigating as the Union flotilla steamed away.

General Finegan's continued belief that he was greatly outnumbered had kept him at bay from the Union defenses. He could not even get the railroad gun close enough to fire again on the city, since the Federals had torn up enough track so he could not repair it in time. The pickets continued to watch for any movement so he could shift his forces to counter it. However, on this Sunday he knew something was amiss when he received word that huge plumes of smoke could be seen coming from the city. Upon closer inspection he "discovered it was on fire in several places and that the transports were being loaded with soldiers."

Finegan did not hesitate to send in cavalry to ascertain the status of the enemy and what kind of damage the fire had done. Captain Winston Stephens, Company B, 2nd Florida Cavalry, said they did all they could do to stop the flames. "My men were first in the Town & I sent them in every direction & they did all they could to arrest the fire," but they were too late to stop it or engage the enemy. When Finegan arrived, he said there was "evidence of precipitate departure by the enemy, and some quartermaster's stores were left by them, which were taken and turned over to the proper officers."

General Finegan had tried several times to engage his foe in a decisive battle, but the abrupt order by General Hunter would not allow him to try again. However, he would get another opportunity eleven months later near a small hamlet called Olustee in the northeast Florida wilderness, and this time he would obtain results.

What their Blood Bought

As the Union flotilla made its way down the river towards the Atlantic, those on board its crowded ships knew that this arrangement would not be too much of an inconvenience. Once they were able to cross the bar, it would only be a short voyage to Fernandina, where those who wanted to, could disembark. Then the ships could proceed on to Port Royal in less crowded conditions. However, as they got closer to the ocean, those on deck noticed that the sky was changing. Ominous clouds were gathering that would later dispel the notion of a short trip. What these people were witnessing was the beginning of a major storm system in the Atlantic that would force the ships to lie in the mouth of the river for the next two days until its abatement on the 31st. This would cause some passengers to be innovative while others would only grumble.

When the ships reached the mouth of the St. John's, it was obvious to all by now that to continue would be futile. With the storm raging in the Atlantic, staying in a safe place was a wise decision, even if the ships could get over the bar. Given these conditions, the leaders decided they would stay put for the night and see if the weather would clear up enough to proceed in the morning. After the ships had anchored down, Major Strong, the senior officer on the *Convoy*,[1] which held part of the 1st South Carolina, decided to allow some of the men to leave the ship and go on shore to ease the crowding,[2] since there were several empty buildings available.[3] So, 100 men disembarked "to quarter in deserted fisherman's huts till the bar is possible."

While the occupants of the ships could only wait to see if the storm would subside by morning, several people wrote what it was like to be where they were. The *New York Tribune* reporter recorded this scene from the *Boston*: "Six O'clock P.M.—Mouth of the St. John's. A fierce northeast storm is raging upon the ocean. Gun-boats and transports are lying here in safety, waiting until it abates. Again we are witnessing a conflagration. Some of the soldiers have gone ashore ... Much indignation is expressed on board." Dr. Rogers later wrote in his cramped quarters on the *Convoy* that the "wind blew a gale most of the night, the rain poured in torrents, while occasional thunder and lightning added interest to the scene. I enjoyed it much more than part of our men had not gone on shore."

The night passed away without much incident. Except for the grumbling being "expressed on board" the *Boston*, everybody got through with not much discomfort. Though there was a lull in the storm that morning, the leadership decided to stay put for at least one more day, since they felt it was not done in this area yet. Several more companies of the 1st S.C. took advantage of the better weather to go on shore to also quarter in the fisherman's huts. Shortly thereafter they had "built up fires & gone to housekeeping with their wonted promptness." While this was happening, Dr. Rogers and Major Strong left the *Convoy* and went ashore "and designated quarters for every company on board and now they are all drying and rejoicing themselves before blazing fires."

While the men of the 1st dried out on the land and the people of the other ships, both military and civilian, were able to move about the decks, Colonel Higginson wondered about his regiment's future assignment. "Some of the Floridians think that after the taking of Charleston or Savannah we shall be sent here again." In a letter to his mother, he said, "We are ordered back to Camp Saxton—but what to do there we know not. Possibly to do garrison duty for Beaufort—possibly to go thence to Fort Pulaski & relieve the 48th N.Y. for that is one rumor—I hope not true. At any rate I suspect they have corked up our energies for a short time—but if they have much of a fight at Charleston they may need us yet." Whatever the future might hold, his current "orders now are to return to Camp Saxton." While *en route*, "we must necessarily put in at Fernandina on the way, to leave many people & and much property, which will lighten our vessels and make our people more comfortable."

Outside other than the impulsive nature of General Hunter, Higginson contemplated as to why the expedition was so abruptly pulled out. He thought about the impending move against either Charleston or Savannah and that the Federals "simply need every available soldier in S. Carolina." Therefore, "they must have the transport vessels which we necessarily detained." There was also the possibility of massive Confederate reinforcements "from Savannah to dislodge us." Higginson also thought about the possible behind-the-scene efforts of those opposed to the recruitment of blacks in the military, specifically Hunter's new chief of staff, Brigadier General Truman Seymour,[4] who Higginson felt had been heavily influenced by Hunter's former deputy commander, General Brannan. It "is simply a thwarting of our career by ... Seymour now chief of staff to Maj. Gen. Hunter and one of the Brannan stamp."

Regardless of why the expedition was pulled, however, they were going to remain at the mouth of the St. John's River until the weather got better, that is, "2 gunboats & seven transports ... crowded with passangers [*sic*], refugees & their furniture, contrabands ... "[5] Writing on the *John Adams* on the 30th, Higginson said that "the storm is abating, we are in an excellent harbor, & though on some of the boats there is much discomfort, I think we can worry through ... Now, nothing can take away from this regiment the credit of another successful expedition; & if the men can only be made comfortable, a few day's [*sic*] delay makes no difference."

During this time, Colonel Higginson and Dr. Rogers observed differences between the Volunteers and the 6th Connecticut, 8th Maine, or any other units they had seen in the Department of the South and 10th Corps. Higginson said that "on boad [*sic*] the transport with white troops, there is general grumbling & dissastisfaction [*sic*]. Every Captain of a transport who has once taken my regiment wishes to take it again in preference to whites."

That evening Dr. Rogers was in cramped conditions with southern Unionists. He said:

> The Captain of the Convoy insisted on my taking his berth, so that my quarters were very good ... At this moment I am writing in the captain's room with a crowd of homeless women and children around me. One important testimony from them I am glad to record. They prefer to be here with the poorest accommodations rather than on the Boston or Delaware with nice staterooms and a large saloon. And what do you suppose is the reason? Because black soldiers do not offer them insults and they do not feel so secure with the white ones. It is established beyond all controversy, that black troops with worthy commanders, are more controllable than white troops. What they would be with a less conscientious Colonel, I cannot say.

The night of the 30th was just like that of the 29th for everybody, trying to be comfortable as possible while hoping that the weather would permit them to go the next day. When day finally dawned on Tuesday the 31st, those who were up saw the first signs that they might be able to leave. When the sun was well above the horizon, it was obvious that the storm had finally dissipated. When the leadership was convinced of this, the flotilla got ready to make the afternoon high tide. Dr. Rogers recorded, "Our men are coming aboard again and we shall start for Fernandina this afternoon. [Allowing] the men ashore was a great hit. Nearly all are in good condition."

However, the sad part of the morning was that Dr. Rogers had to amputate the leg of John Quincy, the servant of Lieut. Colonel Billings, both of whom had been wounded in Palatka. Rogers diagnosed his ability to survive as "only about one in three, owing to old age and impaired constitution." Acknowledging the day before that he might lose Quincy for a good while, Higginson gave him a compliment by calling him "one of our priests & apostles ... whose eloquence has the scream of the Arab in it ... Several times when we have expected a fight or an expedition we have continued to call out John Quincy for a speech beforehand—but now we must leave him at Fernandina till his foot gets well." Unfortunately that would not be the case, because he would die on April 30.

When the high tide finally allowed the gunboats and transports to enter the Atlantic and head north to Fernandina and beyond, there had to be a certain amount of trepidation among those aboard, primarily the Volunteers. They must have wondered if the whole expedition had been really worth it, since the main goal to get new recruits for the 2nd South Carolina and possibly a third regiment came to naught. Though the mission fell well below the numbers of what was wanted, to gauge if it was successful or not, one must look at the bigger picture—that of whether the opinions of many people were starting to change that blacks, specifically ex-slaves, would make good soldiers and would hold up as well as white units, if not better, when thrown into combat against the Confederates. To fully gauge the impact the Volunteers would have on the war effort, one must ask the pertinent question, what exactly did their blood buy?

The efforts of the Volunteers in this expedition helped to set the stage for more blacks, both slave and free, to don the Union blue. This, in turn, would give bite to the change of the federal government's goal from originally just a political one, the restoring of the seceded states to the Union, to having both political and moral ones: restoration of the states and the abolition of the institution of slavery. Though two more years lay ahead that would be needed to bring this about, the Volunteers and other Union soldiers would slowly but surely advance through the rebellious states, and more and more slaves would be able to rejoice to the words of a certain poem—though not literally but spiritually—that would capture their feelings at the moment of freedom:

> "Oh, praise an' tanks! De Lord he come
> To set de people free;
> An' massa tink it day ob doom,
> An we ob jubilee."

Endnotes

Preface

1 There were two 4th Georgia Cavalry Regiments created during the war. They were distinguished by their respective commander's last name, the first one for Colonel Isaac W. Avery and the second for Colonel Duncan Clinch. I was never able to find out why these two cavalry units had the same number.

Introduction

1 World War II was the last war in which blacks (and other ethnic minorities) were kept in segregated units. In 1948 President Harry S. Truman, acting under his constitutional role as Commander In Chief, ordered the integration of all the armed forces. When the U.S. entered the Korean War in 1950, this marked the first time that blacks and whites fought side by side in the same unit.

2 The Volunteers would be the first black regiment to fight in Georgia and Florida.

Chapter 1

1 Lincoln's opponents were Stephen A. Douglas, Northern Democratic Party; John C. Breckinridge, Southern Democratic Party; and John Bell, Constitutional Union Party.

2 These seized Federal properties were either lightly garrisoned or only had caretakers. At this period in time the U.S. was not at war. The military was very small and could only man these places either with small contingents of troops or just an ordnance sergeant, who looked after the weapons and ammunition stored there, depending upon the strategic importance placed upon them by the national authority. Forts Pickens and Jefferson would be able to hold out not only because of their locations, but because they would have enough troops to defend them until reinforcements could arrive. They would also survive because

the Rebels in these areas would not have any heavy artillery or the means to put them in place even if they had them. Though Fort Sumter would be manned too, its physical location would cause it to have a different experience.

3   The intent of this section is not to give a detailed explanation of initial black attempts to enlist, but to explain generally what took place. To do otherwise would be outside the scope of this chapter, that is, to explain what took place prior to the beginning of the 1st South Carolina Volunteers. For details of the denial of black enlistments, the reader can see what secondary sources I used about black involvement in the Civil War in the bibliography.

4   No blacks fought in the Mexican–American War in either the Regular Army or the state militias. The ones who were in the two previous conflicts were primarily in *ad hoc* organizations.

5   The District of Columbia, the seat of the Federal government, also permitted slavery.

6   Later in the war, 33 counties in western Virginia would vote to secede and form a new Union state called West Virginia. Slavery would still be permitted and it would become the fifth border state.

7   Even with the use of railroads at this point in American history, rivers still played an important role in the economy with the movement of people and goods, but with war it would be troops and supplies. The loss of the border states of Missouri, Kentucky, and Delaware would seriously have hampered these routes of transportation. Since the Ohio River flowed into the Mississippi and also served as the northern border with Kentucky, a Kentucky secession would have obstructed military operations, especially at the confluence of the Ohio and Mississippi, where the Rebels could easily have bottled up river traffic. Missouri too was critical, since its entire eastern border was the Mississippi and its southeastern tip was also at the intersection of these two rivers. Delaware could also have blocked the important flow of traffic of the smaller Delaware River, because upstream from the state was the port of Philadelphia, Pennsylvania, which served as an important transportation hub for the North.

8   A Federal law passed in 1850 to pacify the Southern states, it mandated that any jurisdiction in a free state to which a slave that had escaped was bound to aid the owner in reclaiming his property. The only way after the passage of this law that escaped slaves could guarantee their freedom was to go all the way to Canada or another country.

9   General Thomas W. Sherman is not to be confused with General William T. Sherman, who was at this time in the western theater of operations (the Mississippi River area) and who would later gain fame (or infamy, depending upon one's point of view) for his march through Georgia.

Chapter 2

1   He had been Attorney General during the administration of James Buchanan, Lincoln's predecessor.

2   The planters on the mainland did not move as fast, since they were not in a precarious position as their fellow sea island planters, who could easily be cut off. Once those on the mainland perceived that their plantations too could be subject to the loss of slaves, many would move them inland as 1862 progressed. Though the information does not state it, mainland planters in South Carolina must have moved faster than those in Georgia because the capture of the Port

Royal area was in their own backyard. The presence of a major Yankee base just would have been too tempting for slaves not to escape to.

3 Charles Francis Adams, Jr.'s paternal grandfather was President John Quincy Adams and his great-grandfather was President John Adams.

4 The combination of both military and civilian in the rehabilitation of the freedmen would be later looked on as an early version of what would be called Reconstruction after the war. The early work here would become known as the Port Royal Experiment. The details of this momentous occasion can be found in a book by Willie Lee Rose called *Rehearsal for Reconstruction: The Port Royal Experiment*. Commenting on this confusion of different interests, Charles Francis Adams, Jr., wrote on April 6, "While Government has sent agents down here, private philanthropy has sent missionaries, and while the first see that the contrabands earn their bread, the last teach the alphabet. Between the two I predict divers results, among which are numerous jobs for agents and missionaries, small comfort to the negroes and heavy loss to the Government."

5 The size of the department would change over the course of the war, with parts of it being assigned to other departments as the war progressed and circumstances required it.

6 The fort was located on Cockspur Island at the entrance of the river, which was several miles away from the city.

7 Though Hunter did not know it yet, the major casualties that the Peninsula campaign would later cause would require McClellan to draw on troops from the Department of the South, thus diluting further Hunter's ability to take any offensive action that would have any chance of success.

Chapter 3

1 One of the first individuals who volunteered to go to Port Royal was a physician named John Milton Hawks. He would later serve as a surgeon in the 1st South Carolina Volunteers and the 21st United States Colored Troops. Over 40 years later, he would write a magazine article about his experiences. In part he said: "... in February 1862, I called at the office of the New York Freedmen's Aid Association and volunteered my services as physician to the freedmen on the Sea Islands of South Carolina. Sailing from New York in March, I reported at Hilton Head, S.C. to Edward L. Pierce who was in charge of the affairs of the freedmen, and was assigned to duty on Edisto Island. From there I wrote in March to Major-General David Hunter, suggesting to him that he raise a regiment of Negroes, reminding him what good soldiers they made under Toussaint in Haiti." This quote is placed here in the notes because no other primary source mentions what he is claiming that he did.

2 None of the sources cited for this paragraph say exactly how Hunter was told of Murchison.

3 The sources cited here only say that the names of the men volunteering were entered on a list. Nothing says that they stopped doing their jobs they had on the island, primarily working for the Headquarters. Hunter probably wanted to wait until he had several hundred men signed up before organizing them into a military unit. Their names would have been entered on any list for them since they were illiterate.

4 Edward Pierce had written to Secretary Chase in late April saying that General Hunter had employed another black man named James Cashman to recruit

another 100 men, of which Pierce said he obtained "perhaps twenty-five or fifty." This contradicts what other sources say and therefore is placed here.

5   In this initial attempt to get men to enlist, nothing is mentioned about going to the other Union-occupied islands to obtain recruits, but only in the immediate ones of Port Royal.

6   This individual was Thomas Wentworth Higginson, who would later become the first commanding officer of the reconstituted 1st South Carolina Volunteers. Though he did not become associated with this unit until his arrival at Port Royal from Massachusetts in November, 1862, he soon learned how the regiment first started once he arrived.

7   This was a tactic used by many slave owners to keep their chattels in line. Though the slaves' existence in the U.S. was not good, Cuba was supposed to be far worse in how owners there treated them.

8   In a magazine article entitled "The First Black Regiment" written about 36 years later, Higginson describes a scene similar to what Laura Towne said in her diary in the same time frame, but with a contradictory ending. "On a morning in May, 1862, on Ladies' Island … there stood among the deserted buildings of an old plantation a group …" There was "a squad of white soldiers and a group of negroes—men, women, children—listening to a speech from a white sergeant.… On the present occasion he easily got a hearing, but as soon as he began to explain his immediate object—enlistment—he noticed that the men of military age were gradually slipping away from the group and disappearing in the woods nearby. When he ended his discourse, his audience consisted almost wholly of women, old men, and children. … In this disappointing situation, one tall and erect old black woman, wearing a Madras hankerchief [sic], rose from the step where she had been sitting, came up to him, and said briefly, 'Mas'r, I'se fetch 'um.' She then made for the woods, and in five or ten minutes reappeared, being followed to his great amazement, by a string of sheepish men. She then made every one of these walk up … and give his name … for the muster roll."

9   The only evidence that directly mentions this willful sabotage by Hunter's subordinates is in Higginson's postwar writings. Nothing else also is mentioned about the use of Abraham Murchison on the other islands to counter these rumors spread by the white soldiers.

10   The first part of Lincoln's proclamation repeated Hunter's emancipation order. The second part is this:

> And whereas the same is producing some excitement, and misunderstanding: therefore I, Abraham Lincoln, president of the United States, proclaim and declare, that the government of the United States, had no knowledge, information, belief, of an intention on the part of General Hunter to issue such a proclamation; nor has yet, any authentic information that the document is genuine. And further, that neither General Hunter, nor any other commander, or person, has been authorized by the Government of the United States, to make proclamations declaring the slaves of any State free; and that the supposed proclamation, now in question, whether genuine or false, is altogether void, so far as respects such declaration.
>
> I further make known that whether it be competent for me, as Commander-in-Chief of the Army and Navy, to declare the Slaves of any state or states, free, and whether at any time, in any case, it shall have become a necessity indispensable to the maintenance of the government, which, under my responsibility, I reserve to myself, and, which I cannot feel justified in leaving to the decision of commanders in the field. These are totally different questions from those of police regulations in armies and camps.

11 Lincoln had probably thought that the example he had set concerning General Fremont's attempt at emancipation was enough for all of his generals to understand without him having to get specific. However, when General Hunter did his version, Lincoln knew he had to spell it out once and for all that none of his generals had the authority to say that any slaves were free. Only the president, in his constitutional role as commander of the armed forces, in reference to a wartime necessity, had that authority.

12 Decades later another general would make policy without first seeking approval and would be relieved. In this case, General Douglas MacArthur was fired as commanding general of allied forces during the Korean War by President Harry S. Truman for unilaterally making foreign policy statements which ran counter to Truman's policy.

13 General Hunter did not say how he got hold of the names of these three men or how he decided to go to the 1st New York Engineers.

14 In reality it was not the president but the War Department in the name of Secretary Stanton that would approve or disapprove the nominees for officer commissions.

15 Though this may have sounded like a reactionary tirade by Hunter, his words would prove to be prophetic. By 1864, the Union Army had already created numerous black units with many more to come. Many junior white officers would see this to be the only way they would get promoted and sergeants commissioned as officers. Among the many junior officers who would benefit from the creation of these new units was Charles Francis Adams, Jr., of the 1st Massachusetts Cavalry. Though he was thoroughly opposed to having blacks in uniform, he would become later in the war a colonel commanding the all-black 5th Massachusetts Cavalry Regiment, a move which was ironic, let alone supremely hypocritical, for him to make, to say the least.

16 There were other units in the department, but they were too far away to be considered: the 90th New York Infantry at Key West; the 6th, 75th and 91st New York Infantry, 1st U.S. Artillery (Batteries A, F, and L), and the 2nd U.S. Artillery (Batteries C and K) at Fort Pickens and Pensacola, Florida. The other units that were also available (between Edisto Island and St. Augustine) to provide officers were the 6th and 7th Connecticut Infantry and 1st Connecticut Battery; the 8th and 9th Maine Infantry; the 28th Massachusetts Infantry and 1st Massachusetts Cavalry; the 8th Michigan Infantry; the 3rd, 4th, and 7th New Hampshire Infantry; the 46th, 47th, and 79th New York Infantry; the 45th, 47th, 50th, 76th, and 97th Pennsylvania Infantry; the 3rd Rhode Island Heavy Artillery; the 1st U.S. Artillery (Batteries B, D, and M); and the 3rd U.S. Artillery (Battery E).

17 There is no information that is available on these men.

18 Outside of Captain Trowbridge and Lieutenants Trowbridge and Walker, there is no information that states how long it took to recruit these other men to be officers in Hunter's contraband regiment.

19 This subordinate command included the units from Edisto Island to St. Augustine. It was one of three districts that Hunter had created on March 31, since his command was widely spread out. The Southern District included all the military installations in the vicinity of Key West. The Western District was Fort Pickens (which did not include Pensacola at this time). On June 21, this three-district concept was discontinued. On August 8, Fort Pickins and Pensacola (which had been recently acquired after the Confederates abandoned it) were transferred to the Department of the Gulf.

20 There is nothing in the two biographies about General Stevens or in the regimental history of the 79th Highlanders that specifically states that he chose them because he had been their former commander. However, two of the missionaries, Harriet Ware and Laura Towne, mention this unit in their writings of May 11 and 12. Because of this, one can only come to the conclusion that Stevens did choose them for that specific reason.

21 This is Edward W. Hooper, one of the first missionaries who came to Port Royal in March.

22 In all prior wars, the U.S. Army had only volunteers. Though this draft by Hunter would affect only several hundred men, it was a precursor to what would happen later in the war. When not enough men volunteered, the federal government resorted to conscription (The Confederates did this too). This war was causing casualties on an unprecedented scale.

23 Regardless of their feelings at the time, Todd also said, "It is pleasant to record, however, that very few of the regiment thus disgraced them-selves [*sic*], and in a short time after, when the colored troops became a part of the Union army in the field, they were welcomed by us all as brothers in arms."

24 William H. Seward, Secretary of State.

25 Montgomery Blair, Postmaster General.

26 This momentum still did not mean pending freedom for the slaves in the four Border States, which would also include a fifth when West Virginia was later created. Since the institution was still constitutionally protected, the only way for the slaves to become free in these states would be for the states to do it themselves or for an amendment to be made to the U.S. Constitution.

27 The opinion of many of Hunter's subordinates was not just relegated to the Department of the South. In his excellent two-volume treatise called *The Common Soldier in the Civil War*, historian Bell I. Wiley said that "one who reads letters and diaries of Union soldiers encounters an enormous amount of antipathy toward Negroes. Expressions of unfriendliness range from blunt statements bespeaking intense hatred to belittling remarks concerning dress and demeanor." An example of this is found in a letter written by a Pennsylvania soldier stationed in Virginia in July, 1862. Named Sergeant Enoch T. Baker, he wrote to his wife in reference to information he was getting about the debate to place blacks in uniform:

> Thair is a great controversy out hear about the nigger Question at present if they go to Sending them out hear to fight thay will get Enough of it for it Will raise a rebellion in the army that all the abolitionist this Side of hell Could not Stop the Southern Peopel are rebels to the government but they are White and God never intended a nigger to put white people Down if they would hang a few of the Speculators and leading politicians who are trying to make Presedents instead of good generals the War Wood Soon be over without the help of niggers.

Chapter 4

1 In a matter not found in any official correspondence, Captain Gobin said he had a conversation with a member of Hunter's staff as to why the regiment was organized:

> He informed me ... that the sole object of their organization into regiments was for the purpose of having them on hand when they wished a detail for fatigue duty. A lazier lot of niggers than those around here I suppose never existed. Allow them to remain around

in their quarters, and when you want 40 or 50 to unload a vessel or do any work, you would have to run an hour to get them, and then half of them would run off before you were through. But by organizing them into companies and regiments, they were always kept ready for use, and by sending a detail you received the number needed.

No other primary source corroborates, however, what this staff member told Gobin.

2 Adams is referring to the red pantaloons, a type of pants that Hunter's regiment was issued. A reporter from the *Boston Advertiser* said that the men had been issued blue pants when they were first brought to Hilton Head in May. It can only be surmised here that the Quartermaster department did not have enough blue pants for all of them as their numbers grew, but did have enough of the red pants that had yet to be distributed in the Department of the South because no regiment stationed there wanted them. Since the Union Army was still growing, the various commands were sent in the way of uniforms, weapons, etc., whatever was available. After the active field armies got first pick, the secondary theaters were sent what remained in the supply chain. Later on, as more blue pants became available, the Volunteers would be able to trade their red pants for them.

3 No biography of General Saxton currently exists.

4 Three decades later, Saxton would receive the Congressional Medal of Honor for his work at Harper's Ferry.

5 For a detailed account, see *Rehearsal for Reconstruction*.

6 Smalls had been the pilot of the *Planter* for some time and knew how to operate the vessel expertly.

7 It appears here that Lincoln planted the seed of his thinking without saying it. He probably figured that Stanton would pick up on it and run with it the first chance he got. With the way Saxton phrased his letter, the secretary was able to carry out the president's tacit position and allow the general to form units to: "be detailed by the Quartermaster-General for laboring service with the armies of the United States and ... be clothed and subsisted after enrollment in the same manner as other persons in the Quartermaster's service." If they were needed in the capacity as soldiers from time to time, that was acceptable also, especially "in view of the small force under your command and the inability of the Government at the present time to increase it, in order to guard the plantations and settlements occupied by the United States from invasion and protect the inhabitants thereof from captivity and murder by the enemy. ..." Stanton also authorized Saxton to reoccupy if possible "all the islands and plantations heretofore occupied by the Government, and secure and harvest the crops and cultivate and improve the plantations." For those men who became "employed" by the Quartermaster-General, "who may have been slaves of rebel masters are, with their wives, mothers and children, declared to be forever free." How Stanton was able to state this last section in light of Lincoln's position at the time, I have never been able to find out.

8 Since no biography of Saxton currently exists, I have had to rely on different sources to help fill in various aspects of Saxton's involvement up to this point. The use of *Official Records* on him is indispensable, but in several places they have huge gaps that need to be filled in. These other sources will be used from time to time to help as much as possible.

9 Trowbridge, his brother John and George Walker may have officially been only enlisted men at this time, but I will continue to refer to them with their officer rank.

10 The 3rd Georgia Cavalry Battalion was one of several units that guarded the state's coast against any Yankee intrusion. It would tangle again in November with the Volunteers after they had been reconstituted, but this would not be the end of it. Two months later the 3rd Georgia would achieve regimental status, be renamed as the 4th Georgia Cavalry Regiment (Clinch), and would cross swords with the Volunteers two more times. As far as the area of operations of the 3rd Battalion (and later the 4th) goes, a detailed description of the Confederate units that guarded the Georgia and Florida coasts against which the 1st S.C. would later operate will be covered in Chapter 6.

11 Capers would later be banished to the mainland because of his continued loyalty to Captain Hazzard.

12 New Orleans and a good portion of the state surrounding it fell to Union forces in April, 1862.

13 The Confederate president was Jefferson Davis.

Chapter 5

1 None of the primary sources stated that Captain Trowbridge was able to get resupplied from Port Royal. They also did not say that the Navy helped.

2 Toward the end of his letter, Hunter added this expansion to his thought on martyrdom:

> Whether your intention of hanging me and those of my staff and other officers who were engaged in organizing the 1st South Carolina Volunteers, in case we are taken prisoners in battle, will be likely to benefit your cause or not, is a matter mainly for your own consideration. For us, our profession makes the sacrifice of life a contingency ever present and always to be accepted; and altogether such a form of death as your order proposes, it is not that to the contemplation of which soldiers have trained themselves—I feel well assured, both for myself and those included in my sentence, that we could die in no manner more damaging to your abominable rebellion and the abominable institution which is the origin.

3 Nothing states that this order applied to the officers on St. Simon's Island. Since they were performing this special duty, it is probable that they would have continued it.

4 During this time frame in American political history, political parties did not choose their presidential candidates through state primaries, as they are done today. They were mainly chosen by party leaders. The state primary system would not evolve until several decades later as a means to reform the nomination process by taking power away from party bosses to help end corruption problems and put it in the hands of the rank-and-file party members. It would take, however, several more decades for the old system finally to stop.

5 The original source cited for these names, "The First Freedmen to Become Soldiers," did not give any rank, only name and original unit. In Appendix A (Roster of Officers) of *Army Life*, ranks are given besides other pertinent information. Since the second source shows the ranks of the nine of the original twelve in the reconstituted 1st South Carolina Volunteers, it can only be assumed here that these officers had the same rank in the old Hunter regiment. Of the other three, Henry A. Beach, 48th New York Infantry, would later return and be commissioned as a 2nd Lieutenant on April 5, 1863. No

reason was given why this happened. Maybe he did not want to wait around to see what was going to happen after the Hunter organization was disbanded and went back to his old unit, but later had a change of heart. This is possible because two others were also commissioned as 2nd Lieutenants in April, 1863, meaning that there were three vacancies that needed to be filled. As for James Harrold and John Goddard, both of the 1st New York Engineers, no reason was given as to why they did not return either. Maybe they did not want to wait in seeming limbo, like Beach, and just went back to their previous unit and also did not worry about getting other commissions later.

6   At this point in the history of the Volunteers, there is no information that states whether Company A had returned from St. Simon's Island yet, which it was supposed to do this month. Therefore, there is nothing that shows whether Captain Trowbridge and Lieutenants Trowbridge and Walker knew about their commissions at this time. The return of Company A and therefore the need to evacuate the island by its inhabitants to Port Royal is covered later in the chapter.

7   All of the original sources cited about the return of Captain Trowbridge state either he returned alone from St. Simon's or with his command and the contraband colony.

8   She called it this because these were the remains of a fort built by a Frenchman named Jean Paul de la Ribaudière in the 17th century. It had been made from shells and cement.

9   None of the 3rd Rhode Island Heavy Artillery was stationed on Port Royal Island at the time, but that did not mean that they and other regiments located elsewhere did not get word of its activity.

10 Mr. Ware may have been right about the freedmen's reluctance to enlist, given how they were treated the first time, but he was wrong in his assessment that it would take a while to turn them into soldiers, as Harriet Ware and William C. Gannett were wrong when they rendered the same opinion back in May. Ware said, "I think, too, that it would be very difficult, under any circumstances, to train them into fighting condition under six months, and if they had at the first the prospect of coming into actual conflict with the Secesh, the number who would be willing to enlist would be extremely small. They have not, generally speaking, the pluck to look in the face the prospect of actual fighting, nor have they the character to enlist for their own defense."

Chapter 6

1   During the Civil War, it was not uncommon on both sides for civilians to be directly commissioned as colonels or generals. Some men obtained these ranks because of their competence, while others got them on account of political patronage. The source cited in reference to Billings does not say why he was given this commission; maybe because of his perceived abolitionist stance.

2   Saxton probably sent Beard on this expedition because of his rank just in case it was needed, since Trowbridge was only a captain.

3   Even with these heavy casualties that the Confederacy would suffer beginning with the campaigns of 1862 and would continue to suffer as the war dragged on, except for a brave few, there would be complete political and military opposition to the use of slaves as soldiers. Not until March, 1865, one month before the war would end, did the Confederate Congress finally enact legislation that would permit it, but this would be too little too late.

4   The railroads around which Lee had planned his defensive strategy to
    concentrate forces had not been built where they were for military reasons.
    What he had to work with was a transportation system originally designed for
    civilian economic reasons.

5   In December this unit would be organized along with nine other independent
    cavalry companies to become the 2nd Florida Cavalry Regiment. The Guerrillas
    would be Company K in this new organization.

6   The rest of the coast to Savannah was anchored on the defensive network of the
    city. This was Bryant County, whose border with Chatham County (Savannah)
    was the Ogeechee River, a waterway wide and deep enough to allow Union
    gunboats to threaten a strategically important railroad bridge farther up the
    river. Because of this, an earthen fortress called Fort McAllister was erected to
    protect it. The bridge and fort were close enough to the city that forces from it
    could react quickly if they were threatened from a Federal landing.

Chapter 7

1   In *Official Records* the river is called the Bell.

2   During this time in history, salt was a very important factor in the preservation
    of meat. Many salt-producing operations were set up along the coasts of the
    Confederacy with the blockade in effect. They did not have be set up right
    on the shore, because the many tidal creeks and streams along it were also
    salt water and the preservative could be harvested from them. They were also
    military targets for Union raiding parties. Why the ones the Volunteers were
    going after had not already been previously destroyed by the 9th Maine is a
    good question.

3   It is possible that the Guerrillas did not have enough time to get back in force
    to the shore before Company A left on the *Darlington*.

4   No information is available about the details of this firefight.

5   I consulted different maps, including *The Official Military Atlas of the Civil
    War*, to find this place, but I could not.

6   Trowbridge probably recommended it because he had been previously
    stationed there.

7   None of the primary sources say that this took place, but this was a logical
    thing to do. To have placed these refugees in harm's way any more than was
    absolutely necessary made no sense. They needed a safe place to stay while
    the *Darlington* went on its different raids, so St. Simon's Island with its naval
    protection was the logical place to put them outside of Fernandina.

8   Another source called them the Lamar Mounted Rifles.

9   The information he is talking about here and in the rest of this paragraph
    was a combination of his own observations and other details he learned from
    others later.

10 Only one other source said that the *Darlington* had any artillery on board.

11 One thing I had to deal with was conflicting sources. Beard said additionally
    that they "effected a landing and burned all the buildings on the place and
    captured some arms … Five of the enemy were killed." In his company log,
    Hopkins does not mention anything about a landing. He also said that none of
    his men were killed. This contradiction of information will happen again when
    the Volunteers go up against Brailsford's men.

12 In his version of events, Brailsford said nothing about his plantation being
    burned down. All he said was, "I think the only blood that was spilt on either

side during the day, was a little bull calf of mine that was knocked down by a shell."

13 These men were no more than an armed mob, but no one could doubt that they would have fought bravely once they were shown how to use a musket.

14 These series of actions in no way dilute what they did on St. Simon's Island back in August when they hunted Captain William Miles Hazzard and his detachment from Company D, 3rd Georgia Cavalry Battalion.

15 Though the Army depended upon the Navy for many of its operations along the coast, both in terms of firepower and logistical support, it did have a few ships under its own control. Among them was a gunboat, the *John Adams*, which was a converted icebreaker from Boston; a large transport, the *Ben De Ford*; and the *Darlington*. These vessels were used at the discretion of the department commander, who happened to be at this moment John Brannan. Based upon what Saxton said to Stanton, it is doubtful that Brannan saw the letter.

16 Several of the Union sources being used to write this section are contradictory as to how many companies were actually used. In his later report of this mission, General Saxton said that there were "three companies." Lt. Colonel Beard only gave a number of "160." Given the fact that as of the 12th, the regiment had only 550 men enrolled and Company A had 62 men, not having all the companies numerically proportioned would appear to be the reason for this number. As more men came into the regiment, they would be assigned to the undermanned companies to help bring them up to strength. In her diary, Laura Towne said that "two colored companies" went. In the pension records of Dr. Hawks, he said the expedition was composed of "companies A and B." Since two of the sources concur, while another only said the total number of soldiers going, it is possible that Saxton said in his later report that there were three companies on the expedition, once again hyping it for political reasons.

17 They had probably known about the mill before or during their first excursion, but could not take advantage of it due to what they already had on board in the limited space of the *Darlington*. The amount of lumber available at the Blue and Hall's Mill was probably just too tempting to ignore (let alone to destroy), so it would require another vessel, specifically a large one that could carry a lot, therefore the need for the *Ben De Ford*.

18 Beard did not report any enemy resistance or employees of the mill, but it did not mean that the Volunteers would not be spotted coming into the area.

Chapter 8

1 For a complete history of Higginson's pre-Civil War career, see the following: *Cheerful Yesterdays*, his autobiography; *Colonel of the Black Regiment* by Howard N. Meyer; and *Strange Enthusiasm* by Tilden G. Edelstein. Since this book is about the 1st South Carolina Volunteers, only a brief biography of Higginson is provided.

2 None of the primary sources state exactly when Saxton's letter arrived.

3 Members of one of the Mongolian peoples who overran much of Asia and Eastern Europe under Genghis Khan during the 13th century.

4 Higginson would not hear about the two expeditions until he arrived late in November. On November 10, Chaplain Fowler wrote to Higginson to inform him that it was Fowler and Dr. Hawks who had recommended him to General Saxton and of the success of the 1st S.C.'s first mission in Florida, after Fowler

had just heard about it himself on the unit's return. Higginson would not receive this letter until he was already in South Carolina. It took about 10 days just for Saxton's letter to reach him alone; Higginson left on the 19th. In an ironic twist of timing, within two months of his departure, the first regiment of free blacks raised in the North would begin right in Massachusetts, the eventually famous 54th.

5 The primary sources do not say what mode of transportation he took to New York, either train or ship.

6 This journal he began would chronicle this experience throughout his time in service. He would send it in installments to his wife and mother. It would also serve as the basis for his later book *Army Life in a Black Regiment.*

7 General Hunter would return in late January, 1863.

8 This particular quote came from Higginson's book *Army Life.* In *Civil War Journal*, it says "… and there said my companion is your regiment of Maroons." In Chapter II of *Army Life* he quoted extensively from his journal. However, I have noticed that there were variations here and there from the original. Why Higginson did this is a good question. Maybe he did it for stylistic and publishing purposes. Higginson also probably never thought that his journal would be published, which occurred about 140 years later.

9 The pantaloons were replaced by February 15, 1863.

10 Though described in a somewhat grandiose manner, it still had to have been an impressive sight for the times.

11 When Hawks referred to Higginson's command of "Attention, battalion, shoulder arms." he added that "it seemed to me that he spoke not merely to the thousand men there in uniform, but to the hundred thousand that were to come and did come and 'shoulder arms' in defence of the Union." The 100,000 Hawks speaks of in this quote were of course, only part of the nearly 200,000 that would have enlisted by war's end.

12 This is the name of Higginson's commanding officer in his previous regiment, Colonel Augustus B. Sprague.

13 Higginson was very impressed with Cato's storytelling. In his journal entry for that evening, he wrote, "Probably if I get into the enemy's country, I should be only too glad to put myself as a child into the hands of Ole Man Cato."

14 This also included men from Georgia and Florida.

15 Higginson described the scene this way: "Tugging these wet and heavy boards over a bridge of boats ashore, then across the slimy beach at low tide, then up a steep bank, and all in one great uproar of merriment for two hours."

16 The other paper was called *The Free South.*

17 The paper said he brought back 100 men, but the number quoted by Higginson came from his journal.

18 Higginson had said previously that the 75 recruits from Fernandina appeared better than many of the men from South Carolina. He then added, "Yet they cannot deny that some of the very best men in the regiment are South Carolinians."

19 Another regiment would not begin to be organized until January.

20 Historian Benjamin Quarles never said where he got this quote from, but it seemed quite fitting to place it here.

21 So much information was available about this day that much of it could not be included, so the various events were generally listed.

22 He was really a corporal at the time.

23 This unit was either stationed on Hilton Head or St. Helena Island. The information on this does not specify.

24 Higginson did not say in his journal who these officers were nor what company they were in.

25 These other regiments once again were the 1st Kansas Colored, and the 1st, 2nd, and 3rd Louisiana Native Guards. The 3rd did not begin to be organized until November 24, 1862.

26 More about Colonel James Montgomery will be covered later in the book.

Chapter 9

1 Though different words were used, the music was that of the "Battle Hymn of The Republic." The song was a tribute to the radical abolitionist John Brown, who was hanged in 1859 after he had tried to foment a rebellion by slaves when he seized the federal weapons arsenal at Harper's Ferry, Virginia.

2 Higginson gave a different description of the ordnance on the *John Adams* than that quoted from *Official Records*. He said she had "a thirty-pound Parrott gun, two ten-pound Parrotts, and an eight-inch howitzer." He also said that she had a draft of seven feet.

3 Though none of the original sources explain it, it is possible that Companies D, E, I, and K were not chosen because the most recent recruits from Florida were assigned to them.

4 Lt. Colonel Billings remained back at Port Royal with the other four companies to oversee their training. Higginson took Major Strong because he preferred him over Billings as latter events would testify to this.

5 In *Army Life*, Higginson had said that there was also a fort on Jekyll Island across the bay.

6 On the 24th, Dr. Rogers wrote he had "confiscated a nice bath tub and three new windows for my hospital, which has only shutters."

7 No reason why she was late was found among the primary sources.

8 Higginson did not say which of the six companies were loaded onto the *John Adams*. Later in the chapter of his book that deals with the Hundred Pine, he mentions Company G by name. However, the *Supplement to the Official Records* says that Companies B, C, G, and H went.

9 No information states whether Sutton ever knew this company as the Guerrillas.

10 This is the approximate time when they left, based upon the only time frame given by Higginson when he said, "it was after midnight when we set off upon our excursion" after they had captured Township Landing.

11 Higginson never did say what the newest intelligence was that he received.

12 Again, this is only an approximate time based upon Higginson's time frame. I have to assume that this was the rough time when the gunboat would have passed the first picket station going upriver at night.

13 These points of defense were not of Captain Clarke's original choosing. They were the result of prewar economic activity in logging and railroading. There may have been better places that would have made more military sense, but Clarke had to make the best of things with what he had.

14 The Union regiment on Amelia Island at this time was now the 7th Connecticut Infantry, with Company D guarding the railroad when the 1st S.C. landed at Township.

15 A present-day map shows a place called Reid's Bluff.

16 There was the possibility that the first picket post could have been surprised and neutralized before any of the men got away. It is better to have a multiple warning system in the event something of this nature happening.

17   It is possible here that the three pickets took up post with their horses at the gate in anticipation of the boat landing at Township when they heard her coming up the river. This had to have been done either when the boat landed prior to Township to let off Corporal Sutton and the others of the landing party, or before Sutton arrived. Either way the three pickets escaped capture. The two remaining pickets also had to have remained hidden after the Volunteers started to move inland since Higginson did not mention capturing any Rebels, nor did Bryant say they rejoined the company prior to the fight. Nothing is also mentioned after the 1st S.C. left. It is possible that they continued to remain hidden until the *John Adams* left and then went back to picket duty, waiting for Captain Clarke to arrive and issue further orders. The two pickets also could not get near the boat because the landing was guarded by the remainder of the Volunteers.

18   Not having the advantage of modern communications to target artillery rounds onto the enemy, the 1st S.C. could not have used its superiority in firepower if it was needed when they moved into the interior. Even if they had this ability, the skirmish they were to be shortly engaged in would have been over and the enemy out of range before the first rounds from the *John Adams* would have impacted.

19   Dr. Rogers wrote during the night of the mission that 175 men "had been landed … ten miles above St. Mary's with the Colonel at their heads."

20   Slowly but surely President Lincoln's Emancipation Proclamation would spread to the slaves in the eleven rebelling states, who would learn for the first time that they were finally free.

21   Keeping a tight formation of Civil War infantry units better facilitated command and control if and when they had to go into action, because of the type of weapon they had to use—the musket. Firing it in volleys was the only way for this kind of firearm to be effective against a massed foe.

22   Bryant's account said nothing about being fired upon by the advance guard of the Volunteers.

23   During the Civil War, Union soldiers were paid $13.00 a month. With the Rebels blazing away "at $10.00 a day," that was a lot of firing in comparison.

24   Though on a widely different scale, this can be compared to the battle of Antietam in Maryland the previous September. Though it basically ended in a draw between the Confederate Army of Northern Virginia and the Union Army of the Potomac, the battle was as close to a Union victory as President Lincoln was going to get in waiting for one to occur before he was going to announce his preliminary Emancipation Proclamation to the public.

25   This detachment did not include Companies A and B, which had been the only units of the regiment to have any combat experience up to this point in time when they conducted their raids along the coast in Georgia and Florida the previous November.

26   With the three points that had pickets where the Federals could land, Company K was too small a unit to contain a concerted Union move against the camp. Quick evacuation several miles west along the railroad or all the way to Camp Finegan would have been the only alternative to save the unit intact or as much as possible. Moving back along the railroad in the direction of Finegan was also the only logical step, since it was where the other Confederate forces were; in any other direction, they would have been possibly facing Federal troops. Of course, nothing was ever mentioned in Captain Clarke's evacuation order about the other picket posts. It can only be assumed here that the other pickets were given the order to fall back too and join the rest of the company so they would not be cut off by any other possible Union movement.

27 Higginson said nothing about firing several times more as he moved his men back.

28 Higginson also said, "This I mention because it was the only article of property I ever took, or knowingly suffered to be taken, in the enemy's country, save for legitimate military uses, from first to last; nor would I have taken this, but for the thought of the school, and aforesaid, the temptation of the box. If any other officer has been more rigid, with equal opportunities, let him cast the first stone."

29 It was only done this way since the Rebels did not have enough men and artillery to counter the Union threat. This was the best they could do under the circumstances, to strike at the enemy when the Rebels would be least exposed to return gunfire.

30 Company K could not take advantage of firing at the gunboat from Waterman's Bluff, because she had already passed the high ground before the Rebels could get there.

31 Dr. Rogers said that "we reached St. Mary's before noon."

32 Rogers wrote "As we were about to leave the wharf, bang, bang, bang, went sesech rifles from behind the houses and whistling went the balls over our heads."

33 Rogers also said that "we were not long in sending shot and shell enough to protect our skirmishers …"

34 Even as the Rebels were firing on the boat, the women knew that they would not be fired upon as the boat returned.

Chapter 10

1 He was also the commander of the 7th Connecticut Infantry stationed on the island, which had recently replaced the 9th Maine.

2 He published a history of his company 47 years later.

3 Until the *John Adams* landed at Township Landing, the Rebels could only speculate as to the Union intent. Besides, what Tourtellotte does say in his book as to this intent is being confused in part with the Volunteers' raid up the St. Mary's. This can be understandable since he published it nearly five decades after the fact.

4 To add to the misstatement of the facts, Tourtellotte gave an example that was supposed to have occurred during "the scrapping." He said, "In one case, after vicious tongue lashings on each side the slave took the master prisoner, the chagrin driving the master to desperation, causing a barehanded fight in which the master was assisted by comrades and the slave stretched senseless and in the retreat was left behind at the mercy of his foes."
Higginson accounted for all of his wounded and dead, leaving nobody behind. The first recorded time in which black soldiers became prisoners in Florida was not until February 20, 1864, after the battle of Olustee, some 35 miles west of Jacksonville. It was a Confederate victory, with the Federals retreating several miles in piecemeal fashion before being able to get somewhat reorganized, thus leaving many dead and wounded, both black and white, on the battlefield.

5 These individuals did not see what the Volunteers did on the parade ground in Beaufort, else they might have thought differently. They were only following the lead of Major General George B. McClellan, a Democrat in political party affiliation and a major opponent of black enlistment. In 1864, he was the Democratic Party's presidential nominee.

6 The last time a Union vessel had gone to this place was the gunboat *Ottawa* the previous year, but it was not a successful operation.

7 Dr. Rogers said that knowledge of another expedition up the river was not made known until the day of it around noon. He said, "I have just received a note from the Col., who is ashore, that sets our line officers to making ready in haste for another expedition. We are not yet done with the St. Mary's River and some of the upper settlements."

8 Though Higginson would have loved to travel in the *Ben De Ford* (he was convinced the river was deep enough for her), the boat was too big and "would be unmanageable in the … sharp turns."

9 Higginson did not mention anything about the *Planter* being sent back to St. Mary's to get any brick in his history of the unit, but Dr. Rogers said Higginson did this in a letter the doctor wrote on the 29th around noon. Rogers wrote, "The *Planter* has not yet returned, but has been using her artillery this morning shelling the pickets in the woods I presume."

10 Captain Clarke probably anticipated that it was going to be a long wait for the boat to return and had his men get some sleep while a guard stood watch.

11 Other sources do not list Dent as the commander of Company D during this time, but he is placed here as commander by what William Frederick Penniman said in his memoirs, since he himself was a member of the unit.

12 Rogers also wrote a few things about the trip that Higginson did not:

> Oh, it was a queer night, so queer that more than once I laughed outright, when I thought of the curious fact that T.W.H. and I were so industrious trying to get a peep at real rebels, while they would undoubtedly do something to get a peep at us. In my time I have seen considerable mismanagement of one kind and another, but do not remember that I ever dreamed that so much of that article could be employed in one night on board a steamboat. Among the boat's officers there was no mutual understanding, and it is fortunate for us that the rebels did not know it. But at daylight we did reach Alberti's mills and then came for me an hour of fitful dreamy sleep. I had made three vigorous efforts to sleep during the night, but enjoyed the calm moonlight and strange scenery and spice of danger too much for drowsiness. We passed picket fires and felt the possibility that our return might be obstructed or greatly harassed.

13 According to Higginson, they were able to make it to Woodstock, with all the problems the river afforded, before the Rebel cavalry could get there to warn of the gunboat's approach. His statement also implies that nobody heard the noise of the *John Adams* as she neared the objective.

14 Higginson also said, "I have always been infinitely grateful, both for the credit and for the discipline of the regiment,—as well as for the men's subsequent lives,—that the opposite method was adopted."

15 The two primary sources used to describe the battle of the bluffs, Higginson's *Army Life* and the Penniman memoirs, are contradictory as to which bluffs were used. Higginson's first published account of the St. Mary's River mission was in 1866 as an article in the magazine *Atlantic Monthly*. Penniman did not write his memoirs until about 1901, some 38 years after the engagement. Given the difference in time between the two, Higginson's account is probably more accurate than Penniman's. Both give names of bluffs that exist, while one mentioned in Penniman's version does not (Map of Camden County, Georgia, 1999, Mars Marketing, Inc., Cincinnati, Ohio). Penniman mentions only one bluff, Clark's, while Higginson states four, of which the ones with names, Reed's (not on the map) and Scrubby, he says were used to fire upon

the *John Adams*. As the battle of the bluffs unfolds, Penniman's account will be added in, with appropriate endnotes used when his memoirs digress from Higginson. The map used shows the names of four bluffs: Clark's, shortly after the brickyard; and further down the river three clustered close to each other— Carleton Griffin, Little Griffin, and Scrubby (there is also the possibility that the names of three of them have been changed). I will use endnotes to bring into context what is on the map as opposed to what is described in Higginson's and Penniman's accounts. The main reason probably why the names of them in both accounts differ from the actual names is that Higginson was there only once and did not write the names down until later (most likely when he was writing his initial article of the operation), while Penniman did not write his memoirs until 38 years later when specific details can easily be lacking. His memoirs did not say where he was living at the time; if not in the local area, he wouldn't have been able to consult anyone.

16   This does not correspond with what is on the ground because the first bluff that the *John Adams* comes to is Clark's, the first one after leaving the brickyard. This is where Penniman said the Rebels first engaged the Volunteers.

17   It is most likely here that the St. Mary's picket was the only one on the Georgia side. Anything of a significant nature was miles upriver (the brickyard, Woodstock). All the Georgia Confederates had to do was ride up the trails that paralleled the river and see where the Yankee gunboat went so they could plan an appropriate response.

18   Other sources list Company D at a Camp Brookfield in Glynn County (above Camden County) during this time frame. Company D is used here because of what Penniman said in his reminiscences. The *Supplement to the Official Records* says that Companies C, E, and H were stationed at a place called Camp Tattnail, "located about five miles south of Woodbine, across from Cole's Cemetery," of which the St. Mary's River was part of its area of responsibility. The Supplement also does not say which company had pickets at St. Mary's or who was watching the 1st South Carolina while it was at Woodstock, at the brickyard, and on the bluffs opposing the *John Adams* as she came back down the river. Camp Tattnail is near the center of Camden County. Like Camp Cooper, it served as a base camp in a central area for picket stations on the St. Mary's River and on the Georgia coast portion of the country.

19   In Penniman's memoirs, he gives a different account as to how many men actually engaged the *John Adams*. He says that the reinforcements sent for did not arrive in time and only his squad engaged the 1st South Carolina. He wrote, "By the time they [the reinforcements] arrived the gun boat had gone up as far as Woodstock and returned down the river, though not until some of the boys had a bit of a chance at her." He also claims "that the mere squad, some eight or ten men only, came near destroying her."

20   As previously mentioned, both Higginson and Penniman have different accounts as to how many bluffs from which the Rebels fired. Clark's Bluff is the first one to pass going back downstream after leaving the brickyard as shown on the map, while Higginson says the gunboat passed one bluff before being engaged at the next one. Clark's is several miles upstream from the others that are close to each other (also as shown on the modern map).

21   The Index to the 4th Georgia Cavalry does not have anybody with these initials.

22   Higginson mentions no use of any weapons outside of rifles and cannon against the enemy. He also says nothing about the boat getting out of control after Captain Clifton was killed.

23 Higginson says that it "was Reed's Bluff where we were first attacked, and
    Scrubby Bluff, I think, was next." Penniman says that they first hit them at
    Clark's.

24 Higginson says that the barge swamped shortly after this incident. It was
    then captured and refurbished by the Rebels only to be stolen later by some
    escaping slaves who made it to Union lines. Higginson said that some of these
    men "enlisted in my own regiment."

25 In describing these previous experiences, Dr. Rogers said that he:

> had written thus far when the rebels began firing from the shore and I found myself
> among our soldiers, who replied with a spirit and precision that sent more than one
> poor fellow to the dust. Captain Clifton of the John Adams was shot through the
> head and died instantly. The Major's head escaped by about two inches. Strange to say
> no other incident occurred in this nor in the subsequent firing from the bluffs on the
> Florida shore. The first attack was from the Georgia bluffs. They were both desperate,
> but of short duration. One fellow actually jumped on the flat-boat in tow, and was
> immediately shot by one of our soldiers. I afterwards asked Robert Sutton what he
> was about during the conflict, and found that he was deliberately shooting from the
> pilot house, with two guns, having a man to load one while he fired the other.

Chapter 11

1 There is no record that specifically states which companies of the 4th Georgia
   arrived.

2 Within this time frame, Company B and the other companies had to have been
   there on the St. Mary's at least five days. This does not take into account the
   time it took to ride the distance from Camp Finegan to Cooper (or from any
   other place at the time of notification) and back.

3 Higginson differentiates in how many men he took prisoner, but their disposition
   remained constant. In a letter to his mother, he wrote, "We hv. iron, lumber, rice,
   a flock of sheep, 7 prisoners, a cannon, & a flag." In his journal he said, "I took
   all the men we found in Woodstock prisoners, meaning them for hostages in
   case we got into any serious trouble on the river & then meaning to put all but
   one ashore farther down, but their friends attacked us so vehemently, there was
   no chance for chivalry." In his official report, Higginson stated, "At Woodstock
   I took 6 male prisoners, whom I brought down the river as hostages, intending
   to land them before reaching Fernandina and return them on parole, but in view
   of the previous attack made upon us from the banks this would have seemed
   an absurd stretch of magnanimity, and by the advice of Colonel Hawley I have
   brought them for your (General Saxton's) disposal."

4 Higginson did not give any specifics as to why Hawley said what he did. Dr.
   Rogers adds an interesting part to this experience of the 1st S.C. He wrote,

> The officer in command at Fernandina has no authority to send out a flag of truce
> with prisoners, so we take all ours to Beaufort. I am exceedingly glad of it, since have
> found, through Robert Sutton, that one of them shot a man while he was trying to
> escape to the "yankees." After I had dressed Robert's wound, this morning, he took me
> to the rebel and ingeniously made him say: "No, you are mistaken, the gun went off
> accidently." "And besides he was not killed, but died of fever." "Then," said I, "you did
> threaten to shoot him?" "Yes, but I intended it only as a threat." Robert said, "I know
> you killed him;" and I to Robert, "The testimony of black men is legal now in Florida."

5 During the Civil War, wives of officers (especially senior ones) in the Union Army often joined their husbands when they were stationed in static places as opposed to those assigned to field armies, especially when the armies were on the move.

6 Since he had to take the prisoners with him, he said "the men were delighted. They said, 'Spose we leave dem dar secesh at Fernandina, Gen. Saxby (the soldiers' derivation of Saxton's name) w'ont see them.' As if they were playthings."

7 Prior to being told of Hawley's decision not to accept the prisoners, Rogers had naturally assumed he would. He recorded on January 30 as the *John Adams* was back in Fernandina: "Our comrades on the Ben Deford greeted us heartily and the Provost Marshal was in readiness to take charge of our prisoners. We shall probably take Mr Bessent to Beaufort with us." He also said humorously about Bessent that "he is a wealthy and influential rebel and may become a very important hostage when Jeff Davis begins to hang us."

8 Dr. Rogers wrote on February 1 that Captain Trowbridge and the *Planter* met the *John Adams* in St. Simon's Bay (on the north side of the island) that morning as opposed to what Higginson said, that the *Planter* arrived in Fernandina on January 30, the same day that *John Adams* returned.

9 See Chapter 7, note 2.

10 The Crooked River empties into the Cumberland River, which separates the mainland from Cumberland Island.

11 King's Bay lies between the Crooked and St. Mary's Rivers.

12 In his report of the operation to General Saxton, Higginson did not say that Trowbridge reported running up against any Confederate troops, since the salt works were an important coastal operation to defend. What troops the 4th Georgia Cavalry did have in the area (probably no more than one company) were already dispatched to the St. Mary's River to counter what the Confederates expected to be more Federal aggression after two trips. The Rebel belief of continued Union movements in this area left the salt works on the Crooked River wide open for Trowbridge to destroy. Dr. Rogers confirmed this: "They met with no opposition ..." Based upon the description of the location of the salt works, Trowbridge had to have been guided to it. It is very doubtful that he would have found it just by being told where it was, finding it, and returning to Fernandina in the time he did without help. This help had to have been one of the Volunteers who had prior knowledge as a slave of the salt works and location. Dr. Rogers gives more detail. He says that Trowbridge's detachment had destroyed the salt works "which operation has damaged the rebels the extent of about twenty five thousand dollars. They met with no opposition, but had a hard time dragging their boats through a marsh. The marshes, or savannahs, in this part of the country, which borders the rivers, are almost impossible for human beings, yet many a slave has waded through them toward the north star of freedom."

13 This amount sounds like a little too much for the *John Adams* to handle, especially with all the people, lumber, animals, and other items taken at Woodstock, plus the bricks. With all the jerking around the gunboat had to endure going back downstream (as she did going up), plus all the Rebel gunfire, what amount of bricks there really were had to have been tied down (like the lumber and other items), or they would have gone all over the place. The weight of the bricks alone (not including everything else) had to have put a premium on the boat's displacement (how much clearance the base of the boat needed before she hit bottom and grounded).

14   A civilian specifically appointed to handle police matters with other civilians during a military occupation of an area.

15   Higginson did not say that he got horses or cattle at Woodstock in *Army Life*, as opposed to what he said in his report.

16   He probably still gave several of them to Colonel Hawley; if not, to someone else at Fernandina. He also could have let his men have them.

17   How many of the men were able to sleep while going upriver with the boat getting stuck eight times, let alone with the worry of imminent combat, were most likely very few.

18   Higginson said that Captain Steedman of the steamer *Paul Jones* blew up a portion of the abandoned forts to obtain the iron.

19   The evidence suggests that he wrote his report during the evening on the return voyage.

20   The only unit Higginson knew as fact that he was going up against in the entire St. Mary's expedition was "Captain Clark's company of cavalry." He never said he knew it as Company K, 2nd Florida Cavalry, nor did he specifically say who he had fought in the "battle of The Hundred Pine" in his report or his journal, but only later in the 1866 *Atlantic Monthly* article, "Up the St. Mary's," which was later republished in his book *Army Life*. The surprising part is that Higginson said the Rebels used artillery, whereas in his journal (written three days after his report) he said that "our danger in such expeditions is not nearly so great as one would think as we have cannon & the rebels have not ..." Even though his report is very detailed as to what happened, it does not mean he was not prone to a little bit of embellishment to say that they were engaged by artillery. He probably wanted to put his unit in the best light possible without overdoing it.

21   The details of his report are not repeated here, since they have already been covered.

22   Higginson did not listen to Sutton about continuing to Camp Cooper after getting into the skirmish with Captain Clarke and the end result which took place.

23   This is an example of what I refer to regarding the use of racial epithets by those who worked with the freedmen.

24   She did not say who this soldier was.

25   Higginson also acknowledged this indirectly in his report when he wrote: "Had I listened to the urgent appeals of my men and pursued the fleeing enemy we could have destroyed his camp." But he added that the knowledge of this came too late, because "in view of the darkness, [the enemy's] uncertain numbers, and swifter motions, with [General Saxton's] injunctions of caution, I judged it better to rest satisfied with the victory already gained."

Chapter 12

1   Nowhere in Higginson's writings does he say anything derogatory about Stickney; on the contrary, he gives him accolades.

2   There is nothing that states when Stickney first heard of Saxton wanting to expand Federal lines to the mainland. As the head of the Florida Tax Commission, Stickney was going to have to know eventually so he could prepare to do his "job" as the Florida agent of the Treasury Department. There is also nothing to state how much influence he might have had in the decision to make Jacksonville the target in his "consultations" with Saxton.

3 Higginson added his own thoughts on the economy of human life when he
   wrote on February 23:

> My friends seem anxious about my exposing myself; but they may be assured that I
> am kept under a tight reign [*sic*] in the respect already; never was a man so teased and
> badgered as I was on this last trip. I do not see it, because though naturally enjoying
> danger as much as most men perhaps, I am not such a fool as not to see the value
> of my life to this regiment & through it to the whole movement of which it is the
> beginning & now that I have tested my men & they me, I certainly am not going to
> curtail my work with them by any needless prominence. Usually I am not given to
> setting my heart on immediate results, but I should dread even a wound were it ever so
> slight, if it obliged me to give up the reins but only for a day. So I have every induction
> to caution.

4 Higginson also wrote that his "men looked neat & soldierly in their blue
   uniform (having got rid of the wretched red trousers, which they hated)."
   About a week and a half later he said also that "General Hunter said they had
   much improved so much since the review—but the improvement was chiefly in
   the blue pantaloons."
5 By February, 1863 the northern armaments industry was still not able to keep
   up with the continued growth of the Union Army and the need for more of
   them due to battlefield losses. Many weapons continued to be imported from
   Europe, specifically from Belgium, France, England, Austria, and Prussia.
   According to Gladstone's *Men of Color*, the 1st South Carolina was given both
   Austrian and Prussian muskets though Higginson said in his journal they were
   Austrian. Gladstone mentions also the Austrian as both .54 and .55 calibre,
   though Higginson does not. I can only assume the 1,000 muskets were all
   the same calibre, so I chose the .54 calibre; thus the Model 1854 Lorenz Rifle
   Musket.
6 Both Higginson and Dr. Rogers wrote how weather affected black and white
   soldiers differently, with the winter months being most harmful to blacks.
7 For a detailed biography of Montgomery, see Tom Le Roy Holman's *James
   Montgomery, 1813–1871*, Ed.D. Dissertation, Oklahoma State University,
   1973. On the evening of February 25, Dr. Rogers was able to get some
   bibliographical data from him:

> All this evening I have been squeezing Kansas history out of Col. Montgomery, a
> history with he himself is so completely identified that I have really been listening to
> a wonderful autobiography. Col. M. is a born pioneer. Ashtabula County, Ohio, is his
> native place. Forty nine years ago, Joshua R. Gidding and Ben Wade were young men
> and Montgomery in his boyhood was accustomed to hear their pleading at the bar.
> So you see how birth and early surroundings fitted him for a fiercer frontier life. New
> England life seems puny beside the lusty life born on the frontier. Of the Col. eight
> children two of his sons are to hold commissions in his regiment. They are young but
> as "they don't know the measure of fear" and hate slavery he is sure they will get on.

8 This indicates that their legal status during this period in time was tenuous,
   i.e., they had no real legal standing and therefore anything could be done
   with them at the whim of the Union Army. If I am correct, it was the famous
   Supreme Court case of Dred Scott v. Sandford, also known more famously as
   the Dred Scott decision, that said that blacks, whether slave or free, were not
   citizens of the United States, is what allowed for this to take place. I would not

be surprised if Montgomery told these men that they had to do what he said, that they had no say so in the matter.

9 In a letter to his mother he wrote the next day, Higginson said that Montgomery came back with 120 recruits.

10 In 1864 the 2nd South Carolina's weapons would be upgraded to the .577 calibre Enfield. By this time also, the unit's name would have been changed to the 34th United States Colored Troop. The 1st S.C.'s name would be the 33rd.

11 No last name was given.

12 Higginson made it quite clear concerning guards and respect. He said:

> Machines cannot make soldiers like mine. The very first object is to develop self respect. The Regulations say "all officers of whatever rank are required to observe respect towards guards"—& this is the principle for making good guards. A guard obeys no order save from the officers of the Guard & the Commanding officer. He may shoot his own Captain if he interferes with his duty as a guard. This educates self respect, & as each man is in turn on guard, each man learns it. I allow no man to stand with his cap off, talking to me out of doors; I explain that slaves do that— soldiers give a military salute, which the officer is as absolutely required to return as the soldier to officer. The better soldiers they become the more they are spoiled for slaves.

13 Not once during the war did the Department of the South mount any offensive action against Savannah, except for the capture of Fort Pulaski.

14 According to strength figures ending March 31, the department had 23,385 men spread out among the areas it controlled. Though spread out, Hunter could have drawn up to 20,000 soldiers for a short period of time without harming the ability to defend his command. In this theater of war, the Confederates were more concerned with defense of their strategic seaports, because they just did not have the men and materiel required to recapture the Sea Islands.

15 Saxton did not want to use the 1st and 2nd S.C. in an attack against Charleston because he did not think they would not perform like the white regiments. No, he had an ulterior motive, and that was to use his black phalanx to increase the number of black regiments.

16 There is no evidence that says exactly when Saxton made known his plans to Higginson.

17 Later in the war from mid-1863 onward, Florida would become a vital link in the ability of the Rebels to continue to fight by providing food, primarily beef. This becomes paramount when Texas is cut off as the South's main provider when the Federals finally gained complete control of the Mississippi with the capture of Vicksburg on July 4, 1863.

18 Florida was divided up into districts for military necessity.

19 In late February Saxton told Higginson where his next mission was to be. I place the time here when Dr. Rogers first mentions the expedition on March 3 in a letter, talking about supplies being loaded. From the time of getting permission from Hunter to loading supplies on the 3rd would have required several days to assemble the necessary ships, move several tons of supplies and baggage and properly store them on board, and prepare the two regiments for embarkation.

It is also possible that Saxton waited until this time so that the Volunteers would have enough time to recuperate from their previous mission, allow the new recruits in the regiment to gain more experience in their training, and give

Montgomery some time to properly organize his new command, though he only had two companies at the time.

20 Higginson never did identify who these "one or two others" were.

21 The "larger number" was those who saw an opportunity to become commissioned officers, whereas remaining in their white regiments meant little or no opportunity to advance.

22 Higginson said that Hunter's headquarters at "Hilton Head, in those days, seemed always like some foreign military station in the tropics."

23 For the most recent account of the first two occupations of the city, see *Jacksonville's Ordeal by Fire: a Civil War History* by Richard A. Martin and Daniel L. Schafer.

24 The *Boston* was 225 feet long, 28 feet wide and with a depth of 10 feet, 6 inches. She was a 12-year-old side wheeler with sails and had a water displacement of 630 tons.

25 The reporters most likely got information too from other sources that they had developed over a period of time.

26 There can be no doubt that the reporters also embellished facts.

27 Miss Forten also says personally about Dr. Rogers:

> I am willing to give up my life—which is nothing—but I do not want one so good and noble as he to die yet. This world cannot afford to lose such. And yet he says "let us think how much better is it is to die in this sublime struggle for universal freedom, than to live to see another generation of slavery."

28 This meant that once the Union's base of operations was secure, she would be sent for.

29 Mrs. King said that another woman, Lizzie Lancaster, was going too.

30 Though Higginson wrote in his journal that Montgomery returned on February 23 with the nucleus of his regiment, Tom Holman said in his dissertation that "they had no more left the decks of the *Cosmopolitan* than they were ordered aboard the steamers now headed toward Jacksonville."

31 The newspaper articles written about the expedition strongly suggest there were only two newspapers covering the event. No other papers are mentioned. No names are also given of the correspondents. Though Richard Martin said in his article "*New York Times* Views Civil War Jacksonville" that "these writers in most cases are relatively unknown," this can be extended to reporters of other newspapers too.

32 Issuing them at that time and date did not exactly help much when Miss Forten, a civilian, already knew of the operation, let alone the two other teachers whom she later told.

33 It is somewhat surprising that Du Pont was not told the nature of the mission, let alone the fact that he did not ask what it was about. He would write later to his wife on March 18: "This Colonel Higginson is off with the black troops again. Though they come for certain assistance from me, bringing of course a request from General Hunter, they never tell you where they are going, and the first thing you hear of them somewhere you least expected."

Chapter 13

1 This is the approximate time as to when Saxton wrote his report, since he said in part, "I have the honor to report that I have sent ...," thus giving the impression that he did not compose it until after the ships had left port.

2 The Department of the South was still a secondary theater of operations in early 1863. The latest planned Federal offensive in Virginia under the new commander, Major General Joseph Hooker, had priority in men and materiel, of which he was amazing huge quantities.

3 This was being a little too presumptuous in Saxton's thinking.

4 Though the source only uses "the commanders," it is obvious that this meant Higginson and the *Boston* commander until the boat was anchored and then Colonel Montgomery and the other boat commanders could come aboard the *Boston*.

5 The author of *A History of Company K*, Jerome Tourtellotte, said that "the steamers Boston and Neptune came in bringing a small mail ..." Though he made the mistake of the *Neptune*, the most likely way Company K found out that the expedition was going up the St. John's was when the mail was brought to them. Neither Colonel Higginson nor Dr. Rogers mentioned any mail delivery.

6 This is the only logical reason why the *John Adams* was not in sight. The channel in and out of Cumberland Sound was only wide enough for one vessel to pass through at a time. If the ship had been first or second, her status would have been known. Why the *Boston* and *Burnside* did not wait once they crossed the bar is a good question. Maybe the *John Adams* did not report any problems prior to the other two ships departing and they had planned not to wait on each other but simply rendezvous at the mouth of the St. John's.

7 In *Battles and Leaders*, Watson is listed as an Acting Master while *Army Life* says he has the grade of Lieutenant (which is equal to an Army captain.).

8 Why Colonel Montgomery waited until this time before issuing these men their weapons, the primary sources do not say.

9 This is the time Dr. Rogers said that the *John Adams* arrived on the 9th. However, when Colonel Higginson said "we waited twenty-four hours for her" starting on the 8th, he gave the arrival time much later in the day when he said, "at the very last moment of the tide, just in time to cross that day, the missing vessel arrived." The time given by Rogers is primarily used instead of that by Higginson because Rogers wrote it down when she arrived. This does not diminish Higginson's account in any way, though he first published his version of this mission three years later in the magazine *Atlantic Monthly*. Besides, it is not uncommon for participants of a particular event to give different versions in various details.

10 This is the only explanation given by any of the participants as to why the *John Adams* was late.

11 According to *The Official Military Atlas of the Civil War*, there were a couple of trails leading up to "Pilot Town" on the south side of the mouth of the St. John's and a partial one on the north side. This meant that the convoy could have been observed after the shots were heard, but it would have taken a while for the Rebels to get there to see what was going on (providing someone *was not* already there) and get back over this primitive road network to report what they saw. However, none of the Confederate writings said that this occurred.

12 In *Army Life* and in "Reoccupation of Jacksonville in 1863," Higginson does not specifically give any order of the vessels. However, he does say that a gunboat was in the lead, but does not say which one (*Norwich* or *Uncas*). He also says that the ship he was behind was a gunboat, but again does not specify.

13 This was the term used to describe early water mines, as opposed to the word's later application.

14 Several Union vessels met their fate during the latter half of the Civil War at the hands of these devices on the St. John's.

15 This was most likely the order of travel, since the *Uncas* was the only naval gunboat left. Since the *Boston* would land at an upper pier and the *Burnside* at a lower one, it would make the most sense to have them in second and third positions. The *John Adams* would be last according to this scenario. Since the *Uncas* was first, it would anchor in the river in an overwatch position, while the next two ships would come up to their respective piers and disgorge the soldiers. Then when one of them was through, the *John Adams* would pull up and have the soldiers disembark.

16 For a more detailed account of this operation against St. John's Bluff, see again Martin and Schafer's *Jacksonville's Ordeal By Fire*.

17 Higginson did not mention anything in his writings about a possible fight here. The army–navy task force that had captured the bluff the previous fall was several times larger. Higginson's small force would have found the going very rough, if not impossible, to subdue any reestablished Rebel redoubt, especially if it meant causing many of his men to be killed. Besides, it would have been very difficult up to this point to get replacements as opposed to white soldiers.

18 This is the present-day home of the Jacksonville Jaguars.

19 One thing that the primary sources do not mention, and it is highly probable that Higginson did not think of it either, is that once the ships had docked and had allowed the companies to land prior to them moving out to their assigned sectors, the Confederates could have fired into them, thus causing massive chaos and blocking the ability of the *Uncas*, or the *John Adams* as she moved up, to engage the Rebel defenses. This would have entailed the Rebels knowing that the Yankees were coming, but that did not occur. However, a version of this would take place about two weeks later in the town of Palatka further up the river when a Volunteer detachment would come up against a brilliant Confederate officer named J. J. Dickison.

20 Higginson also wrote in describing this initial scene: "You cannot conceive anything prettier than the effect as we sailed up the beautiful stream, to this pretty town at eight A.M. the children all running out to meet us, the men and women gazing in amusement. All were polite, some overjoyed, some secretly cursing; some of the women hate the black soldiers, others say they have known many of the men all their lives, and it does not seem like being among strangers."

21 Only Dr. Rogers and the *Times* say which companies of the 1st S.C. landed at the wharves, but they differ as to whom.

22 Montgomery said that his "command was assigned to picket duty, on the Rail Road, West of Jacksonville." This is placed here instead of being placed in the main text because of what he said next. After saying that his unit was placed covering the western approach to town, he says that "we had some skirmishing during the day;—the enemy keeping at long range." This second part contradicts all the other firsthand accounts, which said that there was no contact that first day.

23 To say that the Confederates did not hear the flotilla prior to seeing them is based upon a letter that Winston Stephens wrote to his wife on March 16. He said "the pickets barely had time to get out before they landed."

24 The primary source did not say whether their horses were saddled already in order for them to escape quickly. It is possible they were not and the men only had enough time to grab their equipment and saddle them after they were a good distance from the Volunteers.

25 This wharf belonged to the mercantile firm of Cyrus Bisbee and Anthony Canosa.

26 The District of Middle Florida had the other five companies, which were A, D, E, G, and I.

27 This unit was also known under other names. In volume I of *Biographical Rosters*, it was called Brevard's Partisan Rangers, named after its commander, Major Theodore W. Brevard. However, in volume III, it was called the 2nd Florida Battalion. Since Finegan used the name First Battalion Partisan Rangers in his initial report of enemy action, I will continue to use the same name to prevent confusion.

28 Since the Federals controlled St. Augustine, the Rebels basically ceded control of the east side of the river to them, though it did not stop the Confederates from crossing on occasion.

29 In the Organization of Troops in the Department of South Carolina, Georgia, and Florida, dated March 13, 1863, Captain John Westcott is listed as commander and not Asa Stewart. In *Biographical Rosters*, volume III, Westcott is also listed as commander of Company A. The Organization of Troops and *Biographical Rosters* concur with the other three officers. Since Finegan had Asa Stewart as commander and not Westcott in his report of March 14, I will continue to use Asa Stewart's name. Also in the Organization of Troops, Companies A, B, and C are each listed as Company Partisans, while Company D is listed as Company of Rangers.

30 This structure had to be at the edge of town facing the Rebels. Though this was only what the Confederates could see at the time, Higginson had pickets all around the city.

31 There is not any information that says when McCormick specifically arrived, with the remainder of his command *en route*, other than when Stephens wrote to Davis that "the rest of the command followed me" and to his wife Octavia that "the rest followed."

32 Nothing was said about a signal to be given for both Rebel units to withdraw at the same time.

33 There is no evidence stating what start-time Finegan used for his forces to begin moving toward the enemy's lines. The only time the evidence does state is when contact between the adversaries is approximately made. One source says 9:00 a.m.; another 9:30; still another said 10:30, so I will generally say mid-morning.

34 Though on horseback, it would make sense that they advanced slowly. It was most likely that Finegan wanted his cavalry and infantry to make contact about the same time for maximum effect to test the enemy's reaction. If not, the 2nd Florida would have reached the Volunteers way ahead of the slower moving Partisan Rangers.

35 Davis Bryant, Captain Stephens' brother-in-law, learned that the attacking Confederates "tried to bag the outposts but owing to some mistake the infantry did not move fast enough and, in consequence, the cavalry was left to do the whole and succeeded in merely in driving them under of their Gunboats ..." Stephens wrote this later to Bryant: "We moved so fast that the Infantry did not get in the position intended, but they got a running shot at them."

36 Why did not this reflect in Finegan's report of March 14? Didn't he communicate with Brevard as to why he did not link up with him? Would not a commander want to know why one of his subordinates did not do what he ordered him to do? If Brevard had written a report, it got lost in the shuffle of war and did not make it into *Official Records*. Regardless of why nothing is

mentioned in Finegan's report, what I wrote to explain why the infantry did not make it to its assigned destination is the only thing that makes sense, given that the numbers of each side and the difference of the two regiments of the Volunteers are true.

37 No exact time is given for the attack.

38 Nothing is said as to where the attack took place, but the way Finegan described the event in his report of the attack, it sounds like the Partisan Rangers went up against the 2nd South Carolina.

39 Hardly anything on the Federal side was written about this first day of action, which is quite surprising. Except for what Montgomery wrote in a letter and two newspaper accounts, Rebel sources were the principal means used to describe what took place.

Chapter 14

1 Though no information exists to support this, the underlying tone of this sentence to Beauregard is that if there were to be a corruption of the slave population in east Florida, what would the politicians in the other two states (Georgia and South Carolina) under his protection think of his ability to protect them? This could cause Beauregard's own position to be tenuous.

2 There is no mention of the message in *Official Records*. Only Beauregard's reply is present. There is also no date given in his reply when they communicated with him; it was somewhere between the 10th and the 13th. When the two senators received the news, and from whom, is also not provided. It was possible that they also mentioned the economic and political fallout of a massive slave exodus. By contacting Beauregard, they were also protecting their political backsides.

3 The "Organization of the troops in the Department of South Carolina, Georgia, and Florida," dated March 13, 1863, lists the Milton Light Artillery as the only artillery unit in the District of East Florida under Finegan. However, in a letter of gratitude to his command after the Union withdrawal from Jacksonville, dated March 30, Finegan lists two separate units, Dunham's and another one called Abell's company, commanded by Captain Henry F. Abell. Davis Bryant mentions a company in his letter of March 15. Winston Stephens refers to a detachment in a letter to his wife on February 7, but in another one to Davis Bryant dated March 16 he mentions three artillery companies, one of which came from the District of Middle Florida.

   In *Organizational Rosters*, the Milton Light Artillery was divided into two sub-units on March 6, 1863, with Company A commanded by Dunham; Company B by Abell. Since there is a contradiction, I will say that the Milton Light has two artillery companies. This is just one example of several contradictions of units or their commanders in Finegan's command. With these in mind, I had to make decisions as what to call which unit or who to say was in command. One other thing I need to cover is the terms used to refer to units in the artillery and cavalry. During this time, it was not uncommon to refer to the basic artillery unit as a company, though it was also called a battery, which is its modern rendition. The basic cavalry unit was called a company too, though the modern-day term is troop.

4 No information states which company was stationed at Camp Cooper.

5 Company H brought between 60 and 65 men to Jacksonville. There was no number given for Company F.

6 The District of Middle Florida was a quiet area at this time, except for the occasional raid on a coastal salt works operation by a Union naval ship. Given this fact, General Cobb would be able to send more units to aid his counterpart, as he was able to collect those designated for deployment at the nearest point on the railroad so they could be transported to Jacksonville.

7 General Saxton caught this sentiment when he wrote a letter to Secretary Stanton on March 14: "It is my belief that scarcely an incident in this war has caused a greater panic throughout the whole Southern coast than this raid of the colored troops in Florida." The thought of servile insurrection was very real in the minds of many slave owners. There was Nat Turner's rebellion in 1831 in Virginia. Turner, a very intelligent slave, caused a revolt in which he and his followers killed about five dozen whites before the rebellion was suppressed; the participants were either shot or hanged. There was also most recently John Brown's failed raid on Harper's Ferry, Virginia, in 1859. All the surviving participants of this planned revolt were tried and hanged.

8 Though there is no information to prove it, there is reason to believe that the other two commission members continued with their work after Stickney left to go to Fernandina.

9 Dr. Rogers made the same point. He said, "Many of our men were slaves here, not long ago and you can scarcely imagine the horror and dread the secesh have of them."

10 Higginson would later say of Montgomery: "In Colonel Montgomery's hand these up river raids reached the dignity of a fine art. His conceptions of foraging were rather more Western and liberal than mine, and on these excursions he fully indemified [*sic*] himself for an undue abstinance [*sic*] demanded of him when in camp."

11 Stephens would be killed one year later after the battle of Olustee near Jacksonville.

12 There is no reason mentioned why Hawley did not give to Stickney the promised men. This runs contrary to what Jerome Tourtellotte of Company K, 7th Connecticut, said in his history about what Hawley wanted to do when he thought the 1st S.C. was defeated when it went up the St. Mary's in January: "Colonel Joe's anti-slavery sympathies were badly strained and he raved for the opportunity to turn the Seventh Connecticut loose and avenge our colored brothers." None of the original sources say anything except in *Civil War Journal*, when Higginson affirmed that Stickney was supposed to obtain "four white companies & a battery in addition, which Col. Hawley had promised me."

Also, in the "Organization of troops in the Department of the South," dated March 31, there is no mention of an artillery battery assigned to Fernandina at this time. The only possible explanation for this is that this was a composite unit made from men of the 7th Connecticut and several unassigned guns captured from the Confederates in their haste to evacuate Fernandina/Amelia Island on the approach of Union forces in March, 1862.

13 Stickney probably made this decision in consultation with the commander of the *Boston*. Hawley could have been in on this decision too.

14 To say that Stickney first went to Saxton rather than to Hunter is conjecture on my part, but it seems the most plausible explanation given the command structure in the Department of the South at the time. Saxton was Higginson's immediate superior and the first rung in this chain of command. Since the Florida operation was primarily Saxton's idea, he would naturally endorse the troop reinforcement to see his plan be carried out to a successful conclusion. Once this was done, the next step would be to get Hunter's approval.

15 Several of the main characters in this book state this in their writings.

16 In the "Organization of troops," the 1st and 2nd S.C. were not listed as being assigned to Saxton's command (or anybody else's).

17 Hunter probably let Saxton decide what to send to Jacksonville as long as he was still able to defend Port Royal Island, now that he had white regiments under his command. The 6th Connecticut and 8th Maine were probably the most available in terms of how quickly they could get ready to deploy to Florida. The other units assigned on the island were the 4th New Hampshire Infantry; the 55th, 174th, and 176th Pennsylvania Infantry; the 1st Connecticut Battery; 1st U.S. Artillery, Batteries D and M; and the 1st Massachusetts Cavalry, Third Squadron.

18 No reason is given why it took five and six days for the units to get under way. Maybe the transportation was not readily available when it was initially needed, and it took several days before the ships could be consolidated.

19 In his journal Higginson said that "tonight instead of enemies appeared friends … a whole Ct. regiment, the 6th …" Dr. Rogers mentioned the arrival of the 6th also but did not give a time.

20 This problem would have been present with any of the white regiments stationed in the department. Besides, Higginson must have anticipated that this was going to happen. Prior to the arrival of the 6th, the training and use of the Volunteers had been kept separate from the other units, but the use of them together could no longer be avoided given the current situation in Jacksonville. So, the history of the U.S. military had now reached a significant turning point.

21 In a letter to his mother on the 22nd, Higginson said, "I command the whole now—but tomorrow may bring Col. Rust who as Senior Col. will command the post; though I expect that either this will be temporary or we shall go to another post, farther up the river … There is a strong impression that Gen. Hunter is coming down here, on a visit at least—if so he probably will be here in a day or two & my plans will be clearer."
He added, "Everything so far has turned out so consonant with our expectations from this regiment that I hv not much fear of my being seriously thwarted, which would be the case if put under the orders of Colonels of white reg'ts."

Chapter 15

1 No specific time was given as to when the firing began.

2 Rust did not say why the *Delaware* took so long to arrive except that there had been bad weather.

3 It is surprising that Higginson did not mention that Montgomery was junior to him.

4 Different sources gave varying strength levels for each unit. Dr. Walton of the 8th Maine said there were four companies of his unit, three of the 6th Connecticut, and three of the 1st S.C.; in a later report of the Jacksonville operation, Colonel Rust said there were five of the 8th, four of the 6th, and "a portion of Colonel Higginson's colored regiment;" a reporter of *The New York Times* credited the 8th with four, the 6th four, and the 1st S.C. six; and Dr. Rogers said the 8th had three, the 6th three, and the 1st S.C. five. Given this situation, I decided not to use a specific number of companies from each regiment that went on this offensive action.

5 W. H. Andrews, First Sergeant of Company H, described it this way:

March 20, 1863, the Regulars were ordered to report to Gen. Finegan at Jacksonville, Fla, the enemy having taken possession of the city. Went by the Southwestern Railroad to Fort Gaines, Ga. March 21, proceeded down the Chattahoochee River on board the steamer Indian to Chattahoochee, Fla. Remained all night at the arsonal [*sic*]. 22nd, marched 10 miles in the direction of Quincy. 23rd, arrived at Quincy and was received by Gen. Howell Cobb and staff. 24th, took the cars for Gen. Finegan's Command three miles from the city, the enemy's picket line between two and one-half miles this side [west] of the city.

6   Neither this company nor its commander was ever identified.

7   Colonel Higginson added: "But for our early departure, I think the 8th Me would never hear the last of the jokes cut thereon—one being that the officer who saw the tents must certainly have been 'three sheets in the wind' which is one of the cant phrases for inebriation."

8   Lieut. Colonel Billings appears as a very shadowy figure in Higginson's writings. Though second in command, it was Major John Strong who always accompanied Higginson in the 1st S.C.'s actions against the Confederates or had special missions assigned to him. This tends to suggest that Higginson continued not to have much faith in Billings' ability as an officer. Maybe he was sent on this trip with Montgomery to give him direct combat exposure without being able to be in charge of the operation. However, an event that will later be described caused him to be wounded. This incident probably sealed his fate as an officer, because he was dismissed from service by an examining board several months later on July 28, 1863. Major Strong was promoted to Billings' position that same day.

9   Ever since the fall of Fernandina, Jacksonville and St. Augustine in March, 1862, the Confederates had conceded for the most part the eastern bank of the St. John's River above the city to the Federals. Even with the abandonment of Jacksonville twice, the Rebels still did not contest it except for an occasional foray across the river.

10 His name was John Quincy, who "received one through the leg, a little above the ankle, fracturing the small bone and carrying away some of it." The leg was amputated on March 31.

11 There were no civilians present at the time when Braddock and his men were captured. They had probably completed their mission and were spending the night where they were before heading back the next day to Captain Westcott's company.

12 General Finegan was not too happy when he found out what had happened. Though Braddock may have escaped from the Federals, he did not from Finegan's displeasure. Finegan said, "I have ordered the arrest of this officer ... and will ask for trial by court-marshall [*sic*] whenever the proper witnesses can be produced." It might have been better if Braddock had remained a prisoner.

Chapter 16

1   The 1st South Carolina was divided between both the *Convoy* and the *John Adams*.

2   It can only be assumed here that the men had requested to go on land.

3   Prior to the decision to allow the men to disembark, Dr. Rogers had made this observation: "Were this crowded state to last but a few hours there would be no trouble, but it is thick weather and raining like furry [*sic*] and the fleet dare not put out to sea before morning."

4 It is ironic that Seymour would take this position, because 11 months later he would lead another expedition to Florida, of which one-third of his command would be composed of black soldiers. This expedition would culminate in the battle of Olustee, which would be a stunning defeat for the Union forces. It also would have been far worse for Seymour had it not been for the efforts of one of his subordinate units, the 54th Massachusetts Infantry, the first regiment of free blacks from the North. The 54th was given the credit for holding the Rebel army at bay at the end of the battle, thus allowing the Federals to retreat and preventing a possible rout.

5 The gunboat *Paul Jones* had already returned to its previous station on March 28 to continue blockading duty.

Sources

Introduction

LOOBY, Christopher, (ed.), *The Complete Civil War Journal and Selected Letters of Thomas Wentworth Higginson*, pp. 1, 4.

Chapter 1

AMMEN, Daniel, *The Navy in the Civil War*, vol. II: *The Atlantic Coast*, pp. 6-9, 11-45.

BELZ, Herman, *Abraham Lincoln, Constitutionalism, and Equal Rights in the Civil War Era*, p. 103.

BERLIN, Ira, *et al.*, *Freedom: A Documentary History of Emancipation, 1861–1867*, Series I, vol. I: *The Destruction of Slavery*, pp. 11-21.

————, *Freedom: A Documentary History of Emancipation, 1861–1867*, Series III: *The Black Military Experience*, pp. 3, 4.

————, *Freedom: A Documentary History of Emancipation, 1861–1867*, Series I, vol. III—*The Wartime Genesis of Free Labor: The Lower South*, pp. 13, 87, 88.

BERRY, Mary Frances, *Military Necessity and Civil Rights Policy: Black Citizenship and the Constitution, 1861-1868*, pp. 37, 38.

COCHRANE, William Ghormley, *Freedom without Equality: A Study of Northern Opinion and the Negro Issue, 1861–1870*, pp. 10-14.

DAVIS, George B. *et al.*, *The Official Military Atlas of the Civil War*, plate CLXX.

GIBSON, Charles Dana and GIBSON, E. Kay, *The Army's Navy Series*, vol. I. *Assault and Logistics: Union Army Coastal and River Operations, 1861–1866*, pp. XX, XXI, & pp. 9, 14-17.

HENDRICKS, George Linton, *Union Army Occupation of the Southern Seaboard, 1861–1865*, pp. 1-4.

LONG, E. B. with LONG, Barbara, *The Civil War Day by Day: An Almanac, 1861–1865*, pp. 2, 3, 56-59, 1075.

MAYS, JOE H., *Black Americans and their Contributions toward Union Victory in the American Civil War*, pp. 1-10.

NALTY, Bernard C. and MACGREGOR, Morris J., (eds.), *Blacks in the Military: Essential Documents*, pp. 22, 23.

O'REILLY, Miles, (HALPINE, Charles G.), *Baked Meats of the Funeral*, pp. 171, 172.

QUARLES, Benjamin, *The Negro in the Civil War*, pp. 24-30.

REED, Rowena, *Combined Operations in the Civil War*, pp. 8, 23-32.

WELCHER, Frank J., *The Union Army, 1861-1865: Organization and Operations*, vol. I: *The Eastern Theater*, pp. 91, 92.

Chapter 2

AMMEN, Daniel, *The Navy in the Civil War*, vol. II: *The Atlantic Coast*, pp. 35-61.

BELL, Malcolm, Jr., *Major Butler's Legacy: Five Generations of a Slaveholding Family*, pp. 358-361.

BERLIN, Ira *et al.*, *Freedom: A Documentary History of Emancipation, 1861–1867*, Series I, vol. III—*The Wartime Genesis of Free Labor: The Lower South*, pp. 14-18, 87-97.

BLUE, Frederick J., *Salmon P. Chase: A Life in Politics*, pp. 174, 175, 184, 185.

BYRNE, William A., *Slavery in Savannah, Georgia during the Civil War*, pp. 103-106.

DROZDOWSKI, Eugene C., *Edwin M. Stanton: Lincoln's Secretary of War: Toward Victory*, pp. 930-934.

DYER, Frederick H., *A Compendium of the War of the Rebellion*, vol. I, p. 259.

FORD, Worthington Chauncey, (ed.), *A Cycle of Adams Letters*, vol. I, pp. 117, 126.

GIBSON, Charles Dana and GIBSON, E. Kay, *The Army's Navy Series*, vol. I. *Assault and Logistics: Union Army Coastal and River Operations, 1861–1866*, pp. 19-23.

HEARD, George Alexander, "St. Simon's Island during the War between the States," *The Georgia Historical Quarterly*, p. 254.

HENDRICKS, George Linton, *Union Army Occupation of the Southern Seaboard, 1861–1865*, pp. 4-7, 11.

LONG, E. B. with LONG, Barbara, *The Civil War Day by Day: An Almanac, 1861–1865*, p. 1093.

MAYS, Joe H., *Black Americans and their Contributions toward Union Victory in the American Civil War*, pp. 10, 12-14.

MILLER, Edward A., Jr., *Lincoln's Abolitionist General: A Biography of David Hunter*, pp. 96-99.

MOHR, Clarence Lee, *Georgia Blacks during Secession and Civil War*, pp. 105, 107-110, 114-117.

————, *On the Threshold of Freedom: Masters and Slaves in Civil War Georgia*, pp. 68, 69, 70, 71.

MYERS, Robert Manson, (ed.), *The Children of Pride: A True Story of Georgia and the Civil War*, pp. 802, 803, 805, 858.

RIVERS, Larry Eugene, *Slavery in Florida: Territorial Days to Emancipation*, pp. 242, 243.

SCHAFER, Daniel L., "Freedom was as close as the River: African Americans and the Civil War in Northeast Florida," in COLBURN, David R. and LANDERS, Jane L., (eds.), *The African American Heritage of Florida*, pp. 157-160.

THOMAS, Benjamin P. and HYMAN, Harold M., *Stanton: The Life and Times of Lincoln's Secretary of War*, pp. 229-231.

WELCHER, Frank J., *The Union Army, 1861-1865: Organization and Operations*, vol. I: *The Eastern Theater*, pp. 92, 93.

WESTWOOD, Howard C., *Black Troops, White Commanders, and Freedmen during the Civil War*, p. 2.

A Committee of the Regimental Association, *The Story of One Regiment: The Eleventh Maine Infantry Volunteers in the War of the Rebellion*, p. 109.

AMMEN, Daniel, *The Navy in the Civil War*, vol. II: *The Atlantic Coast*, p. 235.

BERRY, Mary Frances, *Military Necessity and Civil Rights Policy: Black Citizenship and the Constitution, 1861-1868*, p. 40.

COCHRANE, William Ghormley, *Freedom without Equality: A Study of Northern Opinion and the Negro Issue, 1861–1870*, p. 24.

DONALD, David, (ed.), *Inside Lincoln's Cabinet: The Civil War Diaries of Salmon P. Chase*, pp. 96, 99, 100.

DROZDOWSKI, Eugene C., *Edwin M. Stanton: Lincoln's Secretary of War: Toward Victory*, pp. 939-943, 952-956, 982.

DYER, Frederick H., *A Compendium of the War of the Rebellion*, vol. I, p. 363.

FORD, Worthington Chauncey, (ed.), *A Cycle of Adams Letters*, vol. I, pp. 169, 171.

GAVIN, William G., *Campaigning with the Roundheads: The History of the Hundredth Pennsylvania Veteran Volunteer Infantry Regiment in the American Civil War, 1861-1865*, p. 74.

GLADSTONE, William A., *Men of Color*, p. 7.

HAWKS, John M., "The First Freedmen to Become Soldiers," *The Southern Workman*, p. 107.

HAYES, John D., Jr., *Samuel Francis Du Pont: A Selection from His Civil War Letters*. Vol. II, *The Blockade: 1862–1863*, pp. 44, 45.

HENDRICKS, George Linton, *Union Army Occupation of the Southern Seaboard, 1861–1865*, pp. 62-64.

HIGGINSON, Thomas Wentworth, *Army Life in a Black Regiment*, pp. 270-273.

————, "The First Black Regiment," *The Outlook*, pp. 521, 522.

HOLLAND, Rupert Sargent, (ed.), *Letters and Diary of Laura M. Towne, Written from the Sea Islands of South Carolina, 1862–1884*, pp. 37, 41-44, 46-48, 53, 70, 71, 73-76.

HUNTER, David, *Report of the Military Service of Gen. David Hunter, U.S.A., During the War of the Rebellion*, pp. 19, 20.

LONG, E. B. with LONG, Barbara, *The Civil War Day by Day: An Almanac, 1861–1865*, pp. 242, 243.

MAYS, Joe H., *Black Americans and their Contributions toward Union Victory in the American Civil War*, pp. 14, 15.

MILLER, Edward A., Jr., *Lincoln's Abolitionist General: A Biography of David Hunter*, pp. 97, 99, 100-102, 105, 109, 110.

MOHR, Clarence Lee, *On the Threshold of Freedom: Masters and Slaves in Civil War Georgia*, pp. 84, 85.

NALTY, Bernard C. and MACGREGOR, Morris J. (eds.), *Blacks in the Military: Essential Documents*, p. 24.

O'REILLY, Miles, (HALPINE, Charles), *Baked Meats of the Funeral*, pp. 174-181, 187, 188.

PEARSON, Elizabeth Ware, (ed.), *Letters from Port Royal, 1862–1868*, pp. 38, 39, 42, 43, 47, 63, 64.

QUARLES, Benjamin, *The Negro in the Civil War*, pp. 108-110.

RICHARDS, Kent D., *Isaac I. Stevens: Young Man in a Hurry*, pp. 378, 379.

ROSE, Willie Lee, *Rehearsal for Reconstruction: The Port Royal Experiment*, pp. 145, 188.

SHERWOOD, Henry Noble, (ed.), "The Journal of Miss Susan Walker," *The Quarterly Publication of the Historical and Philosophical Society of Ohio*, pp. 37-39, 47.

STEVENS, Hazard, *The Life of Isaac Ingalls Stevens*, vol. II, pp. 383-385.

SCHMIDT, Louis G., *A Civil War History of the 47th Regiment of Pennsylvania Veteran Volunteers*, p. 171.

SMITH, John David, (ed.), *Black Soldiers in Blue: African American Troops in the Civil War*, pp. 10, 11, 14, 15.

TAYLOR, Susie King, *Reminiscences of My Life in Camp*, p. 13.

TODD, William, *The Seventy-Ninth Highlanders, New York Volunteers, in the War of the Rebellion, 1861-1865*, p. 170.

War of the Rebellion: The Official Records of the Union and Confederate Armies, Series III, vol. II, pp. 30, 31, 43, 45, 50-56, 58-60, 116-118, 362, 363, 366; vol. XIV, pp. 362, 363.

WARNER, Ezra J., *Generals in Blue: Lives of the Union Commanders*, p. 224.

WELCHER, Frank J., *The Union Army, 1861–1865: Organization and Operations*, vol. I: *The Eastern Theater*, pp. 92, 93-96.

WESTWOOD, Howard C., *Black Troops, White Commanders, and Freedmen during the Civil War*, pp. 57, 58, 60, 61.

WILEY, Bell Irvin, *The Common Soldier in the Civil War*, pp. 109, 119, 120.

ZILVERSMIT, Arthur, *Lincoln on Black and White: A Documentary History*, pp. 85, 86.

Chapter 4

AVERY, Isaac W., *The History of the State of Georgia, From 1850 to 1881*, p. 688.

BAHNEY, Robert Stanley, *Generals and Negroes: Education of Negroes by the Union Army, 1861–1865*, pp. 61-63.

BELL, Malcolm, Jr., *Major Butler's Legacy: Five Generations of a Slaveholding Family*, pp. 361-363.

BERLIN, Ira, et al., *Freedom: A Documentary History of Emancipation, 1861–1867*, Series III: *The Black Military Experience*, pp. 41-45.

CARWARDINE, Richard, *Lincoln: A Life of Purpose and Power*, p. 218.

COCHRANE, William Ghormley, *Freedom without Equality: A Study of Northern Opinion and the Negro Issue, 1861–1870*, p. 16.

CORNISH, Dudley Taylor, *The Sable Arm: Black Troops in the Union Army, 1861–1865*, pp. 79, 80.

DROZDOWSKI, Eugene C., *Edwin M. Stanton: Lincoln's Secretary of War: Toward Victory*, pp. 240-243.

DYER, Frederick H., *A Compendium of the War of the Rebellion*, vol. I, pp. 95, 96.

EVANS, Clement, (ed.), *Confederate Military History Extended Edition*, vol. VIII, Georgia, p. 155.

FORD, Worthington Chauncey, (ed.), *A Cycle of Adams Letters*, vol. I pp. 174, 175.

HAYES, John D., Jr., *Samuel Frances Du Pont: A Selection from His Civil War Letters*. Vol. II: *The Blockade: 1862–1863*, pp. 176, 177.

HEARD, George Alexander, "St. Simon's Island during the War Between the States," *The Georgia Quarterly*, pp. 262-268.

HEWETT, Janet B., et al., *Supplement to the Official Records of the Union and Confederate Armies*, Part I—Reports: vol. 3, Serial no. 3, p. 105; Part II—Record of Events: vol. 6, Serial no. 18, p. 586.

HENDERSON, Lillian, *Roster of the Confederate Soldiers of Georgia, 1861–1865*, vol. III, pp. 185, 188.

HENDRICKS, George Linton, *Union Army Occupation of the Southern Seaboard, 1861–1865*, pp. 55, 56, 71.

HIGGINSON, Thomas Wentworth, *Army Life in a Black Regiment*, pp. 274, 275.

————, "The First Black Regiment," *The Outlook*, pp. 522, 523.

HOLLAND, Rupert Sargent, (ed.), *Letters and Diary of Laura M. Towne, Written from the Sea Islands of South Carolina, 1862–1884*, pp. 83, 84.

HUNTER, David, *Report of the Military Services of Gen. David Hunter, U.S.A., During the War of the Rebellion*, pp. 28-30.

Index to the 4th Georgia Cavalry, C.S.A., p. 8.

LONG, E. B. with LONG, Barbara, *The Civil War Day by Day: An Almanac, 1861-1865*, pp. 246, 247, 255-259.

MILLER, Edward A., Jr., *Lincoln's Abolitionist General: A Biography of David Hunter*, pp. 112-114.

MOHR, Clarence Lee, Georgia Blacks during Secession and Civil War, p. 126.

————, *On the Threshold of Freedom: Masters and Slaves in Civil War Georgia*, pp. 70, 80.

Official Records of the Union and Confederate Navies in the War of the Rebellion, Series I, vol. 13, pp. 244, 245.

PEASE, William H., "Three Years among the Freedmen: William G. Gannon and the Port Royal Experiment," *The Journal of Negro History*, p. 103.

(Port Royal) *The New South*, September, 1862.

QUARLES, Benjamin, *The Negro in the Civil War*, pp. 112-117.

ROBBINS, Gerald, "The Recruiting and Arming of Negroes in the Sea Islands, 1862–1865," *Negro Historical Bulletin*, p. 163.

ROSE, Willie Lee, *Rehearsal for Reconstruction: The Port Royal Experiment*, pp. 26-28, 152, 154, 155, 190.

SCHMIDT, Lewis G., *A Civil War History of the 47th Regiment of Pennsylvania Veteran Volunteers*, pp. 177, 178.

SIFAKIS, Stewart, *Compendium of the Confederate Armies: South Carolina and Georgia*, p. 151.

SMITH, John David, (ed.), *Black Soldiers in Blue: African American Troops in the Civil War*, pp. 17, 18.

STEVENS, A. W., (ed.), *Enfranchisement and Citizenship: Addresses and Papers by Edward L. Pierce*, p. 105.

War of the Rebellion: The Official Records of the Union and Confederate Armies, Series I, vol. 14, pp. 368, 369, 374, 376-378, 487, 576, 592, 625; Series III, vol. II, pp. 292, 346.

WARNER, Ezra J., *Generals in Blue: Lives of the Union Commanders*, pp. 420, 421.

WESTWOOD, Howard C., *Black Troops, White Commanders and Freedmen during the Civil War*, p. 67.

ZILVERSMIT, Arthur, *Lincoln on Black and White: A Documentary History*, pp. 94, 95.

Chapter 5

BERLIN, Ira, *et al.*, *Freedom: A Documentary History of Emancipation, 1861–1867*, Series III: *The Black Military Experience*, p. 43.

BERWANGER, Eugene H., "Lincoln's Constitutional Dilemma: Emancipation and Black Suffrage" in SCHWARTZ, Thomas F., (ed.), *"For a Vast Future Also": Essays from the Journal of the Abraham Lincoln Association*, pp. 26, 27.

CARWARDINE, Richard, *Lincoln: A Life of Purpose and Power*, pp. 218, 220.

COCHRANE, William Ghormley, Freedom without Equality: A Study of Northern Opinion and the Negro Issue, 1861–1870, pp. 35-53.

COLES, David James, Far from Fields of Glory: Military Operations in Florida during the Civil War, 1864–1865, pp. 8, 9.

CORNISH, Dudley Taylor, *The Sable Arm: Black Troops in the Union Army,*
1861–1865, pp. 89, 83.

DENNISON, Frederick, *Shot and Shell: The Third Rhode Island Heavy Artillery*
Regiment in the Rebellion, 1861–1865, p. 114.

DROZDOWSKI, Eugene, Edwin M. Stanton, Lincoln's Secretary of War: Toward
Victory, pp. 240-242.

DYER, Frederick H., *A Compendium of the War of the Rebellion,* vol. I, pp. 363-364.

ELDREDGE, Daniel, *The Third New Hampshire and All about It,* p. 215.

FUTCH, Ovid L., "Salmon P. Chase and Civil War Politics in Florida," *Florida*
Historical Quarterly, p. 163.

HAWKS, John D., "The First Freedmen to Become Soldiers," *The Southern Workman,*
pp. 107, 108.

HENDRICKS, George Linton, Union Army Occupation of the Southern Seaboard,
1861–1865, pp. 32, 47.

HIGGINSON, Thomas Wentworth, *Army Life in a Black Regiment,* pp. 7, 9, 269-271,
275, 276.

————————, "The First Black Regiment," *The Outlook,* p. 524.

HOLLAND, Rupert Sargent, (ed.), *Letters and Diary of Laura M. Towne, Written*
from the Sea Islands of South Carolina, 1862–1884, pp. 92-99.

LONG, E. B. with LONG, Barbara, *The Civil War Day by Day, An Almanac,*
1861–1865, pp. 269-272.

MILLER, Edward A, Jr., *Lincoln's Abolitionist General: A Biography of David*
Hunter, pp. 122-124.

NALTY, Bernard C. and MACGREGOR, Morris J., (eds.), *Blacks in the Military:*
Essential Documents, p. 25.

Official Records of the Union and Confederate Navies in the War of the Rebellion,
Series I, vol. 13, pp. 251, 252, 335, 336.

O'REILLY, Miles, (HALPINE, Charles), *Baked Meats of the Funeral,* pp. 175, 189-201.

PEARSON, Elizabeth Ware, (ed.), *Letters from Port Royal, 1862-1868,* pp. 89, 91-93,
96-98, 100, 101.

PIERCE, Edward L., "The Freedmen at Port Royal," *The Atlantic Monthly,* p. 312.

QUARLES, Benjamin, *The Negro in the Civil War,* pp. 116, 117.

ROBBINS, Gerald, "The Recruiting and Arming of Negroes in the Sea Islands,
1862–1865," *Negro Historical Bulletin,* p. 164.

ROGERS, Seth, "War-Time Letters from Seth Rogers, M.D. Surgeon of the First South
Carolina Afterward the Thirty-Third U.S.C.T., 1862-1865." *MOLLUS,* pp. 2, 3.

SCHMIDT, Lewis G., *A Civil War History of the 47th Regiment of Pennsylvania*
Veteran Volunteers, pp. 200, 217.

SMITH, George Winston, "Carpetbag Imperialism in Florida, 1862-1868," Part II,
Florida Historical Quarterly, pp. 112, 113.

TAYLOR, Susie King, *Reminiscences of My Life in Camp,* p. 15.

War of the Rebellion: The Official Records of the Union and Confederate Armies,
Series II, vol. 14, pp. 388, 390; Series III, vol. 2, , pp. 663, 664, 695.

ZILVERSMIT, Arthur, *Lincoln on Black and White: A Documentary History,* pp.
112-115.

Chapter 6

BALLARD, Michael B., *Pemberton: A Biography,* pp. 85-118.

BERLIN, Ira, *et al., Freedom: A Documentary History of Emancipation, 1861–1867,*
Series III: *The Black Military Experience,* pp. 43-45.

BRIGHT, Samuel R., Jr., Confederate Coast Defenses, pp. 47, 56, 57.

DONALD, David, (ed.), *Inside Lincoln's Cabinet: The Civil War Diaries of Salmon P. Chase,* p. 195.

DOWDEY, Clifford, *Lee,* pp. 175-179.

HAWKS, John D., "The First Freedmen to Become Soldiers," *The Southern Workman,* p. 108.

HEWETT, Janet B., *et al., Supplement to the Official Records of the Union and Confederate Armies,* Part II—*Record of Events:* vol. 5, Serial No. 17, pp. 153-156, 158-160, 162, 163, 415-425, 473-490.

HIGGINSON, Thomas Wentworth, *Army Life in a Black Regiment,* pp. 269-271.

JAMIESON, PERRY D., *The Development of Civil War Tactics,* pp. 211-213.

MANARIN, Louis H., Lee in Command: Strategical and Tactical Policies, pp. 178-180, 571, 572.

PEARSON, Elizabeth Ware, (ed.), *Letters from Port Royal, 1862–1868,* pp. 102-104, 106, 107.

ROMAN, Alfred, *The Military Operations of General Beauregard,* vol. II, pp. 1-19

SAUCER, John S., Unpublished manuscript of the 4th Georgia Cavalry Regiment (Clinch), pp. 2, 3, 5.

SIFAKIS, Stewart, *Compendium of the Confederate Armies: Florida and Arkansas,* pp. 6, 7, 9, 10, 14-24.

SMEDLUND, William S., *Camp Fires of Georgia's Troops,* pp. 70, 74, 115, 138, 292.

TAYLOR, Susie King, *Reminiscences of My Life in Camp,* pp. 14, 46.

War of the Rebellion: The Official Records of the Union and Confederate Armies, Series I, vol. 14, pp. 189-191, 378, 625.

WELCHER, Frank J., *The Union Army, 1861–1865: Organization and Operations,* vol. I: *The Eastern Theater,* pp. 385, 386.

Chapter 7

CANDLER, Allen D., *The Confederate Records of the State of Georgia,* vol. II, pp. 317-322.

CORNISH, Dudley Taylor, *The Sable Arm: Black Troops in the Union Army, 1861–1865,* pp. 79, 86, 87.

HAWKS, John D., "The First Freedmen to Become Soldiers," *The Southern Workman,* p. 108.

HEWETT, Janet B., *et al., Supplement to the Official Records of the Union and Confederate Armies,* Part II—*Record of Events:* vol. 5, Serial No. 17, pp. 414, 420, 422, 424.

HIGGINSON, Thomas Wentworth, *Army Life in a Black Regiment,* p. 2.

HOLLAND, Rupert Sargent, (ed.), *Letters and Diary of Laura M. Towne, Written from the Sea Islands of South Carolina, 1862–1884,* p. 94.

JOHNSON, Robert Underwood and BUEL, Clarence Clough, *Battles and Leaders of the Civil War,* vol. IV, p. 51.

Official Records of the Union and Confederate Navies in the War of the Rebellion, Series I, vol. 18, pp. 438, 439.

PEARSON, Elizabeth Ware, (ed.), *Letters from Port Royal, 1862–1868,* pp. 107, 108.

REDDICK, Marquerite, compiler, *Camden's Challenge: A History of Camden County, Georgia,* p. 154.

SCHMIDT, Lewis G., *A Civil War History of the 47th Regiment of Pennsylvania Veteran Volunteers,* p. 286.

————, *Florida's East Coast. The Civil War in Florida, A Military History,* vol. 1, Part I, pp. 97, 98, 102, 108-111,120,179, 260, 275.

SMEDLUND, William S., *Camp Fires of Georgia's Troops*, pp. 70, 71, 138, 292.

SMITH, J. Harmon, compiler, Breakdown by County of Enlistment of Military Companies from Georgia in the Civil War, n.d.

Sworn statements of John M. Hawks, March 12, 1901; and William James, January 14, 1891 and December 17, 1894. John M. Hawks Pension Folder, Selected Pension Records for 21st, 33rd, and 34th United States Colored Troops.

War of the Rebellion: The Official Records of the Union and Confederate Armies, Series I, vol. 14, pp. 189-194, 338, 363, 368, 388, 390, 624, 625.

VOCELLE, James, *History of Camden County, Georgia*, p. 117.

Chapter 8

AMMEN, Daniel, *The Navy in the Civil War*, vol. II: *The Atlantic Coast*, p. 255.

BERWANGER, Eugene H., "Lincoln's Constitutional Dilemma: Emancipation and Black Suffrage," in Schwartz, Thomas F., (ed.), *"For a Vast Future Also:" Essays from the Journal of the Abraham Lincoln Association*, pp. 26, 27.

BILLINGTON, Ray Allen, (ed.), *The Journal of Charlotte Forten: A free Negro in the Slave Era*, pp. 155, 156, 171-175.

CARWARDINE, Richard, *Lincoln: A Life of Purpose and Power*, p. 219.

COCHRANE, William Ghormley, Freedom without Equality: A Study of Northern Opinion and the Negro Issue, 1861–1870, pp. 35-51, 54-68.

DENNISON, Frederick, *Shot and Shell: The Third Rhode Island Heavy Artillery Regiment in the Rebellion, 1861–1865*, pp. 114, 115, 132, 133.

DONALD, David D., (ed.), *Inside Lincoln's Cabinet: The Civil War Diaries of Salmon P. Chase*, p. 197.

DYER, Frederick H., *A Compendium of the War of the Rebellion*, vol. I, pp. 364, 365.

ELDREDGE, Daniel, *The Third New Hampshire and All about It*, p. 242.

FONER, Philip S., *The Life and Writings of Frederick Douglass*, vol. III, pp. 235, 317.

FORTEN, Charlotte, "Life on the Sea Islands," Part II, *The Atlantic Monthly*, pp. 668, 669.

HAWKES, John M., "The First Freedmen to Become Soldiers," *The Southern Workman*, p. 109.

HIGGINSON, Thomas Wentworth, *Army Life in a Black Regiment*, pp. 2-16, 19, 30-42, 270, 271.

————, *Cheerful Yesterdays*, pp. 249-252.

HOLLAND, Rupert Sargent, (ed.), *Letters and Diary of Laura M. Towne, Written from the Sea Islands of South Carolina, 1862–1884*, pp. 98, 99.

Letter of Daniel Drew Barrow, Company E, 9th Maine Infantry, December 22, 1862.

LONG, E. B, with LONG, Barbara, *The Civil War Day by Day: An Almanac, 1861–1865*, pp. 248, 285, 294-296.

LOOBY, Christopher, (ed.), *The Complete Civil War Journal and Selected Letters of Thomas Wentworth Higginson*, pp. 39-42, 48-51, 53-58, 67, 68, 70-78, 81, 82, 85, 248-252, 255, 370-374.

MEYERS, Howard N., *Colonel of the Black Regiment: The Life of Thomas Wentworth Higginson*, p. 190.

MORRIS, William, (ed.), *The American Heritage Dictionary of the English Language*, p. 1318.

MOHR, Clarence Lee, *On the Threshold of Freedom: Masters and Slaves in Civil War Georgia*, p. 87.

New York Times, January 9, 1863, Schmidt Collection.

PEARSON, Elizabeth Ware, (ed.), *Letters from Port Royal, 1862–1868*, pp. 128-135.

QUARLES, Benjamin, *The Negro in the Civil War*, pp. 180-183.

RIVERS, Larry Eugene, *Slavery in Florida: Territorial Days to Emancipation*, p. 232.

ROGERS , Seth, "War-Time Letters from Seth Rogers, M.D. Surgeon of the First South Carolina Afterward the Thirty-Third U.S.C.T., 1862–1865," *MOLLUS*, pp. 2-4, 6-12, 18.

SCHAFER, Daniel L., "Freedom was a close as the River: African Americans and the Civil War in Northeast Florida," in COLBURN, David R. and LANDERS, Jane L., (ed.), *The African American Heritage of Florida*, p. 171.

SMITH, John David, (ed.), *Black Soldiers in Blue: African American Troops in the Civil War*, pp. 308, 309.

TAYLOR , Susie King, *Reminiscences of My Life in Camp*, p. 18.

THOMAS, Benjamin F. and HYMAN, Harold M., *Stanton: The Life and Times of Lincoln's Secretary of War*, pp. 249, 262, 263.

War of the Rebellion: The Official Records of the Union and Confederate Armies, Series I, vol. 14, p. 390; Series III, vol. 3, pp. 14, 20, 21.

WELCHER, Frank J., *The Union Army, 1861–1865: Organization and Operations*, vol. I: *The Eastern Theater*, pp. 376, 385.

Chapter 9

BARNES, Elinor and BARNES, James A., (eds.), *Naval Surgeon: Blockading the South, 1862–1866. The Diary of Dr. Samuel Pellman Boyer*, pp. 47, 49, 50-52.

BILLINGTON, Ray Allen, (ed.), *The Journal of Charlotte Forten, A Free Negro in the Slave Era*, p. 177.

COGGINS, Jack, *Arms and Equipment of the Civil War*, p. 144.

COLES, David James, Far from Fields of Glory: Military Operations in Florida during the Civil War, 1864–1865, p. 14.

Compiled by a member (TOURTELLOTTE, Jerome), *A History of Company K of the Seventh Connecticut Volunteer Infantry in the Civil War*, p. 76.

Davis Bryant letter, Camp Cooper, FL.

FUTCH, Ovid L., "Salmon P. Chase and Civil War Politics in Florida," *Florida Historical Quarterly*, p. 167.

HARTMAN, David W., *et al.*, *Biographical Roster of Florida's Confederate and Union Soldiers, 1861–1865*, vol. IV, p. 1544.

HEWETT, Janet, (ed.), *Supplement to the Official Records of the Union and Confederate Armies. Part II—Record of Events*: vol. 77, Series No. 89, pp. 732-755.

HIGGINSON, Thomas Wentworth, *Army Life in a Black Regiment*, pp. 62-75.

—————, "The First Black Regiment," *The Outlook*, p. 529.

JOHNSON, Robert Underwood and BUEL, Clarence Clough, *Battles and Leaders of the Civil War*, vol. IV, p. 51.

Letter of Davis Bryant to his brother Willie, February 19, 1863, Stephens Collection.

LOOBY, Christopher, (ed.), *The Complete Civil War Journal and Selected Letters of Thomas Wentworth Higginson*, pp. 79, 80, 82, 86-93.

Map of NE Florida between the St. Mary's River and the St. John's River.

MILLER, Edward A., Jr., *Lincoln's Abolitionist General: A Biography of David Hunter*, pp. 120-129.

Official Records of the Union and Confederate Navies in the War of the Rebellion, Series I, vol. 13, pp. 522, 523; Series II, vol. I, pp. 113, 114l

PEARSON, Elizabeth Ware, (ed.), *Letters from Port Royal, 1862–1868*, p. 136.

Rogers, Seth, "War-Time Letters from Seth Rogers, M.D. Surgeon of the First South Carolina Afterward the Thirty-Third U.S.C.T., 1862–1865," *MOLLUS*, pp. 14-27.

Schmidt, Lewis G., *A Civil War History of the 47th Regiment of the Pennsylvania Veteran Volunteers*, p. 200.

Sifakis, Stewart, *Compendium of the Confederate Armies: Florida and Arkansas*, pp. 10, 154.

Smith, George Winston, "Carpetbag Imperialism in Florida, 1862–1868," Part II, *Florida Historical Quarterly*, p. 261.

The Official Military Atlas of the Civil War, Plate CXLV.

War of the Rebellion: The Official Records of the Union And Confederate Armies, Series I, vol. 14, pp. 195, 390-392; Series III, vol. 3, p. 20

Chapter 10

Blakey, Arch Fredric, Lainhart, Ann Smith and Stephens, Winston Bryant, Jr., (eds.), *Rose Cottage Chronicles: Civil War Letters of the Bryant-Stephens Families of North Florida*, p. 204.

Compiled by a member (Tourtellotte, Jerome), *A History of Company K of the Seventh Connecticut Volunteer Infantry in the Civil War*, p. 76.

Evans, Clement, (ed.), *Confederate Military History Extended Edition*, vol. VIII—*Georgia*, p. 151.

Hewett, Janet B., *et al.*, *Supplement to the Official Records of the Union and Confederate Armies*. Part II—*Record of Events*: vol. 5, Serial No. 17, pp. 74, 265.

Higginson, Thomas Wentworth, *Army Life in a Black Regiment*, pp. 81-92.

Index to the 4th Georgia Cavalry, C.S.A., pp. 8, 15.

Letter of Duncan Clinch (copy), April, 1887.

Penniman, William Frederick, memoirs, pp. 30, 32, 33.

Rogers, Seth, "War-Time letters from Seth Rogers, M.D. Surgeon of the First South Carolina Afterward the Thirty-Third U.S.C.T., 1862–1865," *MOLLUS*, pp. 27-32.

Smith, Harmon, Jr., compiler, Breakdown of County of Enlistment of Military Companies from Georgia in the Civil War.

War of the Rebellion: The Official Military Records of the Union and Confederate Armies, Series I, vol. 14, p. 196.

Chapter 11

Barnes, Elinor and Barnes, James A., (eds.), *Naval Surgeon: Blockading the South, 1862–1866. The Diary of Dr. Samuel Pellman Boyer*, p. 58.

Billington, Ray Allen, (ed.), *The Journal of Charlotte Forten, A Free Negro in the Slave Era*, pp. 181-183, 189.

Blakey, Arch Fredric, Lainhart, Ann Smith and Stephens, Winston Bryant, Jr., (eds.), *Rose Cottage Chronicles: Civil War Letters of the Bryant-Stephens Families of North Florida*, pp. 199, 204, 207, 213.

Compiled by a member (Tourtellotte, Jerome), *A History of Company K of the Seventh Connecticut Volunteer Infantry in the Civil War*, p. 77.

Hartman, David W., *et al.*, *Biographical Roster of Florida's Confederate and Union Soldiers, 1861–1865*, vol. V, p. 1941.

Higginson, Thomas Wentworth, *Army Life in a Black Regiment*, p. 70, 88, 93-95.

HOLLAND, Rupert Sargent, (ed.), *Letters and Diary of Laura M. Towne, Written from the Sea Islands of South Carolina, 1862-1884*, p. 101.

ROWLEY, John L., Company E, 7th Connecticut Infantry, letter from Fernandina, Florida, January 30, 1863.

Letter of Davis Bryant to his brother Willie, February 14, 1863, Stephens Collection.

Letter of Duncan Clinch (copy), April, 1887.

Letters of Winston Stephens to his wife Octavia, February 2 and 24, 1863, Stephens Collection.

LOOBY, Christopher, (ed.), *The Complete Civil War Diary and Selected Letters of Thomas Wentworth Higginson*, pp. 94, 102, 261.

ROGERS, Seth, "War-Time Letters from Seth Rogers, M.D. Surgeon of the First South Carolina Afterward the Thirty-Third U.S.T.C., 1862–1865,"*MOLLUS*, pp. 32-36.

SCHWARTZ, Gerald, (ed.), *A Woman Doctor's Civil War: Esther Hill Hawks' Diary*, p. 43.

War of the Rebellion: The Official Records of the Union and Confederate Armies, Series I, vol. 14, pp. 195-198.

Chapter 12

BILLINGTON, Ray Allen, (ed.), *The Journal of Charlotte Forten: A Free Negro in the Slave Era*, pp. 191, 192.

BRIGGS, Walter De Blois, *Civil War in a Colored Regiment*, pp. 80, 81.

BURTON, E. Milby, *The Siege of Charleston, 1861–1865*, pp. 12-150.

COLES, David James, Far from Fields of Glory: Military Operations in Florida during the Civil War, 1864–1865, p. 14.

FUTCH, Ovid L., "Salmon P. Chase and Civil War Politics in Florida," *Florida Historical Quarterly*, p. 167.

Gladstone, William A., *Men of Color*, pp. 215, 219.

HAYES, John D., (ed.), *Samuel Francis Du Pont: A Selection from His Civil War Letters. Vol. II: The Blockade, 1862–1863*, pp. 441, 497.

HIGGINSON, Thomas Wentworth, *Army Life in a Black Regiment*, pp. 74-76.

————, "The Reoccupation of Jacksonville in 1863," in Civil War Papers Read Before the Commandery of the State of Massachusetts, *MOLLUS*, pp. 467, 468.

HOLLAND, Rupert Sargent, (ed.), *Letters and Diary of Laura M. Towne, Written from the Sea Islands of South Carolina, 1862–1884*, pp. 103, 104.

HOLMAN, Tom LeRoy, James Montgomery, 1813-1871, pp. 181, 183, 184.

Letter from General Hunter to Colonel Joseph S. Morgan, February 7, 1863, Papers of James Montgomery.

LONG, Richard A., (ed.), *Black Writers and the American Civil War: Black Involvement and Participation in the War Between the States*, pp. 137, 138.

LOOBY, Christopher, (ed.), *The Complete Civil War Journal and Selected Letters of Thomas Wentworth Higginson*, pp. 94, 95, 98, 101-108, 262, 263.

MARTIN, Richard A., "The *New York Times* Views Civil War Jacksonville," *Florida Historical Quarterly*, p. 413.

New York Times, January 28, 1863; (via *Philadelphia Inquirer*, March 25, 1863 and April, 1863), Schmidt Collection.

PEARSON, Elizabeth Ware, (ed.), *Letters from Port Royal, 1862–1868*, pp. 163, 164, 167.

RIVERS, Larry Eugene, *Slavery in Florida: Territorial Days to Emancipation*, pp. 88-90, 230, 232, 233, 242, 243.

ROGERS, Seth, "War-Time Letters from Seth Rogers, M.D. Surgeon of the First South Carolina Afterward the Thirty-Third U.S.C.T., 1862–1865," *MOLLUS*, pp. 36, 37, 39, 40, 42, 52, 56-61, 105.

SCHAFER, Daniel L., "Freedom was as close as the River: African Americans and the Civil War in Northeast Florida," in COLBURN, David R. and LANDERS, Janet L., (eds.), *The African American Heritage of Florida*, pp. 157-175.

SMITH, George Winston, "Carpetbag Imperialism in Florida, 1862–1868," Part II, *Florida Historical Quarterly*, p. 263.

TODD, Frederick P., *American Military Equipage: 1851–1872*, vol. I, pp. 135, 136.

War of the Rebellion: The Official Records of the Union and Confederate Armies, Series I, vol. 14, p. 194; Series III, vol. 3, pp. 14, 20, 421, 434, 822.

WARNER, Ezra J., *Generals in Blue: Lives of the Union Commanders*, p. 477.

WISE, Stephen R., *Gates of Hell: Campaign for Charleston Harbor, 1863*, pp. 23-32.

Chapter 13

BLAKEY, Arch Fredric, LAINHART, Ann Smith and STEPHENS, Winston Bryant, Jr., (eds.), *Rose Cottage Chronicles: Civil War Letters of the Bryant-Stephens Families of North Florida*, pp. 213-215.

Compiled by a member (TOURTELLOTTE, Jerome), *A History of Company K of the Seventh Connecticut Infantry in the Civil War*, p. 87.

HARTMAN, David W., *et al.*, *Biographical Roster of Florida's Confederate and Union Soldiers*, vol. I, p. 169; vol. III, p. 1163; vol. VI, p. 1437.

HIGGINSON, Thomas Wentworth, *Army Life in a Black Regiment*, pp. 75-81.

————, "The Reoccupation of Jacksonville in 1863," in Civil War Papers Read Before the Commandery of the State of Massachusetts, *MOLLUS*, pp. 468-470.

JOHNSON, Robert Underwood and BUEL, Clarence Clough, *Battles and Leaders of the Civil War*, vol. IV, p. 51.

Letter of James Montgomery, April 25, 1863.

Letters of Winston Stephens to his brother-in-law Davis Bryant, March 15, 1863; to his wife Octavia, March 16, 1863, Stephens Collection.

LOOBY, Christopher, (ed.), *The Complete Civil War Journal and Selected Letters of Thomas Wentworth Higginson*, pp. 109-111.

MOORE, Frank, (ed.), *The Rebellion Record: A Diary of American Events*, vol. 6, pp. 444, 445.

New York Times (via *Philadelphia Inquirer*, March 25, 1863), Schmidt Collection.

Philadelphia Inquirer, April 11, 1863, Schmidt Collection.

ROGERS, Seth, "War-Time Letters from Seth Rogers, M.D. Surgeon of the First South Carolina Afterward the Thirty-Third U.S.C.T., 1862–1865," *MOLLUS*, pp. 62-65.

War of the Rebellion: The Official Records of the Union and Confederate Armies, Series I, vol. 14, pp. 227, 423, 825.

Chapter 14

Augusta Daily Chronicle and Sentinel, March 25 and 26, 1863, Schmidt Collection.

CADWELL, Charles K., *The Old Sixth Regiment, its War Record, 1861–1865*, pp. 56, 58.

CLANCY, Anne Robinson, (ed.), *A Yankee in a Confederate Town: The Journal of Calvin L. Robinson*, pp. 79, 80, 90, 91.

Compiled by a member (TOURTELLOTTE, Jerome), *A History of Company K of the Seventh Connecticut Infantry in the Civil War*, pp. 76, 88.

DENNETT, Tyler, (ed.), *Lincoln and the Civil War in the Diary and Letters of John Hay*, p. 54.

EVANS, Clement A., (ed.), *Confederate Military History Extended Edition*, vol. VIII—*Georgia*, pp. 151, 156, 157; vol. XVI—*Florida*, p. 54.

HARTMAN, David W., *et al.*, *Biographical Roster of Florida's Confederate and Union Soldiers*, vol. IV, pp. 1544-1557; vol. V, p. 1941.

HIGGINSON, Thomas Wentworth, *Army Life in a Black Regiment*, pp. 81-85, 87, 89, 90.

————, "The Reoccupation of Jacksonville in 1863," in Civil War Papers Read Before the Commandery of the State of Massachusetts, *MOLLUS*, pp. 471, 472.

HILLHOUSE, Don, *Heavy Artillery and Light Infantry: A History of the 1st Florida Special Battalion and 10th Florida Infantry*, p. 52.

Letter of Charles Phineas Lord, 8th Maine Infantry, March 22, 1863.

Letter of Charles Steedman, March 20, 1863.

Letter of Davis Bryant to his brother Willie, March 15, 1863, Stephens Collections

Letters of Winston Stephens to his wife Octavia, March 16, 1863; to his brother-in-law Davis Bryant, March 16, 1863, Stephens Collection.

LONG, Richard A., (ed.), *Black Writers and the American Civil War: Black Involvement and Participation in the War Between the States*, p. 138.

LOOBY, Christopher, (ed.), *The Complete Civil War Journal and Selected Letters of Thomas Wentworth Higginson*, pp. 109-115.

Official Records of the Union and Confederate Navies in the War of the Rebellion, Series I, vol. 13, p. 777.

Philadelphia Inquirer, April 9 and 11, 1863, Schmidt Collection.

ROGERS, Seth, "War-Time Letters from Seth Rogers, M.D. Surgeon of the First South Carolina Afterward the Thirty-Third U.S.C.T., 1862-1865," *MOLLUS*, pp. 64, 68-71.

SMEDLUND, William S., *Camp Fires of Georgia's Troops*, pp. 65, 115, 138, 165, 184, 209, 265, 279.

War of the Rebellion: The Official Records of the Union and Confederate Armies, Series I, vol. 14, pp. 226-229, 435, 824, 825, 829, 837-839, 850, 851.

Chapter 15

ANDREWS, W. H., *Footprints of a Regiment: A Recollection of the First Georgia Regulars*, p. 112.

BLAKEY, Arch Fredric, LAINHART, Ann Smith, and STEPHENS, Winston Bryant, Jr., (eds.), *Rose Cottage Chronicles: Civil War Letters of the Bryant-Stephens Families of North Florida*, p. 216.

CADWELL, Charles K., *The Old Sixth Regiment: its War Record, 1861–1865*, p. 59.

CLANCY, Anne Robinson, (ed.), *A Yankee in a Confederate Town: The Journal of Calvin L. Robinson*, p. 93.

DAVIS, T. Frederick, *History of Jacksonville, Florida and Vicinity, 1513 to 1924*, pp. 129, 130, 132.

HIGGINSON, Thomas Wentworth, *Army Life in a Black Regiment*, pp. 90-95, 97, 269.

Letter of Charles Phineas Lord, 8th Maine Infantry, March 22, 1863.

Letter of James Montgomery, April 25, 1863.

Letter of Winston Stephens to his brother-in-law Davis Bryant, April 18, 1863, Stephens Collection.

LOOBY, Christopher, (ed.), *The Complete Civil War Journal and Selected Letters of Thomas Wentworth Higginson*, pp. 115-118, 120, 267.

LONG, Richard A., (ed.), *Black Writers and the American Civil War: Black Involvement and Participation in the War Between the States*, pp. 138, 139.

MOORE, Frank, (ed.), *The Rebellion Record: A Diary of American Events*, vol. 6, p. 483.

Philadelphia Inquirer, April 1 and 19, 1863, Schmidt Collection.

ROGERS, Seth, "War-Time Letters from Seth Rogers, M.D. Surgeon of the First South Carolina Afterward the Thirty-Third U.S.T.C., 1862–1865, *MOLLUS*, pp. 74-82, 84, 91.

War of the Rebellion: The Official Records of the Union and Confederate Armies, Series I, vol. 14, pp. 234-238, 840, 841.

Chapter 16

HIGGINSON, Thomas Wentworth, *Army Life in a Black Regiment*, p. 97.

Letter of Charles Steedman, March 29, 1863.

LOOBY, Christopher, (ed.), *The Complete Civil War and Selected Letters of Thomas Wentworth Higginson*, pp. 119-123, 268.

MOORE, Frank, (ed.), *The Rebellion Record: A Diary of American Events*, vol. 3, p. 74.

Philadelphia Inquirer, April 9, 1863.

ROGERS, SETH, "War-Time Letters from Seth Rogers, M.D. Surgeon of the First South Carolina Afterward the Thirty-Third U.S.C.T., 1862-1865, *MOLLUS*, pp. 82, 83.

ROSE, Willie Lee, *Rehearsal for Reconstruction: The Port Royal Experiment*, p. 179.

Bibliography

Primary Sources

Manuscripts

Amelia Island Museum of History, Fernandina Beach, Florida.
Barrow, Daniel Drew, Company E, 9th Maine Infantry. Letter from Fernandina, Florida, December 22, 1862.
Bryant, Davis, Letter from Camp Cooper, Nassau County, Florida. A19.16.
Florida State Department of Archives and History. Tallahassee.
Scott, George W. Papers, Map of NE Florida between the St. Mary's River and St. John's River. M87-22.
Schmidt, Lewis G. Collection, M91-10.
Kansas State Historical Society. Topeka.
Montgomery, James, Papers. MS 1095.02.
United States Army Military History Institute, Carlisle Barracks, Pennsylvania.
Rogers, Seth. "War-Time Letters from Seth Rogers, M.D. Surgeon of the First South Carolina Afterward the Thirty-Third U.S.C.T., 1862–1865, MOLLUS. Massachusetts Commandery.
Higginson, Thomas Wentworth, "The Reoccupation of Jacksonville in 1863" in Civil War Papers Read Before The Commandery of The State of Massachusetts, MOLLUS, Boston, 1900. Published By The Commandery.
University of Florida, George A. Smathers Library. Department of Special Collections. Gainesville.
Clinch, Duncan, Papers.
Rowley, John L., Company E, 7th Connecticut Infantry, Letter from Fernandina, Florida, January 30, 1863. Florida Miscellaneous, Miscellaneous Manuscripts Collection.
Steedman, Charles, Letters (copies), Miscellaneous Manuscript Collection.
Stephens Collection.
University of North Carolina, Southern Historical Collection, Chapel Hill.
Penniman, William Frederick, Memoirs.
University of North Florida, Thomas G. Carpenter Library, Special Collections Section. Jacksonville.

Hawks, John M., Pension Folder, Sworn Statements of John M. Hawks, March 12, 1901; and William James, January 14, 1891 and December 17, 1894, Selected Pension Records for 21st, 33rd, and 34th United States Colored Troops (originals in National Archives).

Published

Books

A Committee of the Regimental Association. *The Story of One Regiment: The Eleventh Maine Infantry Volunteers in the War of the Rebellion*. New York: Little, 1896.
AMMEN, Daniel, *The Navy in the Civil War*. Vol. II—*The Atlantic Coast*. New York: Charles Scribner's Sons, 1885.
ANDREWS, W. H., *Footprints of A Regiment: A Recollection of The First Georgia Regulars*. Atlanta: Longstreet Press, 1992.
BARNES, Elinor and BARNES, James A., (eds.), *Naval Surgeon: Blockading the South, 1862–1866. The Diary of Dr. Samuel Pellman Boyer*. Bloomington: Indiana University Press, 1963.
BILLINGTON, Ray Allen, (ed.), *The Journal of Charlotte Forten: A Free Negro in the Slave Era*. New York: W. W. Norton, 1953.
BLAKEY, Arch Fredric, LAINHART, Ann Smith and STEPHENS, Winston Bryant, Jr., (eds.), *Rose Cottage Chronicles: Civil War Letters of the Bryant–Stephens Families of North Florida*. Gainesville: University Press of Florida, 1998.
BRIGGS, Walter De Blois, *Civil War Surgeon in a Colored Regiment*. Berkeley: University of California Press, 1960.
CADWELL, Charles K., *The Old Sixth Regiment, its War Record, 1861–1865*. New Haven, CT: Tuttle, Morehouse, and Taylor, 1875.
CANDLER, Allen D., *The Confederate Records of the State of Georgia*, vol. II. Atlanta: Charles P. Byrd, 1909.
CLANCY, Anne Robinson, (ed.), *A Yankee in a Confederate Town: The Journal of Calvin L. Robinson*. Sarasota, FL: Pineapple Press, 2000.
Compiled by a member (TOURTELLOTTE, Jerome). *A History of Company K of the Seventh Connecticut Volunteer Infantry in the Civil War*. N. p., 1910.
DAVIS, George B., *et al.*, *The Official Military Atlas of the Civil War*. Avenel NJ: Gramercy Books, 1983.
DENNETT, Tyler, (ed.), *Lincoln and the Civil War in the Diary and Letters of John Hay*. New York: Dodd, Mead and Company, 1939.
DENNISON, Frederick, *Shot and Shell: The Third Rhode Island Heavy Artillery Regiment in the Rebellion, 1861–1865*. Providence, RI: J. A. and R. A. Reid, 1879.
DONALD, David, (ed.), *Inside Lincoln's Cabinet: The Civil War Diaries of Salmon P. Chase*. New York: Longman, Green, and Company, 1954.
ELDREDGE, Daniel, *The Third New Hampshire and All about It*. Boston: E. B. Stillings, 1893.
EVANS, Clement, (ed.), *Confederate Military History Extended Edition*, vol. VIII—*Georgia*, by Joseph T. Derry, Wilmington, NC: Broadfoot Publishing Company, 1987.
————, *Confederate Military History Extended Edition*, vol. XVI—*Florida*, by J.J. Dickison. Wilmington, NC: Broadfoot Publishing Company, 1989.
FONER, Philip S., *The Life and Writings of Frederick Douglass*, vol. III. New York: International Publishers, 1952.

Ford, Worthington Chauncey, (ed.). *A Cycle of Adams Letters*, vol. I. Boston: The Riverside Press, 1920.

Hayes, John D., (ed.), *Samuel Francis Du Pont: A Selection from His Civil War Letters*. Vol. 2—*The Blockade: 1862–1863*. Ithaca, NY: Cornell University Press, 1969.

Hewett, Janet B., et al., *Supplement to the Official Records of the Union and Confederate Armies*. Part I—*Reports*: vol. 3, Serial No. 3. Wilmington, NC: Broadfoot Publishing Company, 1994.

————, *Supplement to the Official Records of the Union and Confederate Armies*. Part II—*Record of Events*: vol. 5, Serial No. 17. Wilmington, NC: Broadfoot Publishing Company, 1995.

————, *Supplement to the Official Records of the Union and Confederate Armies*. Part II—*Record of Events*: vol. 6, Serial No. 18. Wilmington, NC: Broadfoot Publishing Company, 1995.

————, *Supplement to the Official Records of the Union and Confederate Armies*. Part II—*Record of Events*: vol. 77, Serial No. 89. Wilmington, NC: Broadfoot Publishing Company, 1998.

Higginson, Thomas Wentworth, *Army Life in a Black Regiment*. Boston: Fields, Osgood and Co., 1870.

————, *Cheerful Yesterdays*. Boston: Houghton Mifflin Company, 1898.

Holland, Rupert Sargent, (ed.), *Letters and Diary of Laura M. Towne, Written From the Sea Islands of South Carolina, 1862–1884*. Cambridge, MA: The Riverside Press, 1912.

Hunter, David, *Report of the Military Services of Gen. David Hunter, U.S.A., During the War of the Rebellion*. New York: D. Van Nostrand, 1873.

Johnson, Robert Underwood and Buel, Clarence Clough. *Battles and Leaders of the Civil War*, vol. IV. Secaucas, NJ: Castle, 1991.

Looby, Christopher, (ed.), *The Complete Civil War Journal and Selected Letters of Thomas Wentworth Higginson*. Chicago: The University of Chicago Press, 2000.

Moore, Frank, (ed.), *The Rebellion Record: A Diary of American Events*. In 11 volumes. New York: Arno Press, 1977.

Myers, Robert Manson, (ed.), *The Children of Pride: A True Story of Georgia and the Civil War*. New Haven, CT: Yale University Press, 1972.

Nalty, Bernard C. and MacGregor, Morris J., (eds.), *Blacks In The Military: Essential Documents*. Wilmington, DE: Scholarly Resources, 1981.

Official Records of the Union and Confederate Navies in the War of the Rebellion. 30 volumes. Washington, DC: Government Printing Office, 1894–1927.

O'Reilly, Miles (Halpine, Charles G.), *Baked Meats of The Funeral*. New York: Carleton, 1866.

Pearson, Elizabeth Ware, ed., *Letters from Port Royal, 1862–1868*. New York: Arno Press and the New York Times, 1969.

Roman, Alfred, *The Military Operations of General Beauregard*, vol. II. New York: Da Capo Press, 1994.

Schmidt, Lewis G., *A Civil War History of the 47th Pennsylvania Veteran Volunteers*. Allentown, PA: Lewis G. Schmidt, 1986.

————, *Florida's East Coast. The Civil War in Florida, a Military History*, vol. I, Part I. Allentown, PA: Lewis G. Schmidt, 1991.

Schwartz, Gerald, ed., *A Woman Doctor's Civil War: Esther Hill Hawks' Diary*. Columbia: University of South Carolina Press, 1984.

Stevens, A. W., ed., *Enfranchisement and Citizenship: Addresses and Papers by Edward L. Pierce*. Boston: Roberts Brothers, 1896.

Stevens, Hazard, *The Life of Isaac Ingalls Stevens*, vol. II. Boston: Houghton, Mifflin and Company, 1900.

TAYLOR, Susie King, *Reminiscences of My Life in Camp*. New York: Arno Press and *The New York Times*, 1968.

TODD, William, *The Seventy-Ninth Highlanders, New York Volunteers, in the War of Rebellion, 1861–1865*. Albany, NY: Press of Brandow, Barton, and Company, 1866.

War of the Rebellion: The Official Records of the Union and Confederate Armies. 128 volumes. Washington, DC: Government Printing Office, 1880–1901.

ZILVERSMIT, Arthur, *Lincoln on Black And White: A Documentary History*. Belmont, CA: Wadsworth Publishing Company, 1971.

Periodicals

FORTEN, Charlotte, "Life on the Sea Islands," Part II. *The Atlantic Monthly*. 13 (June, 1864): 587-596, 666-676.

HAWKS, John M., "The First Freedmen to Become Soldiers." *The Southern Workman*. 38 (January, 1909): 107-109.

HIGGINSON, Thomas Wentworth, "The First Black Regiment." *The Outlook*. (July 2, 1898): 521-531.

PIERCE, Edward L., "The Freedmen at Port Royal." *The Atlantic Monthly*. 12 (September, 1863): 291-315.

SHERWOOD, Henry Noble, ed., "The Journal of Miss Susan Walker." *The Quarterly Publication of the Historical and Philosophical Society of Ohio*. 7 (January–March, 1912), 11-48.

Newspapers

The New York Times
(Port Royal) *The New South*

Secondary Sources

Books

AVERY, Isaac W., *The History of the State of Georgia from 1850 to 1881*. New York: Brown and Derby, 1881.

BALLARD, Michael B., *Pemberton: A Biography*. Jackson: University Press of Mississippi, 1991.

BELL, Malcolm, Jr., *Major Butler's Legacy: Five Generations of a Slave Holding Family*. Athens: The University of Georgia Press, 1987.

BELZ, Herman, *Abraham Lincoln, Constitutionalism, and Equal Rights in the Civil War Era*. New York: Fordham University Press, 1998.

BERLIN, Ira, *et al. Freedom: A Documentary History of Emancipation, 1861–1867*. Series I, vol. I—The *Destruction of Slavery*. New York: Cambridge University Press, 1987.

——————, *Freedom: A Documentary History of Emancipation, 1861–1867*. Series I, vol. III—*The Wartime Genesis of Free Labor: The Lower South*. New York: Cambridge University Press, 1987.

——————, *Freedom: A Documentary History of Emancipation, 1861–1867*. Series III—*The Black Military Experience*. New York: Cambridge University Press, 1982.

BERRY, Mary Frances, *Military Necessity and Civil Rights Policy: Black Citizenship and the Constitution, 1861–1868*. Port Washington, NY: Kennikat Press, 1977.

BERWANGER, Eugene H., "Lincoln's Constitutional Dilemma: Emancipation and Black Suffrage," in Schwartz, Thomas F., (ed.), *"For a Vast Future Also": Essays from the Journal of the Abraham Lincoln Association*. New York: Fordham University Press, 1999.

BLUE, Frederick J., *Salmon P. Chase: A Life in Politics*. Kent, OH: The Kent State University Press, 1987.

BURTON, E. Milby, *The Siege of Charleston, 1861–1865*. Columbia: University of South Carolina Press, 1970.

CARWARDINE, Richard, *Lincoln: A Life of Purpose and Power*. New York: Alfred A. Knopf, 2006.

COGGINS, Jack, *Arms and Equipment of the Civil War*. Wilmington, NC: Broadfoot Publishing Company, 1989.

CORNISH, Dudley Taylor, *The Sable Arm: Black Troops in the Union Army, 1861–1865*. Lawrence: University Press of Kansas, 1987.

DAVIS, T. Frederick, *History of Jacksonville, Florida and Vicinity, 1513–1924*. Gainesville: University of Florida Press, 1964.

DOWDEY, Clifford, *Lee*. New York: Bonanza Books, 1965.

DYER, Frederick H., *A Compendium of the War of the Rebellion*, vol. I. New York: Thomas Yoseloff, 1959.

EDELSTEIN, Tilden G., *Strange Enthusiasm: A Life of Thomas Wentworth Higginson*. New Haven, CT: Yale University Press, 1968.

GAVIN, William G., *Campaigning With the Roundheads: The History of the Hundredth Pennsylvania Veteran Volunteer Infantry Regiment in the American Civil War, 1861–1865*. Dayton, OH: Morningside House, Inc., 1989.

GIBSON, Charles Dana and GIBSON, E. Kay, *The Army's Navy Series*, vol. I. *Assault and Logistics: Union Army Coastal and River Operations, 1861–1866*. Camdon, MA: Ensign Press, 1995.

GLADSTONE, William A., *Men of Color*. Gettysburg, PA: Thomas Publications, 1993.

HARTMAN, David W., *et al. Biographical Roster of Florida's Confederate and Union Soldiers, 1861–1865*. 6 volumes. Wilmington, NC: Broadfoot Publishing Company, 1995.

HILLHOUSE, Don, *Heavy Artillery and Light Infantry: A History of the 1st Florida Special Battalion and 10th Infantry Regiment, C.S.A.* Jacksonville, FL, Don Hillhouse, 1992.

LONG, E. B., with LONG, Barbara, *The Civil War Day by Day: An Almanac, 1861–1865*. New York: Da Capo Press, 1971.

LONG, Richard A., (ed.), *Black Writers and the American Civil War: Black Involvement and Participation in the War Between the States*. Secaucas, NJ: The Blue and Gray Press, 1988.

MAYS, Joe H., *Black Americans and Their Contributions toward Union Victory in the American Civil War*. Lanham, MD: University Press of America, 1984.

MEYERS, Howard N., *Colonel of the Black Regiment: The Life of Thomas Wentworth Higginson*. New York: W. W. Norton, 1967.

MILLER, Edward A., Jr., *Lincoln's Abolitionist General: A Biography of David Hunter*. Columbia: University of South Carolina Press, 1997.

MOHR, Clarence Lee, *On The Threshold of Freedom: Masters and Slaves in Civil War Georgia*. Athens: The University of Georgia Press, 1986.

MORRIS, William, (ed.), *The American Heritage Dictionary of the English Language*. Boston: Houghton, Mifflin Company, 1978.

Quarles, Benjamin, *The Negro in the Civil War*. New York: Da Capo Press, 1989.

REDDICK, Marguerite, compiler, *Camden's Challenge: A History of Camden County, Georgia.* Woodbine, GA: Camden County Historical Commission, 1976.

REED, Rowena, *Combined Operations in the Civil War.* Lincoln: University of Nebraska Press, 1993.

RICHARDS, Kent D., *Isaac I. Stevens: Young Man in a Hurry.* Provo, UT: Brigham Young University Press, 1979.

RIVERS, Larry Eugene, *Slavery in Florida: Territorial Days to Emancipation.* Gainesville: University Press of Florida, 2000.

ROSE, Willie Lee, *Rehearsal for Reconstruction: The Port Royal Experiment.* New York: Oxford University Press, 1976.

SCHAFER, Daniel L., "Freedom was as close as the River: African Americans and the Civil War in Northeast Florida," in COLBURN, David R., and Landers, Jane L., (eds.), *The African American Heritage of Florida.* Gainesville: University Press of Florida, 1995.

SIFAKIS, Stewart, *Compendium of the Confederate Armies: Florida and Arkansas.* New York: Facts on File, 1992.

——————, *Compendium of the Confederate Armies: South Carolina and Georgia.* New York: Facts on File, 1995.

SMEDLUND, William S., *Camp Fires of Georgia's Troops.* Lithonia, GA: Kennesaw Mountain Press, 1994.

SMITH, John David, ed., *Black Soldiers in Blue: African American Troops in the Civil War.* Chapel Hill: The University of North Carolina Press, 2002.

THOMAS, Benjamin P. and HYMAN, Harold M., *Stanton: The Life and Times of Lincoln's Secretary of War.* Westport, CT: Greenwood Press, 1955.

TODD, Frederick P., *American Military Equipage: 1851–1872.* vol. I. Providence, RI: The Company of Military Historians, 1974.

VOCELLE, James, *History of Camden County, Georgia.* Kingsland, GA: The Southeast Georgian, 1967.

WELCHER, Frank J., *The Union Army, 1861–1865: Organization and Operations,* vol. I: *The Eastern Theater.* Bloomington: Indiana University Press, 1989.

WARNER, Ezra J., *Generals in Blue: Lives of the Union Commanders.* Baton Rouge: Louisiana State University Press, 1964.

WESTWOOD, Howard C., *Black Troops, White Commanders, and Freedmen during the Civil War.* Carbondale: Southern Illinois University Press, 1992.

WILEY, Bell Irvin, *The Common Soldier in the Civil War.* New York: Gross and Dudlap, n. d.

WISE, Stephen R., *Gate of Hell: Campaign for Charleston Harbor, 1863.* Columbia, SC: University of South Carolina Press, 1991.

Periodicals

FUTCH, Ovid L., "Salmon P. Chase and Civil War Politics in Florida." *Florida Historical Quarterly.* 32 (January 1954): 163-188.

HEARD, George Alexander, "St. Simon's Island during the War between The States." *The Georgia Historical Quarterly.* 22 (September, 1938): 249-272.

MARTIN, Richard A., "The New York Times Views Civil War Jacksonville." *Florida Historical Quarterly.* 53 (April 1974): 409-427.

PEASE, William H., "Three Years among the Freedmen: William G. Gannon and the Port Royal Experiment." *The Journal of Negro History.* 42(April 1957): 98-117.

ROBBINS, Gerald, "The Recruiting and Arming of Negroes in the Sea Islands, 1862–1865." *Negro Historical Bulletin.* 28(1965): 150, 151, 163-167.

SMITH, George Winston, "Carpetbag Imperialism in Florida, 1862–1868," Part II. *Florida Historical Quarterly*. 27 (January 1949): 261-299.

Theses and Dissertations

BAHNEY, Robert Stanley, Generals and Negroes: Education of Negroes By The Union Army, 1861–1865. Ph.D. dissertation, University of Michigan, 1965.

BRIGHT, Samuel R. Jr., Confederate Coast Defense. Ph.D. dissertation, Duke University, 1961.

BYRNE, William A., Slavery in Savannah, Georgia during the Civil War. M.A. thesis, Florida State University, 1971.

COCHRANE, William Ghormley, Freedom without Equality: A Study of Northern Opinion and the Negro Issue, 1861–1870. Ph.D. dissertation, University of Minnesota, 1957.

COLES, David James, Far From Fields of Glory: Military Operations in Florida during the Civil War, 1864–1865. PhD dissertation, Florida State University, 1996.

DROZDOWSKI, Eugene C., Edwin M., Stanton, Lincoln's Secretary of War: Toward Victory. Ph.D. dissertation, Duke University, 1964.

HOLMES, Tom LeRoy, James Montgomery, 1813–1871. Ed.D. dissertation, Oklahoma State University, 1973.

HENDRICKS, George Linton, Union Army Occupation of the Southern Seaboard, 1861–1865. Ph.D. dissertation, Columbia University, 1954.

MANARIN, Louis H., Lee in Command: Strategical and Tactical Policies. Ph.D. dissertation, Duke University, 1964.

MOHR, Clarence Lee, Georgia Blacks during Secession and Civil War, 1859–1865. Ph.D. dissertation, University of Georgia, 1975.

Unpublished Miscellaneous

Index to the 4th Georgia Cavalry, C.S.A. Bryan-Lang Historical Library, Woodbine, Georgia.

SAUCER, John S., Unpublished manuscript of the 4th Georgia Cavalry Regiment (Clinch).

SMITH, J. Harmon, compiler, Breakdown by County of Enlistment of Military Companies from Georgia. Atlanta: Georgia Department of Archives and History.

IIII 2 5 2019